THE
HISTORY
OF
THE WORLD

THE HISTORY OF THE WORLD

FROM THE DAWN OF HUMANITY
TO THE MODERN AGE

FRANK WELSH

Quercus

Contents

An Aztec Sun Stone made in about AD 1500 represents the Solar Calendar

A detail from a terracotta temple frieze from Civit Alba, Sassoferrato, Italy, shows Gallic warriors fleeing

Image painted on silk c.1000 of Taizu, first emperor of the Northern Song

The German empire is proclaimed in the Hall of Mirrors in the palace of Versailles, 1871

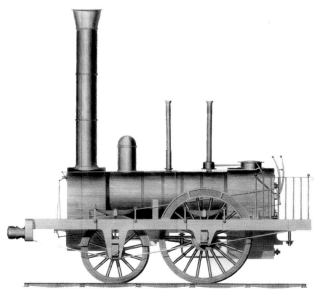

The Planet locomotive that ran on the Liverpool-Manchester railway in 1830, typical of the early steam locomotives

East German troops erecting the Berlin Wall in 1961

Introduction

Dr Samuel Johnson made an excuse on behalf of all authors apologizing for not devoting more time and effort to their work: *'Indolence, interruption, business, and pleasure all take their terms of retardation; and every long work is lengthened by a thousand causes that can, and ten thousand that cannot, be recounted.'*

Apologies and Explanations

In attempting so large a topic as 'The History of the World' – almost certainly a near-impossibility to complete satisfactorily – some explanations are required. Even touching on some of the salient historical and cultural points of all the world's civilisations demands not just a broad brush, but an industrial spray gun. Such a book would be impossibly dull and unreadable: details are essential and while the excellent pictures almost alone tell the story, the text must also strike home with some telling blows: the crew list of a Babylonian river boat or the teaching methods of Charlemagne's court, the relative prices of slaves and civet cats are worth more than smooth generalisations on the course of history.

But history is not a subject for the sensitive. I have frequently used the words 'man' or 'mankind' to include the whole of humanity in a way some may find objectionable; it is a toll we pay to time and space. Others may find that insisting on the antiquity of the world is anathema; other, more rational, persons may be shocked by religions being treated as historical rather than spiritual subjects, or offended by omissions. My apologies to all such in advance: I have attempted never to be inadvertently offensive.

In choosing to refer to periods as BC and AD rather than BCE and CE, for exactly the same periods, I follow British conventions: but when dealing with much longer periods the use of BP – Before the Present – seems more logical. I have avoided such expressions as 'Native American,' nonsensical as it is: American Indians refer to themselves either by their ancient ethnicities (e.g. Ioux, Cheyenne) or simply as 'Indians'. In South Africa Blacks, Whites and Coloureds are established and recognised classifications, although Khoi-San is no more than a convenient portmanteau word.

No history of the world can hope to be impartial or comprehensive; the subject is too great, and any writer is restricted by his own background, (please take 'or her' for granted) his command of language and the sources of his own experience. This book may be labelled 'Eurocentric' or even Anglocentric, certainly a Chinese writer would have a different perspective, and even a French, American or Irish historian would offer alternatives, but there is some reason for Anglo-centricity. English has become the world language, and the medium of international communication (although in a century or two it may well be displaced by Chinese): British practice and concepts have shaped most successful systems of government; American/English language and ideas form the foundation of commercial and financial practice. And perhaps most importantly the world's team games, especially that international passion, soccer, are British inventions, insidious advocates of otherwise outdated ideals of sportsmanship and fair play.

Genesis

When should a history of the world begin? For Archbishop James Ussher of Armagh (1581–1656), the question did not exist, since he had proved the date and time of Creation to be the morning of Sunday 23 October 4004 BC. His method was simple. The Bible, the veritable Word of God, as prepared for King James I of England and VI of Scotland states that Nebuchadnezzar, king of Babylon, died 3,442 years after the world began; the Archbishop knew from unimpeachable history that the king died in 562 BC; add the two together, and you have it! Unhappily – or this book would be much shorter – Ussher was a few billion years out (a date of 13.75 billion years ago now seems to be accepted) and the question remains to be answered.

The period could be usefully contracted to cover the history of humanity, but here the evidence is patchy and the dates conjectural. One generally accepted sequence suggests that it began some two million years ago when one branch of the australopithecines – the southern great apes – developed some skills in stone working which helped their descendants to thrive in Africa, where it all began. About 1.5 million years BP *Homo erectus*, a much more advanced creature than any of the great apes, wandered over vast distances, reaching China and Java in the east,

LEFT *A hand axe from the Lower Palaeolithic period, dated to around 750,000 BC. Tools like this, used to cut up animal carcasses, were made by carefully flaking pebbles of stone or flint.*

ABOVE *A Bronze Age terracotta vase, made in around the 15th century BC and found in Barca, Slovakia. The earliest pottery vessels, from China and Russian Far East, date from c.15,000 BC.*

and France, Spain, England at the other end of the continental land mass. The tools he developed were so useful that they passed on almost unchanged for more than a million years, to 100,000 BP, by far the longest period of human history and spread over all the inhabited world. They were first unearthed by the 18th century antiquary John Frere (1740–1807), Fellow of Gaius College, Cambridge, and of the Royal Society, who had identified what proved to be a hand axe, the multi-purpose tool that enabled man to survive. 'Axe' is perhaps misleading, since the tool, usually triangular but sometimes ovoid or circular, with one or two cutting edges up to 25 centimetres (10 in) long, could be used for slicing or scraping as well as chopping or cleaving, with smaller flakes serving as spear points or for finer work. The 'hand' simply signifies the absence of a haft, a later development.

Recent research into genetics has replaced pre-historical guesswork by respectable hypotheses. In the half century or so since Crick, Watson, Franklin and Gosling worked out the structure of DNA, the nucleic acid that serves as a genetic code of instructions, palaeogeneticists have established the pattern of human evolution beyond reasonable doubt. One of their most astonishing conclusions is that every living person is descended from a single female, 'Mitochondrial Eve' – so called since mitochondrial DNA is passed only matrilineally from mother to child – who lived in Africa perhaps about

200,000 years ago. Our latest common male ancestor is believed to have existed more recently, perhaps as few as 5,000 years ago when the Sumerian civilisation was flourishing; we are all truly related to one another.

Palaeoanthropologists debate the existence of possible sub-species and, since no studies change more rapidly than those of prehistory, clarifications are doubtless on their way. It may be, for example, that *Homo erectus* in Eurasia was paralleled by *Homo ergaster* in Africa. One or the other was the ancestor of Heidelberg Man, *c.*500,000 BP, now generally accepted as the ancestor of both Homo sapiens sapiens, modern man, and of Neanderthal Man.

Neanderthals diverged from the parent stock in Europe and near-Asia, and since they interbred with modern man – all non-Africans are estimated to have between 1-4% of Neanderthal DNA – they may perhaps be called the first Europeans. Distinctive physically, with the pronounced eyebrow ridges and powerful jaws of Heidelberg Man, they were also taller and stronger than modern Europeans, with probably a rather larger brain. In spite of these presumable advantages Neanderthals failed to prosper and died out in *c.*20,000–30,000 BP, displaced by modern man, those other descendants of the Heidelbergers. Another near relative has only very recently (2010) been identified, the *Denisova hominin*, discovered in Siberia. Denisovans and Neanderthals appear to have shared a common ancestor and subsequently moved into different territories. Denisovans, Neanderthals and modern man were contemporaries, and some present-day Melanesians derive up to 6 percent of their genetic makeup from Denisovans.

Travelling Man

It seems therefore that the human race is about 200,000 years old, and for rather more than half of that period remained in its birthplace, Central Africa. Perhaps about 85,000 years ago, although opinion differs substantially, adventurous emigrants crossed the Bab al Mandab, the 20 mile (32km) wide strait at the southern end of the Red Sea, then probably at least fordable, if not dry, and began populating the rest of the world. If they then turned right, and wandered off into Arabia and Southern Asia, they would have been discouraged to come across the remains – if indeed they were not caught in it – of a monstrous volcanic eruption in Sumatra, which produced the effect of a nuclear winter over the whole of the region, covering much of it with a thick layer of volcanic ash.

Survivors, and members of the second great emigration, which began about 60,000 BP, made it to the southern continent of Sahul, the land mass that then joined New Guinea and the islands to Australia, arriving 40,000 years ago, or even earlier. On the way they may have come across a related group, the recently identified small species Homo floresiensis, nicknamed the Hobbit, less than a metre (3.3 feet) tall, with small brains but employing surprisingly 'modern' tools. 'Hobbits' died out about 12,000 BP and some argue that they were in fact a taxon of modern man. Even at that time, with the lower sea levels, a journey from the mainland must have involved several sea passages of some distance: there have always been some humans unable to resist the lure of the far horizons. The original Australian population was later very little disturbed until the arrival of Europeans in the later 18th-century Australian blood lines remained very much those of the earliest arrivals, with their traditions and technology evolving almost independently of outside influence.

Movement onwards into Europe came after 60,000 BP, with some branching off to the Indian sub-continent where they encountered descendants of the first migration, producing a genetic division with contemporary northern Indians, who have a strong admixture of much later arrivals. Moving slowly over the millennia, humanity went on north and west, into Central Asia, up the Danube Valley, into France and Spain, across the Channel to England and through North Africa, hunter-gatherers, living off the land, and the sea. Fishing, by bone hooks and corded fibres, weirs and nets – Australians even devised kite-hauled nets – provided a more reliable source of protein than game. Perhaps about 14,000 BP the Bering Straits were crossed and the population of America begun, while more recently, about 800 AD enterprising Polynesians sailed across the Pacific Ocean to become the first New Zealanders.

A Changing World

Scholars, intent on tidying up the messy hinterland of history, have arranged events in neat sequences: Palaeolithic to Neolithic, Chalcolithic, Bronze and on to Iron, subdivided into cultures, as Gravettian, or Magdalenian. The history of undisciplined humanity however does not flow as a tranquil river, but as an uncertain stream with frequent extensive ponds or waterfalls: some Australian aborigines choose to live as did their ancestors 20,000 years previously: nineteenth century Japanese, possessors of the world's finest steel technology, used straw horse shoes: even today a local farmer, discovering a loose post, will use a convenient rock to bash it back, rather than finding a sledgehammer. As far as possible I have therefore avoided compartmentalising the evolution of human society.

At some stage language developed and with it poetry, philosophy, and history; but how, and when, are conjectural. It seems likely that music accompanied language, and that rhythm was an early source of aesthetic pleasure, for musical instruments are found among the earliest artefacts. As human society evolved, the world itself was changing. When the first modern humans arrived in Europe, some time after 40,000 BP they found a warmer climate, attested by the magnificent Chauvet Cave paintings of c.32,000 BP. These depict prides of savage lions hurtling towards their prey and rhinoceroses locked in combat, as well as cave bears and inquisitive horses. It was a hunter's paradise where herds of mammoth, reindeer, bison and aurochs (early wild cattle) roamed, making it easy for organised hunts to drive into natural or prepared traps, with the assistance of willing dogs. Bones were plentiful enough to use as fuel, and meat, if enough of the fat is eaten, is a healthy enough diet, as contemporary Inuits and Lapps (Sami) can witness, although edible plants were available. The 'Iceman Ötzi', a later survivor of this culture, flourished on a diet of game, mountain goat, chamois, berries and mushrooms, together with some bread or porridge. Indeed, when farmers replaced hunter-gatherers, average height and weight were perceptibly reduced.

These earliest European societies died out or retreated when about 25,000 BP a particularly cold phase began, during which the northern hemisphere was covered by a polar ice cap extending from Ireland to the Urals, as far south as latitude 50 degrees N. The limestone caves of south western France provide evidence of altered conditions. Only a couple of hundred miles from the Chauvet caves the Lascaux paintings of c.17,000 BP show herds of cattle, deer and horses replacing the large predators. A quite sudden temperature rise c.14,000 BP brought a return to warmer and damper conditions, the retreat of the ice cap and the start of a notable rise in sea levels, flooding such land bridges as the Straits of Dover and leaving the shoreline some four hundred feet higher than in the glacial period. About 12,000 BP an even more rapid increase in temperatures – and, given our current concern with global warming the rapidity is notable – brought a dramatic change within a single lifetime. The North African and Arabian deserts were covered with plant life, the grasslands bloomed and the forests grew nearer the Pole.

Communications with the Past

Attempts to understand our forebears, in any other than an aridly intellectual fashion, are best made by emulating them. So simple an activity as gardening, picking wild fruit or fishing, produces the same triumphs and frustrations as those experienced by the earliest hunter-gatherers. Every mother has shared in the same prime human experience and death is mourned and commemorated today as it was in the earliest days of humanity. Moving onwards in time, the most modern stock breeder congratulating himself on a successful calving, or the rabbiter inspecting his snares, is re-enacting the experience of his Neolithic predecessors. Riding a pony in the Himalayas or any wild region, sailing a small boat out of sight of land, all serve to remove oneself from the present and to share, in less extreme circumstance, the fears of pioneers and explorers: while do-it-yourself, I am told, or camping with small children repeats the discomforts and satisfactions of the first hut builders. More seriously, anyone with basic sensitivities is still impressed by the spirituality of any ancient religious site, from cave to cathedral.

With the first representational art communication in another direction becomes possible and we find that the popular idea of Stone Age Man gnawing mammoth bones in a cave needs readjustment. Probably due to Europeans fossicking for fossils and pre-historic artefacts for longer and more industriously than their fellows in other parts of the world, the earliest known representational art is itself European. From as early as 40,000 BP the former Africans settling in Europe and Near-Asia were producing accomplished works of art. The quality of the Chauvet Cave paintings is unequalled, while the contemporary carved 'Lionman' – a twelve inch long ivory figurine found in Swabia – has compelling power, is matched by the charm of the elegant little ivory horse discovered nearby, along with impressive ivories of mammoth, bison and bear. These works may well have had a religious significance, but they also exude an almost light-hearted quality of pleasure in craftsmanship.

RIGHT *A burial from the Neolithic age at Rössen, central Europe. The Rössener culture flourished between 4,600–4,300 BC and represented a cultural shift to a settled agricultural existence.*

recent, serve as sites for therapeutic ceremonies, where the shaman is entranced in a ritual dance to inspire his curative powers. Special powers too may have been attributed to those who could use the tally-sticks that acted as records, or perhaps served as lunar calendars.

Less conjecturally we can see that better methods of hunting evolved, with barbed harpoons and spear throwers, often themselves striking works of art which show a delight in the decoration of everyday objects.

Both men and women were concerned with personal appearance. As well as the hairstyles of the various Venuses, some burials contain complicated jewellery. At Sunghir, near Vladimir, the remains of an older man and two children, dated about 25,000 BP, are adorned with literally thousands of beads, ivory bracelets and pendants and have caps and belts decorated with foxes' teeth. We usually encounter these works of art visually, encased in a museum or more often in an illustration, removed from their original context. When we do have the opportunity to stand among monuments, to feel the carvings, as on the engraved standing stones near Penrith, in the North of England, breathing the same damp or dry, warm or cold air that swept past them several millennia ago, the historical experience becomes much more direct. Even more so later, in the fifth century BC, or in the medieval churches, at a time when contemporary cultures are well-recorded, and we may know the languages used by the craftsmen, such close contact is better than the text books or museums: the Molossian dogs in the Athens Kerameikos may still be available for stroking.

Written records allow another, but not necessarily clearer, view of the past: records of victories, whether on Egyptian third-millennium BC papyri or in 21st century AD headlines, are often well distanced from the truth. The most accurate records are often accountants' receipts or merchants' tallies. Language, too, needs interpretation: many valuable Sumerian and Egyptian records exist, but only the most dedicated scholars can understand the varied complexities of meaning that words and symbols might have had for the original writers. Try, for example, defining the word 'democracy' as understood today and as encountered in nineteenth century authors.

Three contemporary languages, Chinese, Greek and Hebrew, take us directly as far back as the first millennium BC and provide – with some effort – a direct contact with their ancient cultures. To attend a performance in one of the remaining Greek theatres, if we have read something of the period's history and studied the text, is to share the experience of the 5th century Greek, down to the majestic sounds of the classical language: but remember to take a cushion. Latin brings us closer to the present day, not as a spoken language but as the foundation for ideas and concepts that have become part of our everyday life, as ad infinitum to mathematicians, ultra vires, cui bono and a score of others for lawyers, even vox pop for radio and television producers.

A different type of historical continuity is found in legal and constitutional documents – Magna Carta being the famous example – which have taken their place in laws and institutions. Some at least of Magna Carta's provisions are still strikingly relevant, and could do with being much more widely applied. On Free Trade for example: 'All merchants to have safe and secure exit from, and entry to England, and the right to stay there and to move about by sea as well as by land'. And, most particularly 'No free man shall be... in any way destroyed... except by the lawful judgement of his peers or by the law of the land.'

There is nothing light-hearted about the 'Venus of Hohle Fels', which may be as early as 40,000 BP. The enormous breasts and belly, the prominent vulva of the ivory figurine all symbolise fecundity. Several thousand years later the 'Venus of Willendorf' and the 'Venus of Dolni Vestonice', the world's oldest known ceramic, continue the tradition, but slimmer and more naturalistic forms also develop. The Brassempouy pouting head could come from a comic strip, but the number and ubiquity of female figures, and the absence of any male representations – even the Lionman may be female – substantiate the presence of a maternal deity and the richness of the regional culture. At the same time the cave-paintings, with their shaman-like representations and their focus on the hunt suggest a male cult, perhaps accompanied by thaumaturgic rites like those celebrated today by the Botswana Bushmen (San). The Kalahari caves which house their paintings, some comparatively

The 'Temple Scroll' is one of the longest of the Dead Sea Scrolls, which were written in around 150 BC to AD 70 . It contains regulations on Jewish religious ritual and practices, including sacrifices and the design of the perfect temple.

Cambridge University celebrated its 800th anniversary in 2010: in 1229 King Henry III of England gave the new institution, and its sister university at Oxford, a helping hand by sending an open letter to the masters and students of the University of Paris:

'Because of the many tribulations and difficulties you have undergone under the evil law of Paris, we, humbly suffering with you, desire out of reverence for God and the holy church, piously to aid you in restoring your condition to its due liberty. Therefore we announce to your community that, if it pleases you to come to our kingdom of England and make this the permanent centre of your studies. Whatever cities, boroughs or towns you chose to elect we shall assign to you, to be set aside for that purpose, and we shall in every way give you cause to rejoice, as is fitting, in the liberty and tranquillity which is pleasing to God and which ought to be fully sufficient for you.'

Moving closer to the present, the next stage of historical perspective might be called 'grandmother's spectacles' – the world as perceived two generations previously, transmitted by people we have known personally, who used words in senses we understood. Thus my own view of late 19th- and 20th-century history is coloured by my grandparents' attitudes: Garibaldi and Gladstone were heroes, Lloyd George very nearly so; Ramsay MacDonald was suspect. Fair dealing and compassion were more important than equality, self reliance and community action more reliable than government intervention.

Then we have the evidence of our own experiences, usually more impressionistic than objective: watching the Jarrow protest marchers or receiving one's first gas mask gave an unmatched flavour of the period, but do not help with impartial analyses of the causes and consequences of World War II. Having been bombed by both the Luftwaffe and the Irish Republican Army also tends to breed resentment, which needs to be consciously rejected. Finally there comes a time when the pressure of actuality sets in. We are too near the events to see clearly, as history becomes reportage and the sheer volume of information uncontrollable. For the purpose of this book I have chosen this moment as being 11 September 2001, when the attacks on the New York World Trade Center and Washington, DC changed the course of history.

FARMERS TO EMPERORS

	6000 BC	5000 BC	3000 BC	2000 BC	1500 BC	1000 BC
THE MIDDLE EAST	*c.7000 BC* First settlement at Jericho established *c.6800 BC* Large settlement at Catal Huyuk, Turkey *c.5300–3050 BC* Egyptian Predynastic Period	LEFT *Egyptian hieroglyphs carved in stone* *c.3500 BC* The first cities develop in southern Mesopotamia *c.3300–3000 BC* Hieroglyph script developed *c.3100 BC* Upper and Lower Egypt united; Memphis founded *c.3000 BC* Uruk is the largest settlement in the world	*c.2686–2181 BC* Old Kingdom Period *c.2620–2503 BC* City of the dead at Giza constructed *c.2334 BC* Sargon of Agade conquers Mesopotamia, starting the Akkadian empire *c.2300 BC* Harkaf's expedition to Kush *c.2000 BC* Indo–European peoples (Archaeans) settle in Greece; Minoan palaces are built on Crete	*c.1792–1750 BC* Babylon becomes the greatest power in Mesopotamia *1696–1654 BC* Hammurabi of Babylon establishes first legal code *c.1650–1550 BC* 'Asiatic' dynasty founded at Hyskos *1600 BC* Emergence of Mycenaean civilization *c.1595 BC* Babylon destroyed by the Hittites *c.1550 BC* Foundation of the Kingdom of Mitani	*1504–1492 BC* Egyptian empire reaches its greatest extent under Thutmose I *c.1450 BC* Mycenaeans conquer Crete *1352–1336 BC* Legend of Gilgamesh written **13th or 12th century** BC Legendary Trojan War waged against the city of Troy by the Achaeans *1176 BC* Invasion of the Delta region by the 'Sea Peoples' driven off	*900–800 BC* First Greek city states founded *c.796 BC* Assyrian empire founded by Tiglath-Pileser *c.747 BC* Start of the Nubian dynasty of Pharaohs *729 BC* Babylon occupied by the Assyrians *c.671–651 BC* The Assyrians occupy Egypt *612 BC* Fall of the Assyrian empire *586 BC* Jewish captivity in Babylon
INDIA AND CHINA		*c.5000 BC* Hunter–gatherers become pastoralists in Indus Valley region *c.3200 BC* The first ranked societies are found in the Longshan culture LEFT *White pottery pitcher dating from the Longshan culture*	*c.2600–1900 BC* Indus Valley civilization flourishes *c.2205–1766 BC* Traditional dates of the Xia dynasty, the first dynasty in China to be mentioned in historical chronicles	*1900 BC* Indus cities enter their decline *1600–c.1122 BC* Period of the Shang dynasty	*c.1500 BC* Aryans, semi–nomadic people from Central Europe, migrate into the Indian subcontinent *1122 BC* King Wu of Zhou founds the Western Zhou dynasty	*771 BC* Zhou capital moves to Louyang, marking the start of the period known as the Eastern Zhou, which runs to 255 BC
AFRICA AND THE AMERICAS		*4500–2500 BC* Period of Saharan fertility	*c.3000–2500 BC* Domestication of alpacas and llamas. Root crops grown in the Andes *2500 BC* Herdsmen move into the Sahel	*c.1250 BC* The Olmec of Mesoamerica live in chiefdoms ruled by powerful hereditary elite		*590 BC* Meroë, on the east bank of the Nile, becomes the capital of Nubia, northeastern Africa
OLD EUROPE AND ROME	*c.6000 BC* Emergence of settled cultures in the Danube Basin. High quality ceramics and metal working produced	*c.4300 BC* Slow decline in Old European cultures. *c.4000 BC* Evidence of written language *c.3300 BC* Copper smelting starts in Central Europe RIGHT *The standing stones of the Stonehenge ancient monument, Wiltshire, England*	*c.2500 BC* Bronze is made in Central Europe	*c.2000 BC* The Wessex culture flourishes in Britain *c.2000 BC* The main stage of Stonehenge is completed in Britain	*c.1600 BC* First boats using planked construction are built on the River Humber, England	*c.1000 BC* Urnfield cultures spread to Europe *c.750 BC* Beginning of Hallstatt ('Celtic culture') of Central and Western Europe *c.753 BC* The traditional date of the foundation of Rome *616 BC* Etruscan hegemony in central Italy

6000BC – 500AD

550 BC Cyrus the Great founds the Achaemenid Persian empire

539 BC The Babylonian empire conquered by Cyrus the Great

490 BC Greeks defeat the Persians at the Battle of the Plains of Marathon

480 BC Greeks halt the Persians at the Battle of Salamis

431–403 BC Peloponnesian War between Sparta and Athens

359–336 BC Reign of Philip of Macedonia

330 BC Achaemenid Persian empire occupied by Alexander the Great

323 BC Alexander the Great dies in Babylon

321–316 BC Alexander's empire breaks up as his generals seize territory

312 BC Seleucus I captures Babylon and founds the Seleucid empire

167 BC Jewish Maccabees revolt against rulers

160 BC– AD 224 Parthian Empire

142–63 BC Judea independent, then conquered by Rome

6 BC Birth of Christ

AD 30–33 Christ's ministry as recorded in the Gospels

AD 40–70 St. Paul brings Christianity to Rome

AD 70 Jerusalem rebellion suppressed by Trajan: final destruction of the Temple

LEFT *The Palace of Xerxes at Persepolis, which is believed to have been badly damaged when Alexander the Great destroyed Persepolis in 330* AD

559–479 BC Lifetime of Confucius

550–450 BC Lifetime of Buddha and Mahavira

518 BC The Achaemenid Persians conquer the Indus Valley

c.304 BC Macedonia cedes the Indus Valley to Chandragupta Maurya

261 BC Conquest of Kalinga in eastern India by Ashoka marks the zenith of the Mauryan empire

221 BC Start of Qin (Chin) dynasty

209–202 BC Civil War; Qin overthrown and Han dynasty established

c.185 BC Mauryan dynasty collapses

c.120 BC Chinese Imperial University founded

AD 220 Deposition of last Han emperor; China splits into three kingdoms

AD 220–590 China's 'period of disunion', with constant warfare and nomad invasion

AD 320 Foundation of the Gupta kingdom

AD 350 Indian traders and refugees establish Kingdom of Funan around the Mekong Delta

AD 375–467 Gupta Empire extends over northern India

c.500 BC Monte Alban becomes a Zapotec ceremonial centre

c.480 BC Taruga, Nigeria, flourishes as an iron–working centre

400–300 BC Iron working is established in the east African highlands

c.200 BC The city of Teotihuacan is founded in southern Mexico

c.100 BC The Moche state comes into being in coastal Peru

LEFT *Carving of the mythical bird, Quetzal Mariposa, at Teotihuacan, Mexico*

c.AD 350 Fall of the kingdom of Meroë; King Ezana of Axum converts to Christianity

c.AD 500 From this date Monte Alban and the Moche state are in decline and Teotihuacan now has a population of over 100,000

AD 1–100 The kingdom of Axum emerges in northern Ethiopia

480 BC Foundation of Roman Republic

390 BC A tribe of Gauls destroy Rome

343–290 BC The Samnite Wars establish Rome as the dominant power in Italy

264–241 BC The First Punic War between Rome and Carthage

216 BC Rome is defeated by Hannibal

202 BC Carthage defeated by Rome

49 BC Caesar invades Italy

48 BC Roman invasion of Britain

44 BC Caesar murdered. Augustus becomes Emperor

RIGHT *A 19th century painting of the Roman defeat at Teutoburg in* AD *9*

AD 133 Hadrian's defensive wall across northern Britain is completed

AD 167 Lombard invasion of Italy across frozen River Danube

AD 207–284 Collapse of Roman Imperial rule

AD 406 Vandals, Suevi and Alans invade Gaul

AD c.450 Anglo–Saxon migrations to Britain begin; Slavs raid and settle in the Balkans

AD 410 Visigoths under Alaric sack Rome

AD 476 Deposition of the last Emperor Romulus Augustulus marks the symbolic end of the Western Roman Empire

LEFT *Statue of Roman emperor Julius Caesar*

AD 286 Diocletian divides the Roman Empire into east and west

AD 313 Constantine's Edict of Milan confirms toleration of all religions

The River Civilizations

■ Emergence of settled cultures in the Danube Basin *c.*6000 BC ■ Farming begins in the Fertile Crescent of Mesopotamia *c.*6000 BC ■ Uruk develops into the first of the Mesopotamian city-states *c.*4300 BC ■ First signs of a written language *c.*4000 BC ■ Rise of Assyria *c.*1800 BC

The earliest Eurasian civilizations developed in the floodplains of the great rivers, such as the Danube, Nile, Euphrates, Tigris and Indus. As well as providing people with essential water, abundant level land was available for grazing and for cultivating crops, while fish and game augmented their diet.

In whatever part of the world they chose to wander, the most readily available food source to Neolithic man was fish: from Europe to Australia mounds of oyster shells commemorate the courage of the first humans to pioneer that particular food source.

First Civilizations of Old Europe

Widely separated communities adapted to their changing environment, exploring new techniques, not always with the same degree of success, as human ingenuity adapted itself to local circumstances. Farming first developed in Anatolia, where cattle and sheep were domesticated and the seeds of native cereals and peas cultivated as early as the ninth millennium BC. A small spring was enough to encourage a settlement. At Jericho in Palestine, which claims the longest period of habitation in the world, a quite large defended village had been built as early as 7000 BC, while further north, Jarmo in Kurdistan was flourishing at an altitude of around 3,300 feet (1,000 metres). Only a few hundred years later quite large settlements were emerging, most notably at Çatal Höyük, in Anatolian Turkey, with an estimated population of 7,000, and farmers were moving westwards, through the Aegean to Central Europe and onwards to Spain and across the English Channel. The most extended of the new cultures emerged in and around the Danube Basin about 6000 BC.

Bringing with them wheat and barley seeds, peas and domesticated livestock, the people of what is generally known as 'Old Europe' inhabited planned villages, with substantial timber houses, containing ovens, with living spaces separated from their animals – mainly sheep and pigs, but with some cattle – probably as comfortable as any to be found in that region for the next 6,000 years. Their sophisticated products, which included woven cloth and a wide range of pottery, give some idea of their social structure. Few works of art are more mysterious than the figurines. They come individually or grouped, male and female, young and old. One set is placed in a raised bowl, perhaps an architectural reference: another group of 12, has six of either gender (the males differentiated both by size and by sexual characteristics) and of different ages; all but one of the females are clothed. Manufactured with careful skill, they are clearly important symbols, but whether religious, social, or domestic is open to question. One Danubian community, the Cucuteni, produced what could be a 'Parliament of Women' – 21 small but majestic female terracotta figures seated in a circle. From the same region, two very different monochrome figurines, a seated man with his head in his hands – a prototype 'Thinker' – and a woman, head raised to the sky and hands poised on one knee, display a contemplative sensibility that few later artworks can surpass. Danubian society may have been matriarchal, and certainly technical developments increased the social importance of women's work. Spinning, weaving, pottery, and breadmaking, in the form of unleavened flatbreads, were all added to the domestic agenda, while milk from the household animals could be poured into pots, enabling older children to feed the babies, enhancing women's freedom – and allowing them to take on all those extra tasks.

Danubian pottery is uniquely diverse, going far beyond utilitarian pots and dishes to include a variety of stands, shallow double-dishes, delicate ladles and covered pots, all suggesting that some meals were served with elegant formality – perhaps another proof of a female-centred culture. Cheerfulness, too, keeps breaking in, with a stemmed cup in the form of a girl with hands clasped around her waist, or a small animal, which could serve as anything from a bonbon dish to a knife rest.

LEFT *The fired-clay male figurine commonly known as the 'Thinker', made by the Neolithic Hamangia culture of Romania, c.5000–4600 BC.*

Old Europe was one of the first societies to develop a written language, although the evidence is slight – some clay tablets dated about 4000 BC with pictographic symbols arranged in what appears to be a meaningful order. The Danubians were also among the first metallurgists; the mass of metal discovered in that area – more than six tonnes of copper goods and several kilos of gold – is greater than that found in all the other regions of Europe and the Levant combined. Sophisticated jewellery and clothing hinted at some social distinctions, but these were not reflected in high-status housing; all domestic accommodation was workmanlike, but with no pretensions to even modest distinction. In time the villages became very large, extending over as much as 400 hectares (1,000 acres), but they remained villages without much in the way of communal centres of administration or religion, and usually without more than the most basic defences. Without over-population, and with agricultural techniques helping to combat land exhaustion, societies remained generally peaceable.

What caused Old Europe's slow decline, from century 4300 BC, is unclear. A brisk cold spell, between 4100–3800 with more frequent flooding and soil erosion might have depressed the economy, but there was certainly some violence from raiders who began crossing from the steppes over the rivers, the first of those 'barbarians' who were to disrupt established civilizations. By that time Old European societies were developing in different forms,

ABOVE *A wall painting (c.6000 BC) of hunters stalking game animals from the large Neolithic settlement at Çatal Höyük in Anatolia. Perhaps the first 'town' in the modern sense, at times the settlement had a population of as much as 10,000 people.*

notably evident in such ritual enclosures as Stonehenge and Avebury, and the extraordinary Maeshowe chamber tomb on Orkney. Planked boats found on the River Humber show how megaliths could be moved by water.

The Land Between the Rivers

No one society could rightly claim to be the prime originator of civilization, for all contributed to improving the human condition. Some 6,000 miles (9,600 km) away, on the other side of the world, the inhabitants of what is now Japan had already produced what may well be the world's first pottery, and were living in substantial villages. On the Bolan Pass, in the hill country between Pakistan and Afghanistan, the residents of Mehrgarh had established a mixed farming system. Their small, mud-brick villages housed people and animals, and provided storage for their cultivated grain and dried dates. Their technology did not extend to ceramics, but did include the delicate art of drilling teeth, the first example of dentistry.

ABOVE *One of the two main panels on the Royal Standard of Ur, a box-like artefact discovered in one of the royal graves at Ur in present day Iraq, dating from around 2600 BC. The scene, dubbed 'Peace', shows servants parading animals and goods in front of dignitaries. A companion scene of 'War' is on the other side of the standard.*

But the best documented, and the most influential, advances were made in the Asian Fertile Crescent, extending from the Persian Gulf to the Eastern Mediterranean, following the course of the twin rivers, the Tigris and the Euphrates. Travellers could move upriver on the Tigris to Anatolia and then on to the Black and Caspian Seas, giving access to Central Asia. The Euphrates, the western stream, led on to Aleppo and the shores of the Mediterranean – the greatest trade route of the ancient world – and then south through Lebanon and Palestine to the Egyptian empire. By sea, it was a simple passage to the mouths of the Indus River – and Egypt and the Indus valleys were the homes of the other great contemporary cultures.

In northern Mesopotamia – the 'Land Between the Rivers' – the rainfall is consistent enough for reliable cropping, but cultivation in the southerly flood plain depends upon the spring floods and subsequent irrigation, shaping therefore two types of society: the Sumerian and Babylonian in the South, distinguished by their scientific originality and urban magnificence and the northern Assyrians, famous warriors and empire builders. Distinctions are never quite so convenient, the Babylonians were quite capable of sustained violence and the northern Halaf craftsmen produced exquisite early pottery – but the triumphal savagery illustrated on the Assyrian reliefs, of impaled victims, mangled corpses, and prisoners writing in agony, has no equivalent in the southern cities of Sumer.

All within a few dozen miles of each other, the earliest of these, viewed from 8,000 years later, seem attractive societies. Their myths relate how the god of Eridu, Enki-Marduk, was fond of beer, which led him into trouble when man

was created, and a junior goddess, who had also imbibed, is allowed to try her hand. She moulds six creatures, but all lack some essentials: a solution is needed, and all are found a suitable post; the blind girl is made a singer, while the individual lacking sexual organs becomes a civil servant.

The goddess Ishtar was charged with protecting sexual desire: when she takes a trip to the underworld, the Earth grows cold:

> *'No young man impregnated a girl*
> *in the street*
> *The young man slept in his private room*
> *The girl slept in the company of her friends.'*

Much the same agreeable impression is given by the grave goods – children being buried with their toys, or a young man with a dog in his lap – and even the dog has a bone between its teeth.

This pleasantly relaxed life style centred on the city of Uruk, by *c.*3000 BC the world's largest settlement, bigger than Athens at the height of its power, three millennia later, and the centre of a mixed population, traders and residents from many regions. Its prosperity is shown by the development of written communications – not for literary reasons but for prosaic accountancy, the recording of quantities for such trade items as grain, beer, or metals, handled by a trained bureaucracy, providing security for an extensive trade, but surely annoying to the operators of riverboats, required to ship a scribe as supercargo.

Uruk's civilization – and the word is now certainly appropriate – continued to be generally peaceful for most of the fourth millennium; surprisingly no power structure, no overriding authority, seems to have developed: all classes rubbed along together. If it has survived the recent upheavals, the Warka

Vase in the National Museum of Iraq in Baghdad epitomizes Uruk life, with goddess Ishtar (at this time named Inanna) receiving the tribute of a naked man, the leader of a procession of powerfully-built fellows bearing gifts. Inanna was worth propitiating, since she ensured:

'That its people would eat splendid food,
That its people drink splendid beverages,
That those bathed (for holidays) would rejoice
in the courtyards…
That acquaintances would dine together…'

It was perhaps too good to last, and later cities developed into monarchies, and even into empires. Hegemony moved upstream to the region of Akkad, where a dynasty was founded by Semitic-speaking newcomers from Arabia. The imperious crowned head of an Akkadian king, perhaps the famous Sargon (c.2334–2278 BC), with a ceremonial wig and curled beard, epitomizes a new era when dynasties ruled the cities. His scribes, who may

well have exaggerated, claimed that Sargon and his successors established some control over all Mesopotamia and the surrounding region, but without great disruptions: local city government continued, but the idea of a king/emperor was generally accepted. What followed was often to be repeated; the monarch assumed the responsibility and the privileges of the local gods, and appropriated the temples' property. Unity was expressed by imperial standards – of value, measures, laws and also of language, as the Akkadian language replaced Sumerian, which however survived as a learned language, much like Latin in early modern times.

And, as with subsequent empires, Akkad declined, harassed by rebellions and invasions with the leadership returning to Ur where some of the finest ancient works of art were produced (e.g. the gold and lapis-lazuli ram in the British Museum) before Ur, too, succumbed: the temptations offered by rich cities were too great for the nomadic Arabian tribes. The next great empire began in the small town of Babylon, where the long reign of Hammurabi (1792–1750 BC) remains famous for his extensive legal code, the foundation of much subsequent law, which covered family, contract, financial and criminal law, court procedure and punishment in great detail. This first

WRITING

'Because the messenger's mouth was heavy and he couldn't repeat the message,
The lord of Kulaba patted some clay and put words on it, like a tablet -
Until then, there had been no putting words on clay.'
(FROM THE SUMERIAN EPIC POEM *ENMERKAR AND THE LORD OF ARATTA*)

Writing develops according to need. A hunter-gatherer group will find it useful to have a few common signs – rather like the chalk marks that English tramps once used on gateposts to show whether the householders were kindly or not – but more complex societies need records. Traders have to record deliveries, keep accounts, send out bills; tax gatherers must calculate assessments and acknowledge payments, and all in a form which will be intelligible to others. Priests and magnates want to issue laws, encourage obedience and proclaim their own power. Once a written language is widely understood, others then take to writing for pleasure or are driven by cultural pressure, and literature begins.

In all probability, writing began independently in various parts of the world – China , Egypt, and the Americas almost certainly – but the Sumerians have left the most prolific records, beginning in the late 3000s BC and continuing

for three millennia – and the records, thanks to the longevity of the clay tablets, much greater than that of paper or parchment, have proved extraordinarily permanent. The art of writing and notation had to be taught, and therefore many of the earliest texts are dictionaries and word lists. Each city had facilities to train scribes, who then became an élite. In earlier days the written word had real power, often magical, as when fragments of holy books were worn as protective charms, and the ability to proclaim laws, human or divine, without fear of contradiction conferred real authority. But scribal centres also produced original literature, and the Sumerians certainly had the edge when it came to both the quantity and quality of their early literature.

The principal epic, of Gilgamesh, predates the Bible and Homer, with the standard version edited in about 1300–1000 BC, using parts of earlier works from 1,000 years previously. Gilgamesh was probably a real person, king of Uruk about 2700 BC and the epic tells of the hero and his companion Enkidu's adventures among monsters, giants and gods, culminating in Gilgamesh's lone quest for the secret of eternal life.

A Sumerian clay tablet, using pictograms to record stores of commodities. These pictograms later developed into cuneiform script, the earliest writing system.

Mathematics

Babylon's legacy is not expressed in great buildings, or even in works of art but in literature, science and mathematics. Beginning as early as 3000 BC, Sumerians were mastering simple arithmetic and geometry and developing aids to calculation, tables of squares and cubes, using that very useful sexagesimal system, combining decimals and duodecimals. That absolute foundation of all modern mathematics, geography and chronology – the 360 degrees in a circle, the 60-second, 60-minute and 24-hour divisions of time – are all Babylonian inventions. Their astronomers were the first to realize that planetary movements were periodic and therefore mathematically predictable: the movements of Venus, recorded in a seventh-century BC text, were probably made much earlier. They knew the lunar influence on the tides and, more than 2,000 years before Galileo, Babylonians had established the rotation of the Earth and its movement around the Sun. Being essentially a trading people, they combined astronomy with astrology to forecast lucky and unlucky events, and produced tables for calculating rates of interest.

The cuneiform system of wedge-shaped characters inscribed on clay with a reed pen made constructing numerals easy, and with the use of positioning to indicate value and gaps where we might use a point, simple arithmetic was possible, but fractions presented some difficulties. One essential was lacking, the idea of zero, which had to wait, probably until the sixth century AD for the Indian invention of today's numeration.

This cuneiform tablet, found in the Mesopotamian city of Uruk and dating from around the third to the first century BC, is an astrological table, decorated with images of a woman, a raven and a star.

episode of Babylonian rule was short lived: by 1531 BC Hammurabi's dynasty was at an end.

While the Mesopotamian south was enjoying such splendours, clouds were gathering in the north. The higher lands around the two rivers, today's northern-Syria and Iraq, were developing a notably individual culture. The Hurrians, who flourished between 2,500–1,300 BC, produced the first musical notation (c.1800 BC), and in one Kikkuli, the first author to write a treatise on horse-training. Remaining as a congeries of city-states until c.1500 BC, Hurrian culture strongly influenced the neighbouring Hittites and

Assyrians – both Indo-European – before uniting into an extensive short-lived empire, that of Mitanni, extending some 500 miles (800 km) inland from the Euphrates to the Mediterranean. Mitanni was forcibly but gradually conquered by the Hittites, who swept south to destroy Babylon at some time before 1500 BC with help from the Assyrians, the rising power to the East. The Babylonians demonstrated great powers of recuperation and flourished under a foreign occupation, that of the Kassites, an Iranian tribe, who stabilized a new Babylonian state, which endured until c.1155 BC.

The Rise and Dominance of Assyria

In northern Mesopotamia, the land of wooded hills and grassy plains, the Assyrians had absorbed Sumerian culture, and continued to use the Akkadian language in diplomatic business, exchanging ambassadors between Egypt, Babylon, the Hittites and less significant magnates. Trade with Anatolia and the East passed through their capital at Ashur, which was ruled by a board of city merchants, which evolved by the 1300s BC into an ambitious kingdom, dealing on equal terms with the neighbouring empires. Babylon constituted the main rival, admired for its culture, but permanently in contention for leadership. Under the Assyrian monarchs Tiglath-Pileser III (746–722 BC) and his successor Sargon II, ruling from the new capital of Nineveh, the triumphant Assyrian years began, recorded not only in boastful texts:

'I filled the broad plain with the corpses of their mighty men, with their blood I dyed the mountains like scarlet wool … A pile of heads against his city I set.'

but also in the series of reliefs describing victories and the pleasures of the hunt. Unlike Egyptian reliefs, those of the Assyrians are vividly naturalistic, especially in their representation of animals: horses gallop, lions stagger under the impact of arrow-shafts, and gazelles and hares are carried off to the kitchen. Kings are not shown as larger than life, but as accompanying their soldiers into battle, or conferring with their counsellors. But there is no mistaking royal power, stamped on the peoples' consciousness by those massive winged bulls that stood at the palaces' entrances.

At its peak the Assyrian empire extended from the Persian Gulf to the Mediterranean and the Red Sea. Provincial governors were supervised by imperial inspectors, with proclamations and orders travelling along the fine roads connecting the capital with Susa in Elam and Anatolian Gordium. Among the Assyrians' more consistent enemies were the Medes, from present-day Iran, the Egyptians and the Babylonians. In 701, an Egyptian attack, made in alliance with King Hezekiah, king of the small but strategic state of Judea, was repelled, and two years later Babylon itself was sacked by the Assyrians, and its whole population, or at any rate its more prominent members deported to Nineveh. Egypt remained a constant threat, but Assyrian magnificence came to a sudden end in 612 BC, when a coalition of Babylonians, Medes and Scythians from the north overwhelmed Nineveh and re-established Babylonian rule, with the great city once again becoming civilization's leader. A new empire, more splendid than before, arose only years later under Nabopolasser, 'son of nobody', as he described himself. This was the period of Babylonian magnificence, with the great ziggurat, the 'Tower of Babel', the Hanging Gardens of Babylon, and gorgeous palaces. Even the streets and gates of the city – the imposing Ishtar Gate being the best example – were lavishly ornamented, with glazed tiles, gold, silver, and

lapis-lazuli decorations symbolizing Babylon's present wealth and ancient culture. There can have been nothing in the ancient world to compare with the magnificent entrance to the city, from the Festival House, through the Ishtar Gate, down the Processional Way to the palaces, temples and ziggurats. Those towering structures, raised tier upon tier, were stairways to heaven, enabling the priests to access the divinities – and since the gods were local, also proclaiming the wealth and power of the city and its rulers. The Hanging Gardens, one of the Seven Wonders of the Ancient World, was probably a ziggurat with cultivated terraces, but since ziggurats were constructed

ABOVE *King Ashurbanipal of Assyria, who ruled from 685 to 627 BC, shown stabbing a rampaging lion in the belly during a hunt, from a bas-relief (c.645–635 BC) in the Nineveh Palace.*

of baked mud brick, nothing remains but huge piles of rubble, and some fanciful reconstructions. Babylon's heyday was splendid but brief, as recounted in Jewish history. In 597 BC, Nebuchadnezzar deported thousands of Jews to Babylon: in 539 BC, Cyrus the Great, King of Persia took the city and released the captives.

Early Empires

■ Earliest farming communities in South Asia *c.*6000 BC ■ Narmer unites Upper and Lower Egypt *c.*3100 BC ■ Growth of cities in the Indus Valley *c.*3000 BC ■ 'Sea Peoples' threaten Mediterranean region *c.*1100 BC

The civilizations of the Indus and Nile Valleys could hardly be more different. Egypt was a centralized autocracy, surviving for 3,000 years, with a divine, omnipotent monarch ruling a highly organized state, while the Indus was home to several independent municipalities, trading with each other and the outside world, without the need for defensive or collective endeavours: one left records of unparalleled detail, while the other disappeared almost without trace.

The first farming communities in Southern Asia developed at sites such as Mehrgarh in the mountains of Baluchistan as early as 6000 BC and spread from there into the Indus Valley in the fourth millennium.

Civilizations of the Indus Valley

It is difficult to consider the Indus Valley cultures between 4000 and 2000 BC dispassionately; the consistent charm and humanity is overwhelming. No grandiose Egyptian monstrosities deface the region: no ambitious and aggressive Mesopotamian rulers contend for dominance; the cities lack complex defences, great temples or public buildings – but the houses were equipped with bathrooms, toilets, main drains and constant water supply. Natural resources were prolific. The great river system, helped by irrigation, provided consistent water supplies throughout the 2,000-plus miles (3,200 km) of the system. Available crops ranged from basic cereals, through temperate-zone fruits such as grapes, almonds and figs to tropical dates. The world's most abundant sources of semi-precious stones – lapis-lazuli, carnelians, turquoise – were found within easy reach, as were 'fish-eyes' (pearls) and copper.

The archaeological record begins before 5000 BC, with small villages of hunter-gatherers turning into pastoralists – goats were the first animals to be domesticated (always excepting the dog which domesticated itself in very ancient times, and then collected other creatures into the folds). Local barleys and wild wheat varieties (emmer, einkorn) were encouraged, and by 3000 BC ceramics had developed to a high standard, both technically

and aesthetically. Figurines display what might be thought of as distinctively 'Indian' features. The early stylized female forms develop into seductive long-legged, high-breasted girls with hair either elaborately styled or flowing free. The area covered by settlements was vast – the best part of 1,000 miles (1,600 km) north into the Himalayas and even beyond the Hindu Kush, and perhaps half that distance from west to east. But unlike the other great culture-regions of Egypt, Mesopotamia, Anatolia, or Iran, the Indus never developed into anything resembling an empire. The city-state, a metropolis and its hinterland, remained the model.

Harappa and Mohenjo-Daro are today the most visible of the Indus cities that grew after 3000 BC. Some 400 miles (640 km) apart, and showing some local differences, both towns and the few other excavated sites have in common a well-considered and beautifully engineered town plan, with residential and public quarters methodically arranged. Water supply and sanitation were priorities: in Mohenjo-Daro no fewer than 700 domestic wells have been found, each serving two to three houses, all carefully constructed with specially shaped bricks. Many houses also had bathing and sanitary facilities, the bath on an inclined platform, some with a toilet either furnished with a seat or the still-common squatting privy. All the waste from each house was drained into a common network of sewers, which fed into cesspits and soakaways. Since this complex infrastructure had to be constructed before any building was begun, a sophisticated planning

LEFT *Terracotta statue of a 'mother deity' from the Indus River site of Mohenjo-Daro, c.2500–1800 BC.*

This seal, which was found during the excavation of Mohenjo-Daro in the 1920s, is thought to show a deity named Pashupati, who was regarded as 'Lord of the Beasts': a rhinoceros, an elephant, a tiger, goats and a bull can all be clearly made out. The god is seated in a yogic position.

system was essential, while the continuous supervision and repair work demanded a well-organized municipal government with access to advanced engineering techniques.

Indus prosperity was underpinned by trade, and especially in luxuries. Agate, alabaster, chalcedony, jasper, chert, steatite, and seashells were processed and assembled into fine jewellery or precisely measured weights: cotton, linen and jute fabrics were woven. Stone-ware bangles – much sought after - were mass-produced by a sophisticated technology; highly crafted ceramics were made by experts to fine tolerances. These products were exported, mainly to Mesopotamia, starting their travel either by cattle-drawn carts (another Indus first) or river boat, thence by sea through the Persian Gulf, calling at Arabian ports, notably Oman. Records, presumably of provenance, were attested by merchant's seals, which bore some indications of a writing system, still undiscovered: but perhaps the Indians were too busy enjoying life to want to write about it, or to leave vainglorious inscriptions. This impression is justified by the justly-famous bronze statuette, usually known as the Dancing Girl, long-legged, wearing bangles and nothing else but an elaborate hairstyle. She stands, hand on hip, head defiantly thrown back: –- the seductive charm of India epitomized.

From about 1900 BC the Indus cities simply closed down, although life continued normally in the villages. There seems to have been no violent upheaval, although that was to come later. Perhaps the cause was related to radical alterations in the river's course, which could have affected the irrigation works; but for whatever reason, one of the ancient world's finest civilizations came to a quiet end, possibly assisted by a change to cooler weather, but certainly associated with new arrivals from the West. The newcomers who moved from the steppes to succeed the Harappans, harass the Babylonians and invade Egypt, and who went on to populate all Europe, were Indo-Europeans, who called themselves 'Araya' – Aryans. They brought with them new and improved livestock, most significantly the horse, and with the horse, wheeled vehicles. It may be that mounting a horse, thereby raising oneself above people on foot, prompts aggressive feelings, but whether by force or more peacefully, the new people supplanted the old.

The immigration did not stop, but continued for over 5,000 years, with new waves, all originating in the same area – the Central Asian Steppes – and especially the region north of the Black and Caspian Seas. And all spoke variants of the same original language. Today, from Ireland to Bangladesh – and much further afield in cultural colonies such as the Americas and Australia – Indo-European languages are spoken; the most widespread, English (or variants thereof) is used as an official or as a second language by more than 2 billion people. Other new languages, such as Finno-Ugric, came with later immigrants, but the only survivor of an original European tongue is Basque, a language isolate (i.e. with no related languages).

Another language group came from the South. Hebrew and Arabic are Semitic languages: like 'Aryan', overlaid with spurious racism, the word 'Semite' has become misapplied, to signify one particular group whose liturgical language is Semitic, revived in the 19th century to become the national language of the State of Israel.

A New Culture on the Nile

Egypt was unlike any other ancient empire: its vast size, extending 2,000 miles (3,200 km) from tropical Africa north to the Mediterranean and the Levant, and west and east into Libya and the Sinai Peninsula, was much greater than the Mesopotamian or Anatolian states. Equally unique was its continuity. For a period of perhaps 4,000 years after 4000 BC, the people of the Nile Valley enjoyed a settled existence, living for much of the time in a well-regulated state – a record for almost any period of human history. The artistic achievements of the empire are more impressive and varied than those of any other ancient civilization, and their influence on world history similarly significant.

The Nile was the key to all Egyptian history. In an otherwise arid climate, the annual floods between August and September provided a subsequent growing season of exceptional productivity, which enabled an unmatched cereal harvest. As the Sahara – once an extensive savannah supporting a variety of wildlife – dried up as the climate changed, its inhabitants moved towards the tempting Nile Valley. This formed a very extensive oasis, which once the seeds and techniques of cereal cultivation had been passed on, became the ancient world's granary, a magnet for all surrounding populations. Before its promise could be fulfilled, the seasonal floods had to be controlled by extensive irrigation, which demanded large-scale labour: and that in turn needed a strong central organization.

In the earliest stages settlement was tentative: by the time structured societies were evolving Old Europe had already diminished to the point of extinction. The third millennium BC saw the development of towns and their unification into two separate states, Upper Egypt, centred around Hierakonpolis and Thebes, and Lower Egypt, the Nile Delta, rule over which was symbolized by two separate crowns. When the first identified kings appear, traditionally with Narmer-Menes, who united Upper and Lower Egypt in *c.*3100 BC, what might be called the 'Classical Egyptian Period', that of the Great Pyramids and the Sphinx, began around the Nile-Delta capital of Memphis.

the marvellous constructions, also injected a constant stimulus into the economy. Not only kings and royal families, but civil servants and priests invested huge sums in pyramids, stelae and memorial shrines (mastaba), which were filled with grave goods to support the dead during their sojourn in the realm of Osiris. A constant demand, well beyond that of the living population, gave employment to labourers, craftsmen and artists.

So extended a realm and so complex a society could not be run by a centralized government, even one with so skilled a bureaucracy, especially when the capital at Memphis, near the present-day metropolis of Cairo, was located at the downstream extremity of the river. Accordingly, from *c.*2350 BC the territory was divided into provinces, administered by a governor, the 'nomarch'. Often almost a viceroy, nomarchs enjoyed great respect, as one boastfully recorded for posterity:

' *…nobody like myself existed before nor will he exist…I was the one who found the solution when it was lacking…I am the hero without equal.'*

Nomarch Ankhtfi had perhaps something to brag about, since in the early 2100s BC he had been faced with a crisis, a civil war with neighbouring nomarchs and a shortage of food. The crisis passed and from 2055 BC a cultural renaissance began, with the upstream city of Thebes becoming important, as the royal armies pushed south into Nubia. During the long reign of Amenemhat III (*c.*1831–1786 BC) irrigation, defensive and mining works underpinned what future Egyptian generations came to look upon as the 'classical' age of literature, and which combined vast projects with increasing elegance.

If the first cause of Egypt's prosperity was the Nile inundation, the second was the river's function as a trade route, navigable without interruption for 600 miles (960 km) to the first cataract, and onwards, with portages, into the heart of Africa. From the Delta any part of the Mediterranean could be reached, with land routes into the Western Desert, the Levant and Anatolia.

Trade links with the Levant increased in importance after *c.*2000 BC, with armed expeditions alternating with treaties, as Egypt began to function as an Ancient World power: and inevitably therefore into conflict with the other powers, such conflict usually taking place in the Levant, in the corridor between the desert and the Mediterranean. The wars of Thutmose III (r.1480–1425 BC) proved extremely profitable. The booty from one major battle included 894 chariots (two covered in gold) and 200 suits of armour. Yet battles could be lost as well as won, as his successors were to discover. Egypt had become a military autocracy, with the Pharaoh represented as a heroic conqueror, heading a professional army, his status celebrated by the colossal statues that began to be erected throughout the realm.

Organizing so extensive a state, adjusting to the seasonal fluctuations of the Nile, maintaining irrigation works and constructing grandiose monuments required a large labour force, which had to be fed, housed, and controlled; and therefore a considerable number of skilled administrators. Egyptian mathematics were eminently practical and scribes prepared for promotion by studying such texts as the Rhind Papyrus, which elucidates such everyday problems as allocating workmen's rations, force-feeding geese, calculating shipping capacity or the relative strengths of beer and designing pyramids.

ABOVE *A golden panel from the back of Tutankhamun's throne depicts the seated King, with his queen, Ankhesenamun, anointing him with perfume, beneath a floral pavilion. The rays of the sun god Aten shine on the couple, giving them the sign for life, the Ankh.*

Egyptian civilization sprang into existence with amazing speed; the first artefacts, such as the Narmer palette, demonstrate a mastery of linear elegance and within three centuries the characteristic monumental tombs, stacked with grave goods appear. Uniquely for that period, the architecture has a known creator, King Djoser's chancellor Imhotep, famous as an astronomer, architect, writer and physician. The Saqqara complex with the Step Pyramid and ritual buildings is Imhotep's and its limestone cladding ensured its survival: unlike Mesopotamia's mud-brick Egyptian stone was to be permanent. Between Djoser, *c.*2620 BC, and King Menkure (d.2503 BC) the great city of the dead at Giza was constructed, with not only the necropolis but the remains of the workers' village, a well-organized settlement, being preserved. Egyptians' obsession with death and the after life, which inspired

Ordinary life was not much affected by a new dynasty of 'Asiatics' the Hyskos, who ruled in the north for a century after 1650 BC, paralleling separate rule from Thebes, where the 18th dynasty of the New Kingdom initiated a brilliant era, symbolized by the start of the Karnak Temple complex. Since the Egyptian dynasties that came after systematically obliterated all the Hyskos's monuments, their most enduring legacy – apart from some interesting Minoan-style murals – was the introduction of the horse and chariot. Asian gods survived better, including the widely popular Astarte, probably helped by the influence of the impressive Queen Hatshepsut (r.1473–1458 BC). Her successors increased the country's reputation abroad by successful wars in the Levant and massively impressive monuments at home. Egypt had become not only uniquely prosperous but increasingly cosmopolitan. This new openness to the outside world led to the central hiatus in Egyptian history, the Amarna period.

In 1357 BC , King Amenhotep IV (r.1352–1336 BC) changed his name: he would henceforth be known as Akhenaten, the human-divine form of the living sun, the 'Aten' the one and only god: all other divinities, including Osiris, the god of the underworld, quailed before the over-powering light. An entirely new capital was begun at Amarna, midway between Thebes and Memphis, financed by stripping the orthodox priests of much of their wealth. The new religion was shortlived. Orthodoxy returned within 20 years, and the surviving relics of the Aten-cult, of Akhenaten, and his beautiful wife Nefertiti, were destroyed. Their heir Tutankhaten renounced his father's heresy, changing his name to Tutankhamun, and moved back to the capital at Memphis, where his tomb has yielded the most famous examples of Egyptian art.

However shortlived the heresy had been, it had left royal prestige badly impaired, inspiring Rameses II (r.1279–1213 BC) to restore the dynasty's reputation. Rameses became the most famous of the warrior kings, but more due to his remorseless self-publicity than actual military talent; his one great battle of Kadesh, against the Hittites, was no better than a drawn match, but was

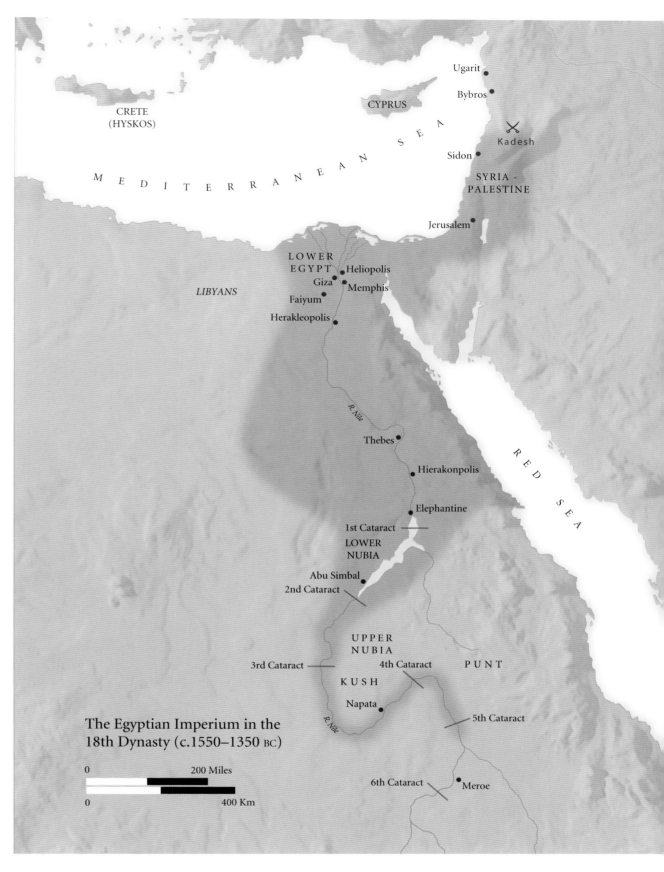

The Egyptian Imperium in the 18th Dynasty (c.1550–1350 BC)

presented for domestic consumption as a glorious victory, described in many lengthy inscriptions and commemorated in enormous statues of the god-king. Rameses' monuments were erected all over the land, from the Delta to the rock temples of Abu Simbel in Nubia. When even more self-promotion was required, Rameses commandeered the statues of previous Pharaohs, obliterating the original inscriptions. His was a hard act to follow, and in the century after Rameses' death no fewer than 13 Pharaohs ruled over a fragmenting empire.

At the beginning of the 1100s BC new invaders disturbed the whole of Asia Minor. The 'Sea Peoples' – probably from the Aegean and Syrian coast – using a new type of ship, had overthrown the Hittite empire, occupied Cyprus, and settled in Anatolia. In 1176 BC, they launched a massive attack on Egypt, which was repulsed, but Egypt now had new and formidable neighbours in

Palestine in the shape of the Assyrian empire. An obsession with maintaining a foothold in the Levant dragged Egypt into a series of needless and usually unsuccessful wars. An unprecedented humiliation came when a royal princess was married to the ruler of a modest kingdom – Solomon of Israel-Judah. The last 900 years of Egyptian independence saw only two relatively brief periods of rule by traditional Egyptian dynasties.

The first of the foreign rulers were Libyans, whose Pharaoh Sheshonq (r.945–924 BC) managed to restore some royal authority, but the Libyan kings were never able to rule unimpeded. The next dynasty came from the southern borders of the empire in Nubia. Nubians and Libyans at least came from neighbouring regions, which had long experienced Egyptian authority, but when the country was integrated first into the Persian realm and then under their Greek successors the continuity of Egyptian culture was broken.

The key to a real understanding of Egypt's past only came with the deciphering of the Rosetta Stone.
Found in 1799, this stele, dating from 196 BC, contained parallel texts in hieroglyphs, Demotic, and
classical Greek. Painstaking work by French and English scholars unlocked the mystery.

Egypt, Nubia and Kush

Although geographically in the continent of Africa, Egypt has followed the course of the Nile to focus on the Mediterranean, to become part of the history of Europe and Asia. Threats and opportunities have come from the north, across the sea or through Sinai, and the capital has traditionally been sited on the Nile Delta. But Egypt of the Pharaohs also extended 2,000 miles (3,200 km) south, past the Nile cataracts into the states of Nubia and Kush, in what is now Sudan. To the earlier Pharaohs it was the 'unknown' south. One adventurous nobleman, Harkhuf, was sent in about 2300 BC on four expeditions, together with his father and a priest. He brought back 300 donkeys laden with 'every good product,' (i.e. incense, ebony, grain and ivory). Even so, his most exciting tidings concerned a 'dancing dwarf from the land of the spirits'. An enthusiastic king demanded the dwarf be forwarded with every care: 'let excellent people sleep beside him in his den. My majesty desires to see this dwarf more than the gifts of Sinai and of Punt.'

So evidently rich a territory had to be acquired: Pharaoh Pepi II immediately mounted two invasions, killing 'a great number of chiefs' children and excellent commanders,' and placing the newly acquired territories under a Viceroy 'the Prince of Kush' who, with the peoples' cooperation, founded a prosperous client state. Kush developed its own bureaucracy and government, which carried out extensive public works, including highly individual pyramids. At the same time a profitable trade was also being carried out in Punt – modern Somalia – as gold, ivory, cattle and slaves were exchanged at the market established at the second Nile cataract, convenient for the southern capital at Thebes.

Isolated from the upheavals of the mid-second millennium, Kush-Nubia was able, when northern conditions were disturbed, to ensure a sort of unilateral declaration of independence in 1075 BC. For 300 years the Kushites preserved conservative Egyptian traditions and continued lucrative trade until, once again confronted by revolutions in the north, with four contenders for the throne, the southerners intervened to restore traditional stability.

Around 750 BC the kings of Kush struck north, becoming involved in the civil wars then raging in that region by seizing control of all the Nile Valley as far as 1,800 miles (2,900 km) north of the Kushite capital. The three successive Kushite Pharaohs of the 25th dynasty have become famous as the 'Black Pharaohs', with their distinctive features recorded in their monuments. Allied with the Judaean King Hezekiah, the Egyptians invaded Syria in 701 BC, provoking an Assyrian assault on Egypt. In 664 BC, after 40 years of intermittent fighting, in which the Assyrians drove south to Thebes, the Black Pharaohs withdrew to their capital at Meroë, situated downstream from Khartoum, very much nearer Central Africa than the Mediterranean, and with easy access to the Red Sea coast. They were succeeded in the north by Pharaoh Psamtek I (r. 662–610 BC), who repulsed the Assyrian invasion, enabling Egypt to resume its traditional orientation towards the Mediterranean.

Meroë owed its long prosperity, illustrated by its surviving 200 pyramids, to its position as an entrepôt, where tropical African produce and slaves could be exchanged for iron, manufactured in its bloomeries and furnaces from Sinai ores. In about AD 300, Kush eventually succumbed to the neighbouring and equally ancient kingdom of Axum, in Northern Ethiopia. Bordering on the Red Sea itself, Axum formed another trade nexus between Central African and the outside world.

BELOW *Mural in the tomb of the Pharaoh Amenhotep in Thebes showing Nubian women in the entourage of an Egyptian princess. By the mid-seventh century BC, the former vassal state of Nubia held the reins of power in Egypt.*

*c.*2000 – *c.*350 BC
Persians and Greeks

■ Indo-European peoples settle in Greece *c.* 2000 BC ■ Eruption of Thera precipitates decline of Minoan civilization *c.* 1500 BC ■ Cyrus of Persia begins his reign 559 BC ■ Xerxes defeated at the Battle of Salamis 480 BC ■ Philip II becomes king of Macedon 359 BC

From the late second millennium BC, bronze – an alloy of copper and tin – became widely available, although still as an élite product. Its use transformed warfare, making the heavily armoured and well-drilled infantryman king of the battlefield. When in the fifth century BC Asia and Europe met in their first conflict it was more than a clash of arms, but one between two very different civilizations. Persians were imperial, organized and autocratic; Greeks argumentative, democratic and exceptionally innovative, and the Greek victory shaped Europe's future.

Even more than in other countries, the history of Greece is also that of its geography. Land travel in the rugged and mountainous peninsula has always been difficult, but seagoing comparatively easy, with short passages around the coastline often the easiest mode of transport.

The First Civilizations of the Mediterranean

In Greece, as elsewhere, the original inhabitants were succeeded, probably in about 2000 BC, by Indo-Europeans, who may well have made a stop-over in the Troad, the Anatolian region round ancient Troy. They came speaking a language that developed, over the centuries, into Greek. The Achaeans, as the later Greeks called them, built strong fortifications on top of strategic hills – the Athens Acropolis was originally one of these – and subjugated the existing farmers. Over mainland Greece, around 20 of these mini-states evolved, all very small: the most prominent, claiming some sort of hegemony, was Mycenae, on the Peloponnese, with a population of perhaps 50,000.

The Mycenaeans had some more civilized neighbours, the Minoans, on the island of Crete, a short sea journey to the south. Crete is centrally situated, with access to the Levant, Egypt and any part of the Aegean Sea. From the third millennium Cretans, originally arriving from the mainland in the 6000s BC as part of that initial migration, developed trade over all this area, north to the Greek mainland and south to the African coast, with colonies in Cyprus, Palestine and the smaller islands. Given the size of the boats, some 60 feet (18 metres) long, originally oared, with sail coming in the mid-1000s BC, trade was mainly in high-value items, particularly copper.

Of the four Minoan cities – Knossos, Phaistos, Malia and Gournia – Knossos was the largest, and survived many disasters, including two earthquakes and the violent eruption of the Thera volcano, the most devastating natural event of the ancient world, which buried one city under 200 feet (60 metres) of debris and led to a brief period of climate cooling, the equivalent of a nuclear winter. Minoan art is unique and produced outstandingly beautiful and entirely original objects. Their finely painted pottery features such engaging creatures as octopods, and figurines, imposing in spite of their small scale, of bare-breasted goddesses in flounced robes. Élite tombs in stone-vaulted rooms were furnished with jewelled ornaments and weapons, gold masks and amber. It is however the frescoes that decorated the Cretan 'palaces' that are the most remarkable. Featuring flying fish, boys

LEFT *The most famous Mycenaean archaeological find is this finely crafted golden funeral mask, popularly dubbed the 'Mask of Agamemnon', found during excavations of shaft graves by the German scholar Heinrich Schliemann in 1876.*

boxing, the dangerous sport of bull-leaping and particularly the gorgeously dressed smiling women chatting to each other, the frescoes speak of an elegant and relaxed life in the sun.

Whereas the Minoans were primarily traders, the Mycenaeans were dedicated to war. Their architecture was based on grim citadels – the Lion Gate and the 'Treasury of Atreus' at Mycenae are examples, but the civilizing effect of Knossos was also apparent. Nestor's palace at Pylos was equipped with a bathroom, and decorated with frescoes, bolder and less frivolous than those of the Minoans. Their élite, the 'Followers,' were armoured knights, chariot drivers with fantastic boar-tusk helmets, armed with long, heavy lances and rapier-like swords. In search of the essential copper and tin for the manufacture of bronze, Mycenaean traders sailed to Egypt, the Levant and Italy, while their merchandise has even been found as far afield as Britain, once a major source of tin. Mycenaean sub-kings established their own rule throughout the eastern Mediterranean, supplementing trade by the less complex method of piracy – their ships, the antecedents of the Homeric 50-oared vessels, or 'pentekonters,' were some 100 feet (30 metres) long, and equipped with bronze rams.

Such a warrior-culture had little trouble taking over Minoan Crete, which was subjugated by the late 1400s BC, but the single greatest event of Mycenaean times was the Trojan War. Disentangling the historical events from Homer's poetic saga *The Iliad*, probably written in the eighth century BC or later, what is certain is that Mycenae and its colonies were the greatest contributors to the Greek armies, while its King Agamemnon was their leader. Troy was vanquished, but it was a hollow victory. Within two generations after its fall, the power of Mycenae and its associates had crumbled away in the general upheaval caused by the incursions of the 'Sea Peoples'. By this time, newcomers, the founders of Classical Greece, were installing themselves.

These newcomers, the Dorians, settled in mainland Greece and Cyprus, displacing some of the Myceneans, who emigrated to the Anatolian offshore islands of Ionia. Thereafter there was a long period of quiet farming, with many scattered communities producing only the most basic architecture and primitive art until suddenly, about 500 BC, with all the brilliance of a flash of lightning, the richest culture the world has ever seen arose in the Greek city of Athens.

An Imperial Power

Together with the Medes and Parthians, the Persians migrated from Central Asia in around 900 BC, forming a separate state in 700 BC, but one subordinate to the Medes. After the alliance with Babylon had destroyed the Assyrians, King Cyrus II, the Great (r.559–530 BC) began a career of conquest, starting with the Medes, continuing with the rich kingdom of Lydia – whose ruler Croesus, renowned for his vast wealth, created the world's first standard coinage and built the Temple of Artemis-Diana at Ephesus, one of the Seven Wonders of the ancient world – and culminating in the conquest of Babylon, which he entered unopposed. The famous cuneiform inscription on the British Museum's Cyrus Cylinder records this achievement – after a bloody and decisive battle – but it does not, as some enthusiastic propagandists claim, constitute the first declaration of human rights. On the other hand the Persian policy of leaving a thoroughly subjected community to continue with its own traditions is an economic way of running a vast empire, as the British later proved in India.

ABOVE *Fresco of boxing boys from the Minoan settlement of Akrotiri on the small island of Thera (also called Santorini), north of Crete.*

One gesture was portentous. As the Hebrew Bible records, Cyrus freed the Jews from the Babylonian Captivity, who were now able to return, rebuild the Temple at Jerusalem, and begin redacting and writing the Books of the Tanakh (Old Testament), the foundations not only of Judaism but of Christianity and Islam. During their exile the Hebrews had been exposed to other cults and philosophies, and may have incorporated some of these; there is certainly a striking resemblance between Persian and Hebrew flood myths.

Even their most stubborn enemies admired the Persians: Aeschylus (*c*.525–456 BC), the playwright who had fought them on land and sea, praised their unflinching courage; the Greek historian Herodotus (*c*.484– *c*.425 BC) noted that young Persians were taught 'to ride, shoot with the bow and tell the truth.' Above all they must not lie: a gentleman should not get into debt, since a debtor generally lies. They did not fight in armour but in their linen shirts: other disgruntled Greeks complained that the real Persian power lay in their 'archers' – their fine gold coins were marked with a bowman.

The state founded by Cyrus was a genuine imperial power, uniting different cultures, races and languages, over a wide territory, with a well-defined system of administration. Extending from the Nile up the Mediterranean coast to the Black Sea, and overland to the Indus, Persian 'satraps' ruled more justly and tolerantly than any other governors of the day: or, for that matter, than most since. Persian art and architecture reflected Persian values, very different from those of the Assyrians, whose influence is nevertheless clear.

Assyrian reliefs are those of triumphal slaughter and violence, with torture and death depicted in detail: Persian rulers chose to decorate their palaces with dignified processions of retainers and tribute-bearing foreigners, and enjoyed themselves in the 'paradises' (the word is originally Persian), quiet walled gardens of trees, flowers and watercourses

Cyrus' son Cambyses (r.529–522 BC) spent most of his short reign in the conquest of Egypt, which endured until 404 BC, when a revolt restored a native dynasty, but Cambyses' attempt to extend his conquest into Nubia failed. After some family murders, a cousin, Darius (r.522–480 BC), succeeded. Darius consolidated his extensive realm; his account of the construction of his palace at Susa mentions Lebanese cedar, brought by Assyrians, silver and ebony from Egypt, ivory workers and sculptors from Ionia, gold from Bactria, lapis, carnelian and turquoise from Soghdiana, and many others. The imperial road from one capital, Susa to Sardis ran for 1,600 miles (2,600 km), with 111 posting stations: a good chariot could cover the distance in a month. 'Nothing', reported the admiring Herodotus, 'stops these couriers from covering their allotted stage in the shortest possible times – neither snow, rain, heat nor darkness.' Darius also began constructing the palatial complex of Persepolis in 518 BC, combining vast scale (150,000 square yards/125,400 sq m) with the splendour of glowing colour in tiles and paintings.

Darius intended to extend the empire even further, making a sortie across the Hindu Kush into the Punjab and down the Indus, recruiting Indian archers and horsemen to assist in his European wars. Persian armies had to switch fronts well over 2,000 miles (3,200 km) for the next expedition to Thrace, and then to quell a rebellion among the Ionian Greeks. Both these were successful, the empire was consolidated, but the Athenians had attracted Darius's attention by helping the Ionians, and became his next target.

The Greeks were divided between the Ionians on the Anatolian islands, Attic Greeks (with Athens their biggest city) and the Peloponnesians, grouped under Sparta. Most of the Ionian states had accepted Persian rule, leaving independent leadership divided between Sparta, with the most efficient army, and Athens, the richest: but it was Athens that scored the first victory. Furious at their invasion of Ionia, Darius was bent on revenge. At the first opportunity, in 490 BC, he marched a large army towards Athens. The hastily assembled Greek force of 600 hoplites, well-armed and trained infantry, tore through the Persian ranks, charging at the run in a massed phalanx. The surprised Persians retreated, and the Battle of the Plains of Marathon went down in history as a crushing Greek victory.

Dating from the sixth century BC, the 'Cyrus Cylinder' is an ancient clay cylinder that documents the Persian conquest of Babylon in 539 and eulogizes the Persian king Cyrus II. The text is written in Akkadian cuneiform.

Darius died before he could strike back, but in 480 his successor Xerxes (r.485–465 BC) prepared for what should have been a decisive blow, with the largest army ever seen, drawn from all parts of the empire, including Indians.

Showdown at Salamis

It should have been no contest. Xerxes, Great King of the Medes and Persians, Lord of Syria, Chorasmia, India, Egypt, Parthia, Bactria, Lydia, Ionia and many other satrapies, had already crossed into Europe on a bridge of boats, crushing the Spartans' heroic stand at Thermopylae and burning the city of Athens. On the night of 17–18 September 480 he assembled his navy, which included 300 Phoenician and 200 Egyptian ships, together with those recruited from his Ionian subjects. In all, he commanded 1,000 triremes – the latest form of warship, fast oared galleys with crews of more than 200, ship-killers that were armed with three-fanged bronze rams capable of smashing through enemy timbers in one shattering blow. Xerxes' fleet rounded the peninsula of Piraeus and made for the island of Salamis to finish off the last resistance. The Great King, supported by 30,000 of his invincible troops, made ready to view the inevitable victory from the coast and to finish off the thousands of Greeks who might struggle ashore; no prisoners were to be taken; the impertinent Athenians and their allies must be annihilated.

Faced by the Persian ships, 400 nervous Greek crews awaited the assault. What actually happened was recorded by one participant, the poet Aeschylus. His play *The Persians* tells the story, as if from the enemy's viewpoint:

> *Skilfully dashing in, and striking hard,*
> *The Greeks soon changed the surface of*
> *   that sea*
> *Into a single mess of flesh and wrecks,*
> *With bodies washed on every beach*
> *   and shore.*

Queen Artemisia of the Ionian realm of Halicarnassus, ostensibly a Persian ally, held back with her triremes until the Greek victory looked likely before prudently switching sides.

Defeats can be overcome, but humiliation is fatal to supposedly divinely ordained rulers, especially when it takes place in full view of the Great King himself. The subsequent Battle of Plataea, where the Greek infantry routed the Persian host, guaranteed Greek independence. Darius' successors kept the empire together with varying degrees of success for some 130 years, at the cost of extremely vicious family feuds and civil wars; in one of these the Greek mercenary commander Xenophon made his own record of the famous march of the Ten Thousand through the Persian Empire to the Sea.

The reason for the Greek victory at Salamis was their superior ship-handling, which demanded absolute coordination among all the crew, and especially the 170 oarsmen. At the last moment of the charge, the attacking ship had to swerve aside in order to rip down the enemies' side, smashing rowers and hull

RIGHT *Glazed brick bas-relief (c.515 BC) of archers from the Persian royal guard, from a frieze in the palace of Darius I in Susa (ancient Shushan), Iran. These life-sized figures testify to the martial prowess of the Persian Achaemenid empire under Darius.*

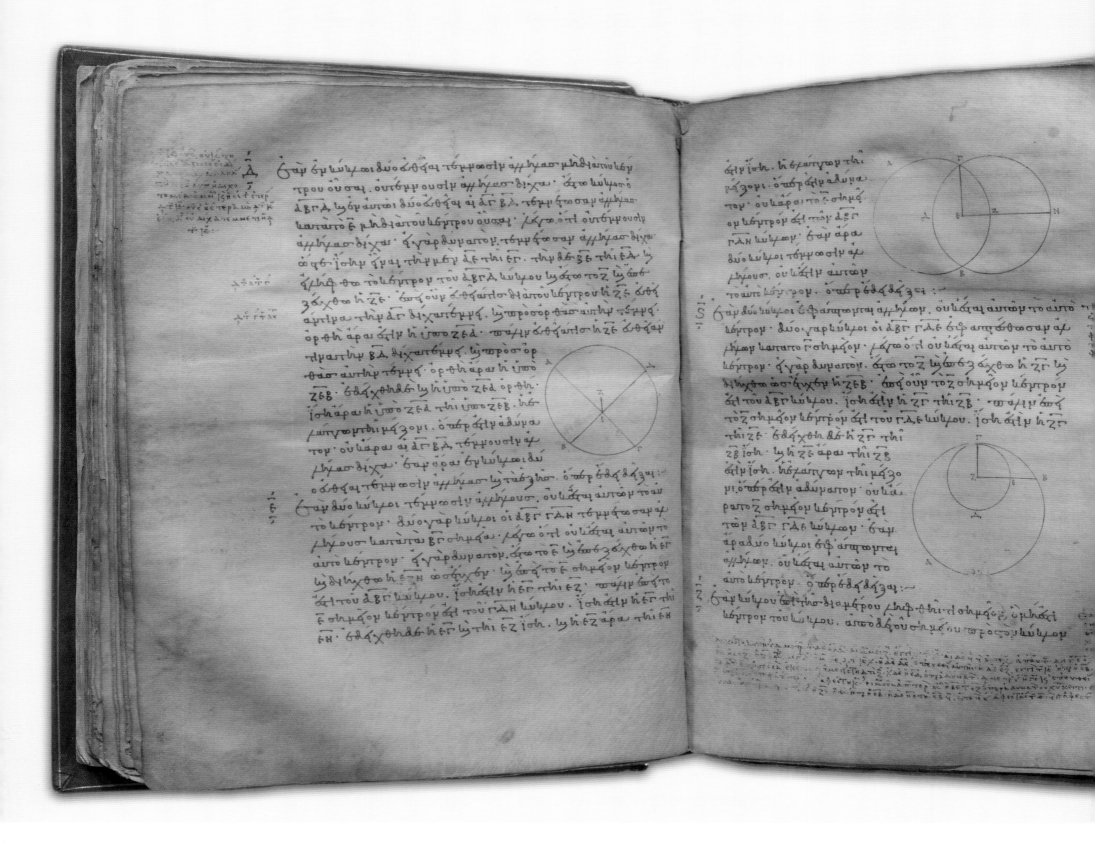

as the bronze ram tore though at a speed of over 10 knots. In order to avoid injury, the oarsmen on the attacking ship had to throw their oars in to avoid killing or maiming themselves. Only a crew with great skill, and complete trust in each other, could do this: and complete trust cannot exist in subjects of autocracies. All the Greek crews were free men: the trireme, like the later longbow, was the weapon of a free but disciplined society and their victory at Salamis ensured the transmission of Greek culture..

The Glory that was Greece

The Ancient Greek experience is central to all later history. Within a relatively short time – some 300 years – and in a geographically limited area – a circle with radius of 250 miles (400 km) from the island of Chios encompasses the entire space between Byzantium and Crete, Sparta and Anatolia – the world changed. Sumerian and Egyptian discoveries were absorbed, the practice of democracy began, the theatre was established as an art form, and permanent references in the visual arts created (Picasso is a good recent example).

Through the Romans, Greek ideas of law and justice shaped all modern legal practice, and Greek philosophers began that restless enquiry into the nature of the Universe and humanity that has characterized all Western cultures.

As in most cultures, the first examples were poetic, with the works of Homer and Hesiod. We have no personal details about the authors, but the Homeric epics remain magisterial works of literature. Sappho was one of the first named poets, and her works remain fresh: for example, her 'evening song':

'All things thou bringest, Hesper, that
the bright dawn did part
Sheep and goats to the fold, and the child
to the mother's heart.'

In Sappho's time – around 600 BC – Greek states developed from monarchies – still confined to small cities – into oligarchies, dictatorships and finally,

Pages from the first printed edition of Euclid's Elements, Elementarum Euclidis, *printed in Greek in 888* AD. *Euclid was a Greek mathematician, often referred to as the 'Father of Geometry', deducing the basic principles of geometry.*

democracies, but by no means in our modern definition of the term.

The concept of a national democracy was to prove the most influential Greek idea – local self-government was an ancient practice, but for two millennia great states had been autocracies, and the idea that momentous decisions should be discussed in open debate was truly revolutionary. Athenian democracy, itself imperfect (no women or slaves could play a part) did not last, and was capable of great folly (demanding the death of Socrates) and in launching major, unsuccessful wars, but the idea of human rights to equality before the law and to a share in decision-making persisted.

Reprieved from becoming a Persian satrapy, the city of Athens erupted in a ferment of intellectual activity. The world has never experienced anything quite like the following century where in a small city world-shaping events took place. Aeschylus was followed within a few years by Euripides and Sophocles; drama joined the world's major arts. Perhaps more important, a young contemporary, Aristophanes, wrote the first comedies. Every subsequent theatrical comic trick – puns, impossible words, patter songs, vulgarity, silly foreigners, mixed with satire equally relevant more than 2,000 years later. The most powerful play – comedy can shift prejudices much more rapidly than tragedy – is *Lysistrata,* in which the Athenian women refuse to sleep with the men unless they ended the current war.

Mingling with the poets were philosophers whose work fundamentally altered subsequent ways of organizing thought, and artists introducing revolutionary elegance and realism. Whereas the individuals behind Sumerian or Egyptian works remain for the most part anonymous – we do know the real names of just a few of the later Bible writers – Greeks proudly proclaimed authorship. The historian Herodotus begins his work 'This is a publication of the researches of Herodotus of Halicarnassus' – and the text that follows furnishes us with much of what we know about the fifth-century BC world. Herodotus was an avid traveller, but was careful to distinguish between his own observations and hearsay (e.g. 'monstrous dogs, men without heads, who have eyes in their breasts, at least as the Libyans say').

Although the works of philosophers, historians and dramatists, Greek may not attract most people's attention, Greek art and architecture are seen everywhere in the Western world. Before the fifth century BC Greek sculpture imitated Egyptian and Assyrian. Within a single generation new forms, in which stone was made to represent ideal human bodies, billowing drapery or violent action, were developed. Previous sculpture 'in the round' had been rare. Mesopotamian artists preferred to work in relief, while Egyptian three-dimensional work was often left attached to the rock-core.

Painting was also radically different to any previous work. Pottery survives much better than plaster or fabric, and we have to rely on the vase paintings to show the moods ranging from savage realism to tender affections experienced by fifth-century Athenians: rarities indeed in any previous art.

Athenian splendour and power continued: within 30 years of Salamis an Athenian thalassocracy – a seaborne quasi-empire – extended over all the Aegean as far as Byzantium. Athens was endowed with its magnificent Acropolis, with the essential line of communication between the city and its harbour at Piraeus secured by the Long Walls. But the rivalry between the Greek city-states continued: notably, a state of war existed between Sparta and Athens for almost 30 years, from 431 to 403 BC. Thucydides, historian and soldier, described the disastrous Athenian attack on the Sicilian colony of Syracuse when the Athenians were pursued into a river. 'The water was fouled at once, but they drank it none the less, a mess of mud and blood; indeed, most of them fought over it.' As hegemony shifted between Sparta and Thebes, Greek unity disintegrated, and the Persians recovered most of their former Greek possessions. When, in 359 BC an effective Greek leader (Philip II of Macedon) appeared he was faced with confusion and dissent in what remained of Greece.

BELOW *Greek hoplites (heavily armed spear-men) portrayed on the frieze of an amphora (jar), probably made somewhere between 565 and 550* BC *in the Attic region of Greece, around Athens.*

336 BC – c. AD 140
Alexander and his Successors

■ Alexander becomes ruler of Macedon 336 BC ■ Death of Alexander 323 BC ■ First Mauryan ruler Chandragupta ascends the throne *c.*321 BC ■ Death of Buddhist King Kanishka of the Kushan empire *c.* AD 140

The campaigns of Alexander the Great consolidated the Hellenistic world, in which Greek language and culture spread from the Mediterranean to the Indian Ocean and Central Asia. New religions and philosophies replaced or merged with ancient beliefs, both in the East and in the cosmopolitan West, disseminated by trade links with India and even to reclusive China. As the earlier empires fractured, boundaries changed and smaller states emerged, but signs of new imperial powers were appearing.

King Philip of Macedon (r.359–336 BC) was regarded by the haughty southern Greeks as a semi-barbarian, remote in his cold and mountainous realm, but they were soon forced to acknowledge his inflexible ambitions and his military genius. He transformed a light cavalry force into a professional army equipped with new weapons and tactics: the Macedonian phalanx became masters of every battlefield for nearly two centuries, supported by organized engineering and artillery divisions, all thoroughly drilled and disciplined. Before his assassination by Pausanias of Orestis, one of his seven bodyguards, King Philip had vanquished the previously independent Greek city states, extended his sovereignty to the Black Sea, and was preparing to attack the old enemy, Persia.

A Legend in his Own Time

His talents and ambitions, plus a dazzling personal charm, were inherited in 336 BC by his son, Alexander (d.323 BC), who had also benefited from tuition by the great philosopher Aristotle (which did not prevent the young king immediately killing off any likely competitors).

Alexander the Great became a legend in his own lifetime and has remained one ever since, the romantic facts of his brief and glorious life eclipsing mere fiction. Bucephalus his horse, the marriage with Roxane, the Gordian Knot and his own beauty, recorded on coins and medals, continue to inspire artists and film directors as much as his military triumphs. Within five years of his accession, Alexander's army had swept through Asia Minor and the Levant, invaded Egypt – the city of Alexandria remains as a testament to his presence, along with many other Alexandrias throughout the Near East and Central

Asia – crushed all Persian resistance and burned their capital of Persepolis. Yet the conquest of Persia was not enough for Alexander, and so he pushed on past the Hindu Kush into India.

Measured in terms of battles won, towns conquered, and enemies slain – all in the space of 12 years – Alexander was one of history's most successful commanders. Yet, like his later admirer Napoleon, he over-reached himself. The sub-kings of the old Indian satrapies submitted, and the Greek influence in their sculpture, the Gandharan, continued for centuries, but the highlanders of the Swat Valley had to be subdued by hard campaigning. The last battle was fought in 326 BC on the Hydaspes (Jehlum) river, against Porus, ruler of a relatively small kingdom. The Indian elephants were terrifying, but Greek discipline prevailed. In one of his generous gestures Alexander left the defeated Porus in charge of enlarged territories, and set off for his next intended conquest, the extensive lands beyond the Ganges. But the reports of a hostile army, said to have 4,000 elephants and 80,000 horses, were unnerving, and the Greek soldiers insisted on returning. Taking the opportunity first to sail down the Indus and reach the Indian Ocean, Alexander then led most of his army home, but he contracted a fever and died on the return journey, at Babylon in 323 BC.

A Hard Act to Follow

Alexander's immense empire, stretching from Macedon and the Aegean through Egypt, Asia Minor to India was fought over by his surviving generals, and it was some 20 years before these disputes were more or less settled. Ptolemaeus, who had already staked out his claim to Egypt, had the easiest

task, taking over the undamaged Persian satrapy, conforming to Egyptian customs, but installing a Greek bureaucracy where efficiency was tempered by corruption, relying on Egyptian cooperation from a people accustomed to foreign occupation. The economy was transformed, widespread irrigation and drainage channels were cut – the Syracusan engineer Archimedes' invention of the rotary screw came in useful here – and such new crops as figs, vines and Syrian corn introduced.

ABOVE *This metope panel from a third-century BC Greek frieze shows Alexander the Great on horseback, about to deliver the coup de grâce to a fallen enemy.*

The capital was moved 10 miles (16 km) north to the new city of Alexandria, where a cosmopolitan population quickly gathered, Africans, Arabs, Phoenicians, northern barbarians, Greeks and Jews mingling, all adopting

Greek as the lingua franca. Alexandria became the world's most brilliant town, with the famous Pharos (lighthouse), and the most extensive library ever collected. Natives of different regions had their own forms of municipal government, notable among them the Jews, but all following Greek laws and customs and speaking Greek. Even the stiff Hebrews had the Bible translated into Greek (the oldest surviving text, the Septuagint, was produced in Alexandria in the first century BC). The last of the Ptolemaic dynasty was the beautiful Cleopatra VII (r. c.69–30 BC).

The ruthless Seleucus I Nicator (in the words of the second-century AD Roman historian Appian 'strong in arms and persuasive in council') originally claimed the lion's share of Alexander's empire, including all the Asian conquests. Sensibly, he reached an accord with the Indian ruler Chandragupta Maurya to withdraw, in return for 500 war-elephants. As well as warring with the other claimants, Seleucus' heirs also had to suppress rebellions by client kings. One such revolt resulted in an independent Greek dominion in Bactria and northern India, which endured for 300 years, while another uprising established an independent Jewish state. More inroads were made by the Parthians, who took Anatolia and much of Iran in the mid-second century BC, and by the Attalids, with their capital at the magnificent city of Pergamon (modern Turkey). The Attalid kings faced troublesome Celtic invaders, who were at that time overrunning Eastern Europe. The Celts eventually settled in what became known as Galatia, the land of the Gauls, and are commemorated in the well-known statue of the 'Dying Gaul', which together with the great altar frieze in the Berlin Museum, exemplifies the art of Pergamon.

Antigonus Monophthalmus ('one-eyed') the third claimant, aided by his son the rapacious Demetrius Poliorcetes, made a determined bid for supreme power, but their successors had to content themselves with sovereignty over Macedon, Thrace and the rest of historic Greece.

India – Cradle of Ancient Religions

When Alexander's armies moved into the Punjab they crossed a religious and cultural frontier. Persian satraps, while formally venerating Ahura Mazda, the great God of Light, and the ancient Persian pantheon, as expanded and codified by Zoroaster in the 15th century BC, had tolerated the diverse religions of their varied subjects; Greek, Egyptian, Phoenician, Jewish and many regional divinities remained undisturbed. But once beyond the Khyber Pass those gods lost most of their power.

The Aryan newcomers had moved down the Ganges plain, integrating with the established population, but assuming a supremacy over these indigenous *Dasa*, who were dismissed as 'dark, flat-nosed, uncouth, incomprehensible and generally inferior'. Over more than a millennium local customs must nevertheless have influenced the Aryans' original culture, which, in later years, shaped all Indian thought and society. The first manifestation of this is the collection of praise-poems known as the Rig-Veda ('In Praise of Knowledge') honouring gods, rulers and past heroes, probably first collected towards the end of the second millennium BC. Much later, sometime before 500 BC (around the same time the Homeric poems were written), the national epic the Mahabharata appeared, along with Hinduism's basic text, the Bhagavadgita – the 'Hymn of the Lord'. The society they describe was firmly stratified: at its head were the priests and scholars (Brahmans) and warriors, followed by farmers, merchants and artisans. Outside this caste system were the *dalits*, or 'untouchables', since any contact meant being defiled. Caste status was hereditary and immovable, except downwards: caste could be lost, but promotion was impossible: you remained in the situation in which it had pleased the gods to place you.

Those gods provided spiritual and emotional sustenance for everybody. Vishnu, appearing on Earth either as the young prince Krishna or the Lord

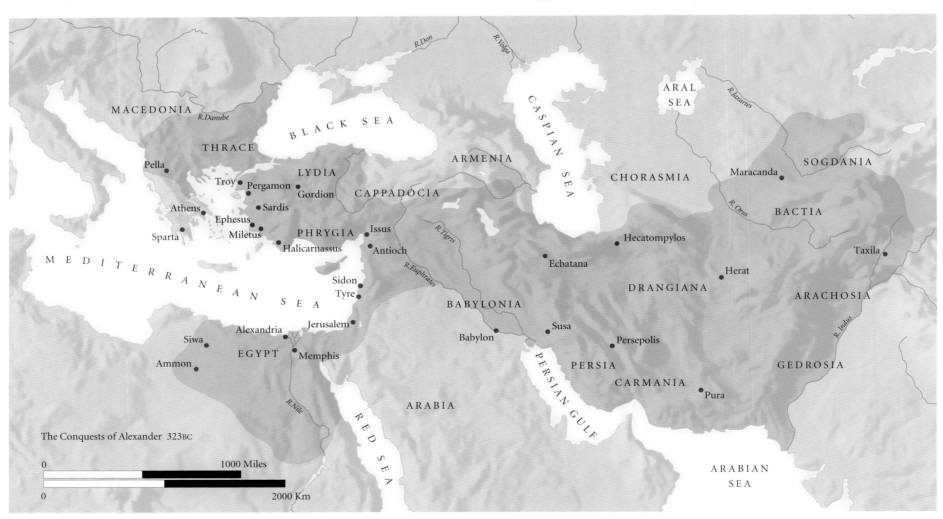

The Conquests of Alexander 323 BC

Rama, was a fabled hero: six-armed Shiva promised fertility and threatened violence; while smiling elephant-headed Ganesh was much beloved as a bringer of prosperity and good living. For some 3,000 years this Hindu culture has underpinned Indian society.

By the time of Alexander's incursion, Hinduism was adjusting to the impact of two new great religious teachers, Siddhartha Gautama, the Buddha, and Mahavira Nataputta, the founder of Jainism, who both worked at sometime between 450 and 550 BC. Buddhist doctrine – dharma – spoke of the annihilation of all human desires and imperfections and the achievement of

ABOVE *Miniature from an early 18th-century Indian manuscript of the Persian epic poem, the* Shahnameh *('Book of Kings'), showing Iskander – the Persian name for Alexander – on horseback, meeting members of the highest Indian caste, the Brahmans.*

'nirvana' – nothingness' and the awakening of the pure soul. Perfection was available to all the poorest and meanest (although one might well believe that those struggling on the brink of extinction would find renunciation rather more difficult). Such a philosophy could never transmute into a persecuting religion, such as Judaism (when given a chance), Christianity or Islam.

THE ZHOU

The first Zhou king formalized the existing system of governance into a prototypical feudal system, with nobles ranked as the equivalents of duke, marquis, baron and count or viscount, but without the same psychological reinforcement of clan loyalties and the ideals of chivalry, that held the later European feudalism together. Each magnate was granted land, servants and the rights to taxation, and each subcontracted the obligations to their subordinates. The population at large was divided into gentry and scholars, farmers, artisans and merchants, and in that order: the classification became permanent and the source of trouble when the 19th-century grandees of the East India Company inserted themselves in Chinese society.

After about 770 BC the Zhou state fragmented from central control to form some 20 or so minor states, and the 'empire' became a respectable fiction, brutally exposed when in 771 BC the Yu emperor was killed in a revolt and the capital moved east downstream to Louang. Regional chiefs acknowledged the emperor's ritual supremacy, but competed among themselves for hegemony: in the process some individual states prospered and consolidated into substantial kingdoms. New technologies were introduced, most notably iron-working about 500 BC, with immediate results in both agriculture and warfare. Communications were improved by the first of the extensive canal network that linked north and south. If any Western visitors had arrived 1,000 years later, in AD 500, they would have seen a very different China, still behind the West in certain aspects, especially urbanization, but swiftly forging ahead.

Rather, the glory of Buddhism has always been its tranquillity and tolerance. Even so, to some Hindus Buddhism represented a heresy to be forcibly discouraged. In its homeland, India Buddhism was never as successful as in its eastern diaspora.

Buddhism has spread throughout the world, but Jainism remains restricted to India; unsurprisingly, since it is no creed for the fainthearted. Jains insist on absolute nonviolence, avoiding harm to any living creature, in truth and justice, asceticism, the renunciation of fleshly pleasures and possessions. Their doctrines and practice have inspired many non-Jains, most famously the Mahatma Gandhi. Both these admirable cults influenced the rulers of the first historic Indian dynasty, the Mauryas of Maghada. The first king – or even emperor, since Mauryan rule extended from Afghanistan to the Bay of Bengal – Chandragupta (r. c.321–297 BC) was a contemporary of Alexander, whom he may well have met. After his deal with Seleucus settled his western borders, Chandragupta was able to assemble his vast realm, which was administered with ruthless efficiency; but on his abdication the first emperor chose to retire to a Jain monastery, in Karnataka, still a centre of pilgrimage.

His grandson Ashoka (r. c.268–231 BC), who established his capital at Pataliputra – present-day Patna – could claim to be the founder of the Indian state. After a violent start to his career Ashoka embraced the principle of both new philosophy-religions, and was able to have his proclamations inscribed on rocks and stone pillars. At least 60 of these are distributed all over the Subcontinent, indicating at a widespread influence, if not direct rule.

Ashoka's edicts combine blameless virtue with good sense and would serve as advice to many modern governments; the first, in the Jain spirit, abolishes capital punishment; another declares that 'All extravagance and violence of language should be carefully avoided'.

Ashoka cultivated trade and diplomatic contacts with other countries: the flag, as so frequently thereafter, followed the trade. His new road, planned with rest houses, wells and shade trees, ran a thousand miles along the Ganges and the Himalayan foothills to Taxila, joining the established trade routes across the Hindu Kush, and eastwards to the coast. Megasthenes, the ambassador of Seleucus who spent some time at the Mauryan court, greatly admired the roads, which were far superior to those in Greece. He also described tame monkeys, speaking parrots, a tree producing wool that was spun into fine threads, and gold-digging ants the size of foxes – the last of these the only far-fetched claim. Mauryan emissaries visited Burma, Egypt, Greece and the Levant, as well as establishing friendly contacts with the kingdoms of southern India.

After the Mauryan empire faded away, within 50 years of Ashoka's death (its memory is perpetuated in the triple-icon figure that independent modern India adopted as its national emblem), the initiative shifted back to the west, at first to the Greek kings of Bactria, one of whom, Menander, expanded his rule into the Punjab, converting to Buddhism. Greek Bactrian coinage, technically much better than the Mauryan, provides what might be called the first, and for many years the last, true portraits of Indian rulers. In Bactria, the Chinese explorer Chang Ch'ien discovered a cultivated society and 'heavenly horses', which were introduced to China's imperial stable. Chang Ch'ien's understanding of Bactria was helped by the fact that the then-current rulers, the Yueh-Chi, were from the Chinese borders. Having been repulsed by the Chinese defences, including the Great Wall, they had established themselves instead on the far side of the Himalayas. Both they and their descendants, who established the Kushan kingdom, enriched the northwest with a mixture of mid-Asian and Persian cultures, but like so many subsequent interlopers, they soon became assimilated into Indian culture.

Around the time of King Kanishka (r. AD 127–140), himself a Buddhist, a great council, only the fourth since Buddha's death, was held under Kushan auspices, dividing the faith into two branches, Hinayana and the more relaxed Mahayana. A flow of Buddhist culture developed, its source in northern India, spreading into Ceylon, throughout Southeast Asia, and on to China, Korea and Japan, and branching into Tibet and Nepal. Indian influences, spreading east and interacting with Chinese cultures, produced a creative synthesis of great magnificence in the nascent states of Indochina.

The First Rulers of China

China, in the traditional translation of its common name 'Zhongguó', is the 'Middle Kingdom', the centre of the world. Hemmed in on two sides by the sea, and on the west by mountains and desert, it is open to the north, to the Manchurian and Mongolian plains. Chinese rule has never extended far beyond the early boundaries of the Han dynasty, but Chinese influence has been widespread. Its vast area, 2,500 miles (4,000 km) or so from southwest to northeast, or from east to west, includes a wide range of climates, from desert and mountain to subtropical coast, and of different cultures. Two great river systems, the Yellow River (Huang He) in the north and the Yangtze in the centre, divide the country geographically and to some extent politically.

Over the last few millennia immigration has been restricted, at least by comparison with that in the West; most Chinese descend from the autochthonous inhabitants, but the open north has experienced invasions and subsequent drastic changes. The best recorded of the early societies developed along the Yellow River, which flows 3,395 miles (5,500 km) into the Yellow Sea. Its fertile soil allowed intensive agriculture, although floods and sometimes dramatic changes in its course could produce major disasters. The first farmers got off to a poor start, and it was not until the art of rice cultivation was introduced from the south that the Longshan culture emerged: it was then that small scale production began of what was to be China's most distinctive manufacture – silk. Cities became quite extensive; Erlitou covered 300 hectares (740 acres) and contained palace compounds, a large walled space with wood-framed buildings approached by flights of stone steps, the pattern for all subsequent palaces; but all lagging well behind the West. If a traveller from Eastern Europe, Egypt, the Indus Valley or Asia Minor had made their way to China in around, say, 1500 BC, they would have found little to admire: no enormous pyramids, or ziggurats towering over the plains, no elegant weapons or armour such as that of Mycenae; no fashionably dressed ladies like those of Knossos; no Babylonian sophisticates discussing literature, the only signs of writing being scratches on animal bones; Harappans would be scandalized by the lack of drainage and washing facilities. The cities were built of timber, not of stone, and their walls, though massive, only of stamped earth. All would have been horrified to find that magnates were buried along with decapitated slaves, slaughtered on the spot. In place of the fragile beauty of Sumerian work of 1,000 years before, there were only grotesquely shaped and decorated bronzes. The pottery true, was of an unmatched fragile beauty, and the cast bronzes, if uncouth in shape, were amazingly well-constructed, and the visitors would have admired the fine lines of the pale jade pieces.

Setting aside the myths of the first Yellow Emperor, and the Xia dynasty, the first records are those relating to the Shang rulers between 1600 and 1050 BC. Their influence covered a wide area of northern China, down the Yellow River to Shandong and, over time, towards the south. On the other great river system, the Yangtze, societies reflected the regional characteristics, with elephant tusks appearing in burials, and towards the end of the millennium, huge bronze statues that are technological triumphs. During this period the shamanistic character of the northern pastoralists was combined with the more sophisticated beliefs of the southerners to produce the ancestral Chinese mind-set. The emperor was a cult figure, intercessor between his subjects and natural and supernatural forces. It was assumed that a better system had once existed and that ancestral wisdom must be regained and those wiser forebears venerated. The protracted line of Shang emperors was abruptly cut off by one of the subordinate rulers, Wu of Zhou, in 1122 BC. Justifying his usurpation, King Wu claimed that the Shang had forfeited 'the mandate of heaven,' due, it was said, to drunkenness:

'His heart was malign. Therefore Heaven sent down destruction on Shang and had no mercy … Heaven is not tyrannical, people themselves draw guilt upon themselves.'

ABOVE *An oracle bone from the Shang dynasty in China, c.14th–13th century BC. The inscriptions were used mainly for divination, but also as a way of recording significant events.*

Wu's doctrine could be neatly summed up in Elizabethan statesman Sir John Harington's wry comment on the mainsprings of power: 'Treason doth never prosper. What's the reason? If it do prosper , none dare call it treason.' However, as well as conferring power, Heaven's mandate demanded obligations from the ruler, to safeguard, shelter and nourish the population.

c.150 BC – c.AD 500
Roman Imperium: Republic and Empire

■ Rome achieves supremacy over Italy *c*.150 BC ■ End of the Punic Wars between Rome and Carthage 146 BC ■ Foundation of the Augustan empire 23 BC ■ Birth of Christ 6 BC ■ Foundation of Constantinople AD 330 ■ Sack of Rome by the Visigoths AD 410

From *c*.150 BC, Rome dominated the Western Mediterranean, and was to extend its hegemony throughout the Western world. The first Roman imperium endured for 500 years before being superseded by the Byzantine Empire in the East and by a patchwork of Frankish and Gothic kingdoms in the West, with some central authority still exercised by the Roman Church.

Latin was the great and enduring gift of Rome, offering access to the whole corpus of Western learning and making the works of Greek philosophers, Arab and Persian scientists, Christian Fathers and Roman poets available to all. A Gaulish-speaking Briton could converse with a Spaniard or Italian in a common language: reliable contracts could be sealed between Jewish and Egyptian merchants: churchmen could conduct disputes on fine points of theology at interminable length. Ultimately Latin evolved into the Romance languages, which include Italian, Spanish, Portuguese and French.

The Rise of Rome

Alexander's wars and their aftermath had left the Western Mediterranean comparatively undisturbed, with the Greek cities in Italy, France, and Spain enjoying continuing independence. The present cathedral at Syracuse, the richest of the Greek colonies, is built with the columns of the previous temple of Athena still in their original place. Further inland, the majestic temple of Agrigentum testifies to the wealth of another Sicilian colony. Colonies spawned subcolonies; thus, Antipolis (Nice) and the Spanish port of Empurias were founded by settlers from Massilia (Marseilles). These all competed with the former Phoenician colonies, independent since the mid-sixth century BC. The largest of these, Carthage, had expanded to control Cyprus, Sardinia, Corsica and the Balearic Islands, along with the island of Malta, home to the world's earliest stone temples. The Carthaginians could also claim a foothold in Western Sicily, and some 200 subcolonies spilling over into the Atlantic.

In Western Italy, the Etruscans preserved the traditions of the Asian civilizations among smaller city-states, including Rome. The Romans were originally descendants of one of the Indo-European tribal groupings that moved into Italy about 1000 BC, bringing with them their language variant, Latin, settling among the Neolithic farmers. By *c*.570 BC the modest hill town had flourished to become the largest central Italian city, with a fine temple of Jupiter Capitolinus and (after 480 BC) a formal republican constitution. Its complex organization, with many checks and balances, ensured an oligarchic government while maintaining a popular assembly, which in spite of many rebellions and civil wars, endured: even today the street furniture of Rome is marked SPQR – *Senatus Populusque Romanus* ('The Senate and the People of Rome').

Overshadowing the whole region were intruders, generally known as Gauls, who were infiltrating all Europe, settling in Anatolia, northern Italy and Spain, and making raids further south, one of which in 390 BC had shocked the Romans by destroying their capital. Once suppressed, as they were in 215 BC, the Gaulish settlers gave little further trouble, while the region was reinforced by Roman veterans, allotted land in a rigidly planned system.

After Rome had mopped up the other Italian states, it vied with Carthage for supremacy and control of the trade routes (with Syracuse a third contender). The Punic Wars between Rome and Carthage began where the Athenians had left off, in Syracuse where the unlucky Archimedes perished in 212 BC. They ended only in 146 BC, after such famous episodes as Hannibal leading his army of elephants through Spain and over the Alps to defeat the Romans at the Battle of Cannae. Yet the Romans eventually won, and added Hispania to their existing province of Cisalpine Gaul.

ABOVE *A wall painting from a house in Pompeii, dated around the 1st century AD, shows a Roman couple, with a scroll and writing materials. It is believed he was a local breadmaker called Paquius Proculus.*

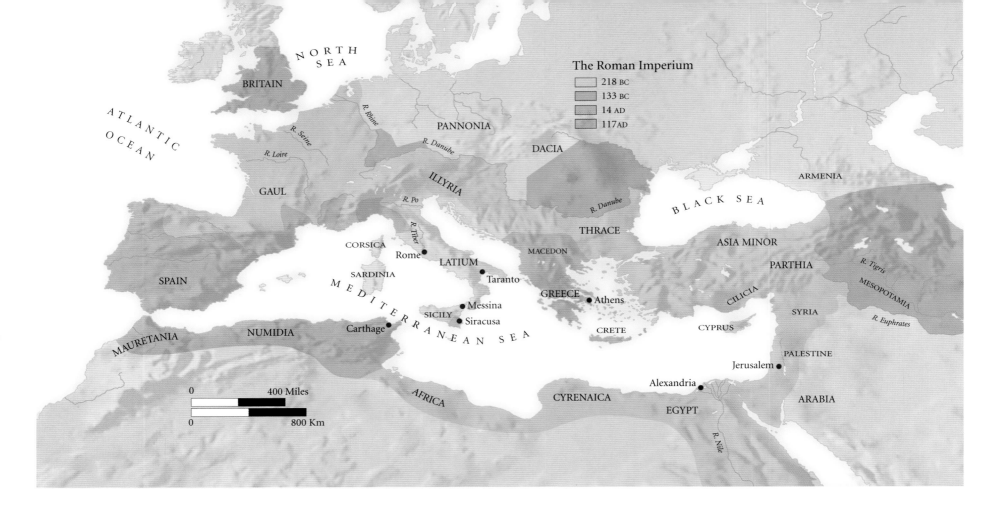

The Roman Imperium
- 218 BC
- 133 BC
- 14 AD
- 117 AD

Roman Expansion

The Greek historian Polybius wrote in c.140 BC that within 50 years 'the whole world fell under the single rule of Rome'. Not perhaps quite all the world as then perceived, since Egypt continued independent, but the Successor empires of Antigonus and Seleucus had been dismembered and by the century's end Roman rule extended throughout Italy, much of Spain and southern France (Provence), Macedonia, Greece and the former Attalid state of Pergamon.

Roman success was due largely to its military organization. All volunteers were entitled to Roman citizenship and to a moderate land-holding after completing their terms of service. Within a few generations, many conquered territories were peopled with loyal Roman veterans. Their infantry tactics, supplemented by their superb engineering skills, were as effective against Hannibal's elephants as against Gaulish cavalry. The inevitable tensions between a constitution based on a republican city-state and a widespread multicultural empire led to internal quarrels and civil wars, with conservatives like Cato attempting to defend republican virtue against both corruption and revolutionary reform. The 'Social War' between Sulla's conservatives and Marius' *Populares* was followed by an uneasy alliance of three rulers (triumvirate): the rich Crassus , the successful general Pompey (Gnaeus Pompeius), fresh from establishing Roman rule in Asia Minor in 61 BC and the coming man Caesar (Gaius Julius), all critically eyed by the intellectual conservative Cicero.

By 49 BC Caesar's reputation was established by his conquest of Transalpine Gaul – France to the Rhine and Channel, and enhanced by his own self-aggrandizing account of the campaign, *De Bello Gallico*. Supported by his loyal soldiers, Caesar took the momentous decision to cross the Rubicon and to march on Rome. Crassus, attempting to match his colleagues' military reputation, had been killed in 53 BC fighting the Parthians, and Pompey was disposed in 48 BC at the Battle of Pharsalus. Adjusting constitutional niceties to practical necessities, Caesar had himself proclaimed dictator for life, and went about grafting a system of personal rule on a republican constitution.

Groups of dissidents, a mixture of Sulla's supporters and recalcitrant republicans, carried on the civil war until their final defeat in southern Spain: within six months of his victory Caesar was assassinated by their sympathizers, on the Ides of March 44 BC.

Yet Caesar had chosen his successor well. His great-nephew Octavian was shrewd and patient. He skilfully eliminated his rivals – his final victory over Mark Antony (Marcus Antoninus) and Cleopatra, the last Pharaoh, is one of history's best-known and most-embroidered stories. Adopting the titles of *Imperator* and *Augustus* ('the illustrious one') Octavian established the Roman Empire which, including its successor, the Holy Roman Empire, lasted for some 1,800 years.

Actual supreme power in the empire was allied to a respect for republican traditions and reinforced by a talented propaganda machine, working at many levels. In literature the most influential was the work of the poet Virgil who described Roman destiny as:

> *'to rule the nations – and you will be given the skill – to impose peace, spare the defeated and cut down the proud with the sword.'*

The message was driven home by grand architecture in Rome itself – imposing monuments and public buildings, such as the Colosseum – but even more significantly, in the newly conquered imperial regions, such as the Porta Nigra in Trier, or Hadrian's Wall. These engineering feats may have crumbled, but Roman literature endured: the final decades BC brought the 'Golden Age' of Latin literature, with such diverse and remarkable authors as Cicero, Horace, Catullus, Lucretius, and Virgil.

Imperialism had its critics, the most biting being the annalist Tacitus, who described a typical Roman conquest (the unsuccessful one of Scotland) 'There they create a wasteland and call it peace.' As with all autocracies, the success of imperial rule depended on the character of the emperor, and

Augustus' immediate heirs – Tiberius, Caligula, Claudius and Nero – were all deeply flawed, though Claudius succeeded where Caesar had failed, in establishing the new province of Britannia. Stability was restored by a series of wise and energetic rulers, of whom Hadrian (r. AD 117–138) was the most versatile and cultivated. He kept the peace, strengthened the frontiers, and commissioned the Roman Pantheon, an engineering and architectural gem. He even wrote verse. His haunting description of the soul on the point of death demonstrates the concision and expressive power of the new Latin:

> 'Anima, vagula, blandula,
> Hospes comesque corporis;
> Quae nunc abibis in loca?
> Pallidula, rigida, nudula,
> Nec ut soles dabis jocos.'

('Little gentle wandering soul, /My body's friend and guest, /Where are you off to now? /Pale, frozen and stripped /No longer sharing jokes.')

Barbarians at the Gates

On the empire's periphery other less-organized societies pressed, with varying degrees of urgency, on the borders. Like the Greeks, the Romans called the outsiders 'barbarians', but while the Greeks applied the term impartially to everyone who did not speak Greek (the word was meant to mirror onomatopoeically the unintelligible babble spoken by foreigners). In Latin the disdain was even stronger: *barbarus* was paired with *immanis* – savage. Yet when it came to savagery, the Romans were second to none – the 'games' staged in the Colosseum have rarely been equalled for cool horror.

The Celtic communities in Gaul and Britannia accepted Roman rule and culture, aided by secure borders. Boudicca's revolt in eastern Britain in AD 60 was decisively suppressed, while the Caledonian tribes were contained behind Hadrian's Wall. A brief attempt to incorporate Germania, east of the Rhine,

BELOW *A detail from a terracotta temple frieze from Civit Alba, Sassoferrato, Italy, shows Gallic warriors fleeing. Like many countries conquered by the Romans, the Gauls became integrated into the Roman way of life.*

as a province was abandoned after the annihilation of an entire Roman army by the German commander Arminius at the Battle of Teutoburg Forest in AD 9, the most complete defeat ever suffered by Rome. The Rhine frontier was mutually accepted and Germanic tribes kept at bay for another 300 years. But before then all Roman society had been revolutionized.

Jews and Christians

Ever since their return from Babylonian exile, Jews had spread all over the Mediterranean and beyond, appreciated as merchants, councillors, charioteers and cavalry, among other qualities. Their religion, although odd, was less so than some of the other brands on offer, and the oddities were politely ignored. But the Jews remaining in Palestine were troublesome. In 167 BC protests against the crude rule of Seleucid vassals were followed by a successful revolt, that of the Maccabees. The inevitable squabbles between the Jewish parties, especially Pharisees and Sadducees, led to Roman intervention, the appointment of the unsavoury Herod as king, and eventually, after constant strife, the forceful pacification by Titus and the final destruction of Jerusalem in AD 70.

The ruin of the great temple marked an epoch in Jewish history. It had been the only place where the priests could legitimately offer sacrifice (although emigrant Jews had already built other temples in Egypt) and Jewish worship had in future to be based on communal services and synagogues, where the sacred texts could be rehearsed and the psalms sung. Jewish resistance continued to the dramatic siege of Masada (AD 72–73) and suppression of the Bar-Kochba Revolt in AD 132, but the second Jewish diaspora had begun.

The great division in world time still today signified by the birth (actually a few years previously) of the prophet Jesus of Nazareth, had passed unremarked, but by the closing years of his first century the Christians (literally followers of the anointed one) were attracting unfavourable notice and official persecution. Paul the Apostle was preaching, often secretly, all over the Eastern Mediterranean, developing as he went the essential doctrines of Christianity, in Greek, the language of the Bible for most Jews, and the lingua franca of the region. Slowly but steadily the new religion found adherents in the Latin West, as far afield as the province of Britannia, but rarely showing much of a public presence.

Paul's Christianity was not, of course, the fully developed set of doctrines embodied in today's Bible, much less the highly evolved practice of the Catholic Church. None of his letters mention, for example, the story of the Virgin Birth, based upon a mistranslation from the Hebrew to the Greek, which had become, two centuries later, an article of faith. Much discussion

LEFT *Found near the southern French city of Lyons in 1897, the Coligny Calendar is an early second century AD lunisolar calendar engraved on bronze in the Gaulish language. Significantly, it uses Roman capital letters and numerals.*

and imaginative creativity was needed before a definitive form of Christianity was generally accepted.

By the mid-third century AD, the empire seemed to be imploding, as the central government faltered under pressure on the frontiers. Nearly 20 claimants appeared in 50 years, the decline being arrested by the Emperor Diocletian: typical of the time he was born in Illyria and avoided Rome as much as possible. In between fighting off invasions, the new emperor began a new era. Yielding to geographical imperatives, rule was divided between four colleagues, two based in the West in Rome and the new centres of Trier and Milan, two in the East in Diocletian's new capital in Nicomedia, just opposite the ancient city of Byzantium. From there a complete reorganization was effected – economic, political, constitutional, and social. The remnants of the old republican system were discarded: the emperor had absolute power and was to be treated as the supreme divinity, only approachable through complex rituals.

The new religion demanded that competitors be eliminated, and both Christianity and the popular Mithras cult were savagely persecuted. How did it happen, then, that within 10 years Christianity was revived, to become the new state religion? Numbers were limited – perhaps five percent of the total population: there was only a restricted physical presence – few, if any, churches and no clear hierarchy.

One plausible answer might simply be that Christianity had a universal appeal in the fourth century. Rulers could rest easy that the new religion did not seek secular power (as in Christ's admonition to 'render unto Caesar the things that are Caesar's'). Older religions were included and traditional centres of previous creeds retained. Ancient seasonal festivals at equinox and solstices were renamed; Christmas took a little juggling with the evidence of Christ's birthday, but Easter was calculated in the Babylonian manner and named by Germanics after a pagan goddess. Perhaps above all the sense of community, of mutual support and eternal hope was decisive. All this could explain a gradual conversion and the future growth, but the suddenness of Diocletian's successor, Constantine, to elevate a modest sect, whose doctrines were little-known and poorly understood, to be the one true religion acknowledged throughout the empire remains a mystery.

Successor State in the East

Any government is defined by the problems it faces, and the solutions it attempts. Constantine's new regime was confronted by unparalleled difficulties. The first step was to define the new religion, but here opinions differed. A passionate discussion had arisen in AD 318 on the exact nature of the Trinity (the Arian doctrine). Nor was there any clear agreement on Christian government, the ranking and appointment of bishops, priests and deacons. The authority of ecumenical Councils, and the pre-eminence claimed by the Bishop of Rome were controversial; if Rome owed its authority to its being the imperial city what should happen now that the Emperor had moved to Byzantium? The Council of Nicaea (AD 325) settled some points, but controversies continued. Arianism remained popular, especially among the barbarians who were holding the frontiers of the Western empire and the divisions between Eastern and Western churches deepened as new doctrines developed in the Roman Church.

Although Constantine disliked Rome, he was determined to reinforce its importance as the historic centre of Christendom, demonstrated during

to Egypt and China, and even into Ethiopia and down the coasts of Africa.

Byzantine arts set new standards of workmanship, including exquisite ivories, gold and silver work, the finest mosaics, not only in the city, but as far afield as Ravenna and Palermo, and, on a much larger scale, statuary such as the bronze horses later taken by the Venetians and set into the façade of St Mark's Basilica. The most influential Byzantine product however was the comprehensive code of laws prepared in the reign of the emperor Justinian (r. AD 518–564) which for more than 1,000 years formed the foundation of all European law. Latin legal tags still encapsulate important principles - 'mens rea,' 'habeas corpus', and so on.

The Eastern Empire began shakily, with 10 emperors in the 70 years after Constantine's death and it was not until AD 408 that Theodosius II was able to offer some stability in a reign of 43 years. Anything approaching sustained order and tranquillity, however, rarely appeared. Those frequent changes of ruler were always accompanied by assassinations, and mob rule often took over any city government. Two factions, the Blues and Greens, originally named after race-going groups, took the place of political parties, and violence was used to settle issues. The 'Nika' riots of AD 532 left 30,000 dead and much of the city in flames. In a sign of the changing times, it was a group of Scandinavian mercenaries led by an Illyrian that suppressed the unrest.

While these domestic difficulties were being settled, external challenges had to be faced.

his brief visit in AD 326, when he consecrated the new basilica of St Peter and endowed a second dedicated to St Paul (S. Paolo Fuori le Mura). The most splendid buildings were naturally those in his new capital, renamed Constantinople; the Milion housed the True Cross, a gift from his mother: St Eirene, the Church of the Holy Peace;the immense Hippodrome was decorated by the 'Serpent Column' first erected at Delphi's temple of Apollo; the new Forum was home to a porphyry column, 100 feet (30 metres) tall, brought from Heliopolis.

Constantinople's splendour was reinforced by these trophies of ancient empires, and protected by the astounding defensive walls erected by Emperor Theodosius. Byzantium may have been an unbalanced choice as the centre of an empire – it was 2,000 miles (3,200 km) and two months' travel from Hadrian's Wall, while the Persians were neighbours in Anatolia – but it was an unequalled centre of trade, throughout the Mediterranean and Black Sea,

War with the Persian Sasanid empire was intermittent, often violent, but never decisive. More threatening, and nearer home, was the threat posed by disgruntled Goths, settled outside Roman territory, but making up a sizeable proportion of Roman forces. Their brilliant young commander in AD 395 was the Visigoth Alaric, confronted by Stilicho, a Vandal, married to the Emperor Theodosius' niece. The future of the Roman Empire was now in the hands of two 'Barbarian' generals. Alaric began by leading his forces to Constantinople itself, thence in a destructive campaign through Greece, before patching up an agreement with Stilicho. Seven years later, there was another invasion, another battle and another truce, the Goth–Vandal confrontation only ending with the murder of Stilicho, and the remarkably well-mannered sack of Rome by Alaric, in AD 410.

The empire would have done much better to agree to Alaric's reasonable demands – a space for his people to settle, and a recognized rank for himself.

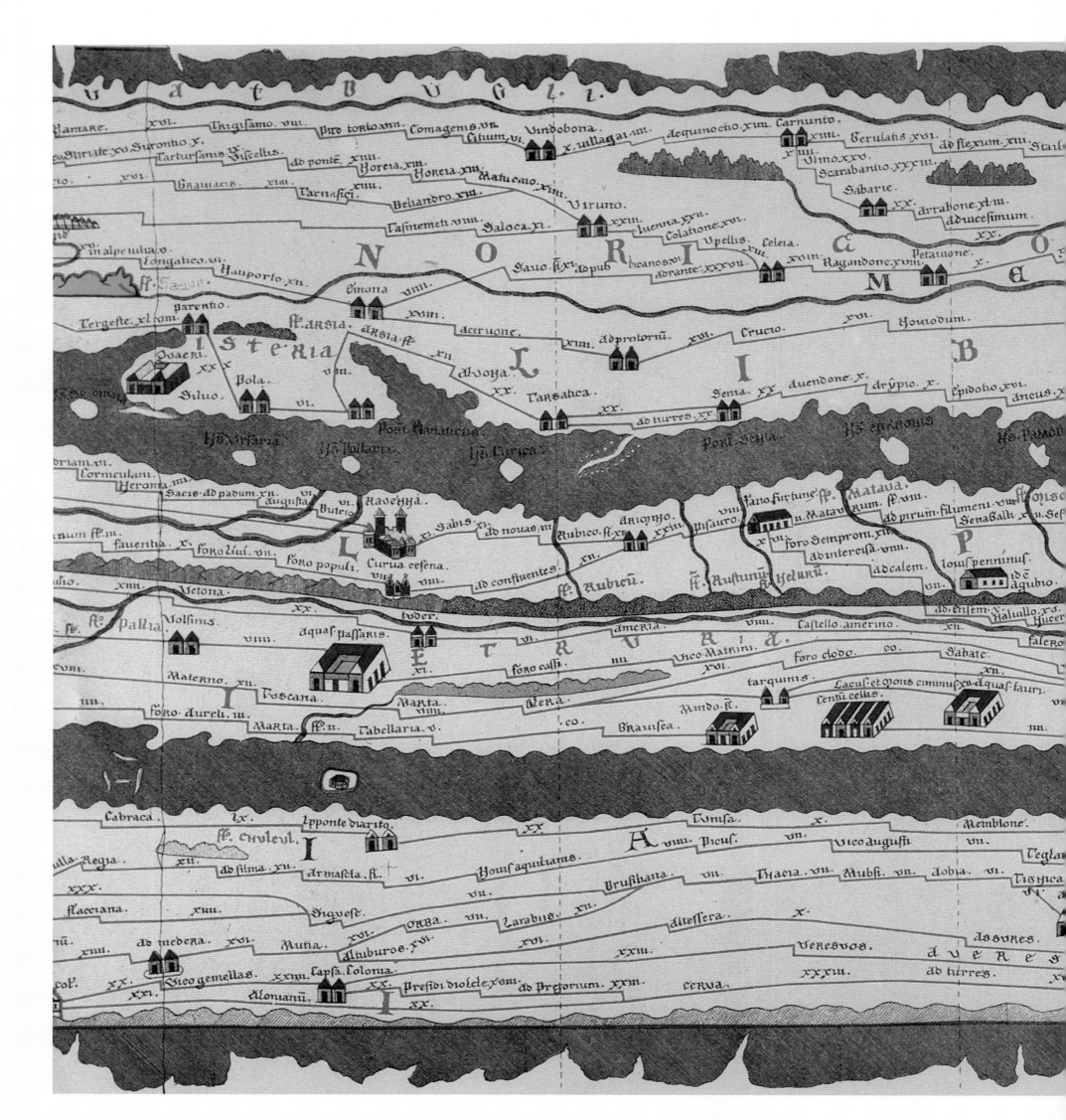

The Tabula Peutingeriana *is a 16th-century copy of a fourth-century* AD *Roman map of the known world. It shows the public roads (*cursus publicus*) built and used by Roman legions, from Britain to the borders of India, and North Africa. This section, the fifth, shows Italy with Rome, the Adriatic coast and North Africa.*

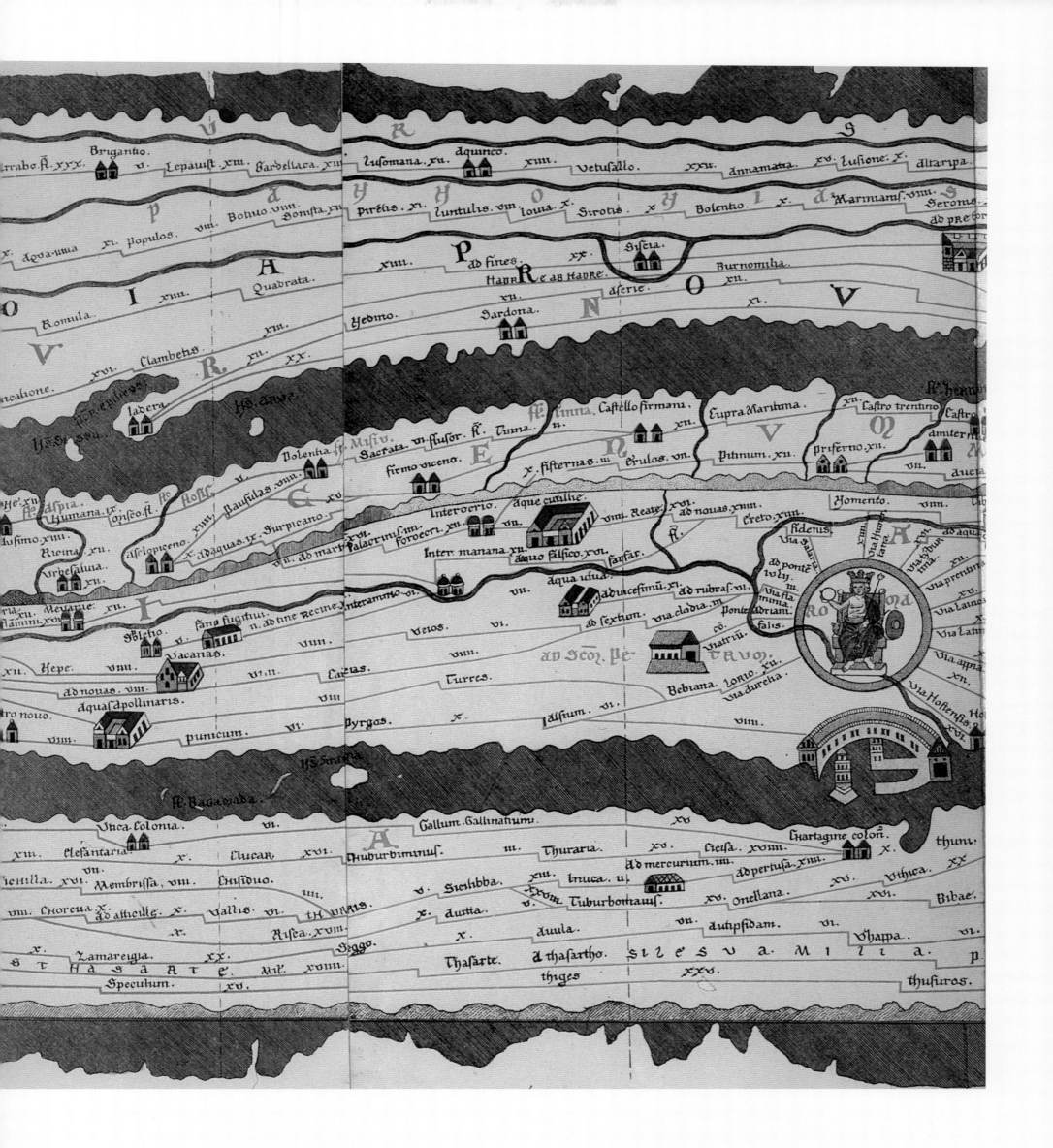

c.1500 BC — AD 1500
Early Civilizations of Africa and the Americas

■ First Olmec settlements in Mesoamerica *c.*1500 BC ■ Classic period of Mayan civilization begins *c.*AD 250 ■ Kingdom of Ghana at its height *c.*AD 800 ■ Pueblo culture thrives in southwestern USA *c.*AD 1000 ■ Rise of Aztec civilization in highland Mexico *c.*AD 1450

From earliest recorded history, North Africa interacted with the Mediterranean and Near East, while the rest of the continent developed separately. The transition from stone to ceramic and metal technology took place only sporadically, while tropical farming required different methods.

Arab traders' regular visits to the east coast brought Islamic doctrines, more advanced technologies and examples of state formation, adapted to traditional African customs. Across the Atlantic, apart from some possible and transitory contacts, the peoples of the Americas evolved their own highly original cultures and civilization, drastically interrupted in the centre and south by the Spanish invasion at the end of the 15th century.

All Africa and her Prodigies

Early African history is complicated by the almost complete lack of written records apart for some travellers' brief descriptions: Ethiopia was the only country with a written form of language, an ancestor of today's Amharic. As early as the fourth century AD Cosmas Indicopleustes wrote that the state of Axum sent expeditions south over the equator, to exchange cattle for gold. In spite of competition from Muslim traders, Christian Ethiopia continued to be not only tolerated but actually supported by Islam. The rugged and mountainous heart of Ethiopia made any attack dangerous, and the Ethiopian Christians, like the Egyptian Copts, went unmolested: Ethiopian bishops were even consecrated in Cairo, and Saladin himself gave the Ethiopians a church in Jerusalem. The Lalibela rock churches commemorate this period, and when the battle with Islam began it was the confident Christians who started it, in the 15th century. It was ended a century later when Muslim forces, now in the form of the Ottoman Turks, devastated the whole kingdom. Some recovery was only possible when the Portuguese, from their Indian settlement in Goa, sent a relief force: Ethiopia entered modern times a sadly damaged state.

Coastal East Africa had been well known, regularly visited and partly colonized since the first century AD, as recorded in the *Periplus of the Erythraean Sea*, whose author visited ports as far south as Zanzibar before changing course for India. At Opone (Ras Hafun in Somalia) he noted the presence of cinnamon and 'slaves of the better sort'; the Axum ruler was 'miserly in his ways.. but otherwise upright, and acquainted with Greek literature'. Abdul al Mas'udi, a Baghdadi scholar, travelled south in AD 916 to the country of Zanj, where the people wear iron ornaments, disdaining gold and silver, and 'speak elegantly'. The iron came from further down the coast in Sofala (Mozambique), where metalworking was the only trade, and was shipped to India. Islam came slowly to Zanj. When the Moroccan Berber scholar and traveller Ibn Battuta (1304–69) visited the region in 1331, he described the thriving entrepôt of Kilwa Kisiwani (in modern Tanzania) as 'one of the most beautiful and well-constructed towns in the world', but its people were still fighting 'a holy war' against their pagan neighbours. Kilwa's prosperity was evident in its buildings, its written languages and coinage, the first ever minted in sub-Saharan Africa. Away from the east coast records are extremely rare. Nor has much been discovered from archaeology, but it seems that most of Africa was sparsely populated, with self-sufficient small communities sometimes forming urban clusters, perhaps not unlike those in the Danube Valley thousands of years previously.

Climatic changes affected Africa dramatically. Between 4500 and 2500 BC increased humidity allowed much of what is now the Sahara to support livestock. When desert conditions returned the herdsmen moved south into the wide band of pasture, the Sahel, that stretches right across Africa from the Atlantic to the Red Sea and permitted the formation of 'Sudanese' type states along the lines of Meroë and Axum. The geographical key to West Africa is the River Niger, which rises in the coastal highlands and flows for 2,600 miles (4,184 km) in a great curve northeast into the Sahel to Timbuktu, then southwest through Nigeria to the Gulf of Guinea, where it forms a wide delta. From the Niger, two main trade routes led north to the Mediterranean. Early trans-Saharan traders used mules, since camels were not seen there until much later, carrying the essential salt and the first African iron. By the mid-first millennium BC, Africans were producing their own iron, a much

Ghana was succeeded first by the Mali empire, more reliably recorded after its conversion to Islam, considerably larger than Ghana, extending from the Atlantic some 1,400 miles (2,250 km) to the interior. Ibn Battuta visited the country in 1352–53 and noted that its people were 'seldom unjust – the Sultan pardons no one who is guilty of it (injustice). There is complete security, neither traveller nor inhabitant has anything to fear from robbers or violent men'. Yet he deplored the fact that 'women servants, slave women and young girls go about quite naked': on the other hand, he mentioned approvingly that boys were chained until they had memorized the Qur'an.

The most widely traded commodities were salt, especially from the Sahara down the River Niger, and slaves. Slavery indeed became the typical African institution, with individuals and families often voluntarily accepting servitude in exchange for security or to satisfy debts. African slaves had always been valued since Egyptian times for their strength and beauty, and, together with animal skins, gold and ivory found ready markets.

Further downstream, urban centres developed among the Yoruba, who became famous as bronze-casters, and between these, smaller settlements on the coast, and the northern empires a network of minor trade routes developed. Extensive trade demanded regulation of weights and measures: when King Toure of Songhay asked a scholar for advice he was told that 'all measures large and small must … conform to a uniform standard', and be frequently inspected. Very precise weights were used to measure gold dust, and were checked against carob seeds: in what can hardly be a coincidence – and may well be evidence of how extensive African trade routes were – the symbols used on Yoruban gold weights resemble very closely those found in the Indus Valley and Mesopotamia, thousands of years previously.

Ancient America: the North

Archaeologists, anthropologists, historians and geneticists still debate the origins and dates of settlement in the Americas, and the constant discovery of new evidence only complicates the argument. Certainly, many adventurous people, having crossed what is now the Bering Straits (but was then a continuous land bridge), made their way south. Some, such as the Athabascan pioneers, went no further than the northwest coast, an area which became relatively thickly populated, and there developed a distinctive language and culture. Fish was the great attraction: although game was plentiful, its capture required considerable effort and the likely expenditure of valuable arrows or spearheads. Using just a few bone-hooks and a length of line, on the other hand, people could easily catch salmon or lake fish, which could be dried, smoked or salted. Early northern groups settled mainly either on the coasts, around the Great Lakes or in the Mississippi Basin.

There was more than enough room for everyone. With no shortage of fresh water, easily accessible timber – no great trees needing to be felled, but branches and saplings readily available for kindling, shelter, and boat-building – clan groups had room for expansion without troubling their neighbours. The almost-sporting character of Indian warfare, where 'counting coup' – striking an opponent and dodging off - was more honourable than wounding or killing, continued until Europeans introduced a new standard of indiscriminate savagery. Chiefs, when needed, were informally elected, but each man retained personal freedom for himself and his family. Combined with a lack of organized religion, early Indian hunter–gatherer society must have been agreeable, possibly explaining why the shift towards pastoralism and agriculture was very slow.

ABOVE *Metalworking, notably bronze casting by the lost-wax method, reached heights of sophistication in medieval West Africa. This plaque is from the kingdom of Benin (in modern Nigeria).*

more useful metal than bronze, which was employed only in decoration. Iron too came from the Sudan, and with it East African institutions of centralized monarchies. Ghana – a long way from the present state of that name, its chief town being in present Mauritania – was the first to emerge, flourishing from *c.* AD 800 as an absolute kingdom, whose people prostrated themselves and sprinkled dust on their heads in the presence of the ruler. Ghana's prosperity was due to gold, 'which grows in the sand as carrots do' (according to a ninth-century Arab commentator). It was of little practical use, but valuable to the Islamic north; more prosaically the state levied heavy taxes on the salt trade. A Córdoban, Abdul al-Bekri, writing in 1067, described the king sitting:

'in a pavilion around which stand ten pages holding shields and gold-mounted swords.'

while the door to the pavilion was guarded by:

'dogs of an excellent breed … wearing collars of gold and silver.'

The Americas

| 0 | 500 Miles |
| 0 | 1000 Km |

convenient currents. There are indeed some similarities between West African and American art, and Mycenaean and Inca architecture, but these are not generally accepted as proof of contact.

Mesoamerica

The Mesoamerican region extended from the valley of Mexico through the central plateau to the Yucatán Peninsula, all within the tropics, but with the 5,000-foot-plus (1500-m) altitude of the Mexico Valley giving a wide range of climates. Chilis, gourds, tomatoes, avocados, pineapples, potatoes and the essential cereal crop, maize, were all developed in the warmer climates of Central and South America: so too were those pleasurable vegetables, nicotiana (tobacco) and cacao (chocolate). The symbiotic relationships between maize, beans and squash gourds was established all over North and Central America. Root crops, such as manioc and potatoes, supplemented maize as a staple, while the reliable stock of fish and small mammals provided animal protein. Carefully managed, and with readily available human fertilizer, three or even four crops a year might be taken, supporting a very high population density.

The first state formations appeared in the tropical lowlands on Campeche Bay, the wasp-waist of Central America, as the Olmec culture developed what became the later Mayan civilization. The first Olmec towns were built in c.1500 BC, following a similar pattern of an immense earth platform aligned north to south, well over 100 feet (30 metres) high, divided by adobe walls and housing the clearest sign of Olmec culture, the enormous stone heads carved from blocks of basalt 10 feet (3 metres) tall, majestic and dignified. Such ritual and social power centres were surrounded by villages, sometimes with such amenities as courts for that other Olmec identifier, the ball-game. 'Game' conveys an unsuitably playful impression of what became an important ritual, which concluded with the ritual killing of the losing team. Cutting out the heart with a knife with a razor-sharp blade made from obsidian (a black volcanic glass) was the preferred method.

Semi-permanent communities formed in the Ohio/Mississippi valleys from c.3000 BC leaving memorials in the thousands of earth mounds found all over the southeastern United States. By c.800 BC a wide variety of food crops were grown, while later the cultivation of maize from AD 800 encouraged population growth and the establishment of at least one Danubian-style great village, at Cahokia (present-day St Louis), rather grandly styled a 'city-state' by some US historians. Unlike the Danubians, the Cahokians raised some impressive mounds and terraces, suggesting a central organization, and practised human sacrifice, but, as with the Danubian communities, Cahokia faded away. The pattern of North American settlement became modest villages, with extensive maize fields and quite extensive arboriculture providing a wide range of nuts and that delicious sweetener, maple syrup.

Some contact with the old worlds must have continued, or even preceded the Bering passage. Similarities with Asian cultures are too numerous to be coincidental and suggest some trans-Pacific arrivals before AD 1200. Plausible arguments have been advanced for cross-Atlantic travel, with similarly

BELOW *Little concrete evidence remains of the Olmecs, one of the first cultures of Mesoamerica , except for a number of colossal stone heads. Many of these have a skull-cap, which archaeologists have linked to the ritual ball-game played extensively in early Central America.*

Olmec cultures were transmitted to such neighbouring territories as that of the Maya in Yucatán and Guatemala and the Zapotec in the high valleys of the Sierra Madre des Sur; by 750 BC the first evidence of Mesoamerican writing was visible. The élite of these societies had access to jewellery, mirrors, decorated pottery, a varied diet and the services of an army of slaves or servants. The most remarkable Mesoamerican achievement was mathematical – the use of zero, beginning some time before the last century BC, reflected in the development of the triple Mayan calendar – 260 days for ritual, 365 days for practical purposes, plus a 'long' calendar of 144,000 days beginning in the year 3114 BC, and estimated to end in December 2012. Mayan writing was an unwieldy system of symbols and numerals, understood only by rulers and scribes, and probably used only for keeping records; the sole fragments of Mayan books that survive are either almanacs, ritual texts, or very basic annals, which might serve as prompts for oral amplification. Certainly after the European alphabet was introduced a rich store of oral culture was revealed.

The Maya and the Aztecs

Some time after AD 500 a new polity was formed in the Oaxaca valley around the impressive Monte Alban site, where a hill top was levelled to provide a 20-hectare (50-acre) platform for official and domestic buildings: some 300 carved stone slabs depicting mutilated corpses suggest that Monte Alban's supremacy was not established peacefully. Armed aggression secured power, but was itself not sufficient to maintain it. Habits of obedience had to be reinforced by a consensual belief, and in Mesoamerica this was demonstrated by constant drama and pugnacity, first in the city of Teotihuacan, on the northeast shore of Lake Texcoco in the Valley of Mexico. Centred on a mile-

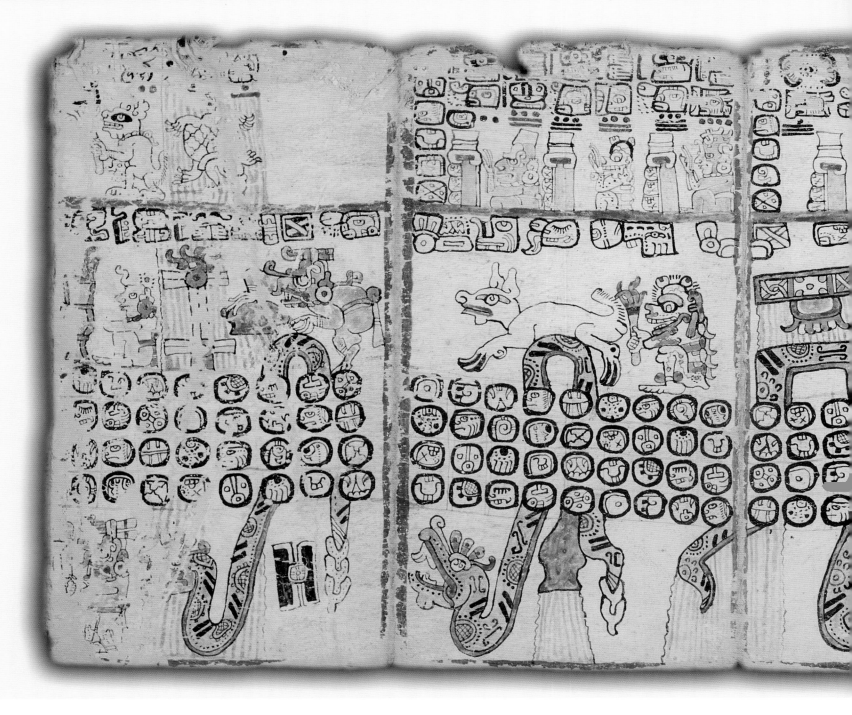

The 14th-century Mayan Codex Tro-Cortesiano (or Madrid Codex), is one of only four surviving such documents from this ancient Mesoamerican culture. Produced on fig-bark paper, and folded like an accordeon, it is a series of divinatory almanacs on various themes. This section shows the God of Death (fourth panel from the left) beating the celestial snake with his axe to make rain. Its scholarly title comes from the Spanish conquistador Hernán Cortés, who brought it back to Spain, and the scholar Juan de Troy Ortolano, who acquired it in the 19th century.

long boulevard connecting three great Pyramids, that of the Sun, the Moon and the Feathered Serpent Quetzalcoatl, the city became one of the world's most populous, with 100,000 citizens, much the same as at the contemporary city of Rome. The Pyramid of the Sun is 700 feet (210 metres) square at the base and 200 feet (61 metres) high. It was meant to inspire awe, and to give the ceremonies carried out on its summit added majesty and mystery. The imposing stairway connected earth with heaven, and continued life on earth depended on the king's intercession with the gods, solemnised with human sacrifice.

Teotihuacan's rulers controlled a large region, but its cultural influence was much more widespread. Some 1,000 miles (1,600 km) separate Teotihuacan from the cities of the Classical Maya in Yucatán, but Teotihuacan was revered as the model of the Mayan cities. In AD 378, a Teotihuacan army marched over 600 miles (965 km) to conquer Mutal/Tikal, one of the most powerful of the 50 or so Mayan city-states in Yucatán, a situation not unlike that of Sumer or classical Greece. And, as in those Old World regions, the Mayan states produced some exquisite art, more delicate than that of the Olmec, and even humorous, carefully observed and using bright colours in the surviving mural paintings. Conflicts between the cities were frequent, the longest and most bitter conflict being that between Mutal and the neighbouring state of Kaan'Calakmul, which continued for more than a century after AD 521. It ended in mutual exhaustion, as successively all the Mayan states fragmented. A period of drought had fatally damaged the fragile ecosystem, which

demanded constant irrigation and careful land management. The northern states – the best known being Chichen Itza – survived better and took their place among the rural communities that had replaced the Mayan cities.

A period of relative calm followed, allowing new skills to be spread. Agricultural productivity – more accurately market gardening - was improved, and metallurgy, hitherto only practised in its most basic form, developed. Some oddities puzzled later Europeans: wheeled vehicles were not developed and wheels were used only on children's toys, and soldiers carried large mirrors. From the early 14th century power was centralized in the Valley of Mexico, and particularly in the lake towns of Tenochtitlán, capital of the Mexica, later the Aztecs, who formed an alliance with their neighbours of Texcoco and Tlacopan – the Triple Alliance. Beginning in the 1450s, aggressive strikes launched by armies of carefully-drilled soldiers forced many smaller states to accept Aztec hegemony. Such wars could either be total combats or semi-ritualistic 'Flowery Wars', fought by extravagantly-uniformed troops according to an established pattern, which nevertheless caused deaths, and, more importantly provided prisoners to satisfy the constant demand for human sacrifices. Such small-scale slaughter, however, was not enough to satisfy demands for flesh and blood at major festivals. When the Aztec ruler Ahuitzotl consecrated the great temple at Tenochtitlán in 1487 he had 20,000 prisoners slaughtered (some estimates are considerably higher) and distributed the more acceptable offerings among his officers and guests.

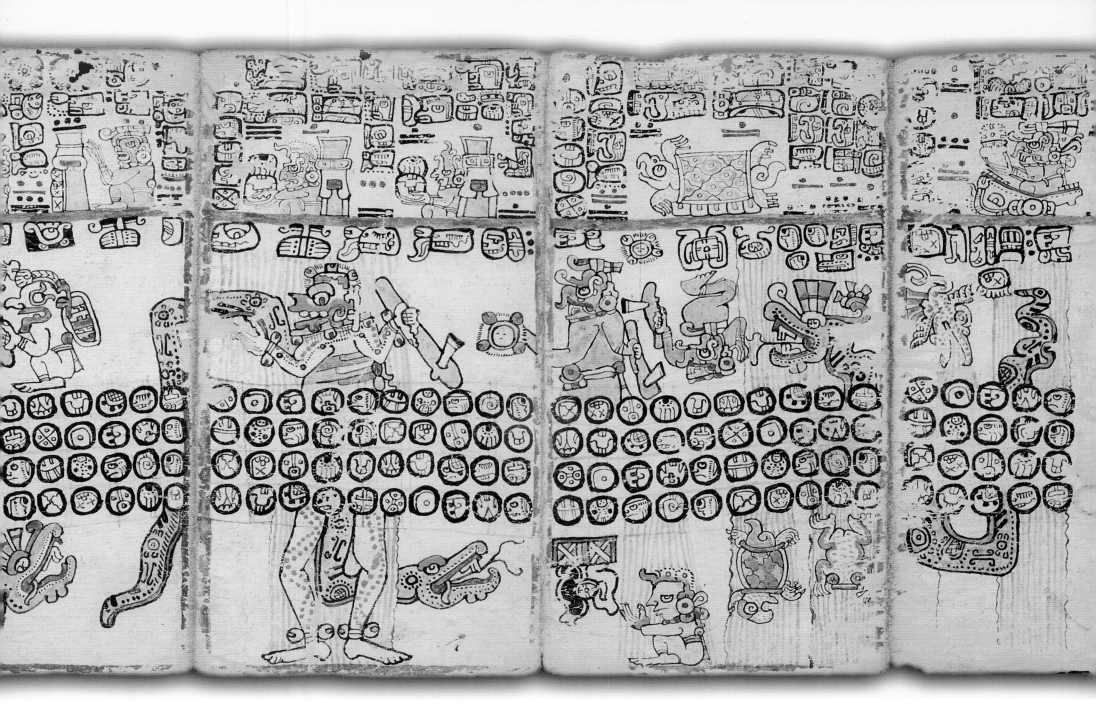

Military service, preceded by training in township schools, was compulsory: failure to capture a prisoner, even as part of a group, was permanently shameful; rank was sought after and distinguished by uniform, nose studs and hairstyles. All of this might be paralleled in the 19th century, even in 20th-century Europe, but Aztec wars were still stone-age combats, the weapons wooden with obsidian blades, without either protective armour, other than padded cotton, or missiles. They were, however, quite violent enough to make the Aztecs extremely unpopular with their smarting vassals and apprehensive neighbours.

South and North

On the west coast of South America, between latitudes 3° North and 14° South a common culture emerged in the short river valleys. The inhabitants, inaddition to the abundant fish, cultivated maize and root crops, and had domesticated the llama and other camelids, permitting the development of the most advanced textile industry, and producing a rich variety of ornaments in precious metals and jewellery. By the first centuries AD, the city of Moche had emerged as the coastal centre, but was supplanted by the highland cities of Wari and Titicaca. Since neither coast nor highland could prosper independently, the inland states founded coastal colonies, linked by well-engineered roads. These, together with the pyramids, temples and colossal status, were later appropriated by the magnificent, but transient, Inca Empire.

On the other side of the continent the Amazonian Indians were – again solidly reinforced by the abundance of fish in the Amazon river – developing their own highly individual system of cultivation based on the creation of 'Indian earth', a rich soil with a very high charcoal content, capable of continued fertility. Manioc and the peach palm were staples and what seems to have been a well-adjusted ecological balance allowed a peaceful and stable society to flourish.

In a very different climate, in the present states of New Mexico and Arizona, a distinctive society was developing as villages expanded into large communities inhabiting multi-storey masonry buildings, often with hundreds of rooms, containing ceremonial spaces and ball courts, with highly finished masonry. For perhaps 400 years, from 800 to 1200, the Pueblo Indians lived surprisingly peacefully in such close proximity, violence being rare, materially assisted by the absence of arbitrary rule or religious authorities. Priests/shamans conducted major festivals and town-leaders emerged, but decision-making seems to have been a communal activity, perhaps assisted by formal male social groups, still particularly common in the United States Their technology was less advanced than that of the Mesoamericans – although their pottery is admirable – but daily life must have been considerably more tranquil. Pressure from nomadic tribes in the north and a prolonged drought in the late 13th century led to more troubled times, and a movement towards the Rio Grande Valley, but Pueblo culture survived – and survives still.

CLASH OF CULTURES

	500	1000	1100	1200

EUROPE

507 Clovis unites much of France

597 St Augustine leads Christian mission to Britain

600 Avar control established in Carpatian Basin

610–641 Emperor Heraclius reforms the Eastern Roman Empire, to become known as the Byzantine Empire

732 Charles Martel defeats Arab invasion at the Battle of Poitiers

771 Charlemagne becomes the sole ruler of the Frankish kingdom

774 Charlemagne conquers the Lombard Kingdom of Italy

800 Charlemagne crowned Roman emperor by Pope Leo III

843 Treaty of Verdun divides the Carolingian empire into three

889 Final breakup of the Carolingian empire

898–899 Magyars invade Italy

962 Otto I crowned Roman emperor in Rome: Holy Roman Empire is founded

BELOW *Modern mosaic depicting Otto I, considered the first Holy Roman Emperor*

1014 Danes conquer England

1016–35 King Canute rules England, Norway and Denmark

1047–90 Normans conquer southern Italy and Sicily

1066 William, Duke of Normandy conquers England

1095 Pope Urban calls the First Crusade at Clermont

1098 Crusaders take Antioch

1099 Crusaders take Jerusalem

1130 Roger de Hauteville (Roger II) crowned king of Sicily, uniting all the Norman conquests in Italy

1149 Second Crusade ends in failure

1169 First Anglo-Normans in Ireland

1187 Saladin defeats Christians at Hattin and recaptures Jerusalem

1190–92 Third Crusade under Richard I: Cyprus captured

1204 Fourth Crusade plunders Constantinople

1215 King John signs Magna Carta

1237–41 The Mongols invade Russia and Eastern Europe. Mongol control permits travel over much of Asia

1248–54 Louis IX leads the Seventh Crusade to Egypt

1261 Byzantines recapture Constantinople: Latin Empire falls

1270 Louis IX dies besieging Tunis on the Eighth Crusade

1287 Mongol embassy to Western Europe

ISLAM AND THE ARAB WORLD

610 Muhammad experiences his first vision

632 Death of Muhammad

636–638 Arabs overrun Syria and Palestine

661–680 Sunni Caliph Mu'awiya founds the Umayyad dynasty

711 Arabs invade Spain

716–717 Arab siege of Constantinople defeated

750 Overthrow of the Umayyad dynasty by the Abbasids

755 Abd-al-Rahman founds the Umayyad emirate at Córdoba

1008–31 The Umayyad emirate at Córdoba collapses into civil war

1071 Seljuk Turks occupy Anatolia

LEFT *Illuminated manuscript dated c.1200 showing a plan of Jerusalem*

1258 Baghdad falls to the Mongols and the last Abbasid caliph is executed

1260 Mamluks expel Mongols from Levant

AMERICAS AND AFRICA

500 The Mayan civilization of Central America peaks in economic prosperity

c.700–1600 Period of the Puebloan cultures of Native American people in the southwestern United States

800–1100 Kingdom of Ghana prospers based on salt trade

800 Uran settlement in Cahokia, Mississippi

916 Cities established on East African coast

1160 The Almohads established as a power on the coast of North Africa

c.1230 The Mali empire in West Africa grows around the upper Niger inland delta

1290 The city of Great Zimbabwe becomes a centre of trade in East Africa

EAST ASIA AND INDIA

552 End of Chinese silk monopoly

590 Yang Jian unites China and founds the Sui dynasty

618 Li Yuan becomes the first emperor of the Tang dynasty

794 Japanese capital of Kyoto founded

802 Foundation of the Khmer empire of Cambodia

907 Final collapse of the Tang dynasty

907–960 Chinese Period of Five Dynasties and Ten Kingdoms

960–79 Song dynasty reunites China

RIGHT *Image painted on silk c.1000 of Taizu, first emperor of the Northern Song*

1226 Much of China occupied by the Mongols under the leadership of Genghis Khan

1258 Korea becomes a Mongol vassal state

1279 Mongols under Kublai Khan defeat the Southern Song and create a new Chinese dynasty, the Yuan

1281 Japanese repel Mongol invasion

500–1600

1300	1400		1500	1600

1302 Crusaders expelled from the Holy Land

1309 Papacy moved from Rome to Avignon

1337 Outbreak of the Hundred Years War between England and France

1360 End of Crusades in the Middle East

1377 Papacy returns to Rome

1378 The Great Schism leads to rival popes at Rome and Avignon

1417 Council of Constance ends the Great Schism of the papacy: Hussite wars begin

1429 Joan of Arc relieves the Siege of Orléans: turning point in the Hundred Years War

1453 End of the Hundred Years War

1455–85 Wars of the Roses in England

LEFT *Statue of Joan of Arc*

1480 Russia (Muscovy) achieves independence from the Tatars

1492 Final conquest of Moorish Granada; kingdoms of Ferdinand of Aragon and Isabella of Castile united

1495 Beginning of the Italian Wars between France and the Habsburgs. Emperor Charles V rules Spain, Germany and South America

1521 Protestant Reformation starts as Luther is excommunicated

1547–84 Reign of Ivan the Terrible as Tsar of all the Russias

1555 Augsburg agreement divides Germany between Catholic and Protestant peoples

1557 Queen Elizabeth I estabishes the Anglican church

1565 Council of Trent establishes Counter-Reformation

1566 The Dutch begin a rebellion against Spanish rule

1588 Philip II of Spain launches an Armada to invade England

ABOVE *Illustration dated 1679 by Dutch artist Jan Luyken depicting defeat of the Spanish Armada*

c.1300 Osman I founds the Ottoman (Turkish) dynasty

1362 Sultan Murad begins conquest of the Balkans

ABOVE *Siege of Constantinople 1453, from a 15th-century illuminated manuscript*

1453 Ottoman Turks under Mehmet II capture Constantinople; Byzantine Empire falls

1501 Ismail I, Shah of Persia, founds the Safavid dynasty

1514 Safavids defeated by the Ottomans at Chaldiran

1516 The Mamlukes of Egypt defeated by the Ottomans at Marj Dabiq

1520 Ottoman Suleiman I becomes sultan

1529 Failure at the Siege of Vienna halts the advance of Suleiman I across Europe

1534 Capture of Baghdad by Suleiman I from the Safavid dynasty

1590 Safavid Shah Abbas concludes peace with the Ottomans

c.1300 Decline of the Pueblo and other farmers of the southwestern deserts of North America

c.1325 Arrival of Aztecs in Mexico

1428 The Aztec empire founded

1438 Pachacutec begins the expansion of the Inca empire

1441–43 Portuguese navigators explore the coast of West Africa

1492 Columbus reaches the Caribbean

1497 John Cabot surveys Newfoundland coast

1519–24 Hernán Cortés conquers the Aztec empire

1524 Giovanni da Verrazano explores the Atlantic coastline of North America

1531–35 Francisco Pizarro conquers the Inca empire

1534–42 Voyages of Jacques Cartier to St Lawrence and Hudson rivers

1575 Portuguese settlement of Angola starts

1592 English participation in transatlantic slavery begins

1368 Yuan retreat to Mongolia; Ming dynasty rises in China

1402–24 Yongle Emperor despatches 'treasure fleets'

1440 Khmer capital of Angkor abandoned

1498 Vasco da Gama reaches India

1469–1539 Guru Nanak founds Sikh religion

RIGHT *A contemporary oil painting of the Portuguese explorer Vasco da Gama*

1519 Babur invades India; he sets up Mughal power in 1526

1539 Suri Afghans of Bihar under Sher Khan rebel and reconquer much of Mughal territory

1542 Mongols invade China: Portuguese traders and missionaries land in Japan

1550 Ming defeat a second Mongul invasion

1557 Portugese occupy Macao

1556 Mughals under Akbar rout the Suri army at Panipat

1576 Mughal conquest of Bengal complete

1592–98 Two invasions of Korea by Japan defeated

1600 The English East India Company is established, followed two years later by the Dutch East India Company

1620 The Forbidden City, commissioned by Wanli Emperor, is completed

AD 622 – 1000
The Rise of Islam

■ The Prophet Muhammad flees Mecca for Medina AD 622 ■ Death of Muhammad AD 632
■ Battle of Karbala begins rift between Sunni and Shi'a AD 680 ■ Conquest of Spain by the
Umayyads begins AD 711 ■ Building of Kailasa Temple in India *c.* AD 800

A key date in history is 9 September AD 622, the first day of the Hijrah, Year One of the Islamic calendar, when the Prophet Muhammad quietly left his home in Mecca to seek refuge in Medina. Within a single generation, obscure tribesmen from the Arabian peninsula had established a vast imperium and impressed the faith of Islam on millions. There were now to be three 'Peoples of the Book' – Jews, Muslims and Christians – whose interaction shaped history in Europe and Asia, and continues to be a decisive influence in modern times.

The Roman Empire recognized two Arabias: Arabia Petraea in the north – the present Kingdom of Jordan, with its prosperous cities of Bostra and Petra –and Arabia Felix, the pleasant land of the Yemen, with its ancient kingdoms controlling the far end of the Red Sea and access to the Indian Ocean through the Strait of Bab al Mandab. These two Arabias, separated by 1,000 miles (1,600 km) of desert, were linked on the west by a single land route, a corridor between the Red Sea and the desert.

A New Religion from the Arabian Desert

Midway along that road another track branched east across the Great Arabian Desert to the Persian Gulf: their junction was the city of Mecca, some 50 miles (80 km) inland from the Red Sea port of Jeddah. Mecca had been for centuries a place of pilgrimage for the semi-nomadic tribes coming to venerate the Ka'aba, the massive granite cube that housed the black stone placed there by the prophet Abraham and his son Ishmael (Isaac). When, in AD 612, one of its citizens, the respected merchant Muhammad ibn Abdullah, began to reveal divine instructions he had received from God via the Angel Jibril (Gabriel) – later recorded in the Qur'an – he challenged the cherished beliefs of his community. All compromise failed, and in 622 Muhammad, with his small band of followers, was forced to move 250 miles (400 km) or so further north along the road to the town of Yathrib, renamed Madinat ul-Nabi ('city of the Prophet'; Medina in English) in Muhammad's honour. That journey, the Hijrah, marks the birth of Islam. Eight years of local civil conflict followed, ending with the Meccans subdued and the Ka'aba cleared of its pagan excrescences, and by the time of Muhammad's death (traditionally set in AD 632) the new doctrines were generally accepted throughout Arabia.

Muhammad himself, a modest man, was the 'Messenger', instructed by God to recall 'People of the Book' (Dhimmi) to their rightful duties. God had previously sent great prophets, as Surah (Chapter) 2 of the Qur'an explains:

'We formerly delivered the book of the law unto Moses … and gave evident miracles to Jesus the son of Mary, and strengthened him with the holy spirit.'

Yet men had misunderstood and perverted this teaching: they must now be told to sweep away these accretions and submit to God's will. This essential first duty was expressed in the name of the new religion, Islam ('submission to the will of Allah') and its adherents, Muslims ('those who submit to God').

The aftermath of Muhammad's death transformed the Western hemisphere, and its effects are still felt. Leadership of the Muslim community (Ummah) passed to a series of caliphs ('successors'), the first four of whom were friends or relatives of the Prophet. Although they often quarrelled (the last three were assassinated) they were spectacularly successful in spreading the faith. By 634 Damascus was captured and Jerusalem besieged: three years later the second caliph, Umar, rode into Jerusalem on a white camel, clad only in well-worn robes and guided by the Christian patriarch around the holy city.

Although Islam was spread by invading armies, it did not prevail by force alone. Its mass appeal can be explained by the straightforward guidance

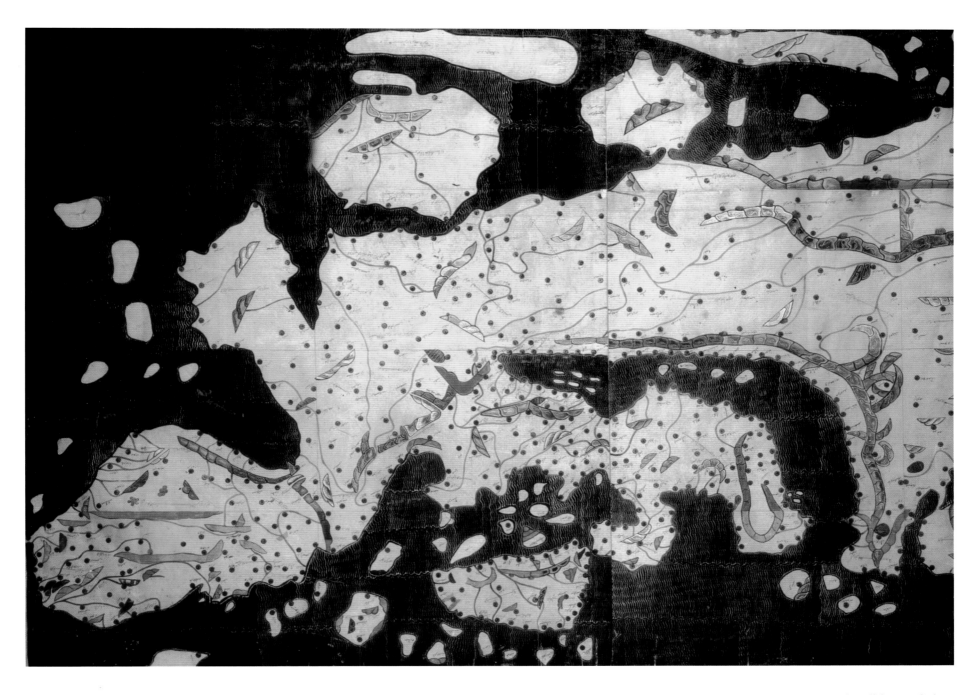

ABOVE *The remarkable world map and 'book of pleasant journeys into faraway lands', customarily known as the* Tabula Rogeriana, *was produced by the Arab geographer Muhammad al-Idrisi for King Roger II of Sicily in 1154.*

and sense of community it offered. All the complex theology of Christianity was swept away, and with it the hierarchy that left lay people well behind a privileged priestly class. All believers were equal before God (as they had been in the early Christian Church) and holy men – and some women – were venerated. Observances were simple: the Five Pillars of Islam – belief in the one God, prayer, fasting, charity and pilgrimage, plus such duties as 'jihad' (the endeavour to convert unbelievers), hospitality to strangers and prohibitions on alcohol and forbidden foods – were all that was required. The Muslim Ummah dwelt in the Dar al-Islam, the 'Abode of Peace', which, within a century of Muhammad's death, extended from the Pyrenees for 6,000 miles (9,600 km) throughout North Africa through the Middle East, and over the Hindu Kush.

The people absorbed, often not unwillingly, into the Peace of Islam were granted a recognized status, protected by the law, called upon for taxation, and given opportunities for advancement. Just as it took only three generations for a Mughal official's grandson to become the first president of Independent India in 1947, the Arab Mansur, procurator of Byzantine Syria, had a son who continued to hold that office under the caliphs – and

a grandson who became a Christian monk in Palestine. Arabic (like English in India) was the official language of Islam, but only a small minority of Muslims were Arabs.

The Golden Years

The first split in Islam did not take long to appear. After the fourth caliph, the Prophet's son-in-law and cousin Ali ibn Abu Talid was murdered by his opponents in 661 and his son Hussein killed by fellow Muslims in the Battle of Karbala (in present-day Iraq) in 680, his supporters, the Sh'iat Ali ('the party of Ali', hence the term 'Sh'ia') began a war against the traditionalists – the majority Sunni. Their often savage dispute continues today, most notably between Sh'ia Iran and Sunni Iraq, with Hussein's death commemorated every year with grieving processions, cries of 'Hussein', and flagellation. Ali's successor, the Sunni Caliph Mu'awiya, founded the first Islamic dynasty of the Umayyads, with their capital in the ancient city of Damascus, where a magnificent mosque was built in AD 715. Demonstrating the period's continuity, it was built on the site of a Roman temple, which had been replaced by a Christian church, and retained the dedication to St John the Baptist, venerated by Christians and Muslims alike.

In 750, the Umayyads were eliminated in a palace coup by Al-Saffah, the founder of the Abbasid dynasty, who moved the capital to the fine new Islamic city of Baghdad, in Persian Mesopotamia.

After the Parthian interlude, a true Persian dynasty had been founded by Shapur I in AD 240 and endured in what was to be the usual Persian pattern of absolute autocracy succeed by declining autocracy, followed by chaos and a return to absolutism. Under two of the later Sasanian kings, Chosroes (Khusrau) I and II, their capital Ctesiphon became a haven for scholars, philosophers and writers and a centre of international trade: Khusrau II was the recipient of a splendid set of Indian chessmen, with ruby and emerald pieces. Sasanian prosperity was based on a well-organized administration and effective taxation, which had begun under Cyrus, and was to continue under Islamic rule, since the new caliphs were well aware of the benefits of a constant income and domestic stability.

By the time of Caliph Haroun-al-Rashid (AD 786–809), the central character in the tale of the *Arabian Nights*, Baghdad had become a cosmopolitan and cultivated city, one of the world's largest, with all the advantages of Persian culture, strategically situated on the main east–west and north–south trading routes. Spices from India, silks from China, gold and slaves from Africa, and skilled artisans from the Levant and Europe flowed into the new capital.

Life in Baghdad in the early 800s was a very different from that in Damascus, Persian rather than Arabic, with its first family of viziers, the Barmakids (originally Buddhists) and many of its merchants coming from the east, Afghanistan and Turkestan, and from Arabia and the Levant. Scholarship and discussion were encouraged in the House of Wisdom, an observatory was constructed and scientific research flourished. The caliph's court developed diplomatic relations both with Byzantium and with the Holy Roman Emperor Charlemagne's court at Aachen (Aix-la-Chapelle): in a splendid gesture, Haroun once sent an elephant to Charlemagne.

Baghdad's glory days did not last. The Caliph's power depended increasingly on non-Arabs, Turkic troops whose revolt caused the capital to be moved to Samarra, and a vigorous persecution of dissenters, Muslim, Christian and Jewish to begin. The greatest of the Baghdadi philosophers, Al-Kundi, died 'a lonely man' in AD 867. Today nothing more than the reputation lingers: with the exception of a few desolate remnants, almost all the Abbasid buildings have been destroyed.

After the erosion of the Caliphate, local Persian rulers founded new dynasties which produced some of the world's most astonishing and original architecture. The Samanids of Khorasan in northeastern Iran – whose rule extended over the Oxus to Bukhara and Samarkand – and the Buyids in central Iran, centred on Isfahan, presided over an eruption of creativity, reflected in the multitude of great towers. Round, square and octagonal, soaring up to 200 feet (60 m), these could be either starkly simple or, like the slender tower of Damghan, entirely covered in intricate ornamentation. A new literary culture was created by the poet Firdausi (940–1020) whose epic 'Book of Kings' is the foundation of Persian literature. Firdausi, writing after more than three centuries of Arab rule, wrote in consciously pure Persian, but in exile, at the court of the notoriously ferocious son of a successful ex-slave Mahmud of Ghazni. One of his companions in what is now Afghanistan was the famous scholar Al Buruni, who translated Indian learning into Arabic and calculated the dimensions of the Earth with remarkable accuracy. Ibn Sina (980–1037) born at Bukhara, worked at the Samanid court, producing medical treatises and his encyclopaedia of Greek philosophy, *The Book of Cure of Ignorance*. Known in the west as Avicenna, he is a major figure in the recovery of classical learning in the west, revered by subsequent Christian scholars. The Persian mathematician Musa Algoritmi gave his name to the word 'algorithm' and the title of his treatise *al-Jabr* to 'algebra'.

Al-Andalus: Spain under Muslim Rule

The Byzantines made no great effort to hold on to Egypt. A few small-scale battles were followed by a capitulation in 642 and the construction of an Arab base, which became the notable city of Fustat near Cairo. In the south, a treaty was easily arranged with the Nubians, but in the West the Arabs faced a more dangerous potential enemy.

The Berbers – who had been Egypt's 'Libyans' – had inhabited the whole of the southern Mediterranean coast around into the Atlantic for many centuries. Integrated into the Roman empire as 'Numidians' – the most famous of the Christian Fathers, St Augustine, was a Berber – they retained a strong sense of national identity. Some years of tough fighting were needed after an Arab capital, which became the splendid city of Kairouan in Tunisia,

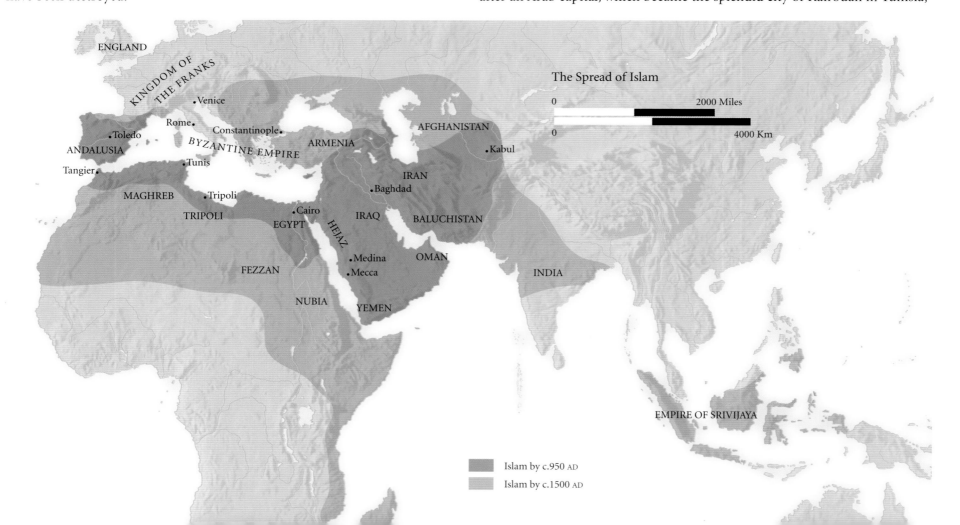

The Spread of Islam

| 0 | | 2000 Miles |
| 0 | | 4000 Km |

ENGLAND
KINGDOM OF THE FRANKS
Venice
Rome
Constantinople
AFGHANISTAN
Toledo
BYZANTINE EMPIRE
ARMENIA
Kabul
ANDALUSIA
Tunis
Tangier
IRAN
MAGHREB
Tripoli
Baghdad
TRIPOLI
Cairo
IRAQ
BALUCHISTAN
EGYPT
HEJAZ
FEZZAN
Medina
OMAN
Mecca
INDIA
NUBIA
YEMEN

EMPIRE OF SRIVIJAYA

■ Islam by c.950 AD
■ Islam by c.1500 AD

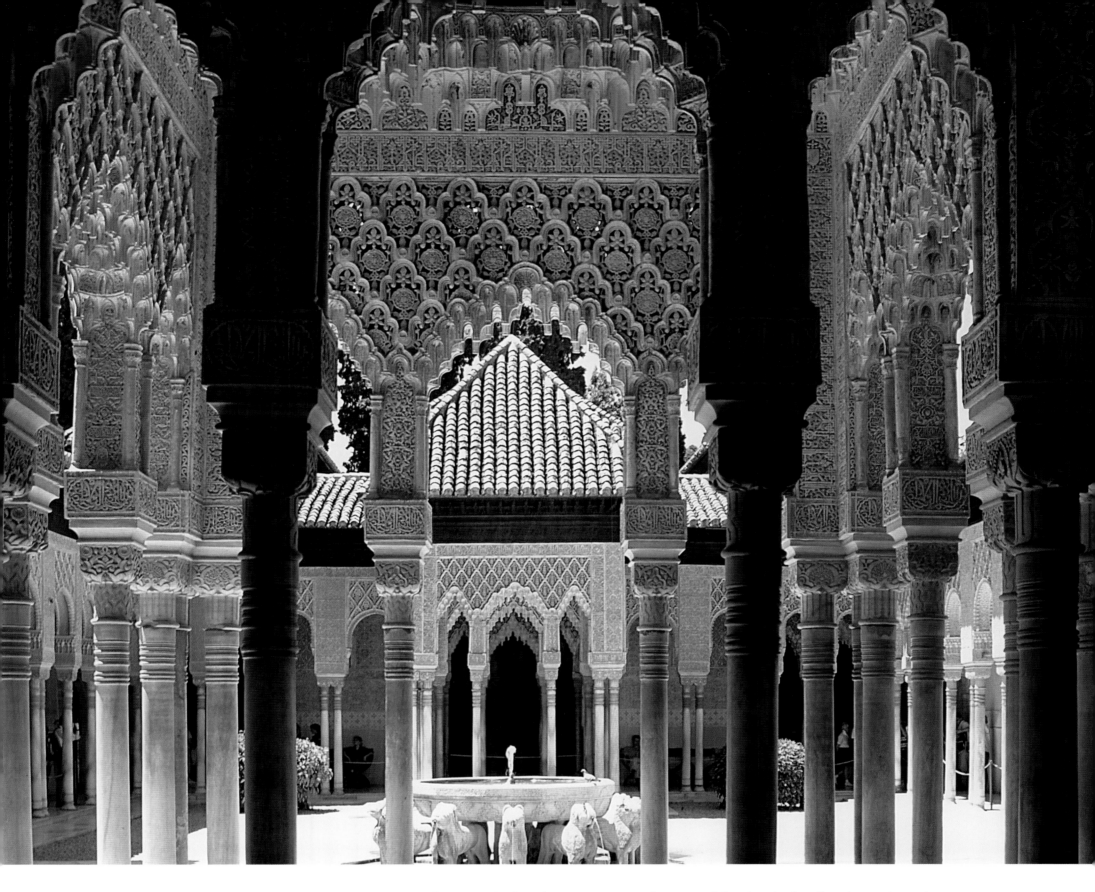

was established in Berber territory, but from the 670s an alliance evolved, and Berber forces formed the spearhead of Islamic advances in Africa.

The most notable of these was in 711 when a Berber commander, Tariq ibn Ziyad, led his own men across the straits to the Rock of Tariq 'Geb-al-Tariq' – Gibraltar – and onwards into Spain. In few months southern Spain as far as Toledo was occupied by Tariq's men. Anxious to avoid the credit going to the Berbers, the Arab Emir followed the next year to complete the conquest and to dispose of the inconveniently successful Tariq. Pressing on through Spain into France, the Muslim armies were finally stopped by Charles Martel at the Battle of Poitiers in 732: but it had only taken 20 years for southern Spain to become the Muslim emirate of Al-Andalus.

The Arab rulers in North African did not make efficient imperialists. The one essential, cooperation with the Berbers, was never achieved and Berber revolts in Africa were clumsily countered. By the later 700s, all North

ABOVE The Court of the Lions in the Alhambra at Granada. This lavish palace and fortress complex was built in the mid-14th century for the last Muslim rulers of Spain, who were swept away by the Christian 'reconquest'.

Africa east of Algeria was divided between independent Berber states, which included what is now Morocco, founded by a descendant of Ali, and therefore Shiite. The Spanish conquest begun by Tariq was followed by civil war, with undefeated Christian forces in the north remaining a permanent threat. Leadership came first from Abd al-Rahman, a survivor of the general massacres of the Ummayads by the Abbasids, who staged a successful invasion in 755 and proclaimed himself Emir of Al-Andalus in Córdoba. By the time of his death in 788 his dynastic opponent, the Caliph Mansur, paid Abd al-Rahman a deserved tribute. 'Although he had no other support but his statesmanship and perseverance … he founded a mighty empire': and, after all, he had got the better of Charlemagne in the pass of Roncesvalles.

The Arabic text within the illustration reads:

صدر الكتاب ارسطاطاليس

رسطها

الى تصير اليهام من المطا والمثاني ومن

النقاد وغيره على طباع مختلفة

LEFT *Page from a work on the medicinal properties of animals by the 13th-century Persian physician Ibn Bakhtishu. The illumination shows Aristotle (right) and his pupil Alexander the Great. Aristotle's work largely became known in the West through Islamic scholarship.*

Many years of rebellion and civil war still lay ahead in Andalusia – in 814 thousands of rebels were deported to Egypt, where they founded a new dynasty, and to Fez, which they helped to make a brilliant cultural capital – but Córdoba was beginning to be recognized as an unequalled multi-cultural centre. The royal library grew to include 400,000 volumes, produced by the finest copyists and binders, covering sciences, medicine, philosophy, law, warfare, engineering and poetry. Industries flourished; wool and silk textiles, leather goods (notably in Córdoba; *cordobanes* literally means 'cordwainers') while Toledo began its lasting reputation for the very finest steel.

Al-Andalus under the Emirs was in practice independent of the Caliphate, but in 924 Abd al-Rahman III declared himself Caliph, Commander of the Faithful, acknowledging no earthly authority. Medieval Baghdad has all but disappeared, whereas Córdoba remains recognizably the former capital of Al-Andalus. At its height the city was said (somewhat improbably) to contain 200,000 houses, 80,000 shops, 50 hospitals, with separate facilities for lepers and the insane, and 900 public baths. The magnificent mosque-cathedral at Córdoba and the Alhambra in Granada testify to the splendour of the Islamic emirate. Wandering through the Alhambra, looking at figs, vines and olives, the contrast with the bleak grandeur of Charlemagne's cathedral in Aachen, Germany, where a diet of beer, bread and beef was the norm, is starkly evident. But as with Baghdad, the magnificence of Al-Andalus was shortlived.

The major weakness of all pre-modern states was the lack of an efficient taxation system, which hampered effective administration and the maintenance of a disciplined army. Moreover, the Arab caliphs were members of an alien race, governing a mixed population of Goths, Berbers, Christians, Muslims and Jews, plus the original Iberian inhabitants. Reliance was placed on Berbers, northern Spanish Christians, freed slaves and whoever could be economically hired. Government slipped from the caliph's family into the hands of viziers.

Berbers, too, established another rival Caliphate, in Cairo in 969 which became one of the more agreeable of medieval states. The Fatimids, who claimed descent from the Prophet's daughter Fatima, were Ismaili Sh'ia, a branch of Islam that survives peaceably today under the aegis of His Highness the Aga Khan. Astute and active traders, the Fatimids also loved scholarship, and their Al-Azhar University in Cairo could claim to be one of the world's oldest. From the city, the Fatimid caliphs ruled Islamic Africa, and also the Arab Emirate of Sicily, taken from the Byzantines in 831. For some years Calabria formed part of the Emirate, but this marked the limit of the Arab advance in Western Europe.

India before the Mughals

The classical age of Indian art and literature is that of the Guptas, between AD 320 and 460. Sumudra-Gupta (c.335–375) was a great empire builder, who extended Gupta rule from Tamil Nadu to the Himalayas. A Chinese visitor, Fa-hsien (Faxian), who was able to travel peacefully all through India about AD 405 recorded his impressions; the facts he finds noteworthy also give an idea of contemporary Chinese society:

> *'The people are very well off, without poll tax or official restrictions … the kings govern without corporal punishment; criminals are fined according to circumstance, lightly or heavily. Even in cases of repeated rebellion they only cut off the right hand. The king's personal attendants, who guard him on the right and the left, have fixed salaries. Throughout the country the people kill no living thing, nor drink wine, nor do they eat garlic or onions.'*

Buddhist cave-temples in Ajanta, although badly damaged, remain to demonstrate Gupta artists' genius, and the peaceful statues, widespread throughout Southeast Asia, combine to give an impression of celestial bliss and human calm. Not only art, but mathematics and technology flourished: the zero, in the form of a dot, made its first appearance, while the 'rustless' iron pillar near Delhi testifies to the skill of Gupta metallurgists. Traditional ayurvedic medicine was embodied in the Susruta Samhita, with extensive descriptions of surgical procedures, as well as a vast catalogue of advice on all forms of medical practice, including recommendations on balanced diets and aphrodisiacs. Gupta civilization was ended by the Huns, but Gupta learning continued to the Middle Ages in Europe and beyond.

After the Guptas, North Indian rule was divided between a few kingdoms, which continued to impress visitors agreeably; another Chinese, the philosopher Hsuan Tang, admired Indian cleanliness and found 'their disposition is soft and humane, and they are earnestly given to study'; on his return 75 Sanskrit works were translated into Chinese. Tamil Southern India became more prominent from the sixth century, fought over by three rival dynasties which intersected in the north at Gwalior. The cult of the god Shiva, the destroyer and preparer of new birth, became popular, reflected in extensive temple-building. The Rashtrakutas, whose influence extended over all central and western India, left the most impressive monuments in the Ellora temples, cut from the solid rock, and the Mamallapuram Temple, dominating the beach near Madras (Chennai).

The most impressive of the southern dynasties were the Chola, supreme in the east for 200 years after the millennium. For the first time the Tamil south invaded the Aryan north, to amass vast quantities of loot, as well as water from the sacred River Ganges to feed a lake in the new Chola capital. Perhaps the Indian equivalent of the Viking states then forming in Europe, the Chola were aggressive raiders, invading the Maldive Islands, devastating Ceylon and, in their most remarkable feat, striking into Malaya and Indonesia, scattering the regional rulers and once again returning with prodigious amounts of booty to fund their temple buildings. Like the Normans, the Chola were great builders; King Rajaraja I, who died in 1014 constructed the Tanjore temple, the largest in India and his son Rajendra planned another for his new capital, to be named 'The city of the Ganga-conquering Chola'.

The first Arab incursions came by sea, along the familiar trade routes to the Indus estuary, at first peacefully, but in 708 a determined assault was made on the port of Debal (modern Karachi) followed by the subjugation of all the Indus Valley. There, in the regions that today form Afghanistan and Pakistan, still Muslim, the Islamic conquest halted for some 400 years. After the initial bloodshed the victors followed the usual Arab practice of leaving their new subjects to follow their own customs, prosper (if possible), and pay taxes.

BELOW *Interior view of the Buddhist 'Carpenter's Cave' at Ajanta. near Ellora in central India. In later centuries, Hinduism also adopted the Ellora caves as a sacred site, constructing the massive Kailasa Temple there in the eighth century AD.*

AD 407 – 1130
From Gauls to French

■ Goths and Vandals overrun Western Roman Empire AD 407 ■ Charles Martel defeats Muslims at the Battle of Poitiers AD 732 ■ Investiture of Charlemagne AD 800 ■ Kievan Rus state established by Vikings *c.* AD 880 ■ Roger II crowned King of Sicily AD 1300

Europe as we know it today began to take shape some 1200 years ago, as the age of great migrations tapered out and states began to form within natural frontiers. Familiar modern languages evolved as the continent divided between Germanic, Romance and Slavonic speakers, with some individual language groups on the borders. Two more invasions, of Germanic and Scandinavian Vikings and Hungarian Magyars, brought new cultures to France, Britain, Sicily and Central Europe.

Roman Gaul's defensive line on the Rhine finally collapsed in AD 407 under a united invasion by most of the German tribes, which broke through at Mainz and swept south, with the Vandals pressing on into Spain. St Jerome, the translator of the Bible into Latin, took time to lament:

> *'Innumerable savage peoples have occupied the whole of Gaul. All that lies between the Alps and the Pyrenees, the Rhine and the Ocean is devastated by the barbarian.'*

The Gaulish and Roman survivors of that invasion were then united by the imperative need to fend off the threat of Attila's seemingly unstoppable Huns, which was achieved in 451 by the Roman general Aetius, with a formal unity being sealed by Clovis, king of the Salian Franks (r.481–511). His people had occupied the region north of the Loire, and after Clovis converted to Christianity in 493, he could rely on the vital support of the Church, reinforced in 507 by his expulsion of the Arian Goths settled in Aquitaine.

Waves of Incursion

Much of what eventually became France thus came under single rule, supported by the damaged, but still functioning, Roman civil administration. Clovis secured the help of another Goth, Theodoric, who was installed as Imperial Viceroy in Ravenna (r.493–526), where the unparalleled mosaics commemorate the reign of this 'barbarian' king over all Italy.

Roman culture prospered especially in the land between Poitiers and Tours. Venantius Fortunatus, the young Italian chaplain of St Radegunde's convent in Poitiers, left a number of poems including the famous hymns '*Vexilla Regis prodeunt*' and '*Pange lingua, gloriosi, Proelium certaminis,*' which exemplify a society not only preserving some Roman traditions but even beginning to convert the barbarians to civilized amenities. Over to the east, however, more barbarians were arriving.

From the early 500s, new immigrants had been moving west, looking for security and good land. Within a couple of centuries most of the territory between the Baltic and the Danube was populated by industrious Slavs, merging with the Latin and German speakers. Natural features tended to separate the Slavs into distinct groups, which became future states, but which were loosely united between *c.*600 and 800 under the Avars, an elite Turkic group. Perhaps influenced by the Scythians, whose use of gold inspired the story of the Golden Fleece, the Avars were formidable, controlling all the Central European Plain into the Ukraine, and disposing populations as it suited them; one substantial tribe, the Lombards, were deported to North Italy, where they flourished.

Military pressure from the Franks and Byzantines eventually squeezed the Avars out, and was followed by two similarly competing groups of Christians, Catholic German and Orthodox Byzantine missionaries whose successes provoked another division among the Slavs. One final wave of immigrants remained to be accommodated, the Magyars, who swept in to settle in Hungary, completing the kaleidoscopic mix of Central European ethnicities and religions.

Frankish unity was intermittent at best, thanks to the custom of dividing the land between the sons, rather than a single heir. Today's France, Belgium, Switzerland and a slice of Germany were divided into four kingdoms: Neustria, the north west; Austrasia, the east; Aquitaine, the south; and the central kingdom of Burgundy. The Merovingian Frankish kings were reputed to be physically magnificent, long-haired and bold. Clovis' successors may have looked the part, but failed to deliver the performance. Fratricidal feuds, and wars against other groups allowed power to slip into the ready hands of royal officials, 'mayors of the palace', the first of whom to seize power was Charles Martel ('the Hammer'; r.715–741).

Charles won his reputation in 732, when he defeated an Arab invasion in a great battle near Poitiers and drove the invading Muslims back over the Pyrenees. One hundred years exactly after Muhammad's death, this

ABOVE Fought between the cities of Poitiers and Tours, the battle that ended in the decisive defeat of the forces under Abd al-Rahman by Charles Martel marked a key moment in early European history. The Frankish commander is portrayed mounted on his white charger in this fanciful interpretation of the engagement by the 19th-century French artist Charles de Steuben.

engagement marked the end of the Muslim advances in Spain (though they continued in Sicily). Charles Martel used his victory to consolidate his power in Bordeaux, Burgundy and Provence. But although Charles acted as a monarch, a *Princeps*, he never took the title of king: that was left to his son, Pepin III 'the Short' (r.752–768), who consolidated his father's success and began a diplomatic offensive aimed at making the Frankish kingdom the first European power.

An Imposing Figure

Only a few years stand out from the confusing mass of historical dates, and certainly Christmas Day of AD 800 is one, when Charles Martel's grandson, another Charles, was acknowledged by Pope Leo, in St Peter's Basilica in Rome, as 'Charles the Augustus crowned of God, and great and peace-loving Emperor of the Romans'. At well over 6 feet (almost 2 metres) tall, confident and dignified, Charlemagne (*Carolus Magnus*) was an emperor who did not need to affect majesty. Brave, determined and alarmingly energetic, he also found time for a succession of mistresses and more intellectual pursuits.

The process had begun half a century before, when Pope Stephen had appealed for help against the threatening Lombards, the Avar deportees who had adopted Roman customs, learnt Latin, and become more aggressive as they saw their chance of expanding their territories by snatching the Exarchate of Ravenna, a remnant of Byzantine rule adjoining Lombardy. The Lombards had been discouraged, but it was left to Charlemagne to settle affairs definitively, and to become king of the Franks and Lombards in 774.

For some years Charlemagne had more pressing business, beginning with the brutal conversion of the still-pagan Saxons, the northeastern neighbours of the Franks, which took 30 years before massacres and deportations worked and the resentful Saxons knuckled under. The drive against the Spanish Muslims, carried out in cooperation with the local Christian rulers, resulted in the reconquest of Catalonia, Corsica, Sardinia and the Balearics, although the initial defeat of his army by the Basques at the pass of Roncesvalles is much better known from the epic poem *Chanson de Roland*, written in the mid-12th century, which became a key text of the romantic ideals of chivalry.

As well as dealing with Muslims and Pagans, Charlemagne was constantly engaged in defending Frankish boundaries so that the events of 800 came unexpectedly. In April 799, Pope Leo was attacked by a justifiably enraged Roman mob – he was an overbearing and rapacious pontiff – and fled to Charlemagne for sanctuary, meeting him in Paderborn in Lower Saxony. Charles was willing to help, but the Romans demanded that the Pope should be put on trial for his misdemeanours. Leo was escorted to Rome, followed by Charlemagne who arrived in November 800, and convened an assembly which diplomatically ruled that Pope Leo should be permitted to declare himself innocent. That was done on 23 December, and two days later the Christmas Mass was celebrated; Charlemagne was hailed as Emperor and the Roman Empire in the West restored.

Britain in the Carolingian Age

Charles was both conqueror and consolidator. New towns and churches were built, using established Roman skills: his own mausoleum-cathedral at Aachen (Aix-la-Chapelle), one of the few surviving churches of the period, was in the style of San Vitale in Ravenna. Music also came from Italy, with singers trained in the Gregorian modes, but for instruction in Latin language the Emperor sought help from what might seem an eccentric source – northeastern England. In 781, Alcuin, headmaster of the York Cathedral

LEFT Charlemagne's majesty continued to exert a powerful influence over his monarchical successors in Europe. In 1349, the Bohemian king and Holy Roman Emperor Charles IV commissioned this jewel-encrusted reliquary bust of Charlemagne, in an attempt to cast reflected glory on his own rule.

ABOVE *The death of the eponymous hero from a 15th-century illuminated manuscript of the* Chanson de Roland. *This epic poem, the oldest surviving example of French literature, tells the story of the exploits of a warrior-hero in Charlemagne's service.*

School was engaged to instruct Charlemagne's nobles. A man of tremendous energy, writing learned works on grammar, theology and history, as well as poetry and keeping up a constant correspondence with Charlemagne, Alcuin came from a distinguished scholarly line, a grand-pupil of the renowned scholar Bede of Jarrow (673–735) the first British historian, and was clearly a gifted teacher.

Within 10 years at Aachen, Alcuin had introduced the native Frankish nobility to the classical authors, using game-problems ('the three jealous husbands,' or the 'missionaries and cannibals' are the best known) to sharpen their maths. After Aachen, he went on to establish another famous school at Tours, a city still regarded as the most cultivated in France. Being a prototypical headmaster, Alcuin insisted on correct Latin 'old style', by that time very different from that commonly used – it was after all, 700 years since the last classical Latin had been written. Alcuin's Latin became the standard for the written language, which was to remain the vehicle for law, philosophy, science and religion for a very long time, clearly differentiated from popular spoken Latin then developing as the 'Romance' languages – French, Spanish, Portuguese, Italian and that odd eastern outpost Romanian.

England becomes apparent to the European mind only in Carolingian times. The Roman province of Britannia had disintegrated after the legions were withdrawn in 407, leaving the Romanized Britons to fend for themselves. In eastern England, the already-settled Germans, invited to defend Britannia against the 'Saxons', were joined by newcomers fighting their way in a search for land: Angles, Saxons and Jutes from Germany and Denmark. The Romano-British – this was the period of the legendary 'King Arthur' – were pushed westwards to Wales or overseas to Brittany. Ireland and Scotland, which the Romans had never attempted to settle, were able to retain their own form of Christianity, based not on episcopal rule, but concentrated in many scattered monastic communities. British St Patrick and Welsh St David brought Christianity to Ireland and their Irish converts in turn set out to convert Scots and English, establishing a centre at Iona in 563. A generation later, in 597, Pope Gregory, who had admired the beautiful English slaves in Rome in a celebrated pun (*non angli sed angeli* – 'not Angles but angels') despatched a reluctant Benedictine monk, Augustine, to convert the southern English.

By this time, Britain was divided into three main Saxon states, Northumbria, Mercia and Wessex, with leadership passing between Northumbria and Mercia, four smaller kingdoms and a dozen minor statelets. Five Welsh

princes and the quickly reducing territory of Dumnonia – essentially Devon and Cornwall – along with Strathclyde, were holding on while in the north Picts and Scots were merging with Germanic and Norse incomers, eventually to form the kingdom of Scotland. This motley collection of minor states was of little account in the greater affairs of Europe.

The two rival forms of Christianity, Roman and Celtic, now on offer sorted out their differences at the Whitby synods of 664, and both took part in the new missionary drive to convert Europe. The scholar Wynfrith (Boniface) was born, possibly in Crediton (Devon) in *c.*662, and taught in Southampton, where he wrote the first Latin grammar to be published in England. In 716, he set off with a group of missionaries to convert the Germans, in which he was strikingly successful. With the support of Charles Martel, he founded the first bishopric at Fritzlar, was consecrated as Germany's first archbishop, and developed relations with the papacy. Before his death in 754, he had established a functioning episcopalian system throughout Germany. He died aged at least 90, while trying to convert the heathen Frisians.

ABOVE *The Benedictine missionary St Boniface, originally from the English West Country, is famous for converting the Germanic tribes to Christianity. Illumination from a manuscript of 1071–72.*

A demonstration of the emergent new Europe was given in 842 when an alliance between two of Charlemagne's grandsons, Lewis and Charles, took up arms against their elder brother Lothair. Their agreement was made following democratic Frankish tradition, in public, and since one part of the allied troops were old-German speakers while the others were proto-French, the announcement had to be translated for them, making the first record of the new European languages: the first phrase reads:

Old French
'Pro Deo amur et pro Christian poblo et nostro comun salvament, ...
In German
In Godes minna ind in thes Christianes folches ind unser bedhero gealtnissi,
In not very good contemporary Latin
Pro Dei amore et pro Christiano poplo et nostro communi salvamento,
In word for word French
Pour l'amour de Dieu et pour le chrétien peuple et notre commun salut,

The transistion from Latin to French is clear enough, and would be a deal clearer in speech, given the French slurring pronunciation (which horrified the English at the Synod of Whitby).

The Feared 'Men of the North'

Those famous and infamous raiders and colonists, the Vikings, came from three nations, the Swedes, Danes and Norwegians, all known to their victims as 'Men of the North'; fervent prayers came from all the coasts of Western Europe to be delivered '*ex furor Normannorum*'. From the mid-700s, predatory crews of small oared ships set out in the early summer in search of adventure and loot, with a little pleasurable slaughter. The Norsemen – Norwegians – were the first to strike and an unfortunate civilian, a Wessex official, was their first English victim, but Wessex was generally well prepared and subsequent raids chose easier targets.

As had most of the earlier barbarians, Vikings combined a strong consensual discipline with a shocking capacity to violence, allied to wary practicality; they fought to win, but were prepared to compromise. Another vital factor in their success was their skill in boatbuilding. A Viking ship, usually not more than 80 feet (24 metres) long, built in the northern clinker (overlapping strakes) fashion, was eminently versatile, capable of long sea passages and navigating inland waters, easy to beach for overnight stops or a supplementary raid.

By 860, Norsemen and Danes had not only raided as far south as Italy, but had established permanent settlements in Ireland and all the Western Isles. France became the preferred target, attacking successfully up the Seine and the Loire. Little effective resistance was made by the Frankish kings, preoccupied as they were with their own quarrels, (after Charlemagne's death seven emperors and four kings of France reigned before the end of the ninth century), but walled towns and the fortresses of great nobles offered some resistance to the Viking advance. By 912, the French King Charles 'the Simple' was forced to compromise: in return for peace he would cede to the Norse leader Rollo some of the best land in France, the lower Seine, with its capital at Rouen.

This was to become the land of the Northmen, the Duchy of Normandy, its people the Normans (and the Duchy, limited now to the Channel Islands, survives, the present Duke also being Queen of England). A parallel process in King Alfred's (r.871–c.900) England resulted in the Danish invaders being allowed to settle in the east, the Danelaw, with York being the most important town, but acknowledging the sovereignty of the Saxon Wessex kings. In both countries, the new settlers adopted the language and customs of their reluctant hosts, but whereas in Normandy the Frankish tongue, now recognizable as early French was used, the English Danes merged their own language into the similar Saxon, producing the foundation of basic old

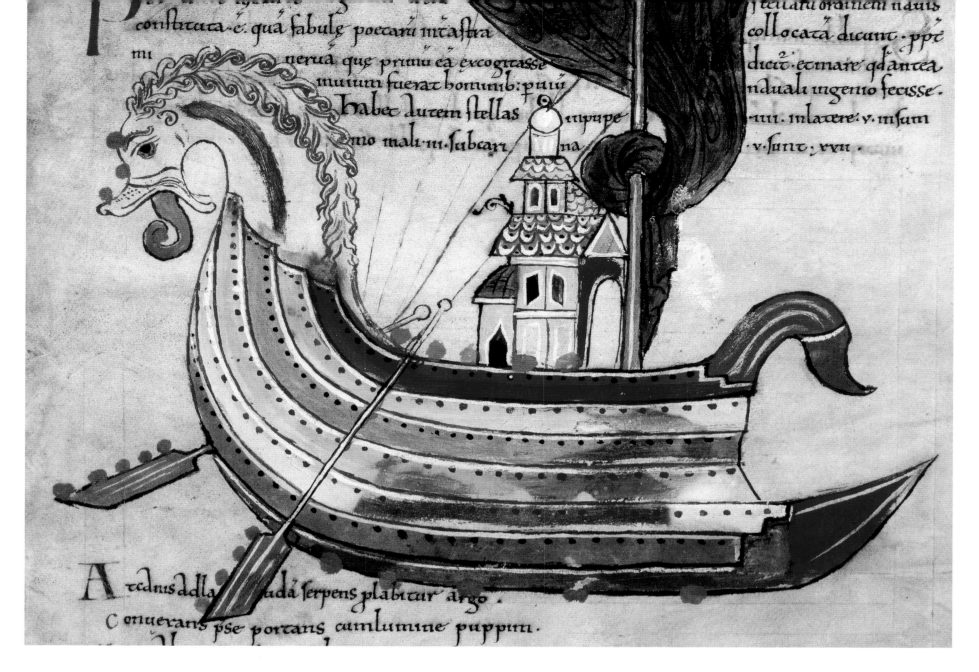

consutata e. qua fabule poetaru mtastra
tui nerua que primu ea excogriasse
muttum fuerat honunib: puu
habet autem stellas in pupe
mo mali m subcari na

A tednus adla uada serpens plabitur argo.
Conuerans ipse portans camlumine puppim.

teltaru ordinem nauis
collocata dicunt. ppe
dicit. etmare qdantea
nduali ingenno fecisse.
uii. mlatere. v. in sum
v. sunt. xvii.

English. The Danes were content with their new status, but the Normans were soon looking for new conquests. The northerners who chose to sail west were traders and farmers, rather than raiders (pickings were much better in the south). Their ships were broad-beamed merchantmen, capable of fitting in a few beasts along with the crew, and navigating the icy seas around the Faroes before moving to Iceland and Greenland. Insatiable curiosity, the hallmark of all adventurers, led Eric the Red and his son Leif south again, to land on the coast of Newfoundland. The Greenland colony was abandoned, but Iceland flourished, becoming the world's oldest continuous democracy.

Swedish Vikings turned their attention eastwards, across the Baltic Sea to the Gulf of Finland and Lake Ladoga from about 750. By the mid 800s, one Rurik, leader of a band known as the Rus, had settled in easily accessible Novgorod, either absorbing or displacing the Slavs established there before moving on to the strategic town of Kiev, the centre of Khazar activities. That enterprising Asian group of warriors-turned-merchants had seized control of the main Russian trading routes and, to preserve a mercantile neutrality from Islam and Christendom, adopted Judaism. From Kiev, the Rus launched a lightning attack on Byzantium in 860; its 'strange swiftness, the inhumanity of the barbarous tribe, the harshness of its manners' staggered the civilized Greeks and announced the arrival of a new force in Eastern Europe.

Notable among Normans, the Hauteville family made a name for energetic violence and ambition combined with diplomatic skill: Robert Guiscard 'the Wily' was the most famous. He and his small band of followers, within a single generation, had made themselves masters of southern Italy, Malta and Sicily, ousting Muslims and Byzantines alike. Claiming absolute authority

for themselves, they were willing to tolerate all religions providing they submitted, and developed Sicily in particular as a brilliant state, well ahead of anything in northern Europe, and matching the Islamic elegance of Al-Andalus. The first Western medical school was founded in Salerno, some 500 years after the Arabs, but rapidly became authoritative. One female doctor – and that was surely remarkable – published a book on women's illnesses and baby care, combined with some cosmetic hints; elderberry, broom, saffron and egg-yolks are advised for lending a golden sheen to the hair. What might be called a family practitioner's handbook appeared in Salerno around 1140, advising the doctor to remember that when feeling the patient's pulse 'that it may well be affected by your presence, or by the thought of your fee' and to tell the patient that he will be cured, with God's help, while confiding to the relatives that the case was indeed serious.

In August 1128, a reluctant Pope Honorius II invested Roger de Hauteville as Duke of Apulia, Calabria and Sicily: two years later on Christmas Day 1130, he was crowned king – under papal suzerainty – of what was then the third largest state in Europe. His new Cathedral at Cefalù near Palermo was an exact contemporary of that then being built far away in England at Durham. Decorated with magnificent mosaics, the interior at Cefalù was equally distant from the massive splendour of Durham; but it was Durham, with its lofty pointed arches that represented the future.

AD 1095 – 1396
The Crusades

■ Pope Urban II proclaims the First Crusade 1095 ■ Recapture of Jerusalem for Christendom 1099 ■ Saladin conquers the Crusader Kingdom of Jerusalem 1187 ■ Soldiers of the Fourth Crusade plunder Byzantium 1204 ■ Decisive Ottoman victory at the Battle of Nicopolis 1396

The series of religious, commercial and political wars known misleadingly as the 'Crusades' had disastrous consequences. Western Europe and Islam became embedded in mutual hostility, the ancient Byzantine civilization was destroyed and the Balkans crushed by centuries of oppressive Turkish rule, while the earlier Muslim cultures declined under militarist autocracies.

The methods used by successive popes to fund the Crusades were applied in their own private struggles and became a prominent cause of the Protestant Reformation. On the other hand some elements of Arab and Persian civilization, from algebra to alcohol, rubbed off on the backward Westerners.

'The Prompting of the Devil'

Europe awaited the end of the first millennium with some apprehension. Even if it did not bring the end of the world, which many feared, the future looked uncertain. Christianity was becoming more deeply divided between the Eastern and Western churches, and while Byzantium was holding firm against Islam, Rome seemed to be disintegrating. No fewer than 25 popes had reigned in the course of the 10th century, many of them perishing violently. All Western Christians allowed the Pope a general respect, but in practical terms the Bishop of Rome was a minor Italian prince, hemmed in by potential enemies. Yet since the Church itself was by a long way the most coherent and powerful institution in Western Europe– when William I of England compiled that methodical survey of his new possessions, the Domesday Book, he found that one-sixth of all lands belonged to the Church – a vacuum at the head was impossible.

A pope's only potential ally was the German Empire, and this institution was also suffering. Ironically it fell to the Saxons, so recently and brutally converted by Charlemagne, to come to the rescue, unite the German duchies, fend off the invasion of Slavs and Magyars from the east, and to help worthy popes to re-establish themselves.

The Saxon Emperor Otto I was consecrated in Rome by Pope John XII in 962; John had been elected at the age of 18 on the orders of his father, the most powerful of the Roman magnates. Under the terms of the *Diploma Ottonianum*, Otto and his successors as emperor undertook to safeguard the independence of the papal states and encourage reform, but this agreement firmly placed the emperor in ultimate control. Reorganization was assisted by spontaneous reforms within the wider Church, especially by two new orders of monks, both based in France, the reformed Benedictines of Cluny and the Cistercians of Cîteaux. Their well-administered abbeys educated a new élite, developed agriculture and technology and provided social services – and became very rich. By an ingenious piece of self-help, the 'discovery' of documents granting great political powers and a large slice of Italy – in fact obvious forgeries – Rome was able to claim more power.

Once the Church was reconstructed and a determined pope was installed, the question first posed at Charlemagne's coronation remained: did an Emperor select/validate a Pope, or vice versa, and did kings or popes appoint bishops? A settlement of that dispute took many centuries, but it became critical in the 11th century. Geography alone made it impossible for a German emperor, whose power-base and responsibilities lay north of the Alps, to control events in Rome, although the young Otto III, whose talents and

LEFT *A watercolour illustration from the* Chronicon Pontificum et Imperatorum *('Chronicle of Popes and Emperors') by Martinus Oppaviensis (c.1450) shows Emperor Otto I meeting Pope John XII.*

energies earned him the title of *Stupor Mundi* ('Marvel of the World') celebrated the new millennium in great style. Papal defiance began with the election in 1073 of an Italian monk Hildebrand as Pope Gregory VII, who proclaimed that it was:

> 'by pride, robbery, perfidy, murder ... by almost every crime at the prompting of the devil'.

that kings attempted to rule, rather than the priests, who should be 'masters of kings and princes.'

ABOVE *Godfrey of Bouillon's capture of Jerusalem in 1099 in the First Crusade, as shown in the 14th-century French manuscript illustration, was to be a short-lived triumph for the forces of Christendom. No subsequent Crusade was as successful; within a century, Jerusalem was in Muslim hands again.*

The first round was settled in Pope Gregory's favour, but a diversion arose when a Cluniac monk, experienced in diplomacy, was elected as Urban II in 1094 with the help of the Norman kings of Sicily. He almost immediately set off on a grand tour, relying on his commanding personality as well as his rank to establish papal authority throughout Christendom. An opportunity was offered when at a conference held in Piacenza an appeal was received from the Byzantine Emperor Alexius Comnenus (1081–1118). Much of the empire's European territory had been occupied by the first Bulgarian Empire, brutally terminated in 1014 by Basil II, the 'Bulgar-slayer,' but a revived Bulgarian state had emerged and Serbian princes were rebelling. These threats were compounded by a new and more aggressive Islamic dynasty. Emperor Alexius' appeal was answered by Urban's proclamation, in 1095, of a bold new enterprise – a holy War of the Cross, a 'Crusade' to retake the holy city of Jerusalem from 'a despised and base race which worships demons.'

The First Crusades

To everyone concerned, the results were unexpected and ultimately devastating. The 'despised and base race' were – not that Urban knew or cared – the Seljuk Turks. The latest of those central Asian invaders that had been moving southwest for thousands of years, the Seljuk tribes produced some outstanding leaders in the 11th century (including the famous Sultan Alp Arslan. patron of the poet Omar Khayyam), who ousted the Baghdadi Caliph and established their own Sunni Muslim dynasty. After an unexpected victory over the Byzantine armies, Turkish emirs ruled most of Anatolia, Persia and the Levant. The newly conquered inhabitants were left unmolested as long as they remained quiescent, and provided young conscripts for the Sultan's army (the *devshirme* system). Christian pilgrims, assisted by members of the new order of St John of Jerusalem, were granted free passage to the Holy Land; hostels, one funded by the King of Hungary, were established in Jerusalem itself. The real enemies of the Turks were not Christians, but the Fatimids, the Shia Muslim Caliphs of Cairo.

The Emperor Alexius defended his frontiers actively. Byzantine gold, plus trade concessions, secured the help of the Venetians, who had recently established themselves as the leading Adriatic sea-power, in ejecting the Normans from the small remaining Greek territories in Italy, and Byzantine troops, aided by foreign mercenaries fought off invasions across the Danube. The emperor had been obliged to finance his wars by confiscating the Greek Church's assets, which lent to his appeal the tempting implication of a possible eventual reunification of the two Churches. What Alexius expected

ABOVE *The defeat of Saladin during the Third Crusade, from the* Chronicle of David Aubert, *a 15th-century illuminated manuscript. Though Saladin lost several battles, there was no final victory and he and Richard I of England signed a truce in 1192.*

was sufficient cash or promises to finance a competent professional force: what the emperor got was mayhem and destruction.

Pope Urban had intended that his Crusade should be formally organized, with Crusaders taking an oath and being granted special privileges, such as the remission of taxes, security against debtors and the grant of 'indulgences,' but some zealots, such as Peter the Hermit and Walter the Penniless jumped the gun,and led their followers overland to the east. Without proper leadership, many bands made themselves unpopular with their hosts. Two other parties, organized by priests, took the easy opportunity of looting Jewish communities on the Rhine and Danube: the worst massacres were committed at Speyer, Mainz and Worms by Count Emico of Leiningen. One honourable exception to this anti-Semitic violence was King Coloman of Hungary, who protected Jews within his realm from the marauding bands.

Emperor Alexius well knew the risks of accepting Western help: his daughter Anna wrote that she dreaded their arrival, knowing as he did:

> *'their … erratic character … and their greed for money.'*

The Crusaders were therefore shipped off as quickly as possible across the Bosphorus, where with help from Byzantine and Armenian forces they eventually, after hard fighting, captured the key city of Antioch. Instead of returning the captured lands to the Emperor, as had been agreed, the Crusaders set up a kingdom of their own, ruled by the most competent leader, the Sicilian Count Bohemond. From Antioch, they fought their way to Jerusalem, held not by the Seljuks but by their enemies the Egyptians: in 1099, the Holy City was stormed, the inhabitants massacred, and a second Western kingdom established; the Crusade was accounted a success.

Crusading Disasters

The Crusader Kingdom of Jerusalem endured until 1187, when a new Muslim commander, the brilliant Seljuk general Saladin, became Sultan of Egypt and Syria and retook Jerusalem. Unlike the bloodbath of Christian victory, Saladin allowed the inhabitants to depart peacefully. Saladin and his most effective adversary – although never a true enemy – King Richard I ('The Lionheart') of England, laid the foundation of the romantic Crusader legend. The old Emperor Frederick Hohenstaufen ('Barbarossa'), the most majestic figure of his time, died before he could come to the aid of Jerusalem, drowned while attempting to cross the Saleph River in Anatolia.

While Richard was fighting in the Levant, his younger brother John tried to secure his English inheritance, but when the time came failed miserably in Normandy and had to agree to the Magna Carta, intended to apply to the feudal barons and 'all free men', a restricted class at that time, but subsequently elevated into a declaration of English liberties. 'Habeas Corpus', the right to be tried before a court and the definition of 'one measure for ale and wine throughout the kingdom' have proved its most enduring benefits.

Crusades continued for over 300 years, and sporadic warfare between Christians and Muslims for even longer. For the Greek empire and for the unfortunate casualties of war and massacre the results were disastrous, for the papacy very nearly so, but, as always in any conflict, many prospered greatly. The demand for weapons and supplies stimulated European industries,

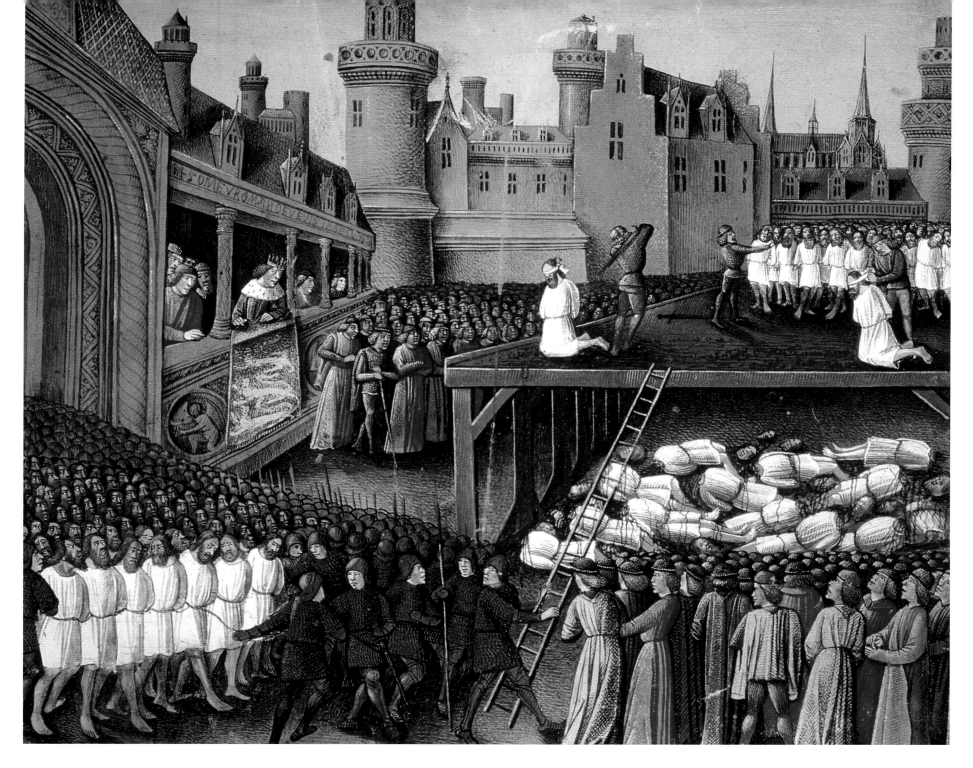

and the introduction of new commodities – silk, carpets, sugar, Chinese porcelain, spices and jewellery – encouraged trade. Venice in particular did extremely well, especially in the Fourth Crusade of 1202–04 when the Crusaders were charged 85,000 silver marks for passage and required to capture the Dalmatian Greek town of Zadar for Venice. The Crusaders recouped their expenses, and very much more, by plundering – again with Italian help – the great city of Byzantium itself, the Christian capital of the Eastern Empire: the four bronze horses now embellishing the portico of San Marco are only the most famous example of the loot. By the end of that crusade the Greek Emperor had been replaced by a representative of the Catholic west, whose territories included all the Aegean coastline and the Peloponnese: Venice was rewarded with slices of the Dalmatian coast and the island of Cyprus, but she had to fight with the other Italian maritime cities, Pisa and Genoa, to hang on to her gains.

Pope Innocent III regretted the bloodshed and looting that resulted from his crusade, but comforted himself with the thought that it was:

> *'the just judgement of God, that the Greeks had been transformed from being disobedient to faithful, from schismatics to Catholics.'*

God, however, did not seem to be benefiting the popes, whose influence declined sharply during the 13th century. Subsidizing crusades and struggling to keep up their position as Italian rulers was very expensive. The old dispute between pope and emperor had been settled in the Church's favour, but only at the price of substituting the insatiably ambitious French princes of Anjou for the German kings in Italy. By the end of the century, it was difficult to persuade anyone to accept the papal throne: for three of the ten years after 1285, the Church was without a leader.

But one excellent source of funds had been discovered: any opponents of the papacy, whether Christian or Muslim, could be dealt with by calling a crusade. Moreover, the necessary subsidies could be financed by selling 'indulgences,' which could only be issued by the Pope, although retailed by such characters as Chaucer's Pardoner, with his stack of pardons, 'comen from Rome al hoot'. Strictly speaking, indulgences were only conditional, and allowed remission of time that would otherwise be spent in Purgatory, where

Different popes took the opportunity to finance official crusades against Venice, against the Emperor Ludwig IV, against the Duchy of Milan, and even against Roman rivals of their own families. Whether or not successful, all these attempts severely damaged the papacy's moral prestige. The military Orders of the Church had, however, done well. The Knights of St John – the Hospitallers – had been joined by those of the Temple of Jerusalem, the Templars, as allies and rivals against the Muslims. Both had ended up wealthy, with the Hospitallers claiming the island of Rhodes, and the Templars building churches and commanderies (London's Temple is the best known) in most parts of Western Europe. Their brother order, the Teutonic Knights, founded in 1190, forcibly converted the pagan Prussians and Lithuanians and established a German-speaking state across the southern Baltic coast, until checked by the now-Orthodox Christian Russians.

The vacuum caused by the decay of Imperial power was filled by national states asserting their independence. England and France both defied papal demands for money and insisted on the rights of kings and other laymen to appoint clergy, but it was France that took royal rights to their logical conclusion by having the seat of the Papacy moved from Rome to Avignon (in 1309), and ensuring that only French Popes were elected.

The Last Crusade

In 1360, the drive to regain the Holy Land was formally ended by a treaty with the Egyptian Sultan, after one last triumphant orgy of looting in Alexandria. It was little more than a formality, since an impressive new power was on the rise. The Osmanli or Ottoman Turks, who stayed in power until the 20th century, took their name from one Osman, who with his son Orkhan (r.1326–62) consolidated their tribal bands into settled communities, seizing the neighbouring cities of Nicaea – capital of the emperor in exile only a century before – and Nicomedia. They remained at heart *ghazis* – religious warriors dedicated to spreading the Muslim faith, but also pragmatists.

In 1346, the Ottomans had taken over most of Byzantine Anatolia and reached the Bosphorus, where they offered themselves as useful allies to the Greeks they had finished attacking. Since a Byzantine family conflict had led to a civil war, followed by an invasion of Thessaly by the Serbian kingdom, a rebellion by Spanish mercenaries, a war with Venice (countered by an alliance with that republic's implacable enemy, Genoa), Turkish help was essential; the emperor-to-be John Cantacuzene sealed the bargain by marrying his daughter to the Turkish Sultan's son. Once over the Bosphorus, the Turks resumed their advance under Sultan Murad I (r.1362–89) forcing the Emperor to cede the remnant of his territories and finally to acknowledge Turkish overlordship. The way was now clear for the Turks to begin the Islamic conquest of Europe; the Serbian Empire was destroyed in June 1389 at the historic battle of Kosovo, by which time Turkish possessions in Europe reached to the Danube, with the Greeks isolated in Byzantium, holding out only on Turkish sufferance.

The tables were turned: Christian aggression in Asia and Africa had been replaced by Islamic penetration in Europe, and the defences were fragile. The most effective Catholic armies, those of the Military Orders, were badly damaged. King Philip IV of France, who was eager to seize their wealth, had plotted against the Templars and secured, on the feeblest grounds, their condemnation for heresy and the abolition of the order: many of the best knights were burned to death and the rest disbanded. The Hospitallers were clinging on in their island of Rhodes, in no condition to help. The Teutonic

ABOVE *The medieval Church was beset with power struggles and schisms. This French allegorical illustration of 1378 portrays the contemporary crisis over the rival popes Urban VI and Clement VII as a Tree of Fortune, with various European states taking sides on its different branches.*

the virtuous dead were obliged to remain until allowed admission to heaven, but most purchasers believed them to ensure their passport to paradise. The idea had developed in the fourth century, but was to be brought to perfection in the 14th century, and was to be a prime cause of the Reformation. Martin Luther's famous '95 Theses' of 1517 were originally entitled 'Disputation on the Power and Efficacy of Indulgences'.

Order had made the fatal mistake of attacking the Catholic kingdom of Poland and suffered a crushing defeat at Tannenberg in 1410. The kingdom of Castile could rely upon the Iberian Orders of chivalry to assist against the local Muslims, but Aragon's strength was diverted to holding on to its Italian territories. France, always the driving force behind all the previous Crusades, was badly weakened after half a century of unsuccessful wars with England and Burgundy.

From west to east the Christian frontier ran along the Danube, held by Hungarians and their unruly subject states and allies. By a dynastic quirk the King of Hungary at the time of Kosovo was the 22-year-old Sigismund of Luxembourg, son of the Holy Roman Emperor Charles IV, who immediately sought help from the other European states. Only one offered much chance of real assistance, the traditional crusading leader, France. Luckily, when in 1394 some discussions began, there was an interval of cautious peace with England, which enabled the Kingdom of France and the Duchy of Burgundy to agree on a new Crusade, to be fought on the Danube; the most magnificent army Europe had seen, with the most expensive armour, silken tents and banners, marched off on the last real Crusade.

Like its predecessors, it failed. At the Battle of Nicopolis in 1396, (in which the Serbs prudently decided to fight on the Turkish side) the crusading army was shattered. Sigismund survived with his reputation intact, and was able to reinforce his power in Hungary, ruling that talented and turbulent people for half a century, a remarkable feat.

ABOVE The Battle near Tannenberg-Grunwald, *a painting (1878) by the Polish artist Jan Matejko (1838–93). This defeat in 1410 saw most of the leadership of the Teutonic Order killed or captured, and shifted the balance of power in Eastern Europe in favour of the Kingdom of Poland and the Grand Duchy of Lithuania.*

As the 15th century began, the prospects for Christendom, East or West, looked gloomy. A militant Islam was threatening the European heartlands and Byzantine power reduced to a shadow. Worse, the Catholic Church was divided, without a single, universally acknowledged pope. Sixty-plus years of consolidation at Avignon had restored papal finances and authority, but sentiment was in favour of a return to Rome: a French pope living under the protection of a French king was a much less powerful symbol than the Bishop of Rome seated on St Peter's throne. So, in 1377, the papacy returned to Rome amid great hopes, which swiftly faded. The next pope, Urban VI, turned out to be so dangerously mad that the cardinals elected an alternative pontiff, who sought refuge back in Avignon. France supported Clement VII in Avignon, while England, Germany, Scandinavia, Hungary and Poland – reluctantly, since the deranged pope had started killing off his opponents – backed Urban.

Some respite was accorded by the death of the Turkish Sultan Bayezid I ('The Thunderbolt') in the invasion of Anatolia by the second wave of Mongols, led by Timur the Lame, but when Timur left for new victories in the East, it would not be long before the Turks were on the move again.

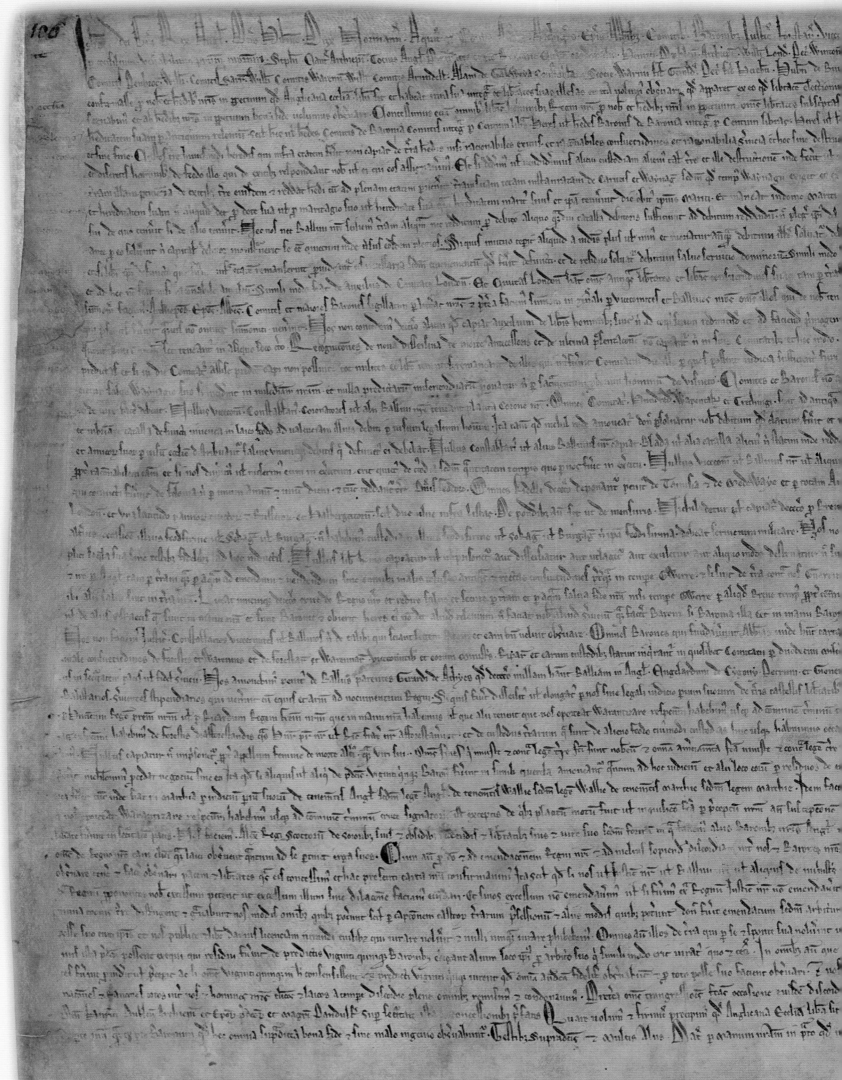

221 BC — AD 1294
China to the Mongols

■ Emperor Shi Huangdi rules China 221 BC ■ End of Han rule AD 220 ■ Jayavarman builds Angkor temples *c.*1180 ■ Genghis Khan becomes Mongol ruler AD 1194 ■ Mamluks defeat Mongols at Battle of Ain Jalut AD 1260 ■ Kublai Khan founds the Yuan Dynasty AD 1271

The shockwaves of the violent eruption of Genghis Khan's Mongols in the 13th century were felt all across the western hemisphere from London to Tokyo. China, which had been developing the world's most advanced technology and perfecting secure imperial rule, was jolted into contact with other societies as a new Mongol dynasty headed by the famous Kublai Khan sent ambassadors to such distant countries as France and England.

All subsequent Chinese history was influenced by the work of the philosopher Confucius (Kong Zi; 551–479 BC), and even today many Asians appeal to Confucian doctrines to justify their own political ideas. Seeing that things in his time were bad and quite likely to get worse, Confucius endeavoured to promote decency, good manners, tolerance and respect for learning. Past standards must be restored and the Emperor must be venerated as representing those values, and as the only hope of stability. Seven hundred years later, the Roman Marcus Aurelius, himself an emperor, was meditating along very similar lines.

The Unification of China

Confucian ideals were ignored by the brief (221–207 BC) and very unpopular Qin (Chin) rulers, the first historic dynasty to begin the unification of China, pushing its influence south to Kuangtung and even into Indochina. The Qin heartland was in the west, horse-breeding country, an excellent base for expansion, which was achieved with what appeared to its contemporaries shocking force; the Qin were (according to a nobleman in the state of Wei):

> *'avaricious, perverse, eager for profit … [knowing] nothing of etiquette, proper relationships and virtuous conduct.'*

The rulers were inspired by the doctrines of the 'Legalist' school, which recommended ruthless severity and draconian punishments, forbade free discussion, banned the publication of philosophical works. The Legalists were the total opposites of the curiously questing Greeks; but their methods were ideal for any ambitious autocrat.

The Qin were predictably successful and by 221 BC Emperor Shi Huangdi ruled most of northern China and had a powerful influence over the rest of the land. China was united culturally as well as geographically by the standardization of weights and measures and the written language; although regional languages and dialects proliferated as they still do, all literate Qin subjects had access to the same texts, which made the imposition of a drastic authoritarian system possible.

The defensive northern works were extended and incorporated into an engineering marvel, the first Great Wall, separating the productive land from the desert, frustrating invasions and keeping the populace under control, while enabling valuable trade to continue and taxes to be collected. The Qin wall although shorter, ran further to the north and east than the present, much later, structure. Most traces of it have now disappeared, but it served its purpose. New imperial roads linked the capital with the south and east coasts and the mountains. All this, however, was done by forced labour at immense cost in human lives. The Legalist doctrines of the Imperial Chancellor Li Si were enforced; opponents of the regime were despatched and offending books – which included most of the accepted Confucian canon - were ceremonially burnt. Today, Emperor Shi Huangdi is perhaps the best known of all, thanks to his magnificent tomb with its regiments of life-sized terracotta warriors, all modelled in detail, with ranks and characters clearly shown in what may be the world's largest and most complete artwork. The whereabouts of the tens of thousands of the victims the Emperor was reputed to have had buried alive is, however, not known.

Qin methods, although effective, did not make for popularity and some years of war were needed before another leading dynasty emerged. The first Han emperor Han Gao Zu (Kao Tsu) began his career as an escaped

convict, but founded a dynasty which lasted for 400 years and which left an indelible impression on Chinese culture and character: to be truly Chinese is to be 'Han'. The Confucian bureaucracy, which endured until the 20th century, emerged: the story is told of how the emperor, pestered with learned quotations and examples, growled:

> *'I conquered the empire on horseback – what is the use of all these Odes and Annals?'*

His chamberlain replied:

> *'True, but it is not on horseback you will keep it … war and peace are two aspects of an eternal art.'*

Emperor Han Wu Ti's long reign (140–87 BC) saw the zenith of Han culture as scholarly assemblies united to form the Imperial University, devoted to studying classical texts and making glorious the teaching of Confucius, so providing 'Filially pious and incorrupt' imperial officers. New cities were developed, not as markets – merchants were always held in low esteem – but as government headquarters, with a fort, palaces and offices in the centre, and dwellings filling in the gaps. The city was formidably walled, as was every structure within: even houses were built with an interior court.

This was the period when Chinese medical practice, already ancient, was codified into the classical texts, with which all practitioners had to be familiar.

Much of the medical philosophy may be disregarded in favour of the practical benefits of a huge and effective pharmacopeia. Sophisticated methods of diagnosis, with particular attention to the pulse, and an understanding of patients, recognizing that some people cannot be treated – those who are 'too proud to communicate' and those who eat and drink to excess – were combined with such techniques as acupuncture only recently accepted in the West. Anatomy, however, was not understood and surgery was primitive, but Chinese medicine has stood the test of time remarkably well.

Administrative competence was much needed since the Han were constantly troubled by Hun attacks; one ambassador, sent on a mission to the Bactrians, suffered ten years in Hunnish captivity, but left a detailed account of his experiences. The imperial envoy Chang Ch'ien returned with two great treasures – the grapevine and news of 'heavenly horses', which another expedition succeeded in bringing back. With improved mounts, and adopting the Huns' costume, and their invention of stirrups, Chinese armies were better equipped. The Chinese never made expert riders, but such equipment as the crossbow, operated by an ingenious trigger mechanism made for good static defence.

Chang's mission marked the start of regular trade between China and the West, along what came to be the Great Silk Road, and which was in fact

LEFT *Under the Tang Dynasty (618–49), the horse came to play a vital role in imperial military strategy, as well as forming a favourite subject for the famous equestrian sculptures and paintings of the period. Many such artefacts have been found in Tang burial chambers.*

several different routes, beginning on the Yellow River, passing through the Jade Gate, before following different tracks over the Pamirs to meet in the Iranian metropolis of Merv. The quantity of fabric produced was greatly increased by mechanization using the draw-loom, where the 3,000 silk warps needed by polychromatic patterns were pre-selected. Since few European products were appreciated by the more expert Chinese, silk had to be paid for in gold, with severe economic consequences for the Roman Empire. When silkworms were smuggled into Europe in AD 552, the Chinese monopoly ended, but trade continued in ceramics, jade, bronzes, and lacquer work. Another Han innovation was the production-line, where lacquer cups passed through the hands of seven craftsmen, supervised – an example of the new bureaucracy – by six officials.

The Han system was amazingly resilient. After the Han rule disintegrated (AD 220), it was 40 years before some order was restored by the Jin (265–420) and Sung (420–490), but for most of the period the border had been forced back to the Yangtze, and the north was ruled by shortlived regimes – no fewer than 17 between AD 304 and 535, of which only three were Chinese (the others being Hunnish, Turkic or Mongol). Yet the invaders were quickly seduced by Chinese civilization and became thoroughly Sinicized themselves.

Unity was restored by the first Sui emperor in AD 590, and symbolized by the construction of the Grand Canal, linking Hangkow on the Yangtze with the Yellow River. Over five million workers were conscripted, and two million died, but the north and centre of China were now permanently linked. Considering what must have been the resultant unpopularity it is not surprising that the Sui did not last long, but were replaced in 618 by the most splendid of the Chinese dynasties, the Tang. Chinese history has known several closed periods, where all contact with the world outside was shunned, but the Tang were unusually open and even cosmopolitan. New art forms – the pottery horses, which superbly embody the equine character, murals and sculpture – were paralleled by a generation of gifted poets. Entertainers, such as jugglers, acrobats and musicians were popular. In practical matters the penal code was revised, and new standards set for the administrative examinations. Poetry became the preferred subject, as in 19th-century England, when a facility for Greek verse and an ability to produce apposite Latin quotations were judged essential for official success. The Confucian bureaucratic system did, however oddly, produce able administrators.

Some previous conquests were lost, and although this was lamented at the time, it reduced the empire to the Chinese heartland, facilitating control, and setting Korea, Indochina and Mongolia free to develop their own states.

The Mongol Empire

At some time about 1194, the Mongol clan leader Temujin was elected Khan of the Mongols, taking the name of Genghis – 'the Strong'. Over the next 30 years he demonstrated strength, undeviating ruthlessness and political clarity,

The Han Empire 87 BC

0   500 Miles
0   1000 Km

XIONGNU   XIANBEI   FUYU
KOGURYO
WEIMO

WUHUAN

YUEZHI

QIANG

R. Hwang Ho

Chang'an

H A N

R. Yangtze

YUNNAN
RANMANG   FUKIEN
ZUO
SUI   MINYUE   FORMOSA
QIONG
KWANGTUNG
AILAO   YELANG   Canton
KWANGSI
DONGSON
HAINAN
R. Gange
Pataliputra
MAGADHA   ASSAM
Calcutta   R. Irrawaddy
Ava
ARAKAN   Pagan
CHINA
Pegu   SEA
R. Mekong
CHAMPA
Bangkok   Angkor
Madras   FUNAN
Andaman Is.
Kavaripattinam   KRA   Saigon

Nicobar Is.
Penang
CEYLON   MALAYA

INDIAN
Singapore
OCEAN   SUMATRA   BANGKA

TARUMA

forging the most extensive empire the world had seen, and slaughtering literally millions in the most violent and sustained massacres perpetrated before the 20th century. To Genghis there should be no such thing as a living enemy: no other sovereign could coexist with the Mongols except as vassals. Once having submitted, the survivors were protected by Genghis' new code of laws: as long as taxes were paid, Muslims, Christians of all varieties, Buddhists or pagans were unmolested and allowed access to all but the highest ranks, which were to be strictly a family affair.

Genghis' troops were light cavalry, capable of staying in the saddle for weeks on end, accustomed to hardship and rapid movement. By 1220, Mongol armies had struck more than 3,000 miles (4,800 km) west, destroying the rich cities of Bukhara and Samarkand. Six years later, after determined resistance, the Chinese Empire submitted, as did Manchuria and Korea. When Genghis died, in 1227, the Mongol Empire, with its capital at Siberian Karakorum, extended from the North Pacific to the Indian Ocean, and was still growing. By 1241, Mongol armies had swept aside Russians, Poles, Hungarians and the Teutonic Knights to reach the shores of the Adriatic. Western Europe took the

ABOVE *The martial prowess of mounted Mongol warriors, who could shoot recurved bows while riding at full tilt, is clear from this illumination in a 14th-century Iranian manuscript, the* Jami al Tawarikh *('Compendium of Chronicles').*

sufferings of its neighbours calmly, and when the Mongols withdrew to settle the next succession, which had to be done formally in council at Karakorum, breathed a collective sigh of relief and concentrated on its fight with Islam.

It was then realized that the Mongols could become useful allies – it was said that many were Christians – so in 1254 King Louis IX of France sent an envoy to Karakorum. The Flemish Franciscan William of Rubruck was politely received, but made aware that one did not negotiate with the Khan – now Möngke, Genghis' grandson – one simply submitted. An object-lesson was given four years later when a Mongol army stormed Baghdad: the 500-year-old Caliphate was destroyed: the Muslim population was slaughtered, but the Christian spared: and it appeared that, perhaps, the Great Khan might agree to an alliance. But the time was not yet ripe.

After Möngke's death in 1259, a disputed succession led to a Mongol civil war. Mongol strength was already divided, as in China Kublai Khan was successfully launching a new dynasty, while in the west the 'Golden Horde' had settled in southern Russia. The new Great Khan Hülegü, could still field a formidable army to attack his next enemy, the Cairo Caliphate, but it was not the force Genghis had commanded, and the Mongols were soundly defeated by the Egyptian Mamluks at Ain Jalut in September 1260. Led by the formidable Sultan Baibars I ('The Crossbowman'), the Egyptians went on the offensive, steadily driving the Mongols back east. Negotiations were now possible, and in 1287 a Mongol ambassador, Rabban Sauma, a Turkish Christian, was sent to Europe. Spending more than a year in negotiations, Rabban was welcomed by the Greek emperor, the French king – who showed him round the newly-built Sainte Chapelle – and Edward I of England, who impressed him as the most effective Western ruler; but he found the cardinals ignorant and unhelpful, willing only to discuss theology, not practical matters.

He did better with the new Pope and the Mongol envoy was able to celebrate Mass in St Peter's during Holy Week: goodwill was everywhere, but no promises of action. Even then the Khan persisted, sending personal letters to the Pope and to the English and French kings. King Edward's reply survives, sending good wishes but saying it was for the pope to decide: but the pope had no armies. The opportunity was lost, and with it the Crusades.

The Fabled Kublai Khan

The most constructive aspects of Mongol rule were experienced in China under the Emperor Kublai Khan, who established a traditionally Chinese administration. Thanks to the usual Mongol tolerance of outsiders and the Chinese capacity for adapting to a change of rulers, China prospered, as witnessed by Marco Polo, during his nearly 20-year residence there from 1275.

The Grand Canal was restored, a stable paper currency established, and the work of previous dynasties consolidated for onward transmission when Chinese rule was reinstated. By then the northern Mongols were thousands of miles away in Russia. The Golden Horde, usually known as the Tatars, settled on the Volga, where they found their Russian subjects amenable, paying their taxes as required and with their prince obeying Mongol laws. Alexander Nevsky, the hero of the fight against the Teutonic Knights, dutifully travelled to Karakorum to render homage to the Great Khan. The Orthodox Church won a new degree of independence and in the absence of an effective Russian central power became the sole national institution, prompting a religious revival; by the end of the 15th century, Mongol rule had faded away and modern Russia began to take shape.

Persia had been devastated by the ferocity of the Mongol attack; as many as 200,000 people may have perished in the sack of Baghdad, but once installed the Khans left the population to their own devices as long as the heavy taxes were paid. The period of Mongol dominance in Central Asia (from c.1260 to c.1340) happened to coincide with the lifetimes of two of the greatest Persian writers, Sa'di and Hafiz. Sa'di in particular was a close friend of two of the Mongols' viziers, both literate and cultivated men, and some splendid

LEFT *The Mongol emperor Kublai Khan (far left) handing over a message to the pope to Western emissaries, including the Venetian merchant Marco Polo. This was allegedly the first time that Kublai Khan had met Europeans.*

architecture offers permanent evidence of the Mongol occupation, notably the magnificent Khan Öljaitü's mausoleum at Soltaniyeh in northern Iran and in the mosques in Kerman and Yazd.

Even after the death of the last Khan, Persia was not free from foreign rule, since the Mongols were succeeded by another Mongol/Turkish dynasty, founded by Timur the Lame (Tamburlaine the Great; r.1369–1405). After the initial violence, symbolized in the heaps of skulls piled before the conqueror, the Timurid rulers left their memorials in magnificent architecture in cities such as Samarkand and Mashhad.

Philosophers and Kings

Philosophers and other intellectuals have always considered it a pleasurable duty to advise people in power. Plato accepted the challenge of instructing Dionysus I, tyrant of Syracuse, and his pupil Aristotle undertook the education of the young Alexander. Neither was notably successful, and their followers do not seem to have done much better, at least in Europe and the West. In the East, however, rulers took their sages' counsels seriously.

It was easy for rulers to agree in principle with Confucius. Yes, they had obligations to their people, especially to keep peace and maintain order, and in return the people had to obey those destined by Heaven to control them. Only those candidates who had proved their merit by demonstrating, through a series of difficult examinations, a mastery of Confucius' teaching would be given administrative posts: their decisions would therefore be impeccable and mandatory. One remark of his contemporary Mencius, who systematized Confucius' work should be inscribed in every library, seminary and *madrasah*:

> *'He who believes all of a book would be better off without books.'*

The thoughts of the sixth-century BC thinker Laozi only run to some 5,000 words, and were specifically intended as advice to rulers. Meditation, restraint, and the suppression of desire are essential, but while the 'Dao', best translated by the Greek word 'logos' – the word, the way, the essence, the truth – is an excellent philosophy, it has not often appealed to those in power.

At best rulers who seriously attempted to follow the philosophers' advice succeeded in perpetuating a prosperous and tranquil society but, the underlying assumption that China was, if not totally insulated from outside pressures, at least in control, with the 'middle kingdom' accepting humble tribute from outside, proved to be a dangerous myth. The earliest Han emperors discovered this when the northern steppe kingdoms demanded to be treated with respect. The 'tribute bearing' missions of the Xiongnu described in the Chinese records were not in reality bringing gifts, but taking them away – a fixed tariff including some 40,000 gallons of wine and 100,000 yards of silk fabric. In return for this levy, the 'barbarians' agreed to stay outside the gates.

Imperial Frontiers

China and India were linked, rather than separated, by the sea. Only a few hundred miles separate Bengal from the natural Chinese border on the upper Mekong river, but neither empire looked in that difficult direction. A land-sea route had been developed in the first millennium BC across the very narrow Isthmus of Kra to the Gulf of Siam where Indian communities had settled in what is now Cambodia, Thailand and Southern Vietnam: a Chinese observer remarked disapprovingly that the Brahmans:

> 'do nothing but study the sacred canon, bathe themselves with scent and flowers, and practise piety ceaselessly.'

The Indo-Chinese Kingdom of Funan endured there until the 600s, with Sanskrit as the official language, trading as far west as Persia. Funan's command of the sea routes was inherited by the Sumatran kingdom of Srivijaya, which, thanks to its strategic position on the Malacca Strait, expanded into Java and Malaysia, with trading posts and colonies as distant as the Philippines. Leadership passed to the Majahabit kingdom of Java, which celebrated the defeat of Sumatra by seeing off a Chinese army despatched by Kublai Khan to reprove the challenging upstarts.

On the mainland, Funan had been succeeded by the magnificent Khmer Empire, based on the fertile rice-growing Mekong lowlands. From the 700s the Khmer prospered peacefully, beginning the extraordinary series of Buddhist temples around Angkor in the ninth century. But over time the cost of fighting dynastic wars and the expense of temple-building broke the Khmer economy. Following persistent Siamese attacks, Angkor was finally abandoned in 1444.

BELOW *The imposing Bayon Temple on the site of the royal city of Angkor Thom in Cambodia, built in the late 12th century by King Jayavarman VII.*

1414 – 1648
Reformation and Renaissance

■ Sigismund presides at the Council of Constance 1414 ■ Gutenberg Bible printed 1455
■ Construction of St Peter's begins 1506 ■ Martin Luther posts his Ninety-Five Theses 1517
■ Council of Trent 1545 ■ Peace of Westphalia ends the Thirty Years' War 1648

The tide of events that swept through Western Europe in the 15th and 16th centuries – comprising successively the Renaissance, the Protestant Reformation and the Catholic Counter-Reformation – transformed not only Europe but also the New World. This period also witnessed the beginning of methodical science, the growth of new technologies such as printing, navigation and gunnery, and the emergence of vernacular literatures.

As Europe staggered into the 15th century it might have seemed to be in terminal decline, and that the future lay with Islam, now extending over 6,000 miles (9,600 km) from the Atlantic and Danube to the Java Sea and from the Volga to Mozambique. The Orthodox Church was subject to the Ottoman Sultan, while the Catholic West was divided between two popes.

A Three-Pope Problem

An Ecumenical Council held at Pisa in 1409 attempted to end the schism by deposing both the 'Roman' pope – actually resident in Ferrara – and the Avignon pretender, living in Perpignan: neither accepted their deposition and since the Council had made their own selection there were now three popes. In such circumstances Charlemagne's successor, the Holy Roman Emperor, was acknowledged as the only competent authority; in 1414 the *de facto* emperor was Sigismund, who as well as being king of Hungary also ruled Germany, Croatia and Bohemia. In this role he was able to prevail upon the Pisan Pope John XXIII, the most widely acknowledged of the three contenders, to call a Council whose authority would be recognized by all western Christians. The Council comprised not only Church dignitaries but also

RIGHT *Pope Martin V leaving the Council of Constance in 1418; the Holy Roman Emperor Sigismund is seen holding the reins of his horse. The council ended almost the almost 40-year Western Schism.*

delegates from all European states. Nothing quite like it had ever been seen, since previous Councils had been concerned only with Church affairs. Sigismund was determined to tackle all pressing problems, including the long war between France and England, and to ensure that the ecclesiastical representatives submitted to his personal control.

Held in the imperial city of Constance over three years, from 1414 to 1417, Europe's first international conference was characterized by its methodical organization, with agendas, agreed minutes, executive committees, plenary sessions and sub-committees. Among the secular delegates were statesmen from Poland/Lithuania and Scandinavia, and Byzantine representatives, with communications being facilitated by the use of a common language, Latin. At the time only France and England could claim to be nations in the modern sense of the word, and presented their cases at the Council with great vigour, denouncing each other's pretensions. In particular, King Henry V had taken great care to instruct the English delegation on how to vote, and supervised their conduct through his own secret agent. In spite of visiting both countries Sigismund failed to reconcile France and England, but did agree a treaty with Henry V that initiated a long alliance between Britain and the Holy Roman Empire.

It was three years before Church unity was restored, the three claimants discharged (John, who actually summoned the Council, came off worst), a new and unquestioned Pope installed

indulgences, and discontent began to simmer. Under Julius' successor, Leo X (1513–21) the need for a massive influx of funds intensified, as the bills began to roll in not only for building St Peter's but also for financing one more crusade against the Turks. Having sold all available church posts – a considerably restricted source of income since the right to appoint the most senior clergy had been diverted to lay rulers – and pawned his furniture, Leo arranged a loan from the Fugger bank of Augsburg, repayment to be made from the sale of indulgences in the archbishopric of Mainz. This was too much for the German monk Martin Luther of Wittenberg, who in January 1517 posted his famous 'Ninety-Five Theses'. Pope Leo was preoccupied with other concerns and resorted to the traditional method of excommunicating the heretic: it had not worked with Hus and did not work with Luther.

Reformation and Counter-Reformation

After the short pontificate of Hadrian VI (the only Dutch pope), Clement VII (1523–34) found himself faced with the continuing problem of Luther, but once again failed to address the issues fuelling growing dissent against the authority of Rome. In 1521, King Francis I of France had begun a war against Charles V, newly elected Holy Roman Emperor, and also King of Austria, Spain and Naples, ruler of Burgundy and Flanders and Lord of the Americas. The war ended only in August 1529, with complete victory for Charles, after battles that had devastated much of Italy and led to the brutal sack of Rome itself in 1527.

The revulsion against indulgences was shared by many faithful Catholics, but there were many other factors in the complex process known as the Reformation. For many years there had been a deep-seated resentment against claims of popes to a supreme power, in politics as in religion, especially when such pretension was accompanied by corruption on a grand scale. Indignation was expressed emotionally in the devout Catholic Dante's epic *Divina Commedia*, and, more practically, in monarchs simply cutting off funds. Franciscan friars, protesting at the Church's enormous wealth, were judged heretical and burnt.

The question was not whether there was to be a thorough reformation, but whether or not it would lead to a schism. The way was now clear for Charles to act as his predecessor Sigismund had done, by presiding over an ecumenical Council, but this could only be convened by a pope, and Clement, perhaps reflecting on the fate of John XXIII, refused to take part. Acting on his own, the best Charles could do was to convene an Imperial Diet, a parliament of ecclesiastical and lay magnates, held at Augsburg in 1530. It might have worked: the Lutherans put forward their doctrinal case, accepted by many Catholics, but without a strong lead from the Pope no agreement was possible. Charles renewed his pleas for a General Council: uselessly, since by the time this was finally convoked at Trent (Trento) in 1545, Protestantism was too firmly established. Clement's papal successors chose persecution, establishing the Roman Inquisition, publishing an Index of Forbidden Books (only abolished in 1966) and confining Jews to ghettos, where they were obliged to wear distinctive clothes. Unlike the Council of Constance, the Council of Trent was unrepresentative; in the later stages, 189 Italian bishops were present, 31 Spanish, 26 French, but only 2 Germans and a single Englishman. Although the door was still held ajar for the reintegration of the Protestants, the main work of the Council, which only adjourned in 1565, was a thorough overhaul of Church practice and doctrines, almost a re-creation of the Catholic Church: but now as a predominantly Italian organization.

and the Catholic Church revived; but a price had to be paid for achieving unity. The new pope, Martin V (1417–31), had been elected not by the cardinals alone, but with the consent of the national representatives, signifying the definitive end of any papal pretensions to universal rule.

Although successful in healing the schism, the Council made one serious error: Jan Hus, the much-admired Rector of Charles University in Prague, was condemned as a heretic and burnt to death. Czech-speaking Bohemia rose in fury against the German emperor, defying the Church and its supporters. Although all ranks, from magnates to labourers, were represented among the Hussites, their strength lay among the peasants, who had formed their own vision of an ideal community, which they transformed into a practical reality in the southern Bohemian city of Tábor. Unable to fight on equal terms with armoured cavalry, masters of the battlefield for centuries, the Hussites devised an entirely new form of mobile armoured warfare: the so-called *Wagenburg*, a mobile fortress of farm carts defended by archers, gunners and infantry armed with spiked flails and billhooks. Over a protracted period of unrest lasting 15 years the Hussites destroyed every Catholic army sent against it until the emperor and pope were eventually obliged to compromise, and the Czechs were allowed to retain their own proto-Protestant church.

Bohemian anger, already simmering against German arrogance, had been ignited by the sale of indulgences, seen as ecclesiastical fraud, just as Chaucer had depicted them a generation earlier, but the warning went unheeded in Rome, as a succession of popes demanded ever-increasing quantities of cash. Julius II (1503–13), for example, had to meet the expenses of buying his election and fighting numerous wars, leading his troops in full armour on the field of battle: he had three daughters to marry off, but his principal expense was in commissioning such artists as Michelangelo and Raphael and in beginning the construction of the magnificent new basilica of St Peter's. Many sincere churchmen were shocked by the widespread sale of

Hampered as he was by conflicting European interests, the Emperor Charles had a free hand in the New World. All Spanish possessions would be unequivocally Catholic, and Counter-Reformation Catholicism, with its splendid architecture and ebullient art appealed to native sensibilities, as demonstrated by the miraculous image of the Virgin of Guadalupe appearing on the site of an Aztec temple. Vigorous protests were made by such writers as Bartolomé de las Casas, planter turned priest, against the mistreatment of Indians, reinforced by the spiritual nourishment provided by the Church which healed some of the more drastic consequences of cultural destruction.

The various reformers active throughout Europe had different visions of the new Church. Desiderius Erasmus of Rotterdam (1466–1536), monk, scholar and good-humoured satirist, had already exposed abuses in his influential tract In Praise of Folly (1509). Luther, with his conservative adaptation of Catholic doctrine inspired by a command of the German language, expressed in such great hymns as 'Ein Feste Burg ist Unser Gott,' prevailed in northern Germany. The subtle (and easily misunderstood) theologian Jean Calvin, converted many French, while in England King Henry VIII (r.1509–47) simply took over as Head of the Church, retaining traditional rites, with some later important modifications. Emperor Charles V, finding his German lands divided between Protestants and Catholics, succeeded in forcing a compromise whereby rulers themselves decided what the official religion of their states should be; as a result, northern Germany became Protestant, forming a bloc with Scandinavia, Holland and Britain, while Austria and the South remained Catholic.

Reformation ideas were disseminated by the new invention of printing with moveable metal type (new to the West, but originating in China), which enabled such works as William Tyndale's translation of the New Testament into English to be distributed cheaply, with revolutionary results. Literacy was common enough to permit prosperous workers to read Bible texts, hitherto decently shrouded in Latin, and to judge for themselves how far their churches had slipped away from the early ideals. Ironically Tyndale was pursued by agents of Thomas More, Erasmus' close friend, condemned for heresy and burnt at the stake. More himself was later executed for treason by Henry VIII and beatified by the Catholic Church, but Tyndale has the more secure memorial in that his translation formed the armature around which the later King James 'Authorized' Version of the Bible was constructed. It was, however, the good Catholic Erasmus who had written:

Martin Luther's 'Ninety-Five Theses' gave voice to widespread discontent in northern Europe over abuses by the Catholic clergy in Rome. Thesis 86 enquired: 'Why does the pope, whose wealth today is greater than the wealth of the richest Crassus, build the basilica of St. Peter with the money of poor believers rather than with his own money?'

'I wish that every woman might read the Gospels and the Epistles of St Paul … Would that the farmer might sing snatches of Scripture at his plough, that the weaver might hum phrases of Scripture to the tune of his shuttle.'

ABOVE *The central figure of Moses, from Michelangelo's tomb of Pope Julius II in the church of San Pietro in Vincoli in Rome. Major building works during Julius' papacy, notably the construction of St Peter's, precipitated a crisis over the sale of indulgences.*

Domestic and international politics intermeshed in Britain. Queen Catherine of Aragon, whose refusal to divorce King Henry VIII led to the Anglican schism, was the sister of the arch heretic-hunter, King Philip II of Spain. When Philip married Catherine's daughter Mary Tudor, Spain became identified with the implacable persecution of supposed heretics during her four-year reign (1554–58) during which Protestant objectors were burnt alive at the rate of one every four days or so. English opinion, previously generally conservative, was sharpened against both Spain and Rome, obliging young Queen Elizabeth I (r.1558–1603) in 1559 to choose between the Reformed Religion and Spain's friendship; correctly divining the mood of her English subjects she chose moderate reform, which brought her into sharp conflict with her subjects in Ireland.

The Normans, like the Romans before them, had balked at the conquest of Ireland, but Viking colonies had been established on the east coast, the largest at Dublin, site of a former late-Roman bishopric. In 1169, King Henry encouraged the Normans who had settled in Wales to obey Pope Adrian IV's command by occupying Ireland, thus establishing what might be called England's first colony. Some control was possible in the coastal towns, particularly in the Dublin 'Pale', where the Irish Parliament was held, but the interior was left to the native Irish, with their own language and traditions, which included a millennium of Celtic Christianity. After Mary Tudor began establishing English settlers in 'plantations', the policy was energetically followed by her sister Elizabeth I, bringing acquisitive Protestant

colonists into violent conflict with the loyally Catholic Irish. Pope Pius V's fierce denunciation of Elizabeth identified Catholicism with treason, and the Spanish raids to support the Church in Ireland identified Irish Catholics with Spain. The stage was set for a persistent and particularly English prejudice against Rome and a long period of violent resentment in Ireland.

Elsewhere, national interests determined alliances. Protestant England remained on good terms with Catholic France, but became a bitter enemy of the Protestant Dutch. The Catholic Emperor Charles fought the French to a humiliating defeat in Italy. In the 17th century, however, religious differences exacerbated political clashes; the Thirty Years' War (1618–48) began as a power struggle between France and the Empire, but the scandalous massacres that accompanied it were facilitated by religious differences; on a much smaller scale, the British campaigns in Ireland, although part of international confrontations, were viciously tainted by doctrinal disputes.

The most lasting effects of the Reformation were less dramatic. Protestants had translated the Latin Bible and Rites into the vernacular, inspiring national literature. The flowering of English drama and poetry sprang in great part from the majestic prose of the new Bible and Prayer Book, and modern German literature's first major figure is Luther. Fighting back, the Counter-Reformation produced the magnificent architecture of the Baroque: Rome, which had been a wolf-infested collection of ruins in the 15th century, was rebuilt; modern music was born in the Italian church as harmony edged out polyphony. But behind the splendour, the papacy became a minor Italian state, and the popes little more than bit-players in European power politics. The energy of the Church was diverted into new and enterprising religious orders, and in particular the Society of Jesus, founded by a group at the University of Paris, and recognized by Pope Paul III in 1540. Carefully selected, well-educated and disciplined, Jesuit teachers and missionaries performed brilliantly, taking the doctrines and practices of the reformed Catholic Church to Japan, Vietnam, China and India and to the new Spanish and Portuguese American colonies. In all these fields, Jesuits demonstrated a sympathetic understanding of local cultures and provided much-needed protection against colonial oppression: all these admirable qualities did not endear them to the governments.

The Renaissance

The Italian Renaissance might almost be called the Florentine Renaissance, since that city was home to so many of its leading figures. (Moreover, at that time, Italy was, to coin a later phrase, 'little more than a geographical expression.') As in Ancient Greece, Italians' first loyalty was to their city, and then to an idea of the magnificent Italian heritage, the Empire of Rome and Latin literature: and Florence was then the largest and richest of cities. The first new humanist story-tellers, Petrarch and Boccaccio, the painters Masaccio, Donatello and Ghiberti and the architect Brunelleschi were all Florentines, and their successors were sheltered by the princely magnificence of the Medici family. It was some time before the new arts spread to other large Italian states, but were quickly taken up in smaller towns, such as Ferrara and Mantua: Baldassare Castiglione's book *The Courtier*, which became the handbook of taste and proper conduct of a gentleman throughout Europe, was written for the court of Urbino. He reviles the French as 'rude and uncultivated,' but good at fighting and insists that a grounding in Greek and Latin is essential for gentlemen.

Northern Europeans may have had much to learn about gentility, and agreed with Castiglione that a decent acquaintance with Latin literature was desirable, but one vital part of the Italian Renaissance could not be exported – the clear blue Mediterranean skies. No such painting as, for example, Botticelli's *Primavera* could be conceived in the darker and damper skies of Northern Europe; nor, for reasons that had more to do with climate than with prudery, was nudity in art a northern speciality. The great painters of the period, Vermeer and Rembrandt, the Holbeins and Dürer, were primarily interior painters.

To some extent Renaissance and Reform intermingled. The Latinist Lorenzo Valla identified the so-called 'Donation of Constantine,' claimed as the foundation of the popes' sovereign rights over Middle Italy, as fraudulent and challenged the accuracy of St Jerome's translation of the Greek Bible, the 'Vulgate', accepted as it had been for a millennium by the Catholic church – a challenge rapidly accepted by the Protestant reformers.

What might be called a return flow, from North to South, occurred in the new art of printing, pioneered by Johannes Gutenberg of Mainz in 1450, reaching Rome 20 years later, and in science and medicine. The spirit of scientific enquiry that had flourished in Oxford with the work of Roger Bacon and William of Ockham was revived by northern savants, most notably Nikolaj Kopernik of Cracow, better known as Nicolaus Copernicus, who put forward a radical new heliocentric model of the universe. Latin names were generally adopted by serious writers, such as the Swiss doctor Theophrastus Bombastus von Hohenheim – Paracelsus – who stressed the need to learn from 'our own interpretation of nature, by long practice, confirmed by experience' rather than poring over ancient texts. The painstaking dissections of the anatomist Andreas van Wesel of Bruges (Vesalius) resulted in the first authoritative study of human anatomy, published in the same year (1543) as Copernicus' great work *On the Revolutions of the Celestial Spheres*. All three had studied at Italian medical schools, but in Catholic countries research was not encouraged: Vesalius was condemned and sentenced to perpetual exile by the Inquisition. The Breton Ambroise Paré, universally acknowledged as the father of modern surgery, was a Protestant, but his skill kept him safe during the religious persecution: constant wars afforded him plenty of practice in improving his techniques.

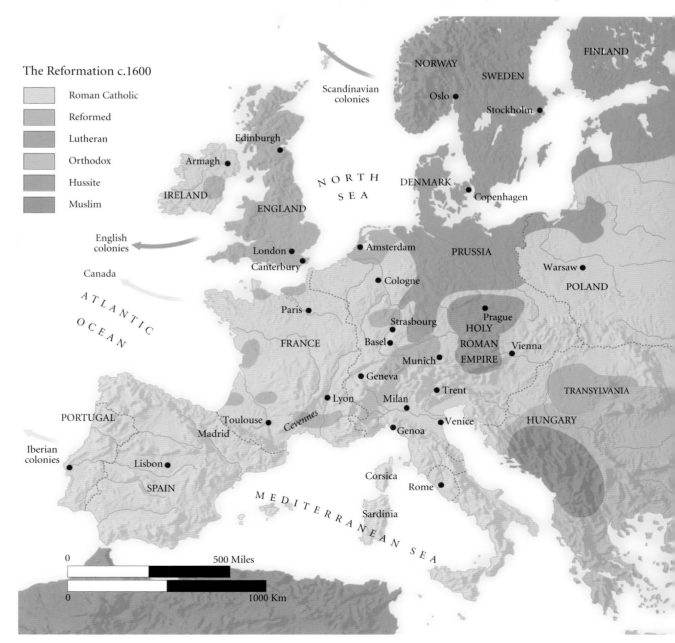

The Reformation c.1600

Roman Catholic
Reformed
Lutheran
Orthodox
Hussite
Muslim

1494 – 1610
New Worlds

■ Treaty of Tordesillas codifies Spanish and Portuguese territorial claims 1494 ■ Vasco da Gama reaches India 1498 ■ Hernán Cortés overruns the Aztec Empire 1521 ■ Conquest of the Incas by Pizarro 1532 ■ First successful English colony established at Jamestown (Virginia) 1608

On 4 June 1494, in the Treaty of Tordesillas, mediated by Pope Alexander VI, Spain and Portugal agreed to divide the world – or at least that part of it still to be discovered – between them. Two months before, Columbus' report of his Atlantic voyage had provoked a lively diplomatic flurry.

The Spanish had found a collection of islands which might, just conceivably, prove to be off the coast of India, but the Portuguese, whose rights had been acknowledged in a previous papal decree, had already rounded the Cape of Good Hope and established good relations with many African rulers. Asked to adjudicate, the pope ruled that all lands west of a line some 1,200 miles (1,930 km) from the Azores were to be Spanish, and to the east Portuguese. No other nation objecting, that should have been that.

Venturing East

The Iberian voyages had been made possible through the union of several different technologies. The cog, the traditional North Sea and Atlantic trading ship, sturdy and seaworthy, had the Mediterranean lateen rig added to its sail plan, allowing the vessel to sail a little closer to the wind: magnetic compasses and sternpost rudders were adapted from Chinese ships, while such Arab and Jewish instruments as the astrolabe and cross-staff allowed more precise navigation. Finally King John II of Portugal himself had prepared a plan for mounting artillery on the decks of a larger type of vessel – the *não* – enabling an impressive firepower to be deployed. The English King Henry VII's ship *Regent* mounted over 200 artillery pieces of different calibres. Such ships could master rough seas and foul weather, hold a steady course and overcome most resistance.

Portugal had begun exploring much earlier than Spain– Columbus himself had served on one African voyage – and by 1424 had discovered first Madeira, followed by the Azores, one-third of the way across the Atlantic. By the 1440s, a modest trade had developed – horses exchanged for slaves – in West Africa, but the ultimate goal was always a passage to India and the East, which Vasco da Gama finally achieved in May 1498. Doubling the Cape of Good Hope, so named by King John, and sailing up the shores of Africa as far as Malindi, da Gama found an Arab pilot to take him to the Indian coast. Thereafter it was constant and pitiless warfare with the Muslim coastal cities.

Alfonso de Albuquerque, the commander, was given the title of Viceroy of the Estado da India, a clear sign of Portugal's intended conquest. Albuquerque was more than willing to effect this, demonstrating the power of his warships by blasting resistance aside and massacring the inhabitants of any city that opposed him. Goa was seized to provide a permanent base in 1510 and other harbours grabbed as opportunities arose. Since at that time the Spaniards were still investigating the unpromising Caribbean islands, Portugal was well ahead, with even better prospects, especially since Pope Alexander's geographical ruling had allotted them Brazil.

By 1530, the Portuguese controlled the western Indian coastal trade with a strategic string of ports, but the adventurers pushed further east, past Ceylon, to the spice islands of Indonesia where the real treasure, more accessible and valuable than gold, was to be found. Nutmeg, cinnamon and ginger were in great demand, but pepper was the prize, essential both in preserving and flavouring European food. All were easily available, since the whole region had become a vast market, supplied by Arabs, Chinese and Japanese merchants trading with local producers.

Permission for a 'factory' – a trading post – had been given to the Portuguese by the ruler of Malacca, on the Malay Peninsula. An attack by Muslims gave Albuquerque the excuse to seize the whole city and the Portuguese proceeded to muscle in; St Francis Xavier, visiting in the 1540s, regretted that the only verb they knew was *rapio*, in all its tenses and conjugations. Treaties were made with those rulers too powerful to bully and quietly, with tacit Chinese consent, the Macao peninsula, near the great port of Canton, was occupied, a unique European toehold in China.

By 1550, Japan had been reached, trading agreements made and a successful Jesuit mission established, too successful indeed for the Shogun Hideyoshi, who brought persecution to a head in 1597 by painfully and publicly executing 26 converts. Trade, under carefully restricted conditions, and the

introduction of new technology, were welcome, but disturbing doctrines capable of destroying traditional Japanese society had to be suppressed.

Moving eastwards, having annexed Timor, the Portuguese were eventually bound to meet Spaniards, sailing across the Pacific from their American share of the world. When this happened, in the Philippines in 1521, the dividing line had to be extended round the globe on the same principle. But by then other European powers had begun to show an interest, and these were not going to defer to any Papal decision, since the Protestant Reformation had taken root. In 1578 Queen Elizabeth I authorized Sir Humphrey Gilbert to occupy any lands on the North American east coast, 'not actually possessed of any Christian prince of people.' Nothing happened on the ground, but Spain had received warning, backed by continuous attacks on Spanish shipping by such raiders as Francis Drake, heroes to the English but pirates to the

ABOVE *Book illumination of 1533, showing the Spanish galleon* La Nostra Sengnora *setting out from the port of Sanlúcar de Barrameda, bound for Venezuela. Broadside guns were then rare, the heaviest pieces pointing fore and aft.*

Spanish, and reinforced by the destruction of the Great Armada in 1588. By the end of the 16th century neither Spain, which had collapsed into economic stagnation in spite – or possibly because – of American gold and silver, or Portugal, annexed by Spain, were in any condition to resist foreign intervention. The Netherlands had achieved independence after a bitter struggle against their Spanish overlords, and both Dutch and English were radical Protestants. By 1602, both countries had chartered East India companies in order to supplant the Portuguese. The Dutch struck first: by 1648 Malacca was Dutch, and the rest of the East Indies followed. The British concentrated on India, relying on diplomacy, and making their biggest gain when Bassein Island and the mainland town of Bombay was ceded as part of King Charles II's wedding settlement with a Portuguese princess.

A few relics of the great navigators remain; Portuguese churches in Macao and Goa reflect the splendid architecture of the home country, but, more enduringly the maize and cassava they brought to Africa from America, which remain a staple food for millions: to say nothing, of course, of tobacco, potatoes and chocolate.

Voyages to the West

The first years after Columbus' discoveries were full of confusion. He steadfastly maintained that the islands he had found were outliers of the East Indies, but if so, where were the great cities, the gold, the spices? His patron Isabella of Castile was worried both about mistreating the 'Indians' and the expense of further voyages. It was however important to reach the true Indies before the Portuguese, but by 1499 when the news of da Gama's successful voyage to India arrived, the exact nature of Columbus' new world was still unknown: it was clearly neither India nor China but some unheard-of region.

It was only in 1513, seven years after Columbus' death, that Vasco de Balboa reached the western coast and claimed the Pacific for Spain, by which time the new lands had been named 'America' in honour of the Italian explorer Amerigo Vespucci, but to the Spaniards they remained Las Indias. And it seemed that they were more trouble than they were worth. The slaves sent back to Spain soon died, and the handful of colonists planted in the Caribbean quarrelled among themselves: Balboa was actually executed by another Spanish commander. Attempting to make the best of it and seeing their Carib slaves obstinately dying, the scattered Spanish colonists despatched slave-raiding expeditions, one of which stumbled into the Yucatán, where they found evidence of an ordered and prosperous Mayan society: the experienced commander Hernán Cortés was sent to report and was told of the existence of a formidable empire, the Aztec.

With a tiny force – 600 men, 16 horses and 10 small cannon – it was unlikely that even Cortés, one of the greatest commanders of his age, could succeed in vanquishing the Aztecs; indeed, but for the devastating effects of a smallpox epidemic on his enemy he would probably have failed. Landing on the Mexican coast in April 1519 and demonstrating Spanish firepower and cavalry in some brisk skirmishes, Cortés recruited thousands of allies from the peoples who had good reason to hate Aztec tyranny. The Tlaxcalan,

BELOW *Hernán Cortés and his men retreating from the Aztec capital Tenochtitlán in 1520. After the city fell the following year, Cortés became governor of the new Spanish territory until 1524.*

neighbours of the Aztec, had been allowed to remain independent with the proviso that they furnished as many subjects as might be required for Aztec rituals; since these concluded with ritual dismemberment and the priest wrapping himself in the victim's flayed skin, the Tlaxcalan were enthusiastic collaborators. With their help and the advice of a Mayan princess, Cortés made his way into the lake capital of Tenochtitlán, which amazed the Spaniards with its sheer size, larger than anything they had seen in Europe. The expedition ended with the Spaniards taking the emperor Moctezuma hostage, and having to fight their way out of the city, barely escaping with their lives

In defeat, Cortés demonstrated his mettle by building a fleet of gunboats, assembling a Mexican army, and besieging the city. It took four months and many casualties before the city that Cortés had called the most beautiful in the world was destroyed, and the last emperor Cuauhtemoc was captured. Aside from the ravages of imported disease, two reasons explain how the Spaniards, with so few men, succeeded in defeating so large and aggressively militant a kingdom. Firstly, the other Mexicans' burning desire for revenge, and consequent readiness to ally themselves with the Spaniards, and secondly the very weakness of Cortés' forces, marooned – literally, since he had burnt his ships on the coast – in a strange world, which obliged their leader to invent new solutions. If the attack had come from across the Pacific, a similar Japanese force would have done as well; without any contact with other cultures the Aztecs were hamstrung by their own rigid concept of warfare.

The Spanish victory was decisive but the results were disappointing. The Aztecs had valued gold only for its ornamental use, and not as a means of exchange, so there were no great mines ready to replenish looted stores. Mayan resistance continued, forcing Cortés to intervene between two rival bands of conquistadores in Honduras before the Mayans were pacified; even then some communities held out for many years. Cortés got little credit for his achievement but, being a true empire-builder, continued his explorations as far north as California, and organized the building of a fleet to cross the Pacific: 40 years after Columbus first sailed a Spanish-American fleet arrived in the East Indies, and found itself immediately embroiled in a war with the Portuguese.

The Conquest of the Inca

Meanwhile, another Spanish expedition was setting off to conquer a much larger empire: in December 1530 an experienced conquistador, Francisco Pizarro, embarked with about 180 men and 27 horses for the great southern empire of the Inca. Unlike Cortés, a Spanish gentleman, Pizarro and his brothers might today be described as rednecks – Pizarro had been a lowly pig-keeper – but the adventurers had gathered enough information about the region known as Biru to secure Pizarro's

ABOVE *Map of the Americas by the 16th-century Dutch master cartographer Theodor de Bry. Clockwise from top left, the portraits in the corners of this ornamental map are of Columbus, Vespucci, Magellan and Pizarro. A huge uncharted 'Terra Australis' was still thought to lie in the far South Pacific.*

appointment as governor of the empire he was to set about acquiring. The Inca state was a newcomer, beginning with the expansion of a tribe living near Cuzco, on the high Andean plateau, which became their capital in the early 15th century. With astonishing speed three generations of Inca had established rule over a vast area of western South America, from Ecuador to Chile. Their power was absolute – the first mythical Inca, Manco Capac, was considered to be a direct descendant of the Sun God, so conferring divinity on all his many successors and their families. Divine favour had to be maintained by human sacrifices, although more limited and decorous than the Aztecs, communities being expected to volunteer their best children for the occasion. Since all the lands and population were at the disposal of the divine monarch, tributes were quietly forthcoming.

Vast areas were devoted to nobles' estates, which were cultivated by impressed labour, which also operated the state textile factories and mines. Food was collected, to be handed out to the populace in hard times, on the Chinese model of the ever-full granary, and also, as in China, a network of imperial highways, furnished with posting stations, ensured communications, using perilous rope-suspension bridges over the mountain gorges. Unlike any other world empire, or even substantial state, the Inca heartland was extraordinarily elevated; the region around the capital Cuzco (which in the Inca language means literally 'navel of the world') is over 7,000 feet (2,130 metres), and settlements continued to the 10,000 foot (3,000 metres) contour, with extensive and beautifully constructed field terraces making agriculture possible. Only physically very fit and adaptable people survived, and constructed a complex infrastructure, culminating in the incredible ritual site of Machu Picchu, at an altitude of 8,000 feet (2,400 metres). Power was exercised responsibly, but implacably. Whole communities could be

MEXICO.

MEXICO. REGIA
ET CELEBRIS
HISPANIÆ NO-
VAE CIVITAS.

Cum Priuilegio.

deported to distant areas as required, and a corps of trained administrators recorded statistics and transmitted messages by the *quipu* system of knotted cords. Problems could be discussed in public with the mummies of deceased Inca, who transmitted their advice through trusted mediums.

Pizarro's little force arrived after a difficult march through Ecuador to find that the Inca empire was in chaos, split apart by a dynastic feud in which one brother had just triumphed; the former Emperor's son, Atahuallpa, with perhaps 20,000 soldiers, was taking his defeated brother Huascar to Cuzco for ritual disposal. Rather than slaughtering the Spaniards immediately, curiosity inspired Atahuallpa to agree to meet the invaders, a grave error, since the invaders charged into the Inca army, captured the emperor, who then made an even more fatal mistake in believing the raiders to be merely bandits who could be bought off with enough treasure. When this was provided – a roomful of gold plus the extensive loot from Cuzco – Atahuallpa was executed: becoming a Christian at the last moment he was not burnt alive but merely garrotted and another brother, Manco, installed as a Spanish nominee. One of the world's most extensive empires was terminated as suddenly as it had arisen.

What followed was pure melodrama. Pizarro's jealous competitor, Diego d'Almagro's attempted coup failed, and d'Almagro was executed. Pizarro was later murdered by Almagro's friends, and his brother Gonzalo seized power by defeating another royal viceroy. This was too much for the Spanish authorities, who despatched an army, and had Gonzalo, in turn, executed for treason. The real winners were the Incas. Manco relinnquished his role as a Spanish puppet to launch a series of rebellions, only brought to an end with the death of the last free Inca, Thupa Amaro, in 1572.

The Viceroyalty of New Spain

The task facing the first Spanish Viceroy, appointed in 1535, was enormous and unprecedented. An entire continent lay open for exploration, and great tracts were already subdued. It was clearly understood that all subjects of New Spain, whether Indians or Spanish (and by now a number were of mixed race) had to be subject to the rule of a clear and just law, and brought within the Catholic Church: and this over vast distances and more than 3,000 miles (4,800 km) from the home country. The Spanish administration met with a fair degree of success. Royal governors and missionaries restrained some of the rapacious brutality of the earlier settlers, and in Mexico memories of the Aztec violence made the change welcome. But New Spain was not the first concern of the Old Country, subjected to the drastic changes begun by the Protestant Reformation.

By a carefully arranged series of dynastic alliances King Charles I of Spain was elected (at great expense) as Emperor Charles V, the most powerful ruler in Europe, with family possessions in Flanders, Burgundy and Austria, Hungary, Bohemia, Sicily and southern Italy: an attempt was even made to include England by marrying his son Philip to Queen Mary Tudor. With so many responsibilities forcing the Emperor into wars with France, and the divisions in Germany between Catholic and Protestant, the still-confused New World was a low priority. The bullion was welcome, but the imperial debts were huge, and the gold was being recovered only slowly by panning in the Mexican rivers, while deep-mined silver needed capital and skilled labour.

LEFT: *An illustration thought to be based on a sketch by the conquistador Hernán Cortés portrays the city of Tenochtitlán, situated on Lake Texcoco.*

Prospects improved in 1545 with the discovery of richest source in the world, almost a mountain of silver, 12,000 feet (3,700 metres) up in the mountains of South America, at Potosí in what is now Bolivia. Silver rather than gold became the real source of Spanish wealth – or as much of it as French and English raiders allowed to reach the home country.

Early Colonies in North America

European intrusions into the northern part of the continent followed a very different pattern from those in Central and South America. Apart from a scattered fringe of Spanish forts, it was over 500 years after the first landings before any form of organized foreign government was attempted. Some time shortly after AD 1000 a single Icelandic crew passed a winter on what is now Newfoundland. The crew found grapes and wild wheat – the northern climate was less challenging a thousand years ago – before they were attacked by the locals, or *skraelings*, as the Norse called them. They were saved by the quick thinking and bravery of one girl, Freydis, who apparently 'bared her breasts, slapped them with a sword and screamed like a hell cat', which frightened off the attackers.

The Spanish voyagers had followed the east coast only as far as Florida, while in the north the Grand Banks cod fisheries, which had been prospering for a century, had confirmed the bleak existence of Labrador. It was therefore sincerely hoped that the two coasts were not connected, and that a passage existed somewhere between the two. The French king Francis I financed both the Italian Giovanni da Verrazzano and the Frenchman Jacques Cartier on five voyages between 1524 and 1543, which discovered the Hudson and St. Lawrence Rivers, but no sea passage to China. They all found the 'Indians' admirable, polite and handsome, and were taken in by the mischievous tall tales of the Iroquois chief Donnaconna, who ended his days in prosperity in France.

The English were the first to attempt to establish a permanent colony in the region that Verrazzano had named 'Arcadia' and the English 'Virginia'. A survey party having reported a friendly welcome – as did almost all the early voyagers – Sir Richard Grenville was despatched in 1585, and, after a little profitable raiding on Spanish colonies, landed his cohorts on Roanoke Island. They did not prosper, failing to retain the Indians' friendship and returned to England, while their 1587 successors mysteriously disappeared without a trace: but their first Governor, the artist John White, left a fine record of the American Indian culture.

ABOVE *A Native American shaman in Raleigh's Virginia colony of Roanoke. Engraving by Theodor de Bry, after a woodcut by the English artist John White.*

Another attempt at Virginia in 1608 was more successful, but precedence as the oldest British colony is claimed by Newfoundland, whose charter dated back to 1587. In spite of the reconnaissance expedition's unfavourable report – 'Nothing to be seen but solitude and a great deal of fish'– a colony was established in 1610. Given the inhospitable climate, they did well to survive, their prosperity based on those ubiquitous fish.

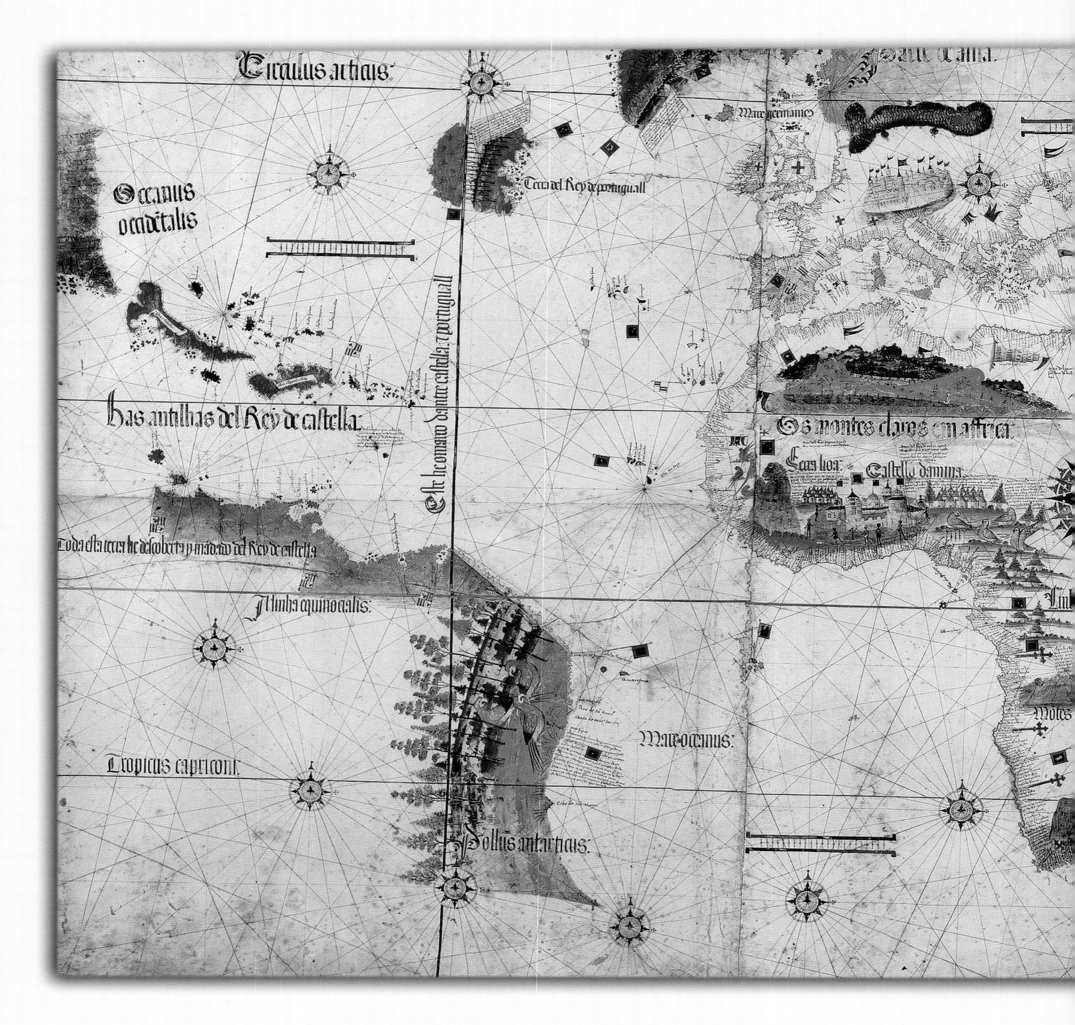

*The earliest surviving cartographic record of Portuguese discoveries
is the Cantino Map of 1502. Clearly visible on the left of the map
is the demarcation line established by the Treaty of Tordesillas,
dividing Spanish claims from those of Portugal. At this stage, only
a fragmentary portion of the coast of Brazil had been explored
and charted – as yet, Europeans had no knowledge of the vast
hinterland that lay beyond.*

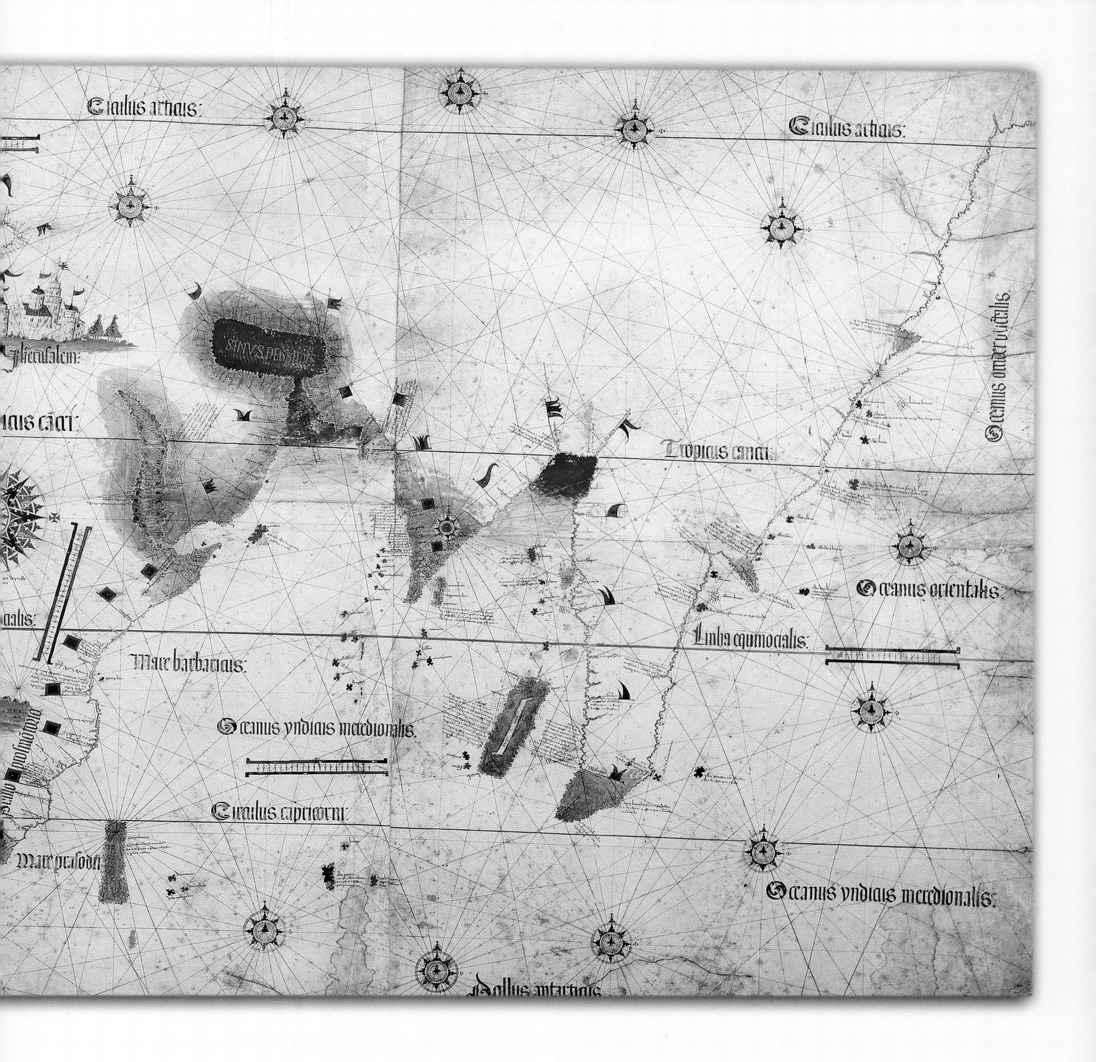

Cirailus arthais:

Cirailus arthais:

Oceanus amereuialis

Jelierusalem:

dais caur:

SINVS PERSIS

Tropicus cancri

Oceanus orientalis

alis:

Linha equinocialis:

Mare barbariais:

Oceanus yndicus meridionalis:

allo palmatoria

Cirailus capricorni:

Oceanus yndicus meridionalis:

Mare prasodu

Pollus antarticus:

1453–1707
Gunpowder Empires

■ Fall of Constantinople 1453 ■ Accession of first Safavid ruler of Persia 1501 ■ Suleiman I ascends the throne 1520 ■ Babur founds the Mughal Dynasty 1526 ■ Ottoman Empire at its zenith 1683 ■ Death of Mughal emperor Aurangzeb 1707

During the 16th century three adjoining Muslim Empires – of Turkey, Persia and India – together with their client states, controlled an area of Europe and Asia that stretched from the Atlantic to the Bay of Bengal.

By 1425, Turkey had recovered from Timur's invasion and resumed its advance in Europe. In 1453, after more than 1,000 years of empire, Byzantium fell. Whereas the Christian invaders had pillaged and destroyed, Sultan Mehmet II ('the Conqueror'; r.1451–81) conserved and rebuilt.

Shadow of God Over All Peoples

The new Ottoman city of Istanbul was carefully planned, with self-contained quarters intended for new immigrants. Christians and Jews were given their own representatives and Italians advised on the new Topkapi Palace, which Mehmet had sited on the model of the Athenian Acropolis. Istanbul was to be not only the centrepiece of the greatest Islamic power, but a cosmopolitan city, uniting Europe and Asia, and playing a leading role in world affairs.

Under Mehmet's successors, who rarely came to power without a general extermination of brothers, cousins and nephews, expansion in Europe continued. Serbia, Bosnia, Herzegovina, Belgrade and Rhodes were all annexed, enabling Sultan Suleiman I ('The Magnificent'; r.1520–66) to claim, over the doorway of the great mosque he erected to challenge Hagia Sophia, the Byzantine cathedral, to be 'mighty with divine power and resplendent with divine majesty … possessor of the kingdoms of the world Shadow of God over all peoples.' If exaggerated, this was nevertheless pardonable, for Turkish rule extended from (very nearly, apart from the Spanish African foothold at Ceuta) the Straits of Gibraltar to the Red Sea and from Adriatic to the Crimea.

Suleiman's contemporaries Charles V and Philip II of Spain, Elizabeth I of England, Ivan the Terrible

of Russia, the Mughal Emperor Akbar, the kings of France and the doges of Venice were usually more than content to remain in good terms with the Sublime Porte, as the Sultan's court was known. Talk of Crusades died out after the Christian victory at the naval Battle of Lepanto (1571) as it became clear that Turkey was a European power, to be dealt with by diplomacy as well as war. Suleiman's attacks on the Habsburg Empire, which brought him to the walls of Vienna in 1529, made him a natural ally of Charles V's enemy, Francis I of France; at one point the Turkish Sultan was joined with Pope Paul IV in making war on Spain.

The most implacable enemies of Turkey were not Christians but fellow Muslims, the Mamluk sultans of Cairo – the successors of Baibars – and the Shahs of Iran. Such foes had to be subdued by force, but it was 40 years before final victory over the Mamluks. In September 1516 Damascus fell, followed in January 1517 by Cairo. Sultan Selim I ('The Grim'; r.1512–20) was able to pray at the great Damascus mosque, the home of the first Caliphate in the eighth century and assume guardianship of the holy sites of Mecca, Medina and Jerusalem. The Ottomans, still regarded by many Muslims as uncouth Turkish upstarts, could now lay claim to the leadership of all Islam.

RIGHT *View of the Siege of Constantinople (Byzantium) in 1453, from a 15th-century French chronicle. After the Ottomans took the city, its new name Istanbul was derived from a Greek phrase meaning simply 'in the city'.*

LEFT *A 15th-century Ottoman miniature portraying Sultan Mehmet II smelling a rose. Mehmet conquered Constantinople when aged just 21.*

The annexation of Egypt brought with it the obligation to protect the sea-trade with India, which had been threatened by Portuguese aggression. Although the Portuguese usually got the better of the sea battles, a compromise was reached in 1562, which enabled an Ottoman expedition to sail to help the Muslim Sultan at Aceh, far distant in Sumatra. It was hardly decisive, but demonstrated the long reach of Turkish power.

In 1534, Suleiman married his favourite concubine, Hurren Sultan, who had already given him five sons. An excited Western observer described the celebrations as

> *'splendid beyond all record … At night the principal streets are gaily illuminated and there is much music and feasting. The houses are festooned with garlands and there are every where swings where people can swing by the hour with great enjoyment … a great tournament in which both Christian and Muslim knights were engaged and tumblers and jugglers and wild beasts and giraffes...'*

Two Britons visited the city in the early 1600s: William Lithgow found the girls 'lascivious indoors, and pleasing in matters of incontinency, who are wont to go bathe themselves in showers twice-a-week' – which must have added to their attractions. Fynes Moryson was, however, horrified by their habit of leaving decaying carcasses, human as well as animal, lying in the streets, 'which must explain the continual outburst of plague.' Istanbul became a world centre, receiving ambassadors from all Europe, playing off one against the other and entering into commercial agreements as with that of the London Levant Company in 1580, which continued for more than two centuries. Perhaps the most famous English visitor was the Lady Mary Wortley Montagu (1689–1782), wife of the British ambassador to Turkey, who brought back to England the practice of vaccination against smallpox and was admitted into the secrets of the seraglio (harem).

Turkish Sultans could claim wide powers, but only intermittently exercise them, having to rely on viziers to implement policies, and to act as regents during the Sultan's frequent absences on campaign. One constant factor overshadowing every Sultan was the doubtful loyalty of his palace guard, the Corps of Janissaries, infantry levied from Christian communities and rewarded with privileges and regular pay: their corps symbol was a spoon stuck in the hat, signifying their right to the communal and generous mess. Once unpaid or dissatisfied, a Janissary rebellion could, however, be fatal to the ruling Sultan. In the field, their fighting prowess was legendary: their discipline and command of musketry was unequalled. By the late 1680s, Ottoman expansion had reached its apogee, with the capture of Crete, the cession of the Ukraine, the maintenance of a border with the Black Sea Cossacks, and was followed by a slow decline.

The Sultans were usually indifferent Muslims, never, for example, making the obligatory pilgrimages to the Holy Places, but as Islam's spiritual rulers were responsible for exterminating heresy, which was a powerful weapon against the neighbouring Shi'a Persians, Turkey's most dogged enemies.

Shah of Shahs

Islam, as practised in Istanbul, was generally a tolerant religion, allowing Jews, Christians and even pagans to live – conditionally – in peace. The various dervish sects – the nearest Christian equivalent might be the Military Orders – were tolerated, as were Sufi intellectuals and mystics, who could be subversive. Nevertheless Islam has been, like Christianity, subject to internal disagreements, quite as bloody and permanent. Shi'a Islam, although in practice differing little from the 'Orthodox' Sunni practice, insists that the rightful caliphs descend from the Prophet's son-in-law and cousin Ali, and his son Hussein, whose death at the Battle of Karbala in 680 is commemorated every year with grieving processions, cries of 'Hussein', and flagellation. Many Shi'a also believe that the 'Twelfth Imam' will appear bodily as a Messiah, which gives an apocalyptic flavour to their expectations; this branch is known as 'Twelver' Islam.

Shi'a, which is professed by perhaps 10 to 15 percent of Muslims, is generally more mystical and emotional than Sunni, but for long periods the two variants of the same faith have, like Catholics and Protestants, coexisted in reasonable harmony. In the early 16th century, however, the contest became fiercer, beginning with the foundation of a new religious state, the Safavid dynasty of Iran, whose name came from a Shi'ite religious brotherhood, and which afforded protection to Shi'a oppressed by the Ottomans. To Istanbul clerics, these were heretics to be exterminated: the Mufti judged that one dead heretic was worth 70 Christians massacred, extirpation being a divine obligation. For their part, the Iranians, conscious of their own splendid heritage and the past glories of Persian civilization, tended to see the Turks as uncultivated barbarians. The first Safavid Shah Ismail (r.1501–24), had to fend off the Uzbek Tatars as well as Ottoman attacks. His forces suffered

LEFT *Persian miniature painting showing Ottoman soldiers parading before the walls of Tiflis (now Tbilisi, capital of Georgia). The Turks captured the evacuated city in 1582 during their military campaign against Safavid Persia.*

particularly from the Turkish gunnery, which had been perfected with European help and had been a decisive factor in the fall of Byzantium. Ismail relied on defence in depth, where the problems of feeding a large cavalry force would limit the Turkish army's ability to remain in the field, which did not prevent the Turks from taking Tabriz and Baghdad in 1534, the latter victory giving Suleiman yet another claim to Islamic hegemony by holding the second seat of the Caliphate.

More Iranian defeats followed until the succession of Shah Abbas (r.1587–1629) and his reorganization of the army along Turkish lines, with the formation of an imperial guard recruited from the Caucasus. Shah Abbas managed to withstand the ferocious Ottoman attacks by strategic withdrawals and tactical surprises, enabling the construction of what became perhaps the most splendid city in the world, Isfahan, with a population of 1 million, 163 mosques and 175 public baths (the contrast with odiferous European cities was striking). The vast Maydan-i-Char presents an incomparable cityscape, with two splendid mosques, the imperial palace and caravanserai, while adjoining arcades and a bazaar demonstrate the city's role as a trading centre, an essential part of the route to India and China. The British assisted in this effort by providing, through the brothers Robert and Anthony Shirley, men, horses and training and by the East India Company's assistance in ejecting the Portuguese from the Strait of Hormuz, marking the start of British commercial enterprise in Persia.

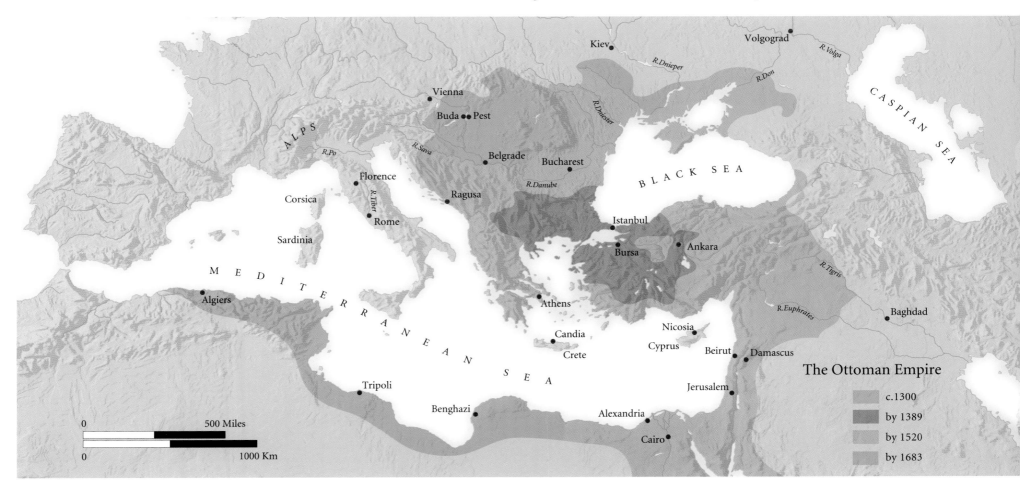

The Ottoman Empire

c.1300
by 1389
by 1520
by 1683

from his ancestry gave him a dubious claim to the much greater realm of the Afghan Shahs of Delhi, which extended down the River Ganges to Bengal. An invasion of India could expect vigorous opposition. Mahmud of Ghazni's conquests in the Punjab had been consolidated by another Afghan, Muhammad of Ghor, who invaded in 1186. In two decisive battles he defeated the strongest Hindu force, the Rajput Federation, took Delhi and pressed on down the Ganges. Five more dynasties succeeded the Ghorids, with varying degrees of success, and when Babur decided to invade in 1525 the Lodi Sultans held the region around Delhi, with the rest of the Subcontinent divided between a dozen Hindu and Muslim states. More wars, some with Persian support, left Babur with a well-trained army and an unexpected military tactic. This was not new, being precisely the same as the *Wagenburg* pioneered by the Bohemians in the Hussite wars, a quickly erected 'laager' of carts mounted with cannon and lined with musketeers, which would repel any attack yet allow the cavalry to pass through in pursuit. With the much improved firearms available to him Babur's armies were irresistible.

Neither Babur nor his men liked the dusty plains of northern India: in a list that reveals Persian preferences he complained that:

> '[The people] have no idea of the charms of friendly society, of frankly mixing together, or of familiar intercourse … they have no horses, no good flesh, no grapes or musk melons, no good fruits, no ice or cold water, no good food or bread in the bazaars, no baths or colleges, no candles, no torches, not a candlestick.'

His followers were persuaded to stay in India by the promises of wealth, but since Babur distributed almost all the plunder among his men, expansion into still unlooted regions was essential if the army was to be kept loyal: and more battles had to be fought with the relations of the Delhi Afghans and the resurgent Rajputs. Babur himself was forced to give up his beloved wine parties and conversations in placid gardens to adopt Islamic orthodoxy and return to the battlefields. He was never able to return to his beloved Kabul, but I am told the garden he planted there still remains a refuge even today.

His son Humayun (r.1530–56), a man of great charm and talent, courage, and ability, never realized other people's capacity for deceit, a dangerous failing in a ruler, not improved by an addiction to opium and a liking for writing poetry. By 1539, he found himself a refugee in Isfahan, sheltered by Shah Tamasp, after his father's empire was seized by another Afghan, Sher Khan (whose name was appropriated by the author Rudyard Kipling for the wily tiger in his work of 1894, *The Jungle Book*). As it turned out, it was fortunate for the Mughals, since Sher Khan reorganized the army and established a methodical civil government.

In the interval, Humayun, with Persian support, had begun to retake his lost empire, and in 1554 he was back in Delhi. Meeting a fate suitable for the scholar and poet, he died after a fall down the library stairs. His son,

The huge and richly decorated mosques of Isfahan demonstrate the theocratic nature of the state. Founded as it was on a religious ideal, great power was appropriated by the *Ulama,* the synod of elders and learned men who defined the law. The Safavid kingdom was comparatively shortlived, but the influence of the *Ulama* continued, to resurface powerfully in the 1978 rebellion against the Shah. Over a century's warfare, Shah Ismail's successors contrived to hold off the Turks, leaving the Persian heartland undisturbed, permitting the intact transmission of the ancient language, culture and civilization.

The Great Mughals

Shah Ismail and the first Mughal emperor, Zahir-ud-din, were almost exact contemporaries and were both men of wide-ranging ability. Better known as Babur ('The Tiger'; r.1526–30), Zahir-ud-din claimed to descend from both Timur and Genghis Khan. He left an autobiography, one of the most impressive documents of the period, which reveals a fallible, conscientious, humorous man who became the greatest ruler of his age. Heir at the age of 11 to Fergana, a small kingdom north of the Oxus (now in Uzbekistan), held by other descendants of Timur, Babur spent the next 10 years in constant warfare, often suffering defeats, before acquiring from an uncle another kingdom, that of Kabul. It was a small power base, but the prestige devolving

Akbar (r.1556–1605), was only 13 years old: but Babur had been no older, and Akbar was as lucky and as gifted, and a good deal more realistic. He was not only a conqueror, but a constructive imperialist: once subdued, the new provinces were integrated into the empire. The acquisition of Gujarat – secured after a cavalry march of 600 miles (960 km) in nine days – brought with it the port of Surat and sea access to Persia and Egypt. Bengal, the richest province of India, was taken by 1576. At Akbar's death, the Mughal empire extended from Afghanistan to the Bay of Bengal and well into central and southern India. Although military power was firmly retained in Muslim hands, Hindus were integrated into the administration. The Rajputs were brought firmly on side, and Akbar married a Rajput princess. His administration formed the model not only for his successors, but for the British when they replaced the Mughal *Raj.*

Akbar's India was huge, supporting a population of perhaps 100 million, at a time when that of Europe was some 50 million, and Britain not more than six million. Expenses, too, were enormous. A standing army of 300,000 was paid, and perhaps half were actually available in the ranks. The world's largest artillery park was maintained, with hundreds of elephants and hundreds and thousands of horses, for most Mughal armies were primarily cavalry. Almost all of the state's income went on maintaining the armies and financing the lavish building programmes. Babur's generous distributions were replaced by a well-organized revenue-collecting system, with collection farmed through a series of officials, and all bearing heavily on the peasant. A French observer remarked that nobody worked in the fields except under compulsion, and rural misery on the edges of flamboyant prosperity remains an Indian characteristic. But all Indian farmers had already experienced 3,000 years at the bottom of an onerous pile, and many of them had seen 600 years of foreign domination, making peasant rebellion unlikely except on those rare occasions when an inspiring leader materialized.

Mughal administration, whether in Delhi, Agra or Lahore, all of which served as capitals, provided a model for the later British *Raj.* Four ministries, War, Finance, Law, and Works, were staffed by officials, often Hindu, graded in military fashion, forming a corps of expert bureaucrats. The 'chitty' became an essential instrument of accounting, and later British civil servants evolved equally complex equations of perceived status by official honours and unspoken social conventions.

All observers were impressed by Mughal splendour. Sir Thomas Roe, sent from London to petition for an imperial 'firman' allowing the East India Company to trade freely, described Akhab's son, Jahangir:

> '*His sash was wreathed about with a chaine of great pearles, rubyes and diamonds, drilld. About his neck he carried a chaine of most excellent pearle, three double (so great I never saw); at his elbowes, armlets set with diamonds; and on his wrists three rowes of several sorts.*'

Sir Thomas insisted that the right course for the English was to remain modest, not hoping to establish forts, like the unpopular Portuguese: 'but if you will profit, seek it at sea and in quiet trade': but quiet trade was not always possible.

Although the dynasty struggled on for another 150 years, Aurangzeb (r.1658–1707) was the last of the 'Great Mughals'. The following century witnessed the reign of no fewer than nine emperors, with at least three of them dying violently.

The history of India's rulers before the British *Raj* is evident in its varied architecture, from the massive Delhi forts and the towering minaret of the Qu'tb Minar of the 14th-century Tughluq Sultans, through Humayun's tomb to the tranquil beauty of the Taj Mahal: close by, Fatehpur Sikri survives as a pristine Mughal city. The memorials of the Mughals' opponents are no less striking – the Rajput palaces and Raja Man Singh's monstrously impressive citadel at Gwalior testify both to the powers ranged against the Mughals and to India's success in uniting and preserving its society – and indeed to the Mughals' successors, the British, in governing the country as a single entity. On a smaller scale the exquisite miniatures and illuminated manuscripts depict the glories of the imperial court and the warriors' magnificence; and, just occasionally, afford a glimpse into the life of ordinary people.

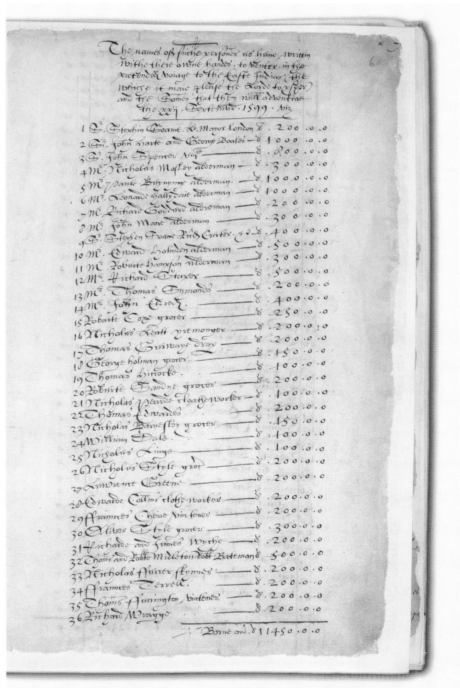

The first subscription list for the British East India Company, 22 September 1599. The company grew to acquire enormous wealth and influence, administering India until the Mutiny of 1857–58, when direct government rule was instituted.

THE MODERN WORLD FORMS

	1600	1640	1660	1680	1700

EUROPE

1603 James VI of Scotland crowned James I of England

1618 The Thirty Years' War starts, primarily between Catholics and Protestants

1629–40 Charles I of England attempts to rule without Parliament

1638 The Ottomans under Murad IV retake Baghdad from Persia

1640 The Portuguese reclaim their independence from Spain

1642–46 In the First Civil War in Britain, Parliament defeats the king

1648 Treaty of Westphalia ends the Thirty Years' War

1649 Charles I executed; the Commonwealth under Oliver Cromwell set up

LEFT *A statue of Oliver Cromwell outside parliament, London, England*

ABOVE *William of Orange arrives in England in 1688, to be greeted by the English lion in this contemporary engraving*

1660 Restoration of the English monarchy under Charles II

1683 Siege of Vienna: the Ottomans defeated

1688 Stuart King James II of Britain replaced by William II of Orange and Queen Mary during the 'Glorious Revolution'

1700 Start of the Great Northern War between Russia and Sweden

1701–14 The War of Spanish Succession involving all major European powers

1707 Act of Union unites Scotland and England as Great Britain

1713 Treaty of Utrecht ends the War of Spanish Succession

1714 Elector of Hanover becomes George I of Britain

THE AMERICAS

1607 Foundation of the first permanent English settlement at Jamestown

1608 French settlers found the colony of Quebec

1625 Barbados becomes the 'richest place in the New World'

1620 The Pilgrim colonists arrive at Cape Cod

1626 The Dutch settle New Amsterdam, later known as New York

1636 Harvard University founded

1656 English capture Jamaica from Spain

1670 The English Hudson's Bay Company established to trade furs with native people

RIGHT *An anonymous 18th century portrait of George I*

1680 Portugal bans the enslavement of Brazilian native peoples

1681–82 La Salle explores the Mississippi and claims the whole area for France

1699 French colony of Louisiana founded

LEFT *A map of New England of 1616, featuring John Smith of Jamestown*

1700 Collapse of Scots colony at Darieb

1701 First treaty between the French and Iroquois

1711 The French sack Rio de Janeiro during the War of Spanish Succession

1716 Spain occupies part of Texas

AFRICA AND OCEANIA

1606 The Dutch 'discover' Australia at what today is called Cape York Peninsula

1626 The French establish an outpost on Madagascar

1642–43 Abel Tasman sails around Australia and names New Zealand

1652 Cape Town founded by Dutch settlers

1672 Dutch officially 'buy' Cape Colony from Khoikhoi

1677 The French build a fort on the island of Gorée, south of the mouth of the Senegal River

1684 Around what today is Zimbabwe, African chief Changamire Dombo builds the Rozwi empire and expels the Portuguese

1698 Oman takes control of Zanzibar

1701 The kingdom of Asante emerges

1713 British slave trade to Spanish America begins

1758–83 Britain and France clash over control of Senegal

ASIA

1603 Foundation of the Tokugawa shogunate in Japan

1609 Dutch rule established in coastal Java

1615 The Manchus unite and begin the conquest of the ailing Ming empire

1627–1658 Shah Jahan builds Taj Mahal and New Delhi capital

1644 Capture of Beijing by Manchurian Qing marks the end of the Ming dynasty

1661 English East India Company base is set up in Bombay, India

1668 The French establish their first factory in India, at Surat

1680 Shivaji dies having established Maratha power

1683 The Manchus conquer Formosa, later known as Taiwan

1697 Western Mongolia is conquered by China

1707 Death of Aurangzeb, last, 'Great Mughal'

1727 Chinese–Russian border fixed by the Kyakhta treaty

1739 Persians defeat Mughals at Karnal and sack Delhi

1600–1820

RIGHT Storming the Bastille, *painted in the last part of the 18th century by an unknown artist*

1740 War of the Austrian Succession starts; accession of Frederick II 'the Great' of Prussia, who raises Prussia to a major European power

1748 Treaty of Aix-la-Chapelle ends the War of the Austrian Succession

1756–63 The Seven Years' War fought by alliances of Austria, France, Saxony, Sweden and Russia against Britain, Prussia and Hanover

1768 War breaks out between Russia and the Ottomans

1772 First partition of Poland between Russia, Prussia and Austria

1783 Russia annexes the Crimea; Treaty of Paris ends the Seven Years' War

1788 Louis XVI summons the Estates-General

1789 French Revolution starts; the Bastille is stormed

1792 Austria and Prussia ally against France

1793 Execution of Louis XVI; a royalist rebellion begins in the Vendee; Spain, Holland and Britain join the First Coalition against France

1795 End of Polish independence

1798 Failed nationalist rebellion in Ireland; the French are defeated by the British at the Battle of the Nile

1799 Napoleon Bonaparte returns to France and seizes power as First Consul

1800 Napoleon defeats the Austrians at Marengo

1802 Act of Union unites Britain and Ireland

1805 British victory over the French fleet at Trafalgar; Napoleon defeats Austro-Russian armies at Austerlitz

1808 Spanish uprising against the French; start of the Peninsular War

1812 Napoleon's invasion of Russia ends in retreat

1813 Napoleon defeated at Leipzig

1814 Napoleon abdicates and is exiled to the island of Elba

1815 Final defeat of Napoleon at Waterloo

1814 Poland united with the Russian empire

1814–15 Congress of Europe sets the political future of Europe

1815–17 Serbian uprisings lead to independence from the Ottomans

---

1741 Bering explores the south coast of Alaska

1759 James Wolfe defeats the French army of Montcalm at Quebec

BELOW The Death of General Wolfe, *painted in 1770. Wolfe died after his victory over the French at Quebec*

1763 Treaty of Paris gives Canada and all land east of the Mississippi to Britain

1773 Boston Tea Party

1774 The First Continental Congress

1775 Start of the American Revolution

1776 Declaration of Independence

1781 French army and navy arrive to besiege British at Yorktown, forcing final surrender

1783 Treaty of Paris confirms US independence; official end of the American Revolution

1787 The Philadelphia Convention adopts the Constitution of the United States

1789 George Washington takes office as the first President of the United States

RIGHT *Portrait of George Washington by Glibert Stuart (1755–1828)*

1803 Under the Louisiana Purchase, France sells province of Louisiana to United States

1807 Britain declares the slave trade illegal

1807 The US Congress passes a law that bans the importation of slaves into the United States. It is largely ignored by the southern states

1810 Mexican war of independence begins

1812–14 United States at war with colonial Britain; Canada defended by colonists and Indians

1815 Brazil becomes an independent kingdom jointly with Portugal

1818 Agreement reached on fixing the US–Canadian frontier on the 49th Parallel

1819 Spain cedes Florida to the United States

1768–71 James Cook's first voyage to Tahiti, New Zealand and Australia

1772–75 James Cook's second voyage in which he circumnavigates the globe

1787 The first freed slaves settle in Sierra Leone

1788 First transported British convicts arrive at Botany Bay, Australia

1792 The first white settlers land in New Zealand

1795 The first British settlers land at the Cape of Good Hope

1803 Penal settlement set up on Van Diemen's Land (Tasmania)

1807 Britain bans the slave trade

1814 Britain acquires Cape Colony from the Dutch

1814 New South Wales, Australia, claims New Zealand as a dependency

1816 Shaka becomes king of the Zulus in southern Africa

1751 Chinese invade Tibet, establishing control over the succession of the Dalai Lama

1757 The British defeat the French at Plassey and Chandernagore

1765 British control Bengal and Bihar

1781 British forces take Dutch settlements in west Sumatra

1793 Emperor Qianlong snubs the British trade mission

1799 The ruler of Mysore, Tipu Sahib, defeated by Cornwallis and killed

ABOVE *The emblem of the society for the abolition of the slave trade*

1809 Ranjit Singh establishes Sikh kingdom

1816 War between Nepalese and British settled

Early Modern Europe

■ Thirty Years' War ends with the Treaty of Westphalia 1648 ■ Execution of Charles I 1649 ■ Defeat of the Ottomans at the Second Siege of Vienna 1683 ■ Outbreak of the Great Northern War 1700 ■ Death of Catherine II ('The Great') of Russia 1796

For many years students were taught that Modern History began in 1485, with the accession of the first Tudor, or perhaps 1492, when Columbus landed in Cuba. More recently, and more plausibly, scholars have tended to identify the origins of modern Europe in the 17th century.

This was the period when European nation-states began to form and when one of today's major powers, Russia, emerged onto the world stage, advancing with astonishing rapidity, well ahead, culturally and intellectually of its current rival, then the British North American colonies.

A Good Question

'Modern Europe began in the cities of Münster and Osnabrück on 28 October 1648. Discuss.' Questions such as this have always attracted history examiners, and exploring answers can be profitable. Certainly the twin Treaties of Westphalia signed in those cities between the German Empire, Sweden, France and their many allies brought Europe's protracted wars of religion to an end. The Thirty Years' War (1618–48) had been a confused and bloody struggle; it can be viewed as Protestant North against Catholic South, or as independent princes against the Austrian Empire and at the end a brisk fight between the old enemies, France and Spain. The treaties formally recognized the Protestant Republics of Switzerland and the United Provinces of Holland, helped to ensure freedom of worship and redefined international frontiers, to the considerable advantage of France. Germany, where the battles had taken place, was devastated, its population reduced from over 20 to perhaps 13 million, with many of the survivors impoverished. Atrocities had been widespread; in particular, the Magdeburg massacre of 1631, in which 25,000 civilians were killed, horrified all Europe.

Pope Innocent X was furious at this tolerance extended to heretics and issued a Bull annulling the treaties. It was simply ignored. Cardinal Richelieu said that in dealing with the Pope 'one must kiss his feet and bind his hands.' The Holy Roman Empire became not much more than a fiction, lending some lustre to the Habsburg rulers of Austria and what remained of Hungary, with the Imperial Diet little more than a debating chamber for the German principalities. The settlement was not permanent: discrimination in individual states remained, notably in Britain, where Catholics' civil liberties continued to be restricted for another 200 years, and France, where a born-

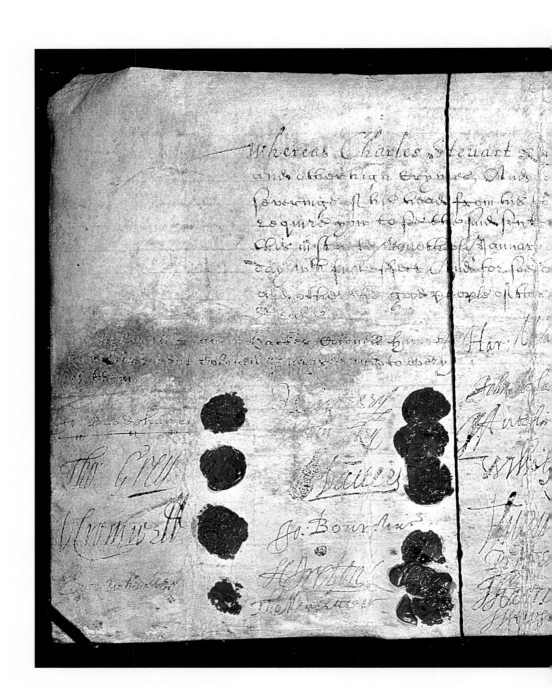

again Louis XIV revoked previously guaranteed Protestant rights, resulting in the emigration of many of the most prosperous and talented French. Wars continued for old-fashioned territorial or dynastic motives. During the remainder of Louis XIV's reign France started four more major European wars, which ended in 1713 with another international treaty, the Peace of Utrecht. France had gained some territory, but ruined her economy in this succession of conflicts, and a new power had emerged on the European scene.

Britain had not been involved in the Thirty Years' War nor represented in the peace negotiations. In the first part of the 17th century the country had been peripheral to European affairs, engaged in no serious land warfare since its defeat in the Hundred Years' War (1453). Queen Elizabeth had been succeeded by James I of England and VI of Scotland, intellectual and cautious in foreign affairs, but inept at handling the fractious English parliament. His son Charles I, sublimely confident in his own divine authority, had provoked the Civil War (1642–51), which ended with his own execution and the emergence of the Commonwealth, under Oliver Cromwell as Lord Protector of a united British Republic. The religious settlement in England had been a compromise between ardent reformers and traditionalists, while that in Scotland had acknowledged the radical, even extreme, popular Presbyterianism. England and Scotland were united, somewhat resentfully, for the first time and resistance in Ireland was crushed. A modern standing army was formed– the oldest regiment of Foot Guards, the Coldstreams,

dates from the Protectorate, as does the organization of a navy strong enough to defeat the Dutch, at that time the unchallenged sea power. In 1658, the Catholic King Louis XIV of France welcomed Cromwell's red-coated New Model Army, cooperating with Marshal Turenne to beat the Spanish – and the royalist British – on the Dunkirk Dunes.

One of the many alternative dates that might therefore be put forward as the start of modern Europe could be 18 December 1655, when Cromwell overruled the Council of State to insist that Jews be allowed to return to Britain. As Lord Protector he was responsible for the welfare of all people as long as they obeyed the law. It was the start of a tolerant ideal, not by any means always realized, but one which became a benchmark of modern civil society.

The collective behind Cromwell's ideals was known as the 'Invisible College', a group of scholars and scientists, mainly Dutch and British but including one surviving Hussite-inspired Czech, Jan Komensky, better known as John Comenius; the industrious polymath, Samuel Hartlib; William Petty, whose economic geography of Ireland inspired a whole new discipline; and the pioneer physicist Robert Boyle. The work of these men and their friends, rising above political and sectarian disputes became the basis of the Royal Society. Another demonstration of tolerance was the fate of Oliver Cromwell's family after the restoration of the Stuart King Charles II in 1660:

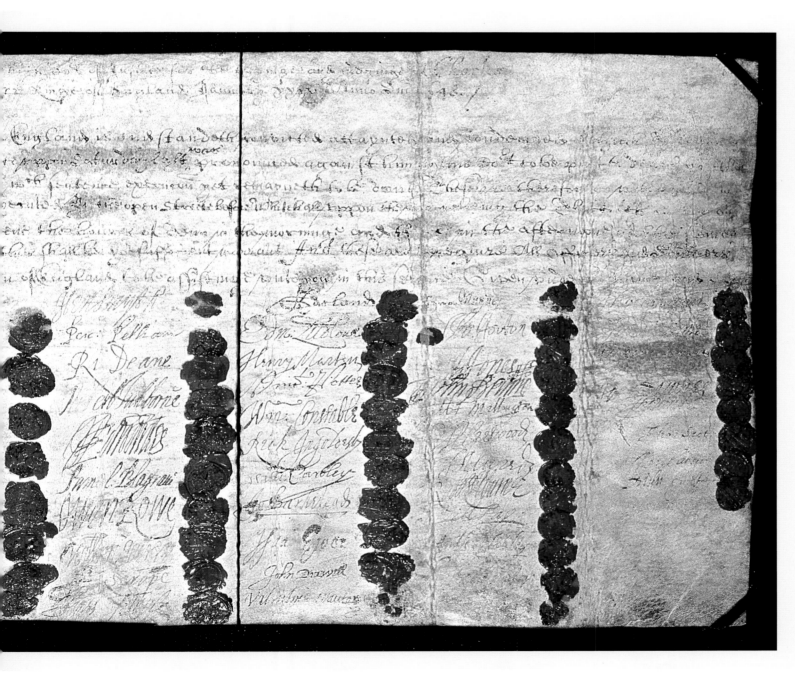

The death warrant for Charles I, signed and sealed in 1649 by the 59 Commissioners who sat in judgement at the king's trial. Under the Restoration, the body of the most famous regicide, Oliver Cromwell, was disinterred in order to be hung, drawn and quartered.

Protestantism, which had initially swept through Hungary, was strenuously suppressed by Leopold, to the extent that Transylvania, which had become independent and Protestant-inclined, looked to the more tolerant Turks for aid. When the Turks began what was to be their final push into Europe in the spring of 1683 one flank of the advance was entrusted to the Transylvanians, fighting alongside Turks and Tatars. In spite of the terrible weather – the 80 wagons carrying the harem ladies were an especial impediment – an enormous army had surrounded Vienna by July. Had heavy artillery taken the place of the ladies, the siege might have been over quickly. No help was to be expected from the French: the Habsburgs, not the Ottomans, were King Louis' enemies. Catholic Bavaria and Protestant Saxony sent troops, but the decisive factor was the arrival of the Polish-Lithuanian cavalry, which after a fierce struggle swept aside the Turkish army: the Polish king, John Sobieski, wrote to his wife:

ABOVE *The final Ottoman challenge to Christian Europe came with Grand Vizier Kara Mustafa's siege of Vienna in 1683. A combined German and Polish force under John Sobieski defeated the Turks at the Battle of Kahlenberg. This painting of the event is by the German artist Franz Geffels (1688).*

'I find it quite impossible to convey to you the exquisite luxury of the Vizier's tents: there are baths, small gardens fountains, rabbits and even a parrot.'

Cromwell's son Richard, the last Lord Protector, died in modest obscurity in Chalfont, aged 86. His younger brother Henry was allowed to retain his Irish estates, and lived peacefully in Cambridgeshire, unmolested by the government, until his death in 1674. If France at this period, under the *Roi Soleil,* represented strong centralized monarchy, Britain was now, having executed one king and on the point of deposing another (James II in 1688), the model of a limited constitutional monarchy.

James II, able and fair-minded, would have made a good king but for a fatal defect; he was a devout Roman Catholic. In 1688, the Whig magnates invited William of Orange, the Protestant Dutch leader, grandson of Charles I and husband of James' daughter Mary, to secure the throne against any revival of a Roman Catholic monarchy supported by the Irish and French. Britain, previously anti-Dutch, now found herself pitted against France. By this stage, Britain was well on the way to becoming a world power, capable of projecting her might to any part of the globe where a battleship could float.

Turkish Decline

Habsburg Austria, much smaller than in Emperor Sigismund's day, was ruled by the unimpressive Leopold I (r.1658–1705) described in unflattering terms by a Turkish envoy as having 'huge white camel's teeth … whenever he speaks, saliva pours … from his camel's lips'. The envoy went on:

'All his dynasty is as ugly as him, and his hideous image is found in all churches and houses and on coinage.'

He also discovered the headless bodies of a favourite ostrich and the Vizier's chief concubine. Those same splendid Ottoman tents, preserved in the Krakow Museum in Poland, still testify to the victory.

Fighting continued, with the Turks usually coming off worst, until a peace was finally settled in 1699: the fact that negotiations had been started by King William III of Britain, was an intimation that Britain was now acting as a European power broker.

William's first attempt at mediation, in 1688, failed in the face of renewed war with the French in which the British, Dutch and Austrians formed a Grand Alliance. Progress depended upon the Turks being convinced that they were losing ground, a conclusion forced upon Istanbul following the Habsburg general Prince Eugene of Savoy's crushing victory at Zenta north of Belgrade in September 1697, reinforced by the fact that in a separate campaign the Venetians had recaptured the Peloponnese and Athens, in the course of which the Acropolis was badly damaged. The peace conference that took place on the Danube in October of the next year was driven by the British delegate, William, Lord Paget, in whom tact was combined with persistence. The Treaty of Karlowitz, a triumph of British diplomacy, concluded after four months of tedious negotiations, signified the end of the Turkish threat. Paget was asked to stay at the Sultan's court, which he did until 1702.

The Emergence of Russia

Another case could be made for identifying the mid-17th century as the start of modern Europe by looking to the east. Russia as a definable country begins with the defeat of the Tatars in 1380 and St Sergius' establishment of his Moscow monastery, followed by the monastic-led expansion which resulted

in the Russian Church's ownership of some two-thirds of the land. Grand Prince Ivan III of Moscow (r.1462–1505) began an invasion of the huge sprawling territory extending from the White Sea and the Ural Mountains to the border of Lithuania, and centred on the ancient city of Novgorod. When Ivan IV ('The Terrible') succeeded in 1547 he was crowned Tsar of all the Russias and began the work of pulling together the dozens of minor principalities, bolstered by the Church's recognition; after Byzantium's collapse the Russian Tsar could claim leadership of the Orthodox faith.

There were some parallels with Charlemagne's situation 800 years previously. Both monarchs claimed an imperium over their part of Christendom and faced the task of assembling many different races, communities and traditions into an acceptable whole. Charlemagne had one great advantage that Ivan and his successors lacked – Latin, not only the liturgical language, but the lingua franca of diplomacy and administration, with a millennium of culture, debate and philosophy to enrich it. 16th-century Russian was only completing its evolution from Old East Slavic, understood by nobody east of the Carpathians, while its written form was totally unfamiliar to most of its population. Ivan IV's own letters – and their authenticity is disputed – are among the earliest examples of quasi-literary Russian. Russia's relative cultural backwardness at this stage is brought sharply into focus when one considers that Ivan was a contemporary of the formidably learned Queen Elizabeth I of England, as well as of Shakespeare and Montaigne. Ironically

ABOVE *Tsar Ivan IV, whose reign (1547–84) saw Russia expand south to the Caspian Sea and east beyond the Urals, was a violent and autocratic ruler. Notoriously, he killed his own son (above) in 1581 during a furious argument, as shown in this work by the 19th-century painter Ilya Repin.*

one of the first notable works in Russian is the autobiography of Petrov Avvakum, a conservative Church leader who was exiled to Serbia before being burnt as a heretic: that was in 1682, yet within 150 years of his death Russia was leading the world in literature and music, surely the most rapid advance of civilization in modern times.

Ivan's first task was to control the boyars, an unruly collection of nobles, by establishing a constitutional two-chamber Council, with gentry and merchants included, reinforced by a secret police charged with sniffing out potential traitors whose estates could be profitably sequestrated. It was a painful process, which earned Ivan IV the sobriquet of *Grozniy*, translated into English as 'the Terrible,' but more accurately 'the Formidable'.

The map of Europe in 1648 was dominated by the Polish/Lithuanian/ Ukrainian Commonwealth, by some way the largest European state and the successor to the medieval kingdom of Poland and Grand Duchy of Lithuania. It was not to last, for Cossack rebellion and invasions from Russia, Sweden

and Germany had sliced off much of the Ukraine and the region of Kiev by 1667. For the time being Russia prudently stayed out of the Thirty Years' War, and as far as possible, avoided clashes with the other eastern giant, the Ottoman Empire. With the first Romanov tsars, Emperor Michael and his son Alexei (r.1613–81), Russia began to assert its leadership in Eastern Europe: the Tsar whose representatives attended the Karlowitz conference was Peter I ('The Great'; r.1682–1725). Lord Paget described the much-altered Russians in 1702:

> '*The Muscovite Ambassador and his retinue have appeared here so different from what they always formerly were that the Turks cannot tell what to make of them. They are all courted in French habit, with an abundance of gold and silver lace, long peruques and, which the Turks most wonder at, without beards.*'

Peter's psychology remains an engrossing problem: he was probably clinically insane, and his behaviour sometimes grotesque – he ordered his son and heir to be beaten to death – but his policies were rational enough. His 18-month sojourn in Western Europe, as far distant as Holland and England, formed his ideas on Russia's future and inspired a programme which ranged from forcing his nobles to shave and dress in French fashions, through insisting that scythes, rather than sickles be used in harvesting, to an organization of provincial and local governments, state control of the Church and subsidies for science and the arts, all consciously modelled on Swedish practice. Russia, although in many respects retaining pre-feudal attitudes abandoned in the West for a millennium, was dragged – albeit only in part – into the 18th century. Conquered territories were stripped of their populations, who were deported as serfs to reward successful Russian officers.

Russian expansion was, however, very distinctively in accordance with contemporary practice. The Great Northern War, the struggle between Russia and Sweden, which began in 1700, was decided by 1710, but spluttered on for another decade, ensuring Russia her first ice-free port, serviceable throughout most of the year, where the tsar began construction of Russia's new capital. Only Louis XIV of France left so architecturally impressive a heritage as Peter of Russia, but with a much finer setting and on a vastly greater scale, a capital city rather than a single palace complex, St Petersburg eclipses Versailles.

Previously Russia had been hemmed in by Turkey, Poland, Lithuania and Sweden: at Peter's death her territory extended along the southern Baltic coasts and into the Gulf of Finland. A commercial treaty with the Shah of Persia was followed by a full-scale Russian invasion and the establishment of access to the Caspian Sea. From 1717, the Russian tsar gained the right to intervene 'to restore order' in Poland at any time. Between 1768 and 1795, the right was exercised three times, with Russia taking a little more of Poland on each occasion. Independent Poland and Lithuania ceased to exist, except, and vitally, in the hearts of the people.

LEFT *Portrait of Tsar Peter I of Russia at the Battle of Poltava by the German painter Gottfried Tannauer (1680–1737). During Peter's reign, Russia modernized its economy and industry and by 1721, it had gained ascendancy over its old Baltic rival, the kingdom of Sweden.*

For most of the 18th century after Peter's death, Russia was ruled, autocratically and effectively, by remarkable women. Both the Empress Elizabeth (r.1741–62) and Empress Catherine (r.1762–96) were German by birth, and between them were responsible for propelling Russia into the centre of European politics. Both came to power as a result of a coup, marching at the head of the guards to depose the previous tsar – very finally for Catherine's husband Peter, murdered on the orders of one of her lovers.

Catherine has exercised the same fascination over subsequent generations as Elizabeth I of England, and there are many parallels between the two queens. Their gifts for choosing talented ministers, playing the game of diplomacy and leadership in war were notable, as was their formidable capacity for learning. Catherine, although a child of the Enlightenment, appreciated how unprepared Russia was for any dramatic change. Her most radical step was to summon a representative commission, on the pattern of the French Estates but without the clergy, to draft a constitution. It proved an impossible task, and in due course the assembly faded, but it did demonstrate for the first time that Russians could elect and run the prototype of a parliament.

Catherine's diplomacy ensured that France, Prussia and Austria all vied for Russian support: the commissariat and the supplies might be primitive, but the sheer weight of numbers made a Russian army formidable enough to defeat the finest soldier of his age, Frederick III ('The Great') of Prussia. After the conquest of the Crimea, Georgia, and what remained of the Ukraine, Catherine was able to take Emperor Joseph of Austria and the ambassadors of all the leading European powers on a tour of inspection (carefully stage-managed by Prince Grigory Potemkin, her chief minister and lover) which included the new cities of Sebastapol and Odessa: Russian fleets were now within three days' sail of either Constantinople or Copenhagen.

Unparalleled as was Russia's precipitous geopolitical advance, it was matched by the extraordinary development of Russian culture. From newly developed literacy the Russian language produced, within 30 years of each other, two of the world's greatest writers, Feodor Dostoevsky and Leo Tolstoy, the multi-talented Nicolas Gogol, and two fine poets in Alexander Pushkin and Mikhail Lermontov. The ancestry of the new writers reflected the opening of Russian society during the 18th century: Lermontov (Learmont) had Scottish forebears; Gogol was Ukrainian; while Pushkin had German, Scandinavian and even African ancestors. Few other countries have ever experienced such a brilliant literary effervescence, which was followed a generation later by an equally gifted group of musicians: Rimsky Korsakov, Borodin, Tchaikovsky, Balakirev and Mussorgsky, all born within 10 years of each other. Certainly Russia's population was huge, but its educated middle and upper class was still very restricted, making this galaxy of genius the more astonishing.

RIGHT *An 18th-century political cartoon from England shows Catherine the Great as the 'Russian Bear' being ridden by her minister Grigory Potemkin, with the English monarchy and parliament opposing her.*

European Imperial Expansion

■ The Pilgrim Fathers found Plymouth Colony 1620 ■ Jan Pieterszoon Coen founds Batavia, capital of the Dutch East Indies 1621 ■ Gold discovered at Minas Gerais in Brazil 1693 ■ British slave trade is officially opened to all private traders 1698 ■ Collapse of the Darien Scheme 1720

The Treaty of Utrecht in 1713 concluded one phase of the intermittent war between Britain and France. Through the acquisition of Gibraltar and Minorca, Britain demonstrated that the Mediterranean was not to be a French lake. Meanwhile in Canada, the British possession of the northeast, Newfoundland, Acadia, Labrador and the Hudson Bay hinterland was conceded, but the interior of North America remained disputed territory between the two rival states.

The privilege of trading with Spanish America – the *asiento* – was granted to Britain, securing the lion's share of the slave trade, and its associated benefits. The American continent was divided between Spain and Britain, with Portugal holding on in Brazil and France attempting to do so in Canada.

A Score of Scattered Colonies

At the start of the 17th century some 1,500 miles (2,400 km) of fertile land had lain available along the eastern seaboard of North America, from the St Lawrence River to the Spanish fort of San Augustino in Florida. Other European nations saw no reason why they should not take it over. The climate was not disagreeable, the land potentially productive, navigable waterways led to the interior, and with the coast provided abundant fish. It seemed however that only the English were prepared, or able, to make a real effort and by the time of Utrecht the whole coast had been marked off as British colonies. God had, it seemed, helped. The hand of God had been 'eminently seen in thinning the Indians, to make room for the English' operating through smallpox, measles, the common cold and similar European diseases, which reduced the Indian population to not much more than a tenth. An opportunity to prosper was offered to all Britons willing to bestir themselves, for religious fanatics and social experimenters to try out their theories in practice. The mechanics were the same in all the colonies. The British Crown assumed possession of the land, there being no 'pre-eminent rulers' with whom to negotiate, and granted it, on conditions, to Chartered Companies and individuals, who evolved some decidedly odd societies: all reflected, to a greater or less degree, in the United States today.

Massachusetts developed as a democratic theocracy, votes being restricted to church members but everyone was required to attend services. The Founders'

children had to demonstrate that they were truly 'born again' in order to be accepted into the community: public evidence of private virtue was therefore essential. There was no aristocracy or even gentry: social status depended on wealth, respectability, intellectual distinction and the gift of oratory; with at least six hours of sermons to be undergone each week this was much appreciated. Penalties for straying were severe. Quakers as well as witches were executed in 17th-century Boston. Connecticut and Rhode Island, Massachusetts' daughter colonies, were rather more liberal, but all shared the same devotion to regular family life, hard work and commercial probity: altogether a formidable recipe for success.

In Rhode Island, the first land was purchased from the Indians, rather than being merely appropriated, but in all colonies some consciences were troubled by the wholesale confiscation of Indian lands and the sometimes brutal treatment of the inhabitants. Virginians had a simple answer, deciding that:

'it is infinitely better to have no heathen among us … than to be at peace and league with them.'

and proceeded to occupy large tracts of land for tobacco plantations. A high proportion of the immigrants were indentured servants, with a number of black slaves arriving in the later years, all encouraging social stratification emphasized with formal codes of manners. The states of Virginia, Baltimore and Maryland had only a shadowy central government, with the administration being devolved to shires. Lacking the rigid Puritan government of the northern colonies, the Chesapeake Bay citizens prospered on tobacco exports, living in a generally cheerful muddle.

ABOVE *Painting showing a group of Puritans about to board ship in Delft harbour to join the* Mayflower *on her voyage to the New World by the 17th century Dutch artist Adam van Breen. The promise of religious freedom took many pilgrims to America.*

To the north, the Dutch colony of the New Netherlands, which surrendered in 1664 to become New York, and the colonies of East and West New Jersey and Delaware, with a mixed settler population of Dutch and Swedes, were already well established with large landholders who fitted easily into British society. New York's constitution was designed by its founder King James II, as Duke of York, with minimal democracy but religious toleration. New Jersey was granted to two of James' supporters, who sold off the western half to a London Company of Quakers. West Jersey was subsumed into the Quaker colony formed by William Penn in 1681. By some way the most original of the colonial constitutions, that of Pennsylvania, was sketched out by Penn himself, with an appointed Legislative Council and a popularly elected Assembly, albeit with only modest powers, providing land in relatively small manageable areas, and offering wide individual freedoms.

Further south lay the colonies of North and South Carolina, granted in 1663 by Charles II to a group of Lords Proprietor one of whom, Lord Shaftesbury, designed the constitution with the aid of his secretary, the philosopher John

Locke. It was an oddity such as only a philosopher might achieve, envisaging an aristocracy of 'landgraves' and 'cassiques' that would guard against 'a numerous democracy.' Naturally enough dissension ensued, culminating in a request in 1714 that the Crown take direct control of those colonies. In their varying degrees however, all the colonies prospered, and by the end of the 17th century were self-reliant in essentials, with export profits, both to the home country and to their neighbours the West Indies, enabling luxuries to be purchased. Prosperous as they were, the commercial importance of the North American colonies was outweighed by the scattered British West Indian islands. Coming late to the Caribbean, Britain had picked up some of the small outer islands, the Lesser Antilles, neglected by Spain. The tiny island of Barbados, occupied in 1625, was said to be the richest

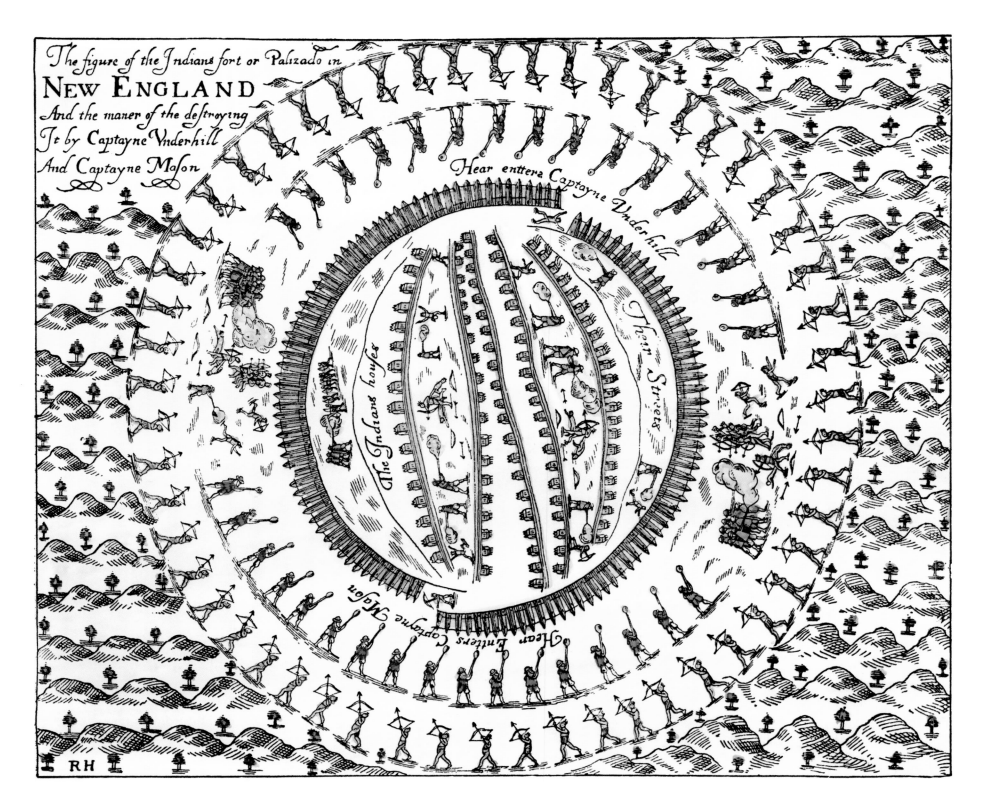

The figure of the Indians fort or Palizado in NEW ENGLAND And the maner of the destroying It by Captayne Vnderhill And Captayne Mason

Hear enttera Captayne Vnderhill

Their Streets

The Indians houses

Hear Enttera Captayne Mason

RH

ABOVE *In 1637, a war broke between English settlers and the Pequot people of Connecticut. With help from native allies, the English exacted brutal revenge for the murder of a trader. This engraving shows their forces attacking the main Pequot village.*

place in the New World, its trade greater than that of all the other English colonies put together, with more white settlers than Massachusetts and Connecticut combined. Most of the whites were indentured servants, contracted to work for a fixed number of years in return for their passage and keep, supplemented by prisoners sent out on similar terms. Sugar was the foundation of prosperity, and profits made it possible to buy slaves.

Slavery

The Atlantic slave trade began in the 15th century, with Portuguese sailors venturing progressively further down the West African coast, opening new opportunities for established African slavers, right on the doorstep without the cost of long overland journeys to the Muslim markets. The protocol was that local rulers would permit a Portuguese trading station, the first being built in 1443, and provide the slaves in return for a share of the profits. At first, opportunities were limited mainly to providing labour for the Spanish domestic sugar industry, or retailing in the North African markets. A Lisbon official was charged with receiving:

'all Moors and Mooresses and whatever other things, which by God's grace may be imported from Africa.'

and ensuring that the correct duty was paid, but this changed rapidly when the American settlements began.

After the first qualms about the morality of slavery had been satisfactorily assuaged, and given the urgent need for labour following the collapse of the Caribbean population, slave imports were allowed, initially for work in the mines and in agriculture, and later in the newly established sugar plantations.

Once the cooperation of African potentates was secured, the only force needed was to defend the trading stations against attacks from competitors, who soon arrived as Dutch, Spanish and English merchants muscled in to find labourers for their own West Indian colonies.

The most profitable trade was developed by the English. Manufactured goods were sent from west coast ports, Bristol and Liverpool being the largest, to the African coastal stations – the first British post was established in 1664 by the simple method of seizing it from the Portuguese – and exchanged for slaves, already gathered in the African traders' baracoons, who were then shipped across the Atlantic. On arrival the sale proceeds were invested in sugar, cotton, rum and tobacco, which were sent back to Britain: three handsome sets of profits on a single round trip without a shot being fired.

All slavery is abhorrent, but the transatlantic trade was more damaging than the traditional inter-African variety. Apart from the sheer volume of the trade, and the havoc caused by the raiding wars, New World slaves were usually placed in labour gangs rather than in households. Brutality was commonplace everywhere, but those sent to Spanish America or Brazil had at last some chance of integration and official recognition: skin shade was an important signifier of social status, but there was none of the disdain for any non-whites rife in the British colonies. All, however, had to undergo the horrors of the Atlantic crossing – known as the 'Middle Passage' in the British trade – which was bad enough for the sailors but infinitely worse for the slaves, shackled in squalid, insanitary conditions with inadequate food.

Most slaves were shipped to the West Indies, while the main North American trade was to the Southern states, but the Yankees of Rhode Island bought as many as 15,000 and a Pennsylvanian Quaker was one of the first importers in that state. The Catholic Church had more doubts about the morality of slavery than most Protestants, but few merchants paid much attention to Pope or pastors: it was not until the 18th century that evangelicals and liberal humanists were able to ignite public concern and begin agitation for the abolition, first of all for the slave trade, then for slavery itself.

Rebellions and Experiments

Among this score of separate colonies, all with their own governments, there was neither any formal communication, nor any competent department of the British government charged with superintending their administration. It was simply assumed that colonies were founded for the benefit of the home country, as expressed in a series of Navigation Laws; colonists should be grateful that they were defended, at the cost of the British taxpayer, by the Royal Navy. The events of 1688, the 'Glorious Bloodless Revolution' were relatively peaceful in America, though decisive. King James had made himself generally unpopular by imposing taxes on sugar and tobacco, aggravated by his grant of a monopoly of slave importation to his Royal African Company. Not only was the price of slaves increased, but the mainland colonies did not receive their fair share. His idea of uniting the New England colonies with New York and New Jersey into a Dominion of New England, and cancelling the previous colonial charters was greatly resented, but there were no organized protests.

New England was enthusiastic for William of Orange. Sir Edmund Andros, appointed by King James II as Governor of his new Dominion, caught attempting to escape in women's clothes, was seized by a rebellious group and incarcerated: he deserves to be remembered affectionately for ending the

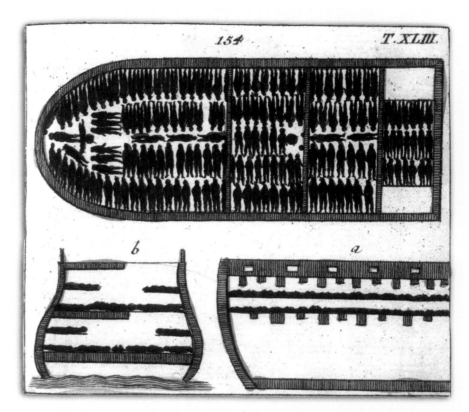

This diagram of accommodation below decks aboard the Liverpool slave ship Brookes in the late 18th century reveals the appallingly cramped conditions endured by captured West Africans on the 'Middle Passage' across the Atlantic. Many slaves died of disease or starvation en route; those who reached their destination faced a life of misery.

Puritan ban on celebrating Christmas. In New York, the ominous-sounding Committee of Safety rejected the royalist government and in Catholic Maryland Governor William Joseph demanded the surrender of all the colonists' guns, provoking the 'Protestant Associators' to force his resignation.

Once the Protestant succession had been established the colonies were ready to welcome a closer association with the home Government. Sir Edmond was restored as Governor of Virginia and Jacob Leister, leader of the New York rebels, was hanged. The Irish peer, Lord Bellomont, the new Governor of Massachusetts was welcomed by the province's poet, Benjamin Tompson, declaring that:

'Our Senators with publick Cares so tir'd, With chearfullness resign to you desir'd.'

What might have appeared as a dress rehearsal for a real rebellion passed off quietly: but the colonists had demonstrated a capacity for revolt.

Two colonial schemes failed. The promise of stability offered by King William inspired an outburst of confidence in Scotland's future, signalled by the foundation of a national bank, the Bank of Scotland, and an attempt at a colonial empire. The Scottish Darien Company intended to establish a settlement on the isthmus of Panama, (which happened to belong to Spain) and national enthusiasm, inspired by the promoters' promise that success would enable its 'Proprietors to give Laws to both Oceans' and to become 'Arbitrators of the Commercial World' raised handsome subscriptions. Badly managed and stupidly planned, it hardly needed English sabotage to ensure that the enterprise was a colossal failure. In March 1700, Spanish forces expelled the intruders from Darien, leaving Scots indignant and downcast, their savings forfeited, eventually to be saved only by complete union in the United Kingdom of Great Britain, in 1707.

Not long after, in September 1715, King Louis XIV died a disappointed man, leaving France near economic ruin, with his heir a five-year-old great-grandson and his nephew Philip of Orleans acting as Regent. An apparently attractive solution to French financial problems was offered by John Law, an ambitious and avaricious Scot who advocated the issue of paper money. His new and successful bank was encouraged by the award of the monopoly of trade with the French settlements in Louisiana, the West Indies and Canada.

In a surge of optimism, new cities, L'Orient in France and New Orleans in America were founded, and a speedy supply of colonists ensured by shipping out convicts, prostitutes and orphans. Public opinion was wildly enthused, and the price of stock shot up. Since Law's bank collected all French domestic taxes, and Law himself was the Controller-General, in charge of the nation's finances, the stock seemed gilt-edged. The bubble, however, quickly burst and by 1720 the bank failed, and France's appetite for transatlantic ventures waned. Neither New Orleans nor Canada attracted new colonists: Louisiana stagnated, but Canada, helped by a high birth rate, prospered modestly.

Iberian America

Two viceroyalties, of New Spain, with its capital at Mexico City, and of Peru, centred on Lima, administered the whole of the vast territory from California to Patagonia. The most senior officials and judges were sent out from Spain, marking a social distinction between *peninsulares* (those born in Spain) and creoles, with attendant jealousies. These were especially marked when the *peninsulares* were members of the religious orders, dedicated to protecting and converting the Indians.

Tough and greedy colonists had been brought up on the previous doctrine, expressed by Pope Nicholas V encouraging Catholic kings and princes:

'to invade, search out, capture, vanquish and subdue all Saracens and pagans whatsoever … and to reduce their persons to perpetual slavery.'

That was clear enough, the colonists considered, but times had changed, and not only humanism but the sheer impossibility of vanquishing and subduing all those millions of Indians persuaded King Philip, a well-intentioned monarch, to insist on Indian rights. Two legally separate realms were created, the Spanish and the Indian, with their own laws and privileges, naturally both subject to the Spanish authorities. Courts dedicated to deciding cases between Indians and Spaniards were enthusiastically, and often successfully, used by Indians to defend their rights.

To a fair extent this worked, and Indian towns and communities retained a considerable independence, while the church missions – the impressive

LEFT *The Religious Toleration Act promulgated by the colony of Maryland in 1649. It granted freedom of worship to Christians who believed in the Trinity, and sentenced to death anyone denying the divinity of Jesus Christ.*

San Augustino in Mexican town of Yurivia, is a fine early example, but the Texan Alamo in San Antonio is the most famous – formed centres of Indian education and nurture. Counter-Reformation Catholicism, with its imagery, colour and processions, and its tremendous capacity for belief, merged with Indian traditions to produce a new Hispanic-Indian culture, more homogenous than that developing in the English colonies.

Brazil followed yet another pattern of settlement and control. Portugal was a considerably smaller and less powerful country than Spain, with even more widespread overseas commitments, stretching right around the African coasts to India, Indonesia and China. With only minimal resources available imperial administration was limited to two centres, in the north at São Luis and 1,200 miles (1,900 km) further south at Bahía, with subordinate captaincies extending to Rio de Janeiro. Effective government over such vast distances could only be ensured in the areas surrounding the main townships, where the missionary orders provided major assistance, building hospitals, schools and orphanages, assisted by the numerous lay confraternities.

The land frontier was ranged over by *bandeiras*, groups of slave-hunting freebooters, who explored the mountains north into the Amazon basin, which they devastated: within 30 years it was estimated that some 2 million Indians perished. Although attacked by the Church and criticized, usually unavailingly, by the government, the *bandeiras* saved Brazil from being occupied by French or Dutch, as well as discovering gold in Minais Gerais. Sugar, however, and later coffee, were to be the major Brazilian exports, and these demanded the importation of black slaves. Brazil developed as a uniquely mixed society, with Portuguese, Indian and African intermarriages and delicate graduation of skin colour.

Portuguese and Dutch East Indies

Portuguese merchants enjoyed a monopoly of European trade in the East Indies for a century, before being faced with competition from the Dutch, during which a chain of trading stations was established, together with the Goa and Macao settlements, a temporary foothold in China and control over much of the island of Ceylon. The Dutch East India Company (*Vereenigde Oost-Indische Compagnie*, or VOC), was headed in the East by the ruthless Governor-General Jan Pieterszoon Coen, with his headquarters at Batavia, on Java. Unlike the American colonies, those of the East Indian Dutch were entirely concentrated on trade and controlled by a commercial company, acting on its own account, and responsible to a board of directors. Profit, not territorial expansion, which usually led to extra expense, was the sole aim.

In spite of this, the Dutch did go some way to settle in their largest possession, the island of Ceylon, but this had already experienced a hundred years of Portuguese occupation and had a large converted Catholic element in its

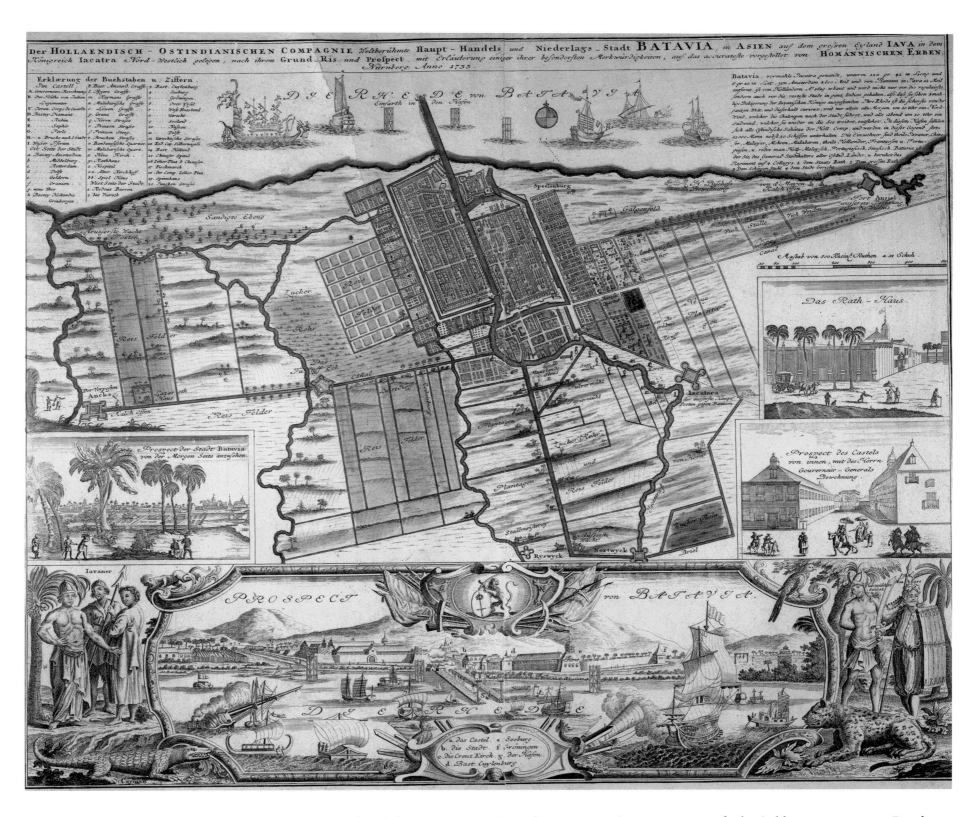

Der HOLLAENDISCH - OSTINDIANISCHEN COMPAGNIE Weltberühmte Haupt - Handels und Niederlags - Stadt BATAVIA in ASIEN auf dem großen Eyland IAVA in dem Königreich Iacatra Nord - Westlich gelegen, nach ihrem Grund Ris und Prospect mit Erläuterung einiger ihrer besondersten Merkwürdigkeiten, auf das accurateste vorgestellet von HOMANNISCHEN ERBEN. Nürnberg Anno 1733.

ABOVE *The port of Batavia on the island of Java was founded in 1621 by the Dutch East India Company and became a key port in its pursuit of the lucrative spice trade. The city is now the Indonesian capital of Jakarta.*

population. One indication of the fixation on profit was the lack of interest demonstrated in Australia, which Dutch navigators kept bumping into, often literally. Even after the wreck of the VOC flagship *Batavia* in 1626 off Western Australia, the exploration of Tasmania – Van Diemen's Land, after its discoverer – and other voyages which by 1644 achieved the charting of almost all the Australian coast from Cape York in the north to the Great Australian Bight, the Company directors found that a continent peopled by 'poor naked people … very bad-tempered,' would not warrant further expenditure.

Since Batavia was only one port in an extensive, highly competitive and well established trade carried on by Indonesian, Indian, Chinese and Muslim merchants, this restricted policy of trade-only was prudent, but Dutch officials found life was more pleasant if they married local girls, especially

in Ceylon. However, it was not easy to find suitable partners, as one Dutch pastor reported:

'This black nation such as they are, are pretty civil upright, regular and orderly in their daily life and conduct … and this is the reason why none of them want to give their daughters in marriage to us, and why the girls themselves are afraid to do so.'

Governor Rijkloff van Goens admitted that life without such comforts could be tedious and frustrating, only made tolerable by vast quantities of beer. Company officials insisted on keeping 'face' by public displays of extravagant pomp, and private 'face' was preserved by an elaborate set of social degrees of precedence: with no real aristocracy, the Dutch attached great importance to distinctions of rank that foreigners found incomprehensible.

1368–1799
Europeans and the Orient

■ Emperor Hong Wu establishes the Ming dynasty 1368 ■ Japan enacts a policy of national isolation (*Sakoku*) lasting 200 years 1639 ■ Manchus overrun China and found the Qing dynasty 1644 ■ Death of the Qing emperor Qianlong 1799

Apart from a brief spasm of withdrawal during the Ming dynasty, China cautiously improved communications with the outside world. Trade flourished under careful control and Chinese inventions – moveable type, the magnetic compass, explosives, the sternpost rudder – were readily adopted in the West, where Chinese goods became widely fashionable. Japan, on the other hand, developed a closed and seemingly unchangeable culture, unknown and ignored by all except her immediate neighbours.

The Mongol Empire disintegrated not long after the great Kublai Khan's death in 1294: between 1307 and 1332, no fewer than nine emperors reigned and peasant revolts spread.

Ming Magnificence

By 1356, the luckiest of the peasant leaders, Zhu Yuanzhang, succeeded in vanquishing the competing warlords and capturing Nanking: 12 years later he established a new dynasty, the Ming, with himself as Emperor Hong Wu (r.1368–98). Zhu had been a peasant and later a Buddhist monk, which had not taught him restraint or gentleness, since he acted as a psychopathic autocrat, having many thousands executed often by the most revolting tortures. Capital sentences were not confined to the offender but could be extended through ten generations, to ancestors and descendants, including cousins. The Confucian system of administration by scholar officials, which had been neglected by the Yuan, was reinstated, and proved a powerful discouragement to dangerously constructive thought. Real talent – and inexpensive since they had no inconvenient families to provide for –was found among the eunuchs, mainly Muslim officials.

The third Ming emperor Yongle (r.1402–24) demonstrated imperial power and dignity by despatching a great fleet to navigate the East Indian archipelago. Commanded by a eunuch admiral, Zheng He, a Muslim of Persian extraction, one of whose forebears had governed the province of Yunnan, the fleet was majestically impressive, comprising 62 'treasure ships' supported by 190 auxiliary vessels, including water tankers, and crewed by some 28,000 men. Gliding into a suitable bay, or one of the few harbours capable of sheltering such a fleet, propelled by giant sweeps – the *yolo*, a cranked oar, was yet another example of Chinese ingenuity – gaily painted,

hung about with banners, the commanders and crew in gorgeous uniforms, gongs and trumpets sounding, Zheng's fleet formed a spectacle such as the world had never before witnessed.

The Ming fleet came not as conquerors, demanding tribute, but as visitors, bringing and receiving presents, while quietly emphasizing Chinese power and influence. Wherever Zheng's ships sailed – in seven successive voyages they reached Ceylon, India, the Persian Gulf and the African coast – they found Chinese communities, established over 1,000 years of peaceful trading. Only once was any serious resistance encountered, from the King of Kotte in Ceylon, who was quickly brought to heel and transported to Beijing to present his personal apologies to the Emperor.

One unquestionable piece of evidence records the amiable intentions of the Ming fleets. This consists of three separate steles dated 1409, found in Ceylon, each bearing a similar text, in Chinese, Tamil and Persian. Each text conveys the same message from his Imperial Majesty, starting:

'Deeply do we reverence Thee, Merciful and Honoured one, of bright perfection wide-embracing, whose Way and virtue passes all understanding, whose Law pervades all human relations …'

and continues in a deeply respectful vein, the only difference being that the Chinese version is dedicated to the Lord Buddha, the Tamil to Devundara Deviyo (an incarnation of Vishnu) , and the Persian to the glory of Allah and his saints. All three deities were treated equally in the matter of presents – gold, silver, silk, scents and ecclesiastical ornaments: in all, remarkable examples of Chinese openmindedness and generosity.

No other realm could offer presents to match those given by the Chinese, but although in the long term trade was doubtless encouraged, the costs of the expeditions were huge and immediate. No sooner had Yongle died than retrenchment set in: 'All building of sea-going ships for intercourse with barbarian countries is to cease forthwith'. Any temptation to resume was countered by the destruction of all relevant records as 'deceitful exaggerations of bizarre things'.Aggravated by a currency crisis and troubles on the northern borders, which led to the capture of Emperor Zhengtong by the Mongols in 1449, the Ming administration tottered and the navy fragmented, ship numbers falling by the end of the century to as little as a tenth: by 1500 it was an offence punishable by death to build a ship with more than two masts: in 1525 an edict ordered all larger ships to be destroyed; but as with all Chinese edicts, exceptions could be purchased, and the trade continued.

Weakening sea defences tempted foreign aggression: pirates and Japanese raiders harassed the eastern and southern coasts, but at the start of the 17th century China remained by far the most populous – at 120 million more than the whole of Europe – and the richest state on Earth, administered by some 100,000 civil servants, reporting to Emperor Wanli (r.1572–1620) secluded in the splendid new palaces of the Forbidden City, communicating with the outside world through a 10,000-strong eunuch corps. The swollen ranks of the élite lived in a luxury unparalleled anywhere else, surrounded by exquisite ceramics, silks and jade, with the most delicious food imaginable, enjoying the new imaginative literature: the novel *Monkey's Journey to the West* remains a great favourite. The peasants, for the most part, survived, and ensuring that so many did was itself a considerable achievement.

ABOVE *Stone sculptures depicting a civil administrator (right) and a military official during the Ming Dynasty (1368–1644). The Ming moved the Chinese capital to Beijing, and built the Forbidden City there.*

The West's first ambassador was welcomed to Beijing in 1601. Matteo Ricci, leader of a Jesuit mission spent the rest of his life in China, consorting amicably with senior officials, translating the works of Confucius into Latin, and preparing the first Chinese world map. The Jesuits' adaptability proved too much for the narrow views of the 18th-century Vatican, who recalled this, one of the most successful Catholic missions.

Yet disturbing signs of change were appearing. Silk weavers and pottery workers revolted and a group of scholars, the Donglin Society, began a reform movement. During the Emperor Wanli's reign the fabric of society held together, but complete collapse was soon to follow. Climate change heralded by the start of the 'Little Ice Age', which caused worldwide cooling

for two centuries, damaged harvests, hitting peasants already impoverished following the devaluation of the copper currency (farm products were sold in copper, but taxes had to be paid in silver). The huge burden of annual government expenses was increased by defence costs, and increased garrisons on the Great Wall. Taxes were steadily rising – seven increases between 1618 and 1639 – while plague ravaged the coastal province of Zhejiang, further decreasing the tax base.

By 1636, local rebellions cohered and evolved a strategy which brought the leaders into control of both the upper Yellow River and Yangtze, eventually gathering for a concerted attack on Beijing, which surrendered without a

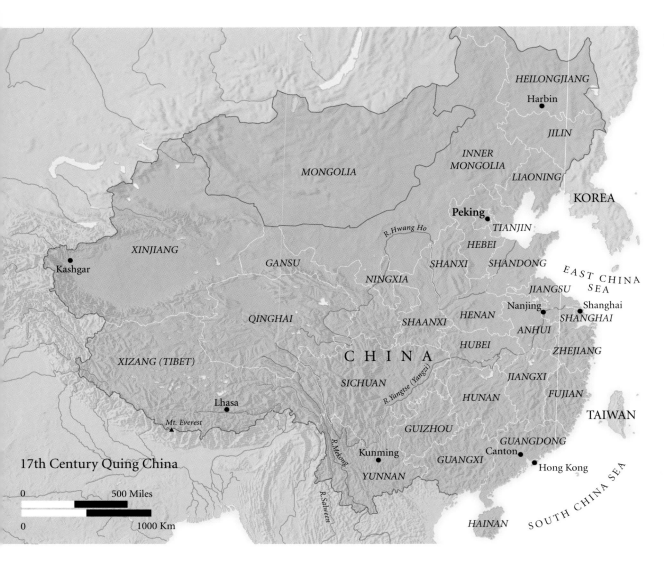

0   500 Miles

0   1000 Km

known as the Qing (Ch'ing). In his proclamation the new Emperor made a brutally frank statement of Manchu aims:

'By keeping peace inside and grabbing outside a great empire is rising.'

The subjugation of China proper was completed in the reign of Nurhaci's grandson Shunzhi (r.1643–61). Since the new emperor was only five years old at the time of his father's death, it was the Regent Dorgon who took Beijing in 1644, and ruled for the next eight years.

Dorgon and Shunzhi were very ready to take advantage of the experienced Chinese civil servants, but kept the military under firm Manchu control, and insisted on external signs of ethnic identity. The Manchu language was retained for official court dress and documents. Tight jackets replaced Chinese robes, Manchu women refrained from distorting their feet into the trotter-like shape affected by Chinese, and Chinese men were obliged to wear their hair in the Manchu style with a shaven forehead and long queue (pigtail). The pure Han Chinese found their new masters crude. Dutch traders were taken aback by meeting one of the highest early Manchu officials, the President of the Board of Rites, guardian of the most sacred traditions, who 'sent for a piece of Pork, which was half-raw, whereof he did eat most heartily, in a slovenly manner, that he looked more like a butcher than a Prince.'

For some years Ming resistance continued in the south, and a naval campaign was fought all along the east coast by the pirate-merchant Koxinga, who founded a trading city in Amoy. In an effort to clear the sea of pirates the Beijing government took the drastic step of clearing the coast of people. The English factor in Surat reported that everybody living near the sea was to be deported inland, and the deportation was brutally enforced:

'The boundary was marked straight with a rope ... a deep ditch was dug ... One step beyond the ditch, and the punishment was death ... Fathers abandoned their sons, and husbands their wives ... sons were sold for a peck of rice, daughters for 100 cash.'

fight in April 1644. The last Ming emperor Chongzhen quietly left the palace and hanged himself, leaving his testament:

'Now I meet with Heaven's punishment above, sinking ignominiously below ...May the bandits dismember my corpse and slaughter my officials, but let them not despoil the imperial tombs nor harm a single one of our people.'

The Manchu: the Last Dynasty

It was not, however, the Chinese bandits who formed a new dynasty, but foreign invaders from Manchuria, the region beyond the Great Wall north of Korea, towards the Amur River and the present Russian frontier. They were hunters and fishers, using reindeer and canoes, growing crops when it suited, but relying mainly on their considerable skills as horsemen and archers. In 1607, the Tungu prince Nurhaci succeeded in forcibly uniting Manchuria and proclaimed himself as Great Khan. He reinforced his military victories by generous rewards to those prominent Chinese, Mongols and Koreans who surrendered, and created a Manchurian state, on a Chinese model, but one which remained characteristically Manchu. The royal family commanded the field armies, organized in eight 'banners' (divisions) of some 8,000 men each. The very names of the first Manchus – Dorgon, Jirgalang and Manggultai, give a flavour of how far removed the new rulers were from the Han Chinese.

Nurhaci turned his forces against Ming China in 1618. When his son Hong Taiji made the transition from Khan of Manchuria to Emperor of China, he took the reign name of Tiancong and declared that his dynasty should be

The tiny Portuguese settlement on the Pearl River at Macao was threatened by these disturbances. Macao was strictly controlled by the Chinese authorities, who made it clear that the Portuguese were there only on sufferance, confined within a strong wall through which provisions were allowed to trickle. The important trade was carried on 60 miles (100 km) or so further upstream in the great city of Canton, capital of the twin provinces

RIGHT *19th-century engraving depicting life at the Qing (Manchu) court. The Manchus adopted many Chinese traditions, but left their Han subjects in no doubt as to who was master.*

of Kwangtung and Kwangsi (Guangdong and Guangxi) which stretch for 800 miles (1,300 km) across the south of China. Guangdong is an odd region, regarded by the rest of China with suspicion and disdain. In part this distrust is due to its remoteness from Beijing, in terrain crossed only by difficult and infrequent passes. The language spoken by the inhabitants is unintelligible to northern Chinese and their customs – typical Cantonese are not scholars, but traders first and last, and will eat anything – are looked upon with distaste.

To vessels making the dangerous passage from the west, the Pearl River is the first safe haven in the Chinese Empire. The first Portuguese ship moored off Canton in 1513, but attempts to obtain official blessing only succeeded in 1557. Although its Portuguese population was never more than a few hundred, Macao was cherished both as a dockyard and way-station on the trade routes from the Indies to Japan, and a centre of missionary activities with its own bishop. Both Dutch and English attempted to muscle in, the Dutch forcibly; the British, with discreet bribery, were more successful. The end nearly came with the coastal deportations, but trade was too profitable

BELOW The semi-legendary 13th-century samurai Minamoto no Yoshitsune, son of Yorimoto, epitomized the ideal honourable tragic hero in medieval Japan, a warrior who killed himself rather than suffer disgrace.

RIGHT The European Factories at Canton in China, painting (c.1800) by the English artist William Daniell. 'Factories' were warehouses established by foreign merchants in the Far East.

for the local authorities to obey imperial edicts, and the judicious gift of an African lion mollified the emperor, who permitted the Portuguese to remain.

China was fortunate in that the two most influential Qing rulers Kangxi (r.1661–1722) and Qianlong (r.1735–99) – better known as Chien L'ung – were able and realistic men who enjoyed exceptionally long reigns, during which Chinese and Manchu were able to adapt to each other, and to the outside world. A true Manchu, a passionate hunter in the Tungu lands, Kangxi ensured Manchu control of the court, but went out of his way to conciliate Chinese intellectuals, encouraging the examination system; his success was proved in that nostalgia for the Ming was allowed to grow fashionable, with Ming resistance celebrated in performances of musical dramas. The writer Kong Shangren described the reception of his own plays before 'famous aristocrats, high officials and talented literati' among whom 'there were a few who sat quietly weeping behind their sleeves – former officials and 'survivors' . When the lanterns had flickered out and the drinking was over, they uttered sighs and went their ways.'

During Kangxi's reign, the borders of China were defined: Formosa-Taiwan, occupied first by the Dutch followed by Koxinga's men, was pacified, Tibet invaded and a compliant Dalai Lama installed; a formal treaty, the first between China and a foreign state, was negotiated with the Russians, using Latin learned from the Jesuits. Trade through Canton was expanded, although still under strict control, and foreign merchants allowed to build warehouses; among these were the English East India Company, destined to become the most dangerous challenge to the Chinese Empire.

Japan

Occupying a similar position to the British Isles, an archipelago lying just off a continent – the shortest land-to-land hop across the Korea Strait is some 30 nautical miles (56 km) – with a long coastline and plentiful harbours, Japan and Britain have always been seafaring nations, and were for long periods cultural provinces of the continent. But the parallel has its limits: Japan's central island, Honshu, is mountainous with more than a dozen summits over 10,000 feet (3,000 metres), and much divided by short and rapid rivers. After the arrival in the last centuries BC of the mainland people known as the Yayoi, Japanese ethnicity and culture has remained mainly homogenous, whereas Angles, Saxons, Danes, Normans and many other peoples since have supplemented the pre-Roman inhabitants of Britain. Bringing with them metallurgy and rice-farming techniques, and gradually displacing the original inhabitants on Honshu, a great number of Yayoi clan units formed, clustering

in the valleys of what condescending Chinese called 'the land of dwarfs'. Chinese characters were first used in about AD 600 to represent the Japanese language, which was itself akin to Korean, with perhaps half the vocabulary also being imported.

Buddhism came from Korea and China in the same period, but as with all other imports, was adapted to Japanese requirements and priorities. Both Buddhism and the native Shinto faith – 'the way of the gods,' or perhaps 'divine essences' - merged with Buddhist philosophy reinforcing the instinct to reverence local or individual deities, including those housed in mountains, trees or streams or enshrined in cult-locations, and especially the ancestors, chief among whom was the Divine Emperor, the descendant of the Sun incarnate, endowed with the Mandate of Heaven.

At some time after 700, the records of beliefs and traditions were prepared in order to validate the Imperial system and a national capital established at Kyoto in 794, where court life was described in the famous *Tale of Genji* and the *Pillow Book* of Lady Sei Shonagon. The emperor, or empress, embodying the soul of the nation, was not expected to concern himself with mundane matters, but to entrust these to a regent, who from 645 was a member of the Fujiwara clan, who held on to power for nearly five centuries, permitting the cloistered court to enjoy the pleasures of Chinese verse, elegant robes, perfumes and literature, looking with distaste at the polloi 'like so many basket weavers in their hideous clothes.'

A violent interruption came in the 12th century, with ferocious civil wars concluding with Minamoto no Yorimoto demanding appointment as

'*Shogun*'– in Europe of that time perhaps 'Earl Marshal' or 'Constable,' but in reality an undisputed autocrat in all matters. In such a system, the Shogunate was open to any local magnate who felt able to mount a successful rebellion, which duly occurred. One rebellion was actually led by an exiled former emperor, Go-Daigo, but the system of temporary Shogunates continued. During the whole period, Japan had been left undisturbed by the outside world, developing its own highly individual culture. Invasions were attempted in 1274 and 1281 by Kublai Khan's Mongol Empire, in two great expeditions, the first with 900 ships, followed by an armada of 4,400, but both were repelled by a combination of storms – the so-called *kamikaze*, or 'divine winds' – and strong Japanese defences. Thereafter Japanese sailors were free to trade all over the China seas, sending a mission to Beijing in 1341, but varying trade with usually successful piracy.

On land, persistent warfare created a militant feudal society, in which some 200 magnates (*daimyo*) employed *samurai*, men-at-arms sworn to loyalty by the code of *Bushido*, forming a caste set aside from farmers and craftsmen, and subject to different courts. Since only *samurai* were permitted to carry weapons their lords had little to fear from rebellions, unlike their counterparts on the mainland, where peasant revolts served to balance perceived abuses of power. Japan's scarcity of natural resources and growing population led to a principle of spareness and frugality in design. Paper matting could substitute for timber, and iron was used only for the magnificent Samurai swords: their armour was leather-based and their horseshoes made from grass. The combination of ingenuity, adaptability, and deferential obedience did much to ensure continuing Japanese prosperity, right up to the present day.

The Age of Enlightenment and the American Revolution

■ Act of Union unites England and Scotland 1707 ■ Jacobite Rebellion 1745 ■ First publication of Diderot and d'Alembert's *Encyclopédie* 1751–72 ■ Seven Years' War 1756–63 ■ Boston Tea Party 1773 ■ American War of Independence 1775–1783 ■ United States Constitution 1787

The Enlightenment, the philosophical, intellectual and cultural movement that transformed Western societies in the 18th century, was essentially the continuation of earlier revolutions. The search for evidence that had stimulated scientific enquiry began by questioning authority: what Aristotle or St Augustine had written was not acceptable as evidence, which must rather be sought by observation, and the results freely published and discussed before conclusions could be reached.

Science flourished under the Protestant Reformation since the only two countries where free research and discussion were permitted – and usually encouraged – were the Netherlands and Great Britain. In France, the lively intellectual life that produced Descartes, Pascal and Montaigne and had seen Diderot and d'Alembert publish their magisterial Encyclopaedia was always prone to suppression by the Church and the *ancien régime*.

A Surge of Ideas

Even French thinkers looked to Britain for a lead. In a single generation, England had executed one king, deported a second and elected a third, which had both shocked and stimulated European opinion. Both the great names in science and philosophy at the start of the 18th century, Isaac Newton and John Locke, were English, but Scottish thinkers soon came to the fore. Scots had taken an independent line during the wars, beginning by siding with the English parliamentarians, but returning to loyal allegiance after the death of King Charles I, furious at having a Stuart ruler, grandson of Mary, Queen of Scots, murdered on the instructions of an English parliament and army (which had just drubbed the Scots at Preston). Scottish loyalty was not rewarded at the Restoration in 1660, when an English form of Church government was imposed, sparking another civil war, which resumed after 1688. Only in 1690 was Dutch William accepted by the Scottish parliament as King of Scotland.

The doctrine of absolute monarchy's 'divine right' had been brutally exposed and succeeded by debate and compromise, for both the 1660 Restoration and the 'Glorious Revolution' of 1688 had been negotiated settlements. In 1707, another negotiation led to the merger of England and Scotland as the United Kingdom, symbolized by the adoption of the Union Flag, incorporating the St Andrew Saltire and the Cross of St George. It was not the end of the dispute, as three subsequent Scottish rebellions proved, but the possibility of a constitutional rule of law in a major country had been demonstrated. The Union led to unprecedented prosperity for Scotland, and able Scots were attracted south and into international attention much more easily than from the relative obscurity of Edinburgh and Glasgow.

Even so, the two of the most prominent Enlightenment thinkers, David Hume and Adam Smith, could have been found at the Edinburgh Poker Club between the hours of two and six, eating at the modest price of one shilling and drinking a good deal of claret. Such informal meetings were the essence of British and American debate, but did not transfer easily to Europe. Hume, a free-thinker who scandalized respectable society, was politely welcomed by King Louis XV, and received elegant

LEFT *A Scottish penny struck in 1797 to commemorate Adam Smith (1723–90), a leading figure of the Scottish Enlightenment. His treatise* The Wealth of Nations *(1776) laid the foundations of modern economic theory.*

tributes from the young future kings, Louis XVI, Louis XVIII and Charles X (who do not however, seem to have benefited from his instruction). Less readable than Hume, Adam Smith's work remains a potent influence. His book *The Wealth of Nations* (1776) caused governments to abandon previous attempts to force trade into a rigid pattern, and his principles can still be usefully applied to modern economic problems.

In France, the Baron de Montesquieu, inspired by a three-year stay in England, was allowed to publish such provoking works as *L'esprit du Loi* in 1748, which extolled the British constitution and proposed that all men, including kings, should obey the same laws. Less respectable French writers such as the energetically prolific Denis Diderot, the encyclopaedist and leader of the *Philosophes*, suffered frequent interference, persecution and even one spell of imprisonment. The thoughtful middle classes accepted the new ideas, but wariness was advisable. In 1767, the young Chevalier de la Barre was sentenced by an official tribunal to have his tongue torn out and to be burnt alive, with one of Voltaire's books hung around his neck. His offences were to have failed to take his hat off at a religious procession and to have sung some heretical verses (a humane executioner only made pretence of removing the tongue, and decapitated the 19-year-old before the burning). Similarly, in 1762, the respectable merchant Jean Calas was condemned to be broken on the wheel for the crime of being both wealthy and Protestant.

Diderot and other popular writers, including Voltaire and Rousseau, went into voluntary exile, Diderot with Catherine II of Russia and Voltaire,

ABOVE *The restless spirit of scientific enquiry fostered by the Enlightenment is captured in Joseph Wright of Derby's famous painting* An Experiment on a Bird in an Air Pump *(1768).*

initially on very friendly terms, with Frederick the Great of Prussia. Their novels, plays, books and pamphlets captured the popular imagination, and continue to do so today: Voltaire's *Candide* (1759) was a powerful satire of contemporary life and letters, while Rousseau's star-crossed lovers in *La Nouvelle Héloïse* (1761) remain a staple of romantic fiction. Writers in Protestant countries had a much easier time of it, but even the blameless Immanuel Kant (from a Scottish family settled in Prussia) had to accept an imposed silence. British reformers tended towards the practical; Arthur Young devoted his researches to agricultural improvements, and young Jeremy Bentham, whose doctrine of Utilitarianism was to shape 19th-century policies, published his first book in 1778.

The First World Conflicts

British philosophers were often honoured – Adam Smith even revered – by public opinion and by government: 'We are all your Scholars,' Prime Minister William Pitt once acknowledged; but their French counterparts were officially neglected. King Louis XV, who succeeded to the throne in 1715, maintained the extravagant lifestyle of his great-grandfather Louis XIV, the *Roi Soleil*. The lavish sensuality of his court is epitomized by François Boucher's nude portrait of the king's mistress, Louise O'Murphy (1752). Louis' government

ABOVE *The Battle of Fontenoy (1745), where troops under Louis XV defeated an Anglo-Dutch-Austrian army under the command of the Duke of Cumberland, ensured the French conquest of Flanders during the War of the Austrian Succession. This painting of the battle is by Pierre Lenfant (1704–87).*

failed to institute the financial reforms that were needed to ensure the country's solvency. Without any organized tax base, but a conglomeration of dozens of different direct and indirect levies, unevenly distributed geographically, applied to different classes of society, and collected haphazardly, only the salt tax – which varied as much as 20-fold according to region – was effective, and accordingly much resented by those who could not avoid it, the peasant farmers.

Court extravagance could perhaps be met from revenue, but the crushing expense was that of war. The conflict between Britain and Spain that began with the so-called War of Jenkins' Ear in 1739 merged into the War of the Austrian Succession, a European war that was also fought in North America and India, complicated by 'Bonnie Prince Charlie's' rising in Scotland, all of which dragged on until 1748. The only real winner was Frederick the Great, in whose reign the country expanded from being a scatter of small states, based on the Electorate of Brandenburg and the Duchy of Prussia, into a European power extending from the Russian border to the North Sea. Neither the French nor the Americans were happy with the Treaty of Aix-la-Chapelle: the Parisians sneered at *la guerre pour le roi de Prusse*, while the

New Englanders resented having to hand back Cape Breton Island, where the formidable fortress of Louisbourg had been captured by colonial and British troops in 1745. Naval press gangs had provoked a serious riot in Boston, which the local militia refused to suppress. Just six years later, war had broken out again.

The Seven Years' War (which actually continued for 9 years, beween1754 and 1763) could well be termed a world war, fought in Europe, North America, the Caribbean, Africa, India and the Philippines. While British forces eventually prevailed in America, one defeat was noteworthy, that of General Braddock's expedition to Fort Duquesne, when his small army of regulars and Virginian militia was shattered by a combined force of French and Indians. Dying of his wounds, the general's last words were 'we shall know better next time'; they were not lost on the Virginian commander, the 21-year-old George Washington. The 1763 Treaty of Paris, marked the end of the first French colonial empire. All Canada, with the exception of two small islands, Saint Pierre and Miquelon, the eastern part of Louisiana, Florida (from Spain) and a number of West Indian islands, were ceded to Britain and French expansion in India was blocked. Although the way was opened for the colonies to expand west towards the Mississippi, a British proclamation defining the lands between the Appalachians and the river as Indian territory antagonized the colonists.

Humiliated after the Treaty of Paris, Louis XV's government was jolted into activity: the navy was upgraded, with some magnificent new buildings on the

Rochefort base, and the army purged. Lorraine and Corsica were ceded to France, establishing what are today's frontiers, with the exception of Nice and Savoy, to be dubiously acquired by Napoleon III a century later. The royal heir, the Dauphin, was married to the Austrian princess Marie Antoinette thereby, it was hoped, ensuring the support of the Habsburg Empire. With the appointment as chief minister of René de Maupeou, tough, able and unscrupulous, vital reforms were attempted: the whole ramshackle edifice of laws, customs, multiple local courts and authorities was demolished and an effective system of governance begun: but only begun, since the death of Louis XV in 1774 brought the inexperienced heir to the throne as Louis XVI. By dismissing Maupeou, halting the reforms, Louis may be said to have signed his own death warrant, since the best chance of avoiding a revolution vanished. By one of fate's little ironies, Charles le Brun, Maupeou's secretary was able to implement the intended reforms, but only some 20 years later as co-Consul with the soon-to-be Emperor Napoleon I.

Revolt in America

Again, everyone believed that the peace would be shortlived and that the North American empire, now so greatly increased, must be defended by a substantial commitment of British troops, since the colonial militia had not distinguished themselves in the latest war, nor during the Cherokee War of 1759 or the then-current rebellion by the Ottawa chief Pontiac. But the estimated cost of some £400,000 per annum was too great a sum for a British government to bear; some contribution from the colonists was expected. For the next few years British governments imposed tax increases on their American subjects, only to abandon them after increasingly indignant colonial protests.

A sugar tax in 1764, actually a tax reduction, but on a widely avoided tax, was followed by a Stamp Duty Act in March 1765. Stamp duty was payable not only on legal transactions, but by innkeepers and newspapers, both lively vehicles of public expression. Mob violence resulted, fuelled by 'strong drink in plenty with Cheshire cheese and other provocations to intemperance and riot.' Stamp Duty officials were threatened with lynching and the first attempt at united colonial action begun by a Stamp Act congress held at New York in October 1765. London had been warned and in March 1766 the Act was repealed after leading to the collapse of two successive British governments. The next administration, headed by Charles Townshend, tried again in May 1767: new revenue duties were imposed and a Board of Customs Commissions established to enforce these, overriding the established law courts. More colonial protests were mounted, including a boycott of British goods, a very effective measure – New York imports dropped to a fifth of their former level – and one that annoyed British manufacturers. In March 1770, all the new duties were revoked, except that on tea. Calm appeared to have been restored, but this proved to be deceptive.

The explanation for the government's havering and equivocation was simply the confused state of domestic opinion, reflected in the fact that there were six different administrations between May 1762 and February 1770. To many Britons, it appeared that the Americans were demanding nothing other than their rights as British subjects. John Wilkes, a talented agitator, kept London in a furore. Elected time after time as MP for Middlesex – the only genuinely democratic parliamentary seat – and consistently rejected by the authorities, Wilkes was making the same point as the Americans and receiving the same rough treatment. In May 1768, soldiers opened fire on a Wilkesite crowd in London, killing one spectator: in March 1770, Boston Custom House guards

shot five members of a besieging mob. An anonymous London pamphleteer, signing himself 'Junius', claimed that the Americans:

'know how to distinguish the sovereign and a venal parliament on one side, from the real sentiments of the English people on the other. They left their native land in search of freedom, and found it in a desert.'

Charles James Fox, an MP at the age of 19, became the leader of pro-American opinion and his party's colours, buff and blue, were adopted as the American uniform. Fox's Cambridge supporters formed the True Blue Club in sympathy: their first toast was 'civil and religious liberty all over the world'. Sympathy, however, was succeeded by boredom. The Americans seemed to be always in a lather of indignation about nothing in particular: the latest London murder mystery was much more interesting, while government attention was then focussed on the impending bankruptcy of the East India Company. An apparent solution was found by reducing the import duty on tea, the Company's main source of income, to a nearly nominal threepence per pound. This lowered the cost from two shillings and seven pence a pound, the price charged by smugglers, to a mere two shillings and enabled the Company to dispose of its tea mountain, estimated at over 30

ABOVE 'The Bloody Massacre Perpetrated on King Street Boston on March 5th, 1770', *an illustrated pamphlet by the American patriot Paul Revere. This incident further fuelled colonists' resentment at direct rule from England and was one of several catalysts for the outbreak of the American Revolution.*

and recognizing Congress as being effectively an American Parliament. Advanced on 1 February 1775, these proposals were probably not too little, but may well have been too late. Before Chatham's proposals were rejected the distinguished constitutional lawyer, Lord Camden, who had been a consistent supporter of the colonists – taxation without representation was 'sheer robbery' – warned that it was:

> *'obvious that you cannot furnish armies, or treasure, competent to the mighty purpose of subduing America'*

and prophetically added:

> *'whether France or Spain will be tame, inactive spectators of your efforts ... is well worthy [of your] considerations'.*

ABOVE Crossing the Delaware *(1851) by Emanuel Leutze illustrates Washington taking his troops across the frozen river on 25 December, 1776, to mount a surprise attack on a group of Hessian soldiers. The attack, now known as the Battle of Trenton, was a turning point in the War of Independence.*

million pounds. Surely everyone would profit? The Americans, however, were more concerned with principle than price, rejecting any 'taxation without representation'. In their protest against the tea duty they had shown themselves willing to pay over the odds for the illegally imported variety, and carried their protests into action when the first cargoes of the new cheaper tea arrived. The Boston Tea Party, on 16 December 1773, saw imported tea dumped in the harbour.

To Lord North's government, who had been congratulating themselves on having solved two problems simultaneously, this was an intolerable affront: mob rule had taken over in Massachusetts. Moving rapidly, Coercive Acts were passed: Boston was closed to trade, the Massachusetts Council, hitherto elective, was to be appointed and the Governor's powers increased, including the right to billet troops as he saw fit. Although not intended to be coercive, the Quebec Act, which regulated Canadian government, extended the border into areas which the colonists had thought their own. To ensure compliance, General Thomas Gage, with nearly 20 years of American experience, had been despatched as Governor and commander-in-chief and found that in practice he could command only in the city of Boston.

The rest of America refused to obey: and a population of one and a half million, with leaders accustomed to fighting French and Indians, could not be suppressed. On 5 September 1774, colonial delegates met in Philadelphia for the First Continental Congress. They were hospitably received 'Flummery, jellies, sweetmeats of twenty sorts, trifles, whipped syllabubs floating islands, fools etc. Wines most excellent and admirable' and left only at the end of October, having repudiated British sovereignty and decided on a complete trade ban with Britain. Not all the delegates were radicals, by any means; in fact the contingent from Massachusetts was regarded by the others with some distrust, on account of its advanced views. London argued over attempting a compromise, or since limited coercion had failed, should it be increased? Lord Chatham – William Pitt the Elder – who had led the successful war against France, was for abolishing all laws objectionable to the Americans

Camden's advice was rejected. Reluctantly, General Gage obeyed London's instructions to break out of Boston; on 18 April 1775, a regiment he had sent to collect gunpowder stores was challenged by a group of militia at Lexington, and the first shots in what was to be the War of American Independence had been fired.

The second Continental Congress, assembled in May 1775, took a decisive step by appointing George Washington as Commander in Chief of an army which did not exist. Washington was indeed the founding father of the United States. Without his dogged reliability, his ability to inspire confidence, commanding presence, complete honesty, allied to tactical genius, the war would never have been won, nor the Republic firmly established. Even to survive the defeats of 1776 demanded all Washington's qualities, left as he was with only 3,000 men. In much the same terms as Oliver Cromwell had complained, Washington pleaded for 'gentlemen and men of character' to be commissioned, rather than those 'not fit to be shoe blacks', regarded by their men 'as no more than broom sticks'.

Congress did more to secure eventual victories by words than by actions. On 2 July 1776 Richard Lee of Virginia successfully moved:

> *'That these United Colonies are, and of right ought to be, free and independent States, that they are absolved from all allegiance to the British Crown ...'*

He added, significantly 'that it is expedient forthwith to take the most effectual measures for forming foreign alliances.' Two days later Thomas Jefferson, also of Virginia, produced a draft Declaration of Independence, at the suggestion of the English radical Thomas Paine. Its preamble has become immortal: 'We hold these truths to be self-evident, that all men are created equal, that they are endowed by the Creator with certain inalienable Rights, that among these life and liberty and the pursuit of Happiness.' Congress amended Jefferson's draft, the most significant alteration being the removal of his denunciation of the slave trade, insisted on by South Carolina and Georgia, in an ominous foreshadowing of future events.

The American Declaration of Independence was adopted by Congress on 4 July 1776 at the Pennsylvania State Hall in Philadelphia. Its famous philosophical preamble owes a great deal to the natural rights theory of government, an Enlightenment principle first formulated by John Locke.

1789–1815
The French Revolution and Napoleonic Wars

■ French Revolution begins with the storming of the Bastille 1789 ■ The Reign of Terror 1793–94 ■ Napoleon proclaims himself Emperor 1804 ■ Battle of Trafalgar 1805 ■ French invasion of Russia fails 1812 ■ Final defeat of Napoleon at Waterloo after the 'Hundred Days' 1815

Revolution has been the most successful of French exports. The example set in 1789 – not only of mounting an initial revolution, but also the ensuing chaos leading to the formation of an autocratic state – was emulated elsewhere throughout the 19th and early 20th centuries.

The cost, human and financial, of the French wars either frightened governments into dour reaction or persuaded them into adopting elements of liberalism. Britain and the USA sheltered the new regimes in Hispanic America, but, lacking any democratic traditions progress was intermittent.

The Estates General

'The French Revolution' often forms another convenient package prepared for writers and examiners to describe a dramatic series of events continuing over some ten years, beginning with the storming of the Paris Bastille in July 1789 and ending with Napoleon Bonaparte proclaiming himself Emperor. As usual, the causes have to be looked for earlier, and the effects analyzed much later. From the first years of Louis XVI's reign, it was obvious that reforms were essential, since the drastic state of national finance could not be ignored and real starvation was threatening, especially in the cities, away from the countryside's meagre resources. But every proposal involved raising taxes, which were levied only on the 'Third Estate' – the population at large. Together with the clergy (the First Estate) and the nobility (the Second Estate), they formed the 'Estates General', the national parliament: and since in France, any descendant of a noble was himself noble (in Britain only eldest sons qualified) clergy and nobility actually controlled a great proportion of the public wealth, all free of taxes. Since the Estates General existed only in theory, having last met in 1614, public discussion had been limited to the regional *parlements*, which had very little resemblance to a British Parliament, being essentially law courts, whose consent to any new laws was mandatory. Although traditionally conservative and protective of privileges, *parlements* – that of Paris being by far the most important – had become infused with the spirit of reform. 'Man is born free … originally men are equal,' the *Parlement* de Rennes declared in 1788, and that:

'one of the first conditions of society is that particular interests should always yield to the general will.'

The parliamentarians insisted that only the Estates General had the authority to deal with the financial crisis. This was too much for the royal court and in May 1788 the *parlements* were suspended, driving their members, including the senior peers and the clergy, into opposition. Those expert propagandists forced the king's hand, and on 8 August 1788 the Estates General was summoned to meet in the following May: but – and it was a big but – they were to meet and vote in separate houses, a signal that the First and Second estates would always outvote the Third estate, which represented the vast majority (some 95 percent) of the French people. France was entering unknown territory.

The Estates General convened on 4 May 1789. After a gap of 165 years, it lacked any comprehensible traditions of assembly or debate: protocol insisted that all should be done as it had been in 1614, down to the details of procedure and costume. The representatives were not natural revolutionaries, but magistrates and local officials, many of whom had never visited Paris: significantly, however, a quarter of them were lawyers. When King Louis received them, it may have been only the second time in his life that he had had seen so broad a cross-section of his subjects, since he had only once before, on a visit to open the Cherbourg harbour, left the environs of Paris and Versailles.

LEFT *A satirical cartoon of 1789 shows the First and Second Estates (a clergyman and an aristocrat) riding on the back of a peasant, representing the Third Estate.*

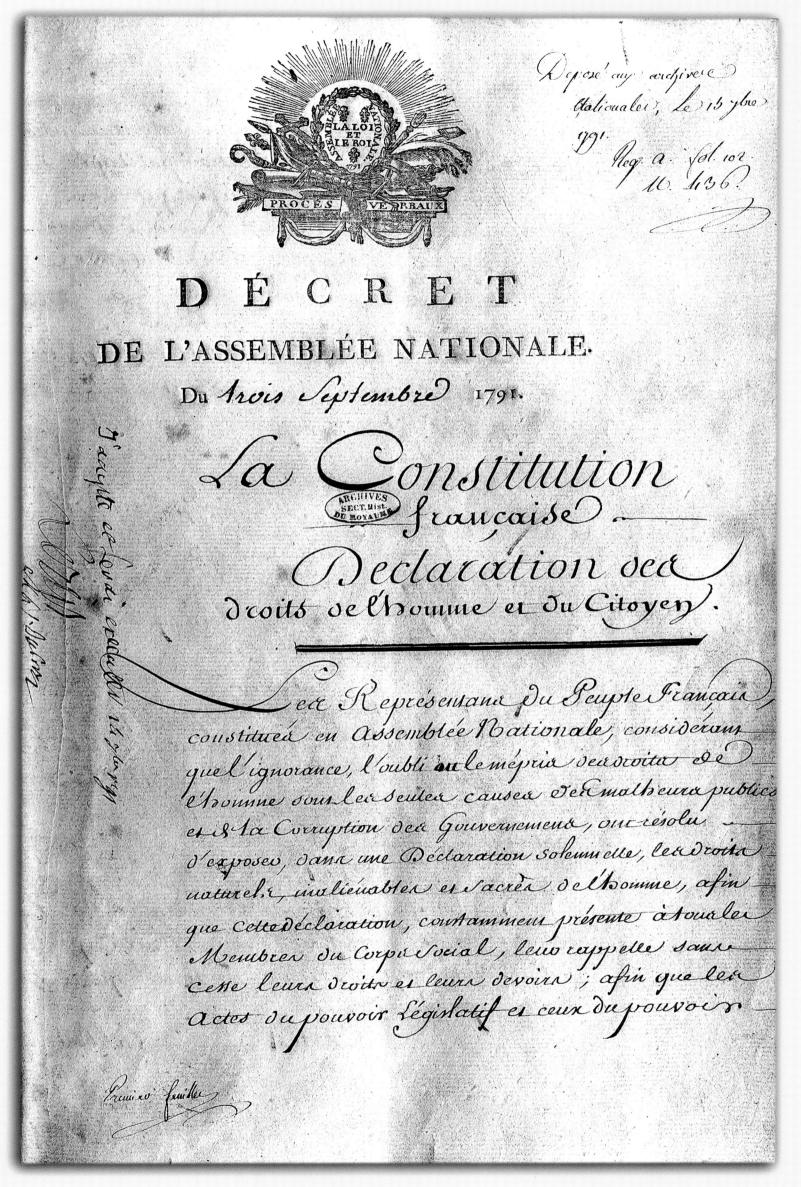

DÉCRET

DE L'ASSEMBLÉE NATIONALE.

Du *trois Septembre* 1791.

La Constitution française

Déclaration des droits de l'homme et du Citoyen.

The Third Estate immediately demanded that the three Orders met together, giving them the possibility of a working majority. When this was refused, they transformed themselves into a National Assembly on 17 June. As in the American Revolution – although that was more a dispute between landlord and tenant than a true revolution – one of the first actions of the National Assembly in August 1789 was to issue a Declaration of the Rights of Man, drafted by Lafayette and his friend Thomas Jefferson, who was US minister in Paris. It was a much less precise document than the American original, and left many questions open. The bold assertion of the first item 'Men are born free and equal in rights' was immediately qualified by the vague statement 'Social distinctions may be founded only upon the general good.'

The history of the next few years are full of 'ifs'. Very few events were inevitable, and mere accident was often decisive. Had Louis XVI been as energetic as his ancestor Henry IV, a respectable constitutional monarchy might have been born that summer, enforced by a spurt of sharp repression; but Louis, who would have made an excellent provincial mayor, was an incompetent monarch. On 23 June, he insisted that the three Orders must remain separate: four days later he retracted – too late, for 170 priests and 50 nobles had already joined the National Assembly. Rumours of a royal counter-attack spread, and on 14 July a Parisian mob, searching for weapons, stormed the Bastille, the ancient fortress in the heart of the capital.

The Fourteenth of July is celebrated as the French national holiday, but at the time it was an apparently inconsequential episode. King Louis, returning from a day's hunting, his usual pastime, wrote in his diary 'nothing'. A week later, another gang of rioters murdered the Paris official responsible for food supplies. When they attempted to bring his head into a City Council meeting at the Hôtel de Ville – a lump of flesh had already been displayed – a messenger was sent out to say the Council was engaged on important business. A more decisive move was made in October, when, inspired by hungry and indignant women, some 20,000 Parisians invaded the Palace of Versailles and forced the royal family back into the city. Ultimate power in France, it seemed, now rested with an increasingly enraged mob.

The Assembly continued to debate a future constitution, beginning with another Declaration of the Rights of Man: those of Woman were briefly considered, but set aside. It continued the debate for two years, meanwhile sweeping away all the most irritating survivals of the ancient regime, in a metaphorical bonfire of privileges, exemptions, special rights and dues, internal barriers to trade and ecclesiastical jurisdictions, all pushed through under pressure from the formidable Comte de Mirabeau. Decapitation, previously a privilege of nobility, would be made available to all offenders with the invention of the guillotine, designed by a royal committee: so popular was the device that public executions were only abandoned in 1939.

Money was raised by confiscating all Church properties and issuing paper money on the security of the proceeds. A whole nation seemed to rejoice at a new dawn. Young William Wordsworth, then walking through France, later recalled the emotions:

> *'Bliss was it those days to be alive.*
> *To be young was very heaven.'*

Bliss lasted for less than a year; in September 1791 the new Constitution was enacted, and the National Assembly dissolved itself before disintegrating in

chaos after more Parisian violence resulted in a pitched battle at the Tuileries, a protracted massacre and the end of constitutional government.

Trying again, a new National Convention was elected to draft another constitution; since less than ten per cent of the electorate voted, it could hardly be called democratic and was quickly overtaken by events. Meanwhile, diverting attention from domestic trouble, war had been declared on Austria and Prussia, and was going badly, until on the 20 April, General Dumouriez gained an unexpected victory over the allies at Valmy. Flushed with revolutionary nationalism and anxious to spread the benefits of French achievement, war was then declared on the rest of Europe, including Britain. King Louis was now an unnecessary embarrassment and was executed in public, with the effective new guillotine, on 21 January 1793 followed in due course by Queen Marie Antoinette. Many Frenchmen were infuriated and armed revolts erupted, notably in the Vendée region of western France: the expense of the war had devalued the paper currency to a fraction of its face value, churches were desecrated and conscription threatened. It took two years' fighting, and extraordinary brutality – the guillotine was too slow, and mass drownings were preferred – before the uprising was suppressed.

Extraordinary challenges demanded extraordinary measures, imposed by the Committees of Public Safety and of General Security, as one faction succeeded another, and sent the losers to the scaffold. No one in public life could feel safe, and when the cold and ruthless Robespierre demanded from the Convention absolute powers to execute anyone, without even the semblance of a trial, his frightened colleagues acted. On 8 Thermidor in the new Revolutionary Calendar (26 July 1794), Robespierre and 70 of his supporters were seized and decapitated in a single day. The Terror had claimed a huge, unknown number of victims – although quarter of a million was perhaps a fair estimate– but was now ended. Once again, France had to find a new way of governing itself.

After a year of consolidation during which peace was made with Holland and Spain and a couple of riots suppressed, yet another new constitution was devised, and to some extent legitimized by a plebiscite. It was too reactionary to suit the Paris agitators, who staged one more revolt, which was dispersed by some well-sited cannon, directed by a young Corsican artillery officer, Napoleon Bonaparte.

Consul and Emperor

The latest Constitution entrusted executive authority to five 'Directors', appointed by a newly-elected Convention in November 1795. For two years it seemed that the revolution really was over, and peace and prosperity established. This was the era of the 'Incroyables' and 'Merveilleuses', rich young men and women sporting extravagant costumes, the girls in diaphanous shifts, with 'directoire' drawers providing minimal cover. The possibility of a monarchist revival was avoided by another coup d'état in September 1797, executed by General Augereau, seconded for that purpose by the useful commander, Napoleon Bonaparte, then busy fighting the Austrians in Italy.

RIGHT *French painter Jacques-Louis David's famous equestrian portrait of Napoleon* (Bonaparte Crossing the Alps; Great St Bernard Pass, 20 May 1800) *conveys the dynamism and charisma of the Corsican career soldier who was soon to brings large tracts of Europe under his control.*

The reconstructed Directory was more concerned with maximizing its members' incomes than dealing with France's serious social and financial difficulties, and was handed a magnificent present when Napoleon returned from his Italian campaign in triumph, with a huge haul of booty and the prospect of new income from the conquered territories. Repression at home combined with military success abroad has always been a favourite solution for incompetent governments, but the Directory felt it prudent to send its successful general a long way off, to a new campaign in Egypt, where he could hardly interfere in Paris. Unfortunately, Napoleon was the only French commander capable of continuing the series of victories in Europe. France became a kleptocracy, a bandit state, raiding new territories including Switzerland and the Papal States, gaining much more loot, but at the cost of near-universal hostility, which led in turn to military failure. Reluctantly, the Directors, who now included the able and thoroughly unscrupulous ex-Abbé Sièyes, recalled Napoleon. After suffering his first defeat, at the siege of Acre by Admiral Sir Sidney Smith, and evading Horatio Nelson's squadron, which had annihilated the French fleet at the Battle of the Nile (Aboukir Bay), Bonaparte returned to France in October 1799.

When Sièyes imagined himself as 'the brain' behind a new regime, with the inexperienced Napoleon as 'the sword', he made a huge mistake. The Convention, now an unrepresentative rump, put together another constitution on the Roman model of a three-man Consulate. One month after Napoleon's arrival in France, a coup d'état resulted in his appointment as First Consul, the unquestioned leader, a new Caesar. That useful device, a referendum, later confirmed Napoleon's position for life by 3,653,600 votes to 8,272. For the next 15 years, under one title or another, Napoleon Bonaparte was the unchallengeable Dictator of France.

History is more often determined by geography, economics, technology or simply climate than by a single person or group, but Napoleon Bonaparte was a great exception. His brilliance as a strategist and his ability to choose subordinates, coupled with a genuine interest in social and educational reforms inspired by a phenomenal energy and a powerful self-confidence,

BELOW *Etching by the artist Francisco de Goya showing Napoleon as a 'flesh-eating vulture' with cropped wings at the mercy of an angry Spanish mob. The hard-fought Peninsular War (1808–14) ended in French defeat.*

enabled him to defy every continental power and inflict a series of crushing military defeats. Nourished by swingeing taxation on conquered territories and massive indemnities, the French treasury was able to bear the enormous expenses of war, and national pride was swollen. The grandiloquent paintings of David, portraying the First Consul in magnificent poses, reflected popular enthusiasm. Even some Britons, who were to be his most persistent enemies, were impressed: the Whig Lord Holland described Napoleon as 'the greatest statesman and ablest general of modern times' and the moderate Tory George Canning wrote:

> *'I am not a panegyrist of Bonaparte, but I cannot close my eyes to the superiority of his talent, and dazzling ascendancy of his genius.'*

Continued victories were essential to maintain the legend of Napoleonic invincibility, and these continued against whatever armies could be assembled by the German powers. By 1802, even Britain was ready to make peace, but it quickly became clear that neither France nor Britain intended to stick to the undertakings made at the Treaty of Amiens, and, without much thought, Britain declared war once more in May 1803.

In reality, Britain could never hope to offer much assistance on the ground to whatever allies could be mustered. The regular army was small and had to stretch to cover Ireland, where a French landing in 1798 had only been overcome with difficulty, supported as it was by an Irish rising, and to defence in Canada and India, while the militia, although keen (Wordsworth and Coleridge were both volunteers) were only available for home service. Strategically the Royal Navy's ships retained control of the world's oceans, but were only occasionally deployable tactically, notably in the destruction of the Danish fleet and bombardment of Copenhagen in 1801. A French invasion looked distinctly possible, as Napoleon began assembling a great army depot at Boulogne, visible across the straits of Dover. Were he to be successful, Bonaparte would come to England as Emperor of the French, having been consecrated by Pope Pius VII on 2 November 1804.

If the attempt had been made, it would probably have meant Napoleon's downfall: 'I do not say they cannot come, only that they cannot come by sea,' was the Royal Navy's answer to a Parliamentary question. Considering a single broadside from a battleship discharged a greater weight of metal than a whole French army's guns, shipping over 90,000 men in thousands of towed lighters with even a couple of English frigates in the offing would have entailed their almost certain annihilation. Nelson's victory at Trafalgar in October 1805, which destroyed the French and Spanish fleets, put paid to that ambition, but Napoleon had already on 13 August shelved the plan in favour of a rapid strike against the German armies. It was to be Nelson's second-in-command at Trafalgar, Admiral Collingwood, who by his patient blockade of European ports played the more decisive role in the eventual French defeat.

The Navy aside, Britain's contribution was to encourage continental coalitions by patient diplomacy and large financial contributions, a protracted process, interrupted by French victories. After 18 months of brilliant campaigning, Napoleon was able to stage a dramatic meeting on a raft in the River Niemen with the Emperor of Russia and the King of Prussia, at which Russia agreed to join the continental boycott of British goods, which it was hoped would counter the Royal Navy's blockade. Prussia was humiliated by the loss of nearly half her territory to France's satellite

ABOVE The Battle of Trafalgar, *painting (1822) by J.M.W. Turner. This naval engagement in 1805 was a vital Allied victory, dispelling the threat of a Napoleonic invasion of the British Isles.*

Confederation of the Rhine and to the new Grand Duchy of Warsaw. One mark of Napoleon's genius was his ability to present revolutionary values of human rights and democracy – scornfully flouted by him in practice – as gifts brought by French armies to oppressed populations. Through conquest bolstered by propaganda, the French Empire extended from the Atlantic to the Adriatic and from Sicily to the Baltic.

It had been gained at tremendous human cost. During Napoleon's wars some 800,000 Frenchmen and half that number of their allied troops were killed. Starvation must have accounted for many more. Since all those wars were fought abroad they were provisioned at the local populations' expense. For every four men there was a horse, which ate ten times as much, and constant advances were essential to draw ahead of the local stocks devoured by the army, leaving the peasants to manage as best they might; and the army that left to invade Russia in 1812 numbered not much less than 800,000.

The first French defeats came, however, in Portugal, after General Sir Arthur Wellesley (the family name had been changed from Wesley in 1798, and Sir Arthur is better known by his later title of the Duke of Wellington) defeated two French armies in the summer of 1808. Napoleon himself had to be called upon to repair the damage, but the following year Wellington was back again, defeating three French marshals and Napoleon's brother Joseph, who had been foisted on the reluctant Spanish to replace King Ferdinand. With the help of Spanish and Portuguese soldiers and *guerrilleros*, who fought

with great savagery, provoked by French atrocities recorded in Francisco de Goya's horrifying etchings, Wellington steadily pushed the French out of the Peninsula. Although, by comparison with the huge commitment to the Russian war, the Iberian front was relatively minor, it was a constant drain on French resources and disturbingly near the frontier of France. By December 1812, when Napoleon was scuttling back to Paris from Moscow, pursued by the Tsar's cavalry and the even more deadly Russian winter, the British armies were just 80 miles (130 km) from the French border.

By then France was exhausted, and disillusioned with Bonapartism. Empire and glory had been bought at too high a price. Conscription, of increasingly younger and older men, was deeply resented – conscripts had to be sent to the depot roped together under armed guard, but many still managed to escape. And although much of the fighting had been done by German and Polish allies, they too were now deserting. From March 1813 Prussia, Austria, Sweden, Bavaria and Saxony joined with Russia in an anti-French coalition. Beethoven's work reflected many others' feelings. In the summer of 1813 he intended to dedicate his Third Symphony (the *Eroica*) to Napoleon Bonaparte. By December, thoroughly disillusioned, he presented 'Wellington's victory' an extravaganza with musketry and cannon, portraying the defeated French slinking away from the triumphant English.

France's defeat at the Battle of the Nations in October 1813 should have been final. Napoleon's heterogeneous force of French, Poles, Italians and Germans was smashed, with 100,000 casualties, by the allied army, with the Austrians bearing the brunt of the struggle. As it turned out, after Napoleon's dramatic but brief return in the Hundred Days of 1815, it needed one more great fight at Waterloo before 22 years of war were ended.

1776 – 1845
A New World Order

■ Surrender of Yorktown brings American Revolution to a close 1781 ■ US Constitution enacted 1789 ■ Spanish-American Wars of Independence 1810–26 ■ Brazil liberates itself from Portuguese rule 1822 ■ Texas wins independence from Mexico 1836

The eight-year conflict known as the American Revolution, or War of Independence, was a complex dispute, in part a civil war between conservatives hoping to preserve the British connection and radicals insisting on independence, but also a frontier fight with Canada, a classic trade quarrel and a straightforward power struggle between empire and colonists.

The war could never have been won by Britain, given the vocal domestic opposition, but it could have been lost by the Americans. Practical independence would still have been attained – denying it would be too expensive – but the 13 colonies would not have become an embryonic nation. Bloodshed and victory were imperative to generate national pride: plus, of course, the expulsion of obstinate dissidents. Spanish America shrugged off imperial rule without too much effort, but then had to sort out the identity, character and frontiers of the new states.

Free and Independent States

What finally tipped the balance in the American War of Independence was, as Lord Camden had forecast, European intervention. Without exception, all Britain's rivals seized the opportunity. France, Spain and Holland formed a 'League of Armed Neutrality', attacking British interests in India, the Mediterranean and the West Indies, vastly increasing the Royal Navy's commitments. In 1777, the Marquis de Lafayette took the frigate *Hermione* to join George Washington: during a brief journey back to Paris he was able to collect several thousand royal troops and a powerful fleet to help the Americans in the summer of 1780. Without French assistance, General Cornwallis' surrender at Yorktown in October 1781 would have been unlikely.

The final peace terms were favourable, thanks in part to Benjamin Franklin, acting as a Peace Commissioner in Paris, who convinced Fox's agent that it was essential to sideline the French by settling the American question first. After two more changes of British government – there were four between January 1782 and December 1783 – and much negotiation the Peace of Paris was concluded in September 1783, acknowledging the Colonies to be 'free, sovereign and independent states' with generous boundaries extending to the Mississippi. How successful the new order would be, remained to be seen.

Independence had been secured, but in name only. It was not until May 1787 that representatives of 12 states assembled (Rhode Island refused to take part). A total of 65 delegates had been appointed, but only 39 stuck it out to sign the Constitution of the United States into existence. The Convention assembled in Philadelphia, with Washington almost automatically elected as President, had many advantages, of which the greatest was familiarity with representative constitutions, on a sufficiently small scale to enable many citizens to participate in an elected legislature. Many states had indeed already established new constitutions after the Declaration of Independence.

The franchise, although restricted, was much more democratic than that in Britain. American literacy too, was higher than in England – Scotland being markedly superior – and informed argument based on such popular journals as Benjamin Franklin's *Poor Richards Almanack* and Alexander Hamilton's *Federalist* was frequent. Nevertheless, the delegates had some difficult times. A major problem was the imbalance between such large states as Pennsylvania and Massachusetts, and the much smaller ones, and whether representation should be proportional to population or equal for all states. James Madison's persistent diplomacy and Benjamin Franklin's jokey good-humour were essential at reaching a compromise: population for the Lower House of Representatives, two members for each State in the Senate. Too much democracy was carefully avoided. There would be no direct elections to the Senate or for the presidency. A balance of power between Executive and Legislature, with a Supreme Court deciding on constitutional problems, was carefully constructed. After more than two centuries and under dramatically changed circumstances the constitution still functions, one of the oldest forms of government anywhere in the world.

When George Washington took office as first President of the United States on 29 April 1789 no trace of government machinery existed: the whole structure of an administration had to be invented. The Treasury was empty,

no system of taxes existed and debt interest was mounting. There was no civil service, and only 80 men in the US Army. Once again, Washington was the essential man: his patient tact and dedication helped to put flesh on the dry bones of the constitution, and within two years the United States had what was, at least potentially, the world's most efficient government.

Within three months of Washington's inauguration the Bastille had fallen and the French Revolution begun; at first enthusiastically welcomed in America, by the turn of the century France appeared as a threat. The French province of Louisiana, comprising the western Mississippi basin to the Rockies and the Canadian border and ceded to Spain in 1763, had been secretly retroceded in 1800. Napoleon, having been frustrated in the East, saw an opportunity of striking against Britain in the West, planning to use the French island colony of Saint-Domingue (modern Haiti) as a base to occupy the mainland. The French invasion force met with unexpected resistance from the newly-freed slaves led by Toussaint L'Ouverture, delaying it long enough to allow an

ABOVE *A contemporary painting by the French artist Auguste Couder shows generals de Rochambeau (right) and Washington giving the orders for the final assault on British positions at the siege of Yorktown in 1781.*

alarmed President Jefferson to attempt to buy the city of New Orleans from France, offering $7.5 million. But Napoleon's patience was exhausted; on 11 March 1803, he decided instead to attempt an invasion of Britain and on 10 April asked for an offer for the whole territory of Louisiana. A price of $15 million was agreed within days; the United States was doubled in size and France gained some much needed cash, even if the actual payment was much reduced, having been made in US bonds, subject to heavy discounts. After the eventual war with Britain in 1812, brought about by the constant armed interference with American shipping involved in blockading the Napoleonic Empire, both the United States and Britain appreciated that their common trade was too valuable to be endangered by antagonism.

The fenators and reprefentatives beforementioned, and the members of the feveral flate legiflatures, and all executive and judicial officers, both of the United States and of the feveral States, fhall be bound by oath or affirmation, to fupport this conftitution; but no religious teft fhall ever be required as a qualification to any office or public truft under the United States.

VII.

The ratification of the conventions of nine States, fhall be fufficient for the eftablifhment of this conftitution between the States fo ratifying the fame:

Done in Convention, by the unanimous confent of the

States prefent, the feventeenth day of September, in the year of our Lord one thoufand feven hundred and eighty-feven, and of the Independence of the United States of America the twelfth. In witnefs whereof we have hereunto fubfcribed our Names.

GEORGE WASHINGTON, Prefident,
And Deputy from VIRGINIA.

NEW-HAMPSHIRE.	John Langdon, Nicholas Gilman.		George Read, Gunning Bedford, Junior,
MASSACHUSETTS.	Nathaniel Gorham, Rufus King.	DELAWARE.	John Dickinfon, Richard Baffett, Jacob Broom.
CONNECTICUT	William Samuel Johnfon, Roger Sherman.		James M'Henry,
NEW-YORK.	Alexander Hamilton.	MARYLAND.	Daniel of St. Tho Jenifer, Daniel Carrol.
NEW-JERSEY.	William Livingfton, David Brearley, William Paterfon, Jonathan Dayton.	VIRGINIA.	John Blair, James Madifon, Junior.
PENNSYLVANIA.	Benjamin Franklin, Thomas M'ifflin, Robert Morris, George Clymer, Thomas Fitzfimons, Jared Ingerfoll, James Wilfon, Gouverneur Morris.	NORTH-CAROLINA	William Blount, Richard Dobbs Spaight, Hugh Williamfon.
		SOUTH-CAROLINA.	John Rutledge, Charles Cotefworth Pinckney Charles Pinckney. Pierce Butler.
		GEORGIA.	William Few, Abraham Baldwin.

Atteft, William Jackfon, SECRETARY.

IN CONVENTION, Monday September 17th, 1787.
PRESENT

The States of New-Hampfhire, Maffachufetts, Connecticut, Mr. Hamilton from New-York, New-Jerfey, Pennfylvania, Delaware, Maryland, Virginia, North-Carolina, South-Carolina and Georgia:

RESOLVED,

THAT the preceding Conftitution be laid before the United States in Congrefs affembled, and that it is the opinion of this Convention, that it fhould afterwards be fubmitted to a Convention of Delegates, chofen in each State by the People thereof, under the recommendation of its Legiflature, for their affent and ratification; and that each Convention affenting to, and ratifying the fame, fhould give Notice thereof to the United States in Congrefs affembled.

Refolved, That it is the opinion of this Convention, that as foon as the Conventions of nine States fhall have ratified this Conftitution, the United States in Congrefs affembled fhould fix a day on which Electors fhould be appointed by the States which fhall have ratified the fame, and a day on which the Electors fhould affemble to vote for the Prefident, and the time and place for commencing proceedings under this Conftitution. That after fuch publication the Electors fhould be appointed, and the Senators and Reprefentatives elected: That the Electors fhould meet on the day fixed for the Election of the Prefident, and fhould tranfmit their votes certified, figned, fealed and directed, as the Conftitution requires, to the Secretary of the United States in Congrefs affembled, that the Senators and Reprefentatives fhould convene at the time and place affigned; that the Senators fhould appoint a Prefident of the Senate, for the fole purpofe of receiving, opening and counting the votes for Prefident; and, that after he fhall be chofen, the Congrefs, together with the Prefident, fhould, without delay, proceed to execute this Conftitution.

By the unanimous Order of the Convention, **GEORGE WASHINGTON, Prefident.**

William Jackfon, Secretary

Resolution to ratify the US Constitution (1787), containing the names of the 39 delegates from 12 states who attended the convention. This agreement supplanted the earlier Articles of Confederation (1781–87).

One grave question remained unsettled. If all were entitled to 'life, liberty, and the pursuit of happiness', were the black slaves not to be accounted human and included? Georgia and the Carolinas fiercely dissented, and the Northern States did not persist. It was left for later decision, not to be discussed before 1808.

Collateral Damage; the Fallout from the American Revolution

The success of the Revolution and the foundation of the United States radically changed the destinies of all other American communities, and even those further afield. Canada was left a population increased by their share of the American 'Loyalist' diaspora, and without the 100,000 refugees Canada would have developed much more slowly, restrained by a small, unenthusiastic French-speaking appendage. The Loyalists, a varied group of professionals, artisans and entrepreneurs, were accompanied by some 2,000 Iroquois under their chief Joseph Brand, who were allotted lands on the Grand River. Unrestrained by a written constitution, with all its amendments, and a Supreme Court, Canada could smoothly absorb not only French law, religion and traditions, but many others, including those of the Indians.

The first modern black African states also emerged from the revolutionary tumult. Thousands of black Americans took their chance to escape slavery by joining the Loyalists, but few remained in Canada once the opportunity was given to cross the Atlantic to the new colony of Sierra Leone, under British protection. Sierra Leone and the neighbouring Gold Coast Colony both formed essential bases for the suppression of the slave trade, and for the development of African political skills. Two generations later, their descendants were writing the first modern African constitution. Another refuge for ex-slaves was provided in the American-backed state of Liberia, while the French failure in Saint-Domingue led to the secession of the western part of the island to form the empire of Haiti.

Integrating the newcomers, and any future British immigrants, with the surviving Indians was an unprecedented task, and one which the British government was inclined to leave to the Canadians themselves. Colonies in general were regarded as an expensive nuisance, and some influential British opinion advised that the Americans should be asked to incorporate the colony. The unsuccessful American invasion during the war of 1812, halted by soldiers led by the Shawnee chief Tecumseh and the Iroquois Major John Brand, later to become the first Indian to be elected to a Canadian parliament, and the furious reaction of the Catholic Québecois to being forced under the rule of a Protestant republic, stifled that possibility. An area rather greater than that of the United States was left to be administered by a governor advised by an appointed council and an elected legislature, working on a tight budget. After much argument, the USA eventually accepted the 49th Parallel of North Latitude as the border with Canada west of the Great Lakes. To the Indians this became the 'Medicine Line', dividing the remorseless persecution of the

US Army from the security provided by the few hundred men of the Royal North West Mounted Police– later the Royal Canadian Mounted Police or 'Mounties'. When the Sioux chief Sitting Bull, survivor of a hundred fights with the US Cavalry, including the annihilation of Custer's troopers at Little Bighorn, finally sought refuge across the Medicine Line in May 1877, his braves were escorted by a whole regiment of US Cavalry; they were welcomed by Inspector James Walsh of the Mounties, accompanied by four constables, walking calmly into their camp.

If Indians could not, as had Brand and his father Joseph before him, be integrated into Canadian political society, then morality as well as economy combined to conciliate those who preferred traditional life, which involved some serious thinking about land ownership and aboriginal rights. Beginning in 1783 and continuing ever since, with the latest in 1984, a series of treaties – agreements is perhaps a more appropriate term – covered the whole area of Canada, recognizing aboriginal rights to land use. They could hardly be truly equitable, but they succeeded in preserving Indian cultures and avoiding the bloody struggles that continued in the USA for most of the century.

Iberian America

The experience of the Spanish colonies was very different. The 13 northern English colonies were racially homogenous, neither the black slaves nor Indians being regarded as having any civic existence; Iberian America was, and often remains, extremely conscious of racial difference, as seen in the plethora of designations for people of mixed race (e.g. *mestizo* for mixed European and Indian, *mulatto* for European and Negro and *zambo* for Indian and Negro). In colonial times, some distinctions were constitutionally legal, but after independence social status was still often determined by skin colour. And while the English colonies formed a tight geographical unit, with easy coastal communications, the Spanish Empire stretched for thousands of miles over North, Central and South America, from San Francisco and the Mississippi to the border of unexplored Patagonia. Over 60 governments, provinces, captaincies-general and intendancies reported through complex lines of communication to the Madrid government, and whereas every English colony already had its own elected, argumentative assembly with up to 150 years experience of self-government in local affairs, no such tradition existed in Spain or her colonies. Reform, however, was on the way.

The southern part of the continent had been neglected, but was now organized as the Viceroyalty of La Plata, (covering modern Argentina, Uruguay, Paraguay and Bolivia). On a narrow strip of land on the south bank of the Rio de la Plata stood the capital Buenos Aires. Once the news of the Spanish King Ferdinand VII's surrender to the French in 1808 arrived, loyalties were split between monarchists and followers of the new liberal junta established at Seville, who proclaimed a new constitution. Buenos Aires declared for Seville, provoking a civil war, during which monarchists were able to take power in Bolivia and Paraguay. In the south, Juan Manuel de

BELOW *The Battle of Maipú was fought on 5 April 1818 by Spanish American rebels led by Argentine general José de San Martín and Chilean independence leader Bernardo O'Higgins against Spanish royalists. The two commanders are pictured celebrating victory in this contemporary painting. The battle proved decisive in establishing Chilean independence.*

Rosas seized power in 1829 to establish a prototypical fascist state, complete with a personality cult, secret police and Church support, setting an example that was to become depressingly familiar. Rosas was eventually brought down in 1852, and after another decade of sporadic fighting around the borders the new Argentine Republic, under liberal presidents, began a period of expansion and prosperity which was to make it one of the world's richest nations.

Apart from some intellectual circles, there was no such general belligerency among the élite that had been experienced in the English colonies, until Spain's disastrous decision to ally itself with the French in fighting Britain. Spanish naval power had been destroyed after Trafalgar and the economic link between America and the mother country destroyed, but Wellington's victories in the Peninsula, and the restoration of King Ferdinand VII in 1814, revived Spanish ambitions to crush colonial bids for independence. Spanish-Americans were divided, with civil wars becoming routine, between republicans and monarchists – perhaps, some suggested with a descendant of the Incas on the throne – between merchants and landowners, and, more importantly, between the Indians and *mestizos* against the creole élite.

Simón Bolívar, who had established a brief republic in Venezuela in 1813, became disillusioned with the arguments between the factions and convinced that any new government must compromise between firm leadership and democracy. In the south, the professional soldier José de San Martín, who had fought alongside the British in the Peninsular War had liberated Chile in a brief campaign and installed his friend Bernardo O'Higgins as president-dictator of a new republic. San Martín's next target was Peru, assisted by the small Chilean fleet assembled by the Scottish Royal Navy officer Lord Cochrane, but this proved more difficult, with sceptical creoles and an undefeated Spanish royal expeditionary force.

Bolívar had been more successful. Enlisting black slaves and *mestizo* guerrillas, and after a terrible march over the Andes, his forces defeated the royalists and entered Bogotá in August 1819. Thereafter the revolutionaries' task grew much easier as the reactionary new regime of King Ferdinand was forced to revert to the liberal constitution proclaimed in 1812 and to negotiate with the colonists. A return to Spanish dominance was out of the question, but the contention between liberals and conservatives, and with the remaining royalist armies, who might well have to fight their way out, still had to be resolved.

San Martín and Bolívar discussed future policy at a meeting in July 1822, which left Bolívar in command to complete the liberation of Peru, with San Martín eventually returning to Europe. Bolívar had now been instrumental in founding several new states, but was disappointed in his principal aim, the establishment of a United States of South America. Even his own creation of Gran Colombia fractured, with Venezuela and Ecuador setting up on their own. On his way to exile Bolívar lamented:

> *'America is ungovernable. Those who have secured the revolution have ploughed the sea'.*

Both Spain and Portugal were invaded by Napoleon's troops, but while the Spanish monarchy sacrificed much of its legitimacy and prestige by surrendering to the French, the Portuguese King João, with his family and staff, moved off to Brazil, escorted by the British fleet. While the war

continued, Portuguese patriotism supported the monarchy, but once peace had been made the King returned to Europe, leaving his son Dom Pedro as regent. Brazilians, however, having tasted independence, refused to return to Portuguese rule and in September 1822 elected Dom Pedro as emperor. Encouraged by Great Britain, Portugal recognized Brazil's independence, with one condition being the abolition of the slave trade. All this had been achieved with little violence, leaving the Brazilian élite united, facing the future confidently.

Mexico

'Poor Mexico!' Porfirio Diaz (president 1876–1911) is said to have lamented: 'so far from God and so near the United States.' Mexican independence began in 1810 with the famous *Grito de Dolores* ('the cry of pain') published on 16 September, now Mexico's Independence Day, by the priest Miguel Hidalgo. It rapidly became a race war, which smouldered on until 1821, when the surviving rebels joined with the conservative leader Augustín de Iturbide to issue a manifesto, the 'Plan of Iguala', a compromise speedily accepted by

ABOVE *In the wake of the 1845 US annexation of Texas, which Mexico considered part of its territory, war continued between the two countries. With the defeat of Mexico at the Battle of Churubusco (1847) and the capture of Mexico city, the country was forced to give up its territories of New Mexico and California.*

almost all, and the Mexican Empire was created. All the central American states agreed to join in what later became the Central American Federation: but without Mexico, for the empire was replaced in 1823 by a republic. The rising had been led by the young General Antonio Lopez de Santa Anna, elected president in 1833.

Among the problems he faced was a rebellion in the province of Texas. Anglo-American settlers had already been peaceably acquiring Texan properties, under liberal conditions: each family was given 72 hectares (177 acres) of arable land and 5,300 hectares (13,000 acres) of prairie pasture; Stephen Austin, who settled 300 families, received a bonus of 26,000 hectares (65,000 acres). English-speaking Texans soon outnumbered the Spanish,

and when Santa Anna announced in 1835 a new decree, centralizing the constitution and reducing states' rights, the colonists rebelled. After a couple of minor, not very competently-led fights, at the Alamo convent in San Antonio and Goliad, which the Texans lost, the Tennessean Sam Houston scored a decisive victory over an army led by Santa Anna in person at San Jacinto. Elected as president of the Republic of Texas, Houston had to decide whether its future should be annexation by the United States or independence: the decision did not come easily.

Establishing a London embassy in an alley off St James' Street, Houston, in his capital of Washington-on-the-Brazos, received a British chargé d'affaires, Captain Charles Elliot, demoted to that unattractive post for the offence of having acquired Hong Kong (see Eastern Superpowers: India and China). Houston and Elliott considered a demarche which would obtain Mexico's recognition of Texan independence, but Foreign Secretary Lord Palmerston refused to consider anything that the United States might interpret as an affront, and the future of Texas was only decided in 1845, when Texas was admitted to the Union as the 28th state.

IMPERIALISM

	1820	1830	1840	1850	1860
EUROPE	**1821** Start of the Greek War of Independence **1827** Battle of Navarino secures Greek independence	**1830** Louis-Philippe elected king of France after the July Revolution; Belgians revolt against Dutch rule **1830–31** Insurrection in Poland suppressed **1832** The Reform Act provides for limited parliamentary reform in Britain; Ottomans recognize Greek independence	**1846–48** Widespread liberal and nationalist revolutions in Switzerland, Poland, Sicily and France **1848** Louis Napoleon elected president of France **1848–49** Revolts against the Austrians fail in Italy; Garibaldi flees to America	**1852** Louis Napoleon becomes Emperor Napoleon III of France **1853–56** Crimean War: British and French halt Russian Black Sea expansion **1855** Alexander II becomes Tsar of Russia and institutes reforms **1859** France and Piedmont win Lombardy from Austria	**1860** Garibaldi invades Sicily and captures most of southern Italy **1861** Russian serfs are emancipated by Tsar Alexander **1864** Schleswig–Holstein War: Austria and Prussia invade Denmark
THE AMERICAS	**1820** Simon Bolívar liberates upper Peru, later renamed Bolivia **1821** Battle of Carabobo; independence of Venezuela **1822** Brazil announces complete independence	**1835** In the southern states of the United States, abolitionists are expelled and mailing anti-slavery literature is forbidden **1836–39** Bolivia and Peru form a brief confederation **1837** The United States officially recognizes Texas as independent. Mexico does not **1837** End of slavery in British colonies	**1845** The United States annexes Texas **1848** Treaty of Guadaloupe Hidalgo ends the Mexican–American War; New Mexico and California, and much of Texas ceded to the US	**1850** California joins the Union as a free state **1854** The Kansas and Nebraska Act gives settlers the right to decide whether to allow slavery in a new territory **1857** The Dred Scott decision outlaws restrictions on slavery in the territories	**1861** American Civil War starts when Confederate forces fire on Fort Sumter **1861–68** New US territories of Nevada, Dakota, Colorado, Idaho, Arizona, Montana and Wyoming created **1862** Argentine Republic founded **1864** France establishes Archduke Maximilian as Mexican king
AFRICA AND OCEANIA	**1822** Liberia is founded for freed US slaves	**1830** French conquest of Algeria starts **1835–36** The Great Trek begins when 10,000 Boers, the Voortrekkers, leave the Cape Colony and go north to seek better livelihoods	**1840** Treaty of Waitangi signed by Maori chiefs **1842–44** Explorer David Livingstone explores central and southern Africa **1843** Start of First Maori War, also known as The Flagstaff War, fought between New Zealand Maoris and Britain	**1852** Britain recognizes Transvaal's independence **1854** Britain recognizes Orange Free State **1855** David Livingstone discovers and names the Victoria Falls **1858** John Hanning Speke discovers and names Lake Victoria	**1860** Start of Second Maori War **1861** Britain annexes Lagos and begins to suppress the Sokoto caliphate
ASIA AND INDIA	**1824–26** First Anglo–Burmese War fought primarily over the control of northeastern India	**1839–42** Disastrous Anglo-Afghan War is fought to counter a perceived Russian threat	**1842** Treaty of Nanking concludes the First Anglo-Chinese (Opium) War, and opens up treaty ports and cedes Hong Kong to Britain **1843–49** Forcible annexation of Sind and the Punjab by Indian government	**1851–75** King Rama IV modernizes independent Siam **1853** US Commodore Perry lands at Edo Bay, Japan **1856–60** Second Anglo-Chinese War **1857** The Indian Mutiny begins with the capture of Delhi and the sieges of Lucknow and Kanpur **1858** Unequal treaties are signed between Japan and foreign powers	**1868** The Meiji restoration in Japan; imperial capital transferred to Tokyo (Edo)

RIGHT *A statue of Simon Bolívar in Paris*

BELOW *A painting of a Zulu attack on a Boer camp by Charles Bell, 1883*

ABOVE *The David Livingstone memorial at Victoria Falls, Zimbabwe*

1820–1900

1866 Prussia defeats Austria in the Seven Weeks War

1867 Dual Monarchy of Austria–Hungary created

RIGHT *The German empire is proclaimed in the Hall of Mirrors in the palace of Versailles, 1871*

1870 Unification of Italy

1870–71 Franco–Prussian War; France defeated and the Empire of the Germans emerges

1878 Congress of Berlin confirms independence of Serbia, Bulgaria and Romania from Ottoman Empire

1881 Tsar Alexander II assassinated; Alexander III reasserts autocratic rule

1885 European powers meet in Berlin and reach agreement concerning Africa. They give Belgium control of the Congo, Germany acquires what is today Tanzania. Britain annexes what today is Botswana. France colonizes Central Africa and establishes a little colony on the northern tip of Madagascar

1899 Hague Conventions ban the most contentious methods of war, including poison gases

1864–70 War of Triple Alliance; Paraguay fights Argentina, Uruguay and Brazil

1865 Confederates surrender at Appomattox; end of American Civil War

1867 Dominion of Canada set up; Russians sell Alaska to the United States for US $7.2 million

1878 Cuban rebellion against Spanish rule

1879–83 War of the Pacific between Chile and Bolivia against Peru

1882 The US Congress puts the Chinese Exclusion Act into effect

1886 After a four-year effort, American troops capture the Apache chieftain Geronimo

1889 Brazil is proclaimed a republic

1893 United States annexes Hawaii

1898 Spanish–American War breaks out as America demands Spain relinquish its control of Cuba

1869 Suez Canal, built by the French, opens

1871 Explorer Henry Morton Stanley finds the ailing David Livingstone at Lake Tanganyika; Stanley continues to explore the Congo region

1877–78 Britain annexes Transvaal

1879 Britain defeats the Zulu kingdom in the Zulu War

1881 First Anglo–Boer War

1884 Berlin conference begins 'Scramble for Africa'

1885 British relieve Khartoum from Madhist attack: King Leopold II of the Belgians becomes King of the Congo

1890 Cecil Rhodes establishes Rhodesia, today's Zimbabwe

1898 Kitchener defeats the Madhists at Omdurman

1899–1902 Second Anglo–Boer War

LEFT *Excavation work for the construction of the Suez Canal. Wood engraving of 1860*

RIGHT *A contemporary illustration of Boers charging to the attack*

1875 Dowager Empress Cixi assumes power in China

1876 Queen Victoria becomes Empress of India

1876 Japan forces the Koreans to accept a trade agreement similar to Perry's demands to the Japanese in 1853

1877 Satsuma rebellion; major uprising of the samurai

1878–80 Second Afghan War; Britain fails to subdue Afghanistan

1884 Franco-Chinese war fought to decide whether France should replace China in control of Tonkin (northern Vietnam)

1887 French Indochina formed

1887 The Yellow River bursts its banks, and the flooding kills 900,000 Chinese

1894–95 Sino–Japanese War fought primarily over control of Korea

1900 Boxer Rebellion in China as nationalists rise against perceived imperialist oppressors

1814 – 1871
Post-Napoleonic Europe

■ Congress of Vienna redraws the map of Europe 1814–15 ■ Louis-Philippe comes to power in France 1830 ■ The 'Year of Revolutions' topples several monarchies 1848 ■ Prussia becomes strongest German state after defeat of Austria 1866 ■ Franco-Prussian War 1870–71

The attempts made in a series of international conferences, beginning in 1814, to reshape Europe after more than 20 years of war met with some measure of success. However, a major legacy of the Napoleonic Wars had been the spread of revolutionary ideas throughout the continent.

A century was to elapse before such another protracted and worldwide conflict broke out, but when it did the maps of Europe and the world were very different, the nature of warfare had changed and the relations between people and their governments were much altered.

'Every Nation for Itself'

When the last signature was fixed to the series of agreements concluded in September 1815 ending the Napoleonic conflicts and drafting a new map of Europe, the soldiers, sovereigns and diplomats assembled in Vienna could justifiably congratulate themselves. A defeated and repentant France, now under a constitutional monarchy, had been accepted as a full participant in the 'Concert of Europe'; a near-approximation to the geographical status quo had been achieved, although Poland had been dismembered and what remained placed under Russian rule, and a new Flemish–Walloon kingdom of Belgium established to check future French ambitions to the north. Tidily, the 300 or so German-speaking states had been reduced to a federation of just 39, with Austria nominally, but Prussia in practice, firmly in control. The Italian peninsula was restored to its former rulers with some minor adjustments, leaving Italian-speakers dispersed over a dozen different administrations.

The emperors of Russia and Austria and the king of Prussia, autocrats all, wanted to go further, and establish a 'Holy Alliance', whose actions would be based on 'The Gospel of our Lord and Saviour Jesus Christ'. To the pragmatic British Foreign Secretary, Lord Castlereagh, it was 'a piece of sublime mysticism and nonsense'. More worrying was these rulers' insistence on frequent further meetings, with very wide agendas, intended to debate current problems and especially those which threatened to overturn established governments. As four of these conventions were held, between 1818 and 1822, the British grew restive. A long-established reluctance to interfere in other countries' domestic affairs was reinforced by a realization that some regimes were so incompetent or oppressive that their people had every right to throw them out. Conservative though British governments were, they appreciated that many cherished customs must be abandoned in the face of public opinion.

Besides, Britain, although the only European gains she achieved were the Maltese islands and the doubtful benefit of governing the tiny North Sea island of Heligoland, had done very well in acquiring colonies – Ceylon and the Cape of Good Hope from the Dutch, as well as some Caribbean islands, and in securing Canada and expelling European competitors from India. Britain, it seemed to many – as it still does today – should avoid too great an involvement in Europe and concentrate instead on opportunities further afield. By 1823, Britain had edged out of the Concert of Europe, and George Canning, Castlereagh's successor, could congratulate himself that 'things are getting back to a wholesome state again. Every nation for itself, and God for us all.'

More formally he made it clear that England 'is under no obligation to interfere or to assist in interfering, in the internal concerns of

LEFT *Illustration by the artist George Cruikshank for Charles Dickens' novel* Oliver Twist *(1839). Dickens was one of a new generation of 19th-century writers and artists who attempted to document social inequality and deprivation.*

independent nations.' And it was up to the British government to decide what constituted, for them, an independent nation. Giving a dramatic example of this Canning announced in 1825 that the breakaway Spanish American colonies were now recognized as independent republics:

'We have called a new world into existence to redress the balance of the old.'

It soon became clear that the clock could not be turned back, even by the most determined autocrat. Political and social ideas inspired such painters as Eugène Delacroix, who depicted liberation struggles and Turkish massacres, or musicians like Beethoven and Verdi (in such operas as *Fidelio*, *Don Carlos*, *Macbeth* and *La Battaglia di Legnano*) celebrating the downfall of tyrants. In literature, Alphonse de Lamartine and Lord Byron were not only producing stirring verse but actually participating in revolts. Goethe and Schiller presided over a move away from naïve *Sturm und Drang* bluster to a measured celebration of humanist values, while Dickens and Balzac exposed greed, hypocrisy and neglect. All helped form the ideas of the younger generation. Even Russian Tsars and the Hapsburg royals became infected

ABOVE *The Congress of Vienna opened in October 1814, the first anniversary of the Battle of the Nations at Leipzig. A grand festival attended by Europe's crowned heads was held on the Prater, the city's main public park by the Danube, to mark the occasion.*

by the new ideals. Britain, especially after the liberal reforms begun by Lord Grey in 1830 and the accession of the 18-year-old Queen Victoria in 1837, provided an example of constitutional rule and a refuge for persecuted continental reformers. John Stuart Mill, a leading advocate of women's rights, resisted both the dogmatic programmes of the Benthamites, with their gospel of utilitarianism, and industrialists objecting to any official intervention in their employment practices. Even that contentious subject, Ireland, seemed to have been settled by the Act of Union in 1802 and the change that made it possible for Catholics to take their parliamentary seats with a clear conscience. This optimism was, however, deceptive.

The postwar settlement endured for only 15 years in France. The next wave of revolution began in July 1830 when King Charles X, grandson of Louis XV, who had 'learnt nothing and forgotten nothing' attempted to overturn an election and restore arbitrary rule. Charles was so clearly in the wrong, and

the near-bloodless coup over in three days, that no intervention was possible. One of the rebel leaders was the old Marquis de Lafayette, emerging once more into history, 50 years after his first meeting with George Washington. King Charles' successor, the Duke of Orléans, who ruled as Louis-Philippe 'King of the French' (r.1830–48) was recognized by Britain and Austria. Tsar Nicholas I, attempting to intervene, was foiled by a Polish rebellion, which led to a year's savage war and the suppression of what remained of Polish independence. Apart from sympathy the British could offer nothing to the Poles, but when civil war broke out in Belgium, the new Foreign Secretary, Lord Palmerston, was obliged to take action. The international conference that began in London in November 1830 proved how effective a revived Concert of Europe could be when France and Britain took a leading role, but it still took eight years of continuous effort and sporadic warfare before a final solution was achieved.

It seemed that each young generation must have its own revolution, and 1845 saw the start of a new, more widespread series of revolts in Switzerland, Poland (1846) and Sicily (1847). The first was settled after a short civil war, the second brutally suppressed, but the third began an Italian revolution, which resulted in the centre of power shifting from reactionary Naples to constitutional Piedmont, and the shortlived Roman and Venetian republics. Poles, Hungarians, Venetians and British rallied to the republicans, who were nevertheless crushed by French, Austrian, Neapolitan and Papal troops. Future battle-lines were thereby clearly defined.

The Second French Empire

France seemed to be repeating the drama enacted there 60 years previously, and now considerably speeded up. It began on 22 February 1848, when a banquet due to be held by the parliamentary opposition was banned. An angry crowd assembled in Paris and shouted slogans. Louis-Philippe dismissed the government the next day: the barricades went up, and on 23 February the King abdicated. The new government divided between conservative republicans and socialists; on 23 June the fighting started, and ended four days later with 10,000 killed or wounded. On 28 October, the constitution of the Second Republic was proclaimed, but a Napoleon had already arrived. This was Louis Napoleon Bonaparte, the great Emperor's nephew, a man of much talent, considerable charm and humanity, although lacking fixity of purpose. The name was enough, and, when the presidential election was held on 10 December 1850, he was elected by a great majority, as Prince President: it had taken less than 10 months for the whole process. But parliamentary democracy and a Bonaparte could not coexist. Eleven months later, ratified by another national vote, the Prince President was installed as Emperor Napoleon III – it being assumed that the first Napoleon's son by his Empress Marie Louise, who died in 1832, had actually reigned as Napoleon II.

In Germany, everything depended on the king of Prussia, the well-intentioned King Frederick Wilhelm IV. The changes in Germany had been generally peaceful and a pan-German parliament assembled in the liberal stronghold of Frankfurt. Most German states wanted him to accept the leadership of a united Germany, but Frederick Wilhelm was reluctant to offend Austria; with its varied population of Hungarians, Poles, Italians, Greeks, Slovaks and Romanians, only the German-speaking section of the Habsburg Empire would be acceptable as members. The conundrum was insoluble and the parliament dissolved to general discontent, especially in Prussia.

European initiative passed to France, where the new Emperor, as a Napoleon, was expected to engineer spectacular military victories. The first, although hardly spectacular, was achieved with the help of Britain and Turkey in defeating Russia in the contrived conflict known as the Crimean War (1853–56), although action was also seen in the Baltic and the Sea of Okhotsk. Austria, sensibly enough, stayed out of an unpleasant conflict, the only beneficial result of which was a drastic reorganization of British military medicine and general goodwill for the Piedmontese for having joined the alliance. Taking advantage of this, Count Cavour, the brilliant Piedmontese Prime Minister, inveigled Napoleon into a secret agreement to expel the Austrians from northern Italy. Three months' very costly fighting in the summer of 1859, with new rifled muskets and cannon causing massive casualties, led to a partial victory, with Lombardy becoming Italian once more as a Piedmontese province: the side effects were the initiation of the Red Cross by the Swiss Henri Dunant, who had seen the battles for himself, and the names of a new colour and a Paris

boulevard, both named Magenta after the bloodiest battle. The real success, and one that shook the world, was that of Giuseppe Garibaldi, who with his 1,000 'Redshirt' volunteers invaded Sicily, swept through southern Italy, brushing aside the King of Naples' armies, and presenting half of the Italian peninsula to King Victor Emmanuel II of Piedmont to form the new united kingdom of Italy, with its capital at Rome.

A New Emperor

As a price of his intervention, Napoleon gained Nice and the province of Savoy for France, but from 1860 his projects were less remunerative. Two inventions altered the course of history in the mid-19th century: the electric telegraph and the breech-loading rifle. Near-instantaneous communication throughout Western Europe, extended to America and the Far East, resulted in rapid decision-making. Countries might be plunged into war, or decide on peace in a matter of hours: and the master of this technique was the Prussian Minister, Count Otto von Bismarck. King Frederick Wilhelm IV had quietly gone mad, and been replaced by his steadier brother King Wilhelm I, who cooperated with Bismarck, beginning with a short war against Denmark in 1864. This was a joint effort between Prussia and Austria, acting under the mandate of the German Federation, with the government of the new territories being shared between them. The treaty forming the joint administration was signed in Vienna on 27 October 1864; converting so seemingly amicable an arrangement into the biggest European war for 50 years looked impossible, but Bismarck arranged it within months. Carefully negotiating France's neutrality, and Italian cooperation, Bismarck manoeuvred Austria into declaring war on Prussia on 11 June 1866. On 3 July, half a million soldiers clashed in Bohemia at the Battle of Sadowa, with a crushing defeat for Austria, helped by the new Prussian breech-loading Dreyse needle gun. The next day, the Emperor Franz Joseph I telegraphed Napoleon asking him to help with 'a peace settlement'; by 26 July the peace terms were agreed, and the map of Europe fundamentally changed.

Italy, whose contribution had been minimal, was rewarded by gaining the whole of the Austrian Italian territories, and now took rank as a European Power. The southern German Kingdoms had sided with Austria, along with some of the mini-states, where suspicions of the new North German Federation, formed with Prussia at its head, provoked them to assemble a confederation of their own in July 1867. It was only a question of time, and not too much of it, before a united Germany would emerge as the strongest European nation. Before this happened France had to be dealt with. Napoleon's

LEFT *A cartoon of 1870 shows the British lion keeping a watchful eye on the Russian bear. British suspicion of Russian expansion at the expense of the moribund Ottoman Empire, especially towards the northern borders of India, was intense throughout the 19th century.*

prestige had suffered a major defeat in his Mexican adventure, when the army he sent to support his protégé the Habsburg Archduke Maximilian, was forced to retreat, leaving Maximilian, who had probably been Mexico's best ruler, to be shot by a firing squad. Napoleon's domestic support was rapidly falling off, forcing his government into a wide programme of liberal legislation, with what seemed great success. Another plebiscite in May 1870 resulted in more than seven million votes of approval. The liberal minister Émile Ollivier felt able to declare on 30 June:

> *'Wherever we look no troublesome questions are apparent: never has the maintenance of European peace been better secured.'*

It took all of Bismarck's talents to provoke France into a conflict, for which no real pretext existed, but on 15 July the French government declared war on Prussia. By 2 September, Napoleon was forced to surrender his armies: it had

ABOVE *French soldiers stand around a cannon in the Place Vendôme during the siege of Paris by Prussian forces in March 1871. The French military proved no match for the well-drilled and heavily armed Prussian army. After 10 months, the Franco-Prussian War ended in humiliating defeat for France.*

taken six weeks for what was supposed to have been Europe's finest military force to be smashed. But the war was not over. On 4 September, a republic was proclaimed, and as the German armies marched on Paris the capital was turned into a huge fortress, which held out against the besiegers for three months while the government decamped to Bordeaux. Fighting continued in some pockets, most successfully around Dijon, where the old hero Garibaldi, leading an army stiffened with his Redshirts, gained what Victor Hugo called the only victory against the Germans by a French general.

The most immediate result of the war was a pan-German enthusiasm which encouraged the southern states to agree to join with Prussia and the

North. As a triumphant gesture, the inauguration of the new Empire of the Germans, with King Wilhelm I as its emperor, was proclaimed in the Hall of Mirrors at Versailles on 18 January 1871, while Prussian guns were still firing on Paris. Outside, a disgruntled French observer commented:

'I wish the Germans joy. We tried emperors, and a lot of good it has done us.'

After an armistice was concluded, a new election managed from Bordeaux returned a government led by the historian Louis Adolphe Thiers, an experienced middle-of-the-road conservative who assembled his administration at Versailles. On 2 March, the Germans entered Paris and marched in triumph up the Champs-Elysées.

In the aftermath of the siege, the Paris municipal government collapsed, and was succeeded on 28 March by a Commune, in much the same way as the extremists had taken over Paris during the first revolution. The rising was ruthlessly suppressed in May, with great violence in which at least 20,000 people died, most killed by the new government's troops; but Thiers was given time to negotiate a peace with Germany. The conditions were severe: France had started the war, and had to face the consequences, which were the sacrifice of her two part-German speaking provinces, Alsace and Lorraine, together with the payment of a massive indemnity, which Thiers, showing remarkable stamina for a man nearing 80 carrying on the government of what was now the Third Republic, began to discharge.

But resentment flourished, as all the previous illusions of France's glories had been shattered and the idea of revenge and restoration was pervasive.

Imperial Affairs

Austria, in spite of her defeat at Sadowa, recovered rapidly without the burden of the Italian provinces and the need to play the big beast in Germany. Kaiser Franz Joseph, encouraged by his wife, the brilliant and wayward Sisi, was able to concentrate on domestic issues. Only months after the battle, in February 1867, an autonomous Hungary was given equal status with Austria as the Dual Monarchy – the Austrian Empire and the Hungarian Kingdom. The division still left a number of minorities. The majority Hungarian Magyars had Ukrainians, Romanians, Croats and Slovenes to neglect or abuse, while Austria was responsible for Poles, Moravians and Czechs. Ten years later, following a series of Balkan wars, the Turkish Province of Bosnia Herzegovina was confided to Austro-Hungarian care, adding more discontented Slavs and Muslims to the emperor-king's responsibilities. In Bohemia, history both repeated and foreshadowed itself: just as in the 14th and 15th centuries Germans and Czechs quarrelled over the status of their languages, German-speakers in the Sudetenland clamoured for supremacy or separation. Searching for the causes of both world wars necessitates delving far back in history.

One small Italian state was all but extinguished in the tumultuous 1860s. Pope Pius IX, consecrated in 1846, had inherited the Papal States, a principality stretching right across the middle of the peninsula, but now integrated into the Kingdom of Italy, leaving the Pope a virtual prisoner in the Vatican. Recovering from what many saw as a humiliation, Pius responded vigorously at the First Vatican Council in 1869, condemning the entire modern world and calling on the faithful to show absolute obedience to his infallible judgement. Many Catholics objected, but the Church revived, missions spread and celestial visions obligingly appeared. The Protestant Churches were also stirred by a religious revival, with open-air services, passionate sermons and spirited songs replacing set services.

At either extreme of Europe, Britain and Russia avoided international complications wherever possible. Administering a vast empire – and dealing with the 'Irish Question' – absorbed most British governments' energies, while in Russia the reforms of Tsar Alexander II (r.1855–81) were slowly restructuring society. Emancipation of the serfs began in 1859 and continued for three years. It was a sensitive task, which included settling compensation to former owners, and allocating lands to the free farmers.

When American slaves were emancipated a few years later, no provision was made for their future but in Russia every family received a small land grant, of between 3.6 and 7.2 hectares (9 and 18 acres) , which could be held communally. In place of services, privileges, and benefits, Russian farming was to be based on cash. Inevitably, prudent and lucky proprietors did well with their compensation, and were able to invest in some of the many new opportunities that increased trade and industrialization brought. So too industrious and clever peasants prospered, and were able to buy lands from their neighbours; the *Kulaks*, the rich peasants who were to become one of the principal targets of the Bolshevik Revolution of 1917, emerged.

BELOW *Coloured engraving of a village in southern Russia in the mid-19th century. Tsar Alexander II tried to forestall revolution from below by reforming from above, emancipating the serfs by 1862. Yet massive discontent and inequality remained in Russia.*

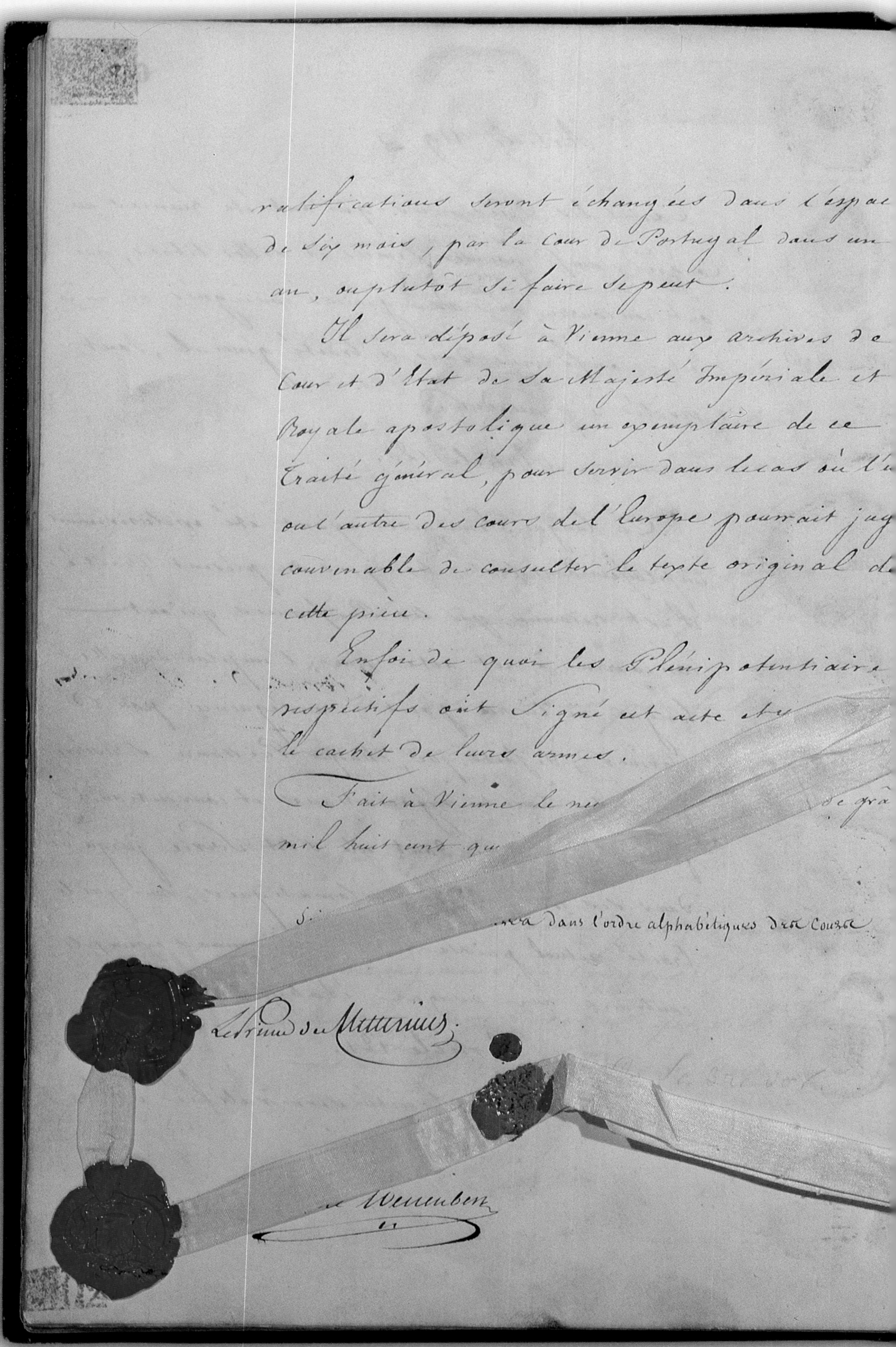

ratifications seront échangées dans l'espac[e]

de Six mois, par la Cour de Portugal dans un

an, ou plutôt si faire se peut.

Il sera déposé à Vienne aux Archives de c[ette]

Cour et d'État de Sa Majesté Impériale et

Royale apostolique un exemplaire de ce

Traité général, pour servir dans le cas où l'u[ne]

ou l'autre des cours de l'Europe pourrait jug[er]

convenable de consulter le texte original de

cette pièce.

En foi de quoi les Plénipotentiaire[s]

respectifs ont Signé cet acte et y [apposé]

le cachet de leurs armes.

Fait à Vienne le neu[f]   de grâ[ce]

mil huit cent qu[inze]

5.   [...]ra dans l'ordre alphabétiques des Cours

Le Prince de Metternich.

Wessenberg

The Final Act of the Treaty of Vienna, signed at the Congress of Vienna on 9 June 1815. The principal architect of the new, arch-conservative order imposed on Europe after Napoleon was the Austrian foreign minister Klemens Metternich, whose main aim was to suppress the forces of nationalism and liberalism.

1730–1856
Eastern Superpowers: India and China

■ Fragmentation of Mughal rule ■ Bengal and Bihar granted to the English East India
Company 1765 ■ First Anglo-Burmese War 1824–26 ■ First Anglo-Chinese War 1839–42
■ The British annex Oudh in northern India 1856

Trade, it was claimed, follows the flag: but in 19th-century Asia the contrary was true. British India began
with a London trading company, and Western relations with China, Indochina, Indonesia and Japan were
driven by enterprising merchants often dragging governments at their heels.

Imperial colonial responsibilities were assumed reluctantly, the ideal being,
as with Siam, friendly relations and free trade. But the geopolitical logic of
governing an Indian empire led inexorably to conflicts, and in particular with
China, where the Qing dynasty was failing to appreciate the scale of change in
the outside world.

The Company *Raj*

China in the 18th century was self-contained, even self-satisfied. The
conquest of Sinkiang, one of Emperor Yongzhen's (1723–35) achievements,
had extended and stabilized the country's borders, while at home the
enormous encyclopaedia *The Complete Collection of Illustrations and Writings
from the Earliest to Current Times,* filled 800,000 pages, printed using copper
type, summarizing all aspects of Chinese culture. The population, greatly
reduced during the change of dynasties, had recovered and expanded, to 178
million by mid-century. The Middle Kingdom, it seemed, could well afford to
ignore the barbarians beyond its frontiers.

A century forward, and the world had changed. A new power was forming
on China's borders in the strange shape of a London-based trading company.
Unlike Manchu China, Mughal India had been shattered, beginning with
raids from Persia and Afghanistan and then by the Hindu Maratha kingdoms.
Founded by the famous Shivaji, who had sealed his power by murdering the
Mughal general in an embrace with his hidden 'tiger claw', a confederation
of Maratha States extended from the Bay of Bengal to the Arabian Sea.
Independent in all but name, the Punjabi Afghans, also in possession of Sind
and Kashmir, and the rulers of Awadh (Oudh), Bijar and Bengal, hemmed in
the Delhi emperors. Some 20 or more foreign trading stations were dotted all
round the coast, from the mouth of the Ganges to the Indus, all depending
on the goodwill of the local ruler, who might or might not be acting as an
agent for the Mughal court.

One such agent was the English East India
Company, given official recognition in 1716 by
an imperial directive, a *firman*, which exempted
it from the petty demands and interference
of local officials, and conferred local revenue-
raising powers. With these privileges came
permission to defend any infringement of its
rights by the small local forces retained at the
Company's stations. Under the leadership of the
redoubtable Robert Clive, the Company's sepoys
(native troops) had already proved their worth,
by defeating their French competitors at the
Battle of Chandernagore, in 1757. Devastated as
they were by the Afghan attacks – such as that in
1737–39, which had claimed 20,000 lives, and a
renewed onslaught in 1756 – the Delhi authorities
paid scant attention to the foreigners' squabbles.
The *nawabs* of Bengal, in particular, had been
administering their eastern region, which had
remained quietly prosperous since the beginning
of the century, until the accession of an aggressive
young *nawab*, Siraj-ud-Daula in 1756. His
attack on the Company, including the infamous
'Black Hole of Calcutta', in which a number of
British captives suffocated during a single night's

RIGHT *A Mughal miniature from the late 18th
century depicts an official of the East India
Company riding in a* howdah *on the back of
an elephant, with an escort of foot soldiers
and mounted Indian retainers.*

confinement, led to quick retaliation, and the opportunity to demand compensation.

After clever diplomacy and one final decisive battle, an agreement was concluded by which a sympathetic *nawab*, recognized at Delhi, was duly installed, a large cash payment made, of which Clive took the lion's share, and most importantly, the Company was granted the *diwani* of the rich provinces of Bengal and Bihar – effectively, rule over some 20 million Indians. In London, governments and shareholders were worried by the possibility of expensive entanglements, but the Indian administration pushed on with its expansion, eliminating the most serious competitor, the southern Deccan kingdom of Mysore. The Mysore ruler, Tipu Sahib, had despatched a diplomatic mission to France in 1788, received by King Louis XVI at Versailles 'with great pomp'. Such an alliance with the enemy had to be terminated, but it took two wars between 1790 and 1804 before Tipu's formidable army was beaten (his clockwork model of a tiger mauling a British soldier is one of the most popular exhibits in the Victoria & Albert Museum), by which date the British *Raj* continued in an unbroken strip from near Delhi to Calcutta and Madras, and across the

LEFT *'Tipu's tiger' in the Victoria and Albert Museum in London. A clockwork mechanism inside this automaton produces noises mimicking the growling of the tiger and the screams of the British soldier.*

continent to the west coast. From then on, British India steadily expanded, attracting the same sort of submission, reluctant or relieved, that the Mughals had formerly obtained from their vassals.

The distinction between Indian and British governments should be made clear. A governor-general was appointed by London, usually a mid-ranking peer, who would not be much missed at home, and given some suggestions as to the policies he should follow. Once in Calcutta, he was advised by a local council, but essentially was an autocrat, with far greater powers than any British prime minister. With a round trip of at least six months, the only practicable method of bringing a governor-general to heel was to recall him. Indian governments therefore were obliged to act in what they saw as Indian interests, and trust that they would be supported by London; among these interests, border security was vital, and defending frontiers implied war.

The first foreign war of British India settled the frontier with Nepal in 1816, and incidentally secured the services of the finest soldiers in the British Army, the Gurkha riflemen, but the next confrontation, with Burma, was more troublesome. For centuries the kingdom of Burma had evolved into the largest state in Southeast Asia, disintegrated, united again, as its disparate races (Mon, Shan, and Burman) prospered and suffered alternately. The appalling King Bodawpaya, squeezed by China and Siam in the East, had expanded aggressively, seizing the territories of Arakan, Tenasserim, Manipur and Assam, which brought Burma against the Indian frontiers. After vain attempts at negotiation, the Indian government was forced into action. The first Anglo-Burmese War (1824–26) was badly conducted and extremely expensive, but the Company's victory resulted in all the recent Burmese conquests being ceded to India.

Settling postwar accounts with the Dutch took until 1824. Ceylon was transferred, with some resistance from the kings of Kandy in the mountainous interior, who had controlled the island for some 1500 years. A later rebellion against particularly ill-judged taxes led to one of those intermittent displays of British colonial stupidity that marred an otherwise laudable record. The safe-keeping of the Buddha's tooth, entrusted to the colonial government, was denounced in London as admitting 'idolatry … an abomination'. The sensible and pragmatic William Gladstone deplored the dogmatic position of the evangelicals:

'we are here as the advocates of good faith …the government had undertaken the responsibility and must accept it.'

The Buddhists were conciliated and Ceylon, in the care of the Colonial Office rather than India, flourished.

Most of the Dutch possessions in the East Indies taken during the war were returned, but the strategic island of Singapore, acquired by the enterprising Sir Stamford Raffles, was handed to the East India Company. Together with the other island of Penang this became the nucleus of the Straits Settlements, administered from the 1860s by the Colonial Office, and one of the most prosperous regions of the East.

Relations with Siam were cordial, helped by the absence of a common frontier and the uncommon wisdom of a succession of monarchs who stabilized Siam's relations with the other South East Asian states, and kept acquisitive Americans, French and British at arms length, while taking advantage of foreign advice and assistance. King Mongkut (or Rama IV; r.1851–75), who engaged Anna Leonowens (of *The King and I* fame) as his children's

RIGHT *French 19th-century cartoon showing an old English hag carrying an opium chest on her back. The East India Company imported opium grown in Bengal to China in exchange for porcelain, silk and tea. The British fought the Opium Wars to protect this lucrative trade.*

governess, established Siam on levels of equality with all Western powers and began modernizing his country whilst preserving its traditional culture. But British relations with Siam's former suzerain, China, were more disturbed.

An Opium War?

Although respectful embassies bringing presents and tributes were allowed to approach Beijing, foreigners coming by sea were obliged to use Canton, and then under many restrictions. Ships could dock only in the permitted season, October to May, and must trade only through the carefully-superintended Merchants' Guild, the 'Cohong'. Foreigners, who included Dutch, Spanish, Swedish and Americans, were allowed to build waterfront warehouses ('factories') and permitted to live there, in a small, restricted area, during the trading season: at other times they must return home, or go to Macao:

Foreign traders developed a parallel organization, accepting the leadership of the British East India Company. Under the supervision of the Hoppo, the Cohong's chief, and the East Indian Company's Select Committee of Supercargoes, generally known as 'the Select' the system worked smoothly. An American merchant praised

'the facility of all dealings with the Chinese who were assigned to transact business with us, [who] together with their proverbial honesty, combined with a sense of perfect security to person and property …

The machinery, however, had to be well-oiled with large and regular payments to Chinese officials.

Western demand for Chinese products was insatiable; porcelain and silks were always wanted, but the trade was driven by the British addiction to tea, a Chinese monopoly. The East India Company could finance Indian expenses by the land revenues, their administration acknowledged to be tolerably fair and competent, skimming off no more of the taxes than was considered reasonable. But the London dividends depended on trading income, where the largest item was the Chinese tea; and tea was also important to the British exchequer since the import duty brought in some three million pounds a year – hence all those American difficulties. Financing tea purchases presented some difficulty, since Chinese traders had only a limited demand for British or Indian goods, chiefly raw cotton and woollen fabric, but were willing to buy any quantity of the excellent Bengal opium. Two further problems: opium was illegal in China and the East India Company banned its direct export. These obstacles were easily overcome, the first by large bribes to the Cohong, the second by selling the opium to private traders, who were then free to find the best market they could, at Canton or smaller ports further up the Chinese coast.

To tidy minds in London, it was a messy and undignified situation, and in 1792 Lord Macartney,

who had already charmed Catherine the Great, was sent on a suitable battleship laden with appropriate gifts, to talk things over with the emperor. The Emperor Qianlong and his officials were taken aback by this shocking assumption of equality, and Macartney was, quite politely, turned away, to travel back through China. He was able to observe conditions there, and reported, accurately and prophetically:

'The Empire of China is an old, crazy, first-rate man-of-war, which a fortunate succession of able and vigilant officers has contrived to keep afloat these one hundred and fifty years past, and to overawe their neighbours by her bulk and appearance.'

He added that once an incompetent regime took charge the ship would drift and ultimately be wrecked '… but she can never be rebuilt on the old bottom.' Subsequently preoccupied with the Napoleonic wars, Britain let the matter drop for the time being. When they had time to consider Indian affairs, which was not often – parliamentary debates were poorly attended – British governments realized that something must be done, and that by 1833 at the latest, being the date at which the Company's current charter expired.

ABOVE *An engraving by E. Duncan shows the British ship* Nemesis *destroying a Chinese war junk in Anson's Bay, 1841, during the first opium war. By 1838, 1,400 tons of the drug were received into China's southern ports, and opium addiction was rife in the country.*

No British administration was ready to take on the enormous responsibility of running India, which the Company seemed to be doing rather well. It had developed into an imperial power in its own right, ruling over a population much larger than that of the home country, and deploying a standing army and navy that made it the equal of many great states. Such a role was quite incompatible with that of a trading company; all the Company's commercial activities were to cease, in India and in China, ' with all convenient speed'.

The next step was to regularize the position at Canton, and prospects were not hopeful. One more attempt to contact Beijing had been made by another embassy, also rejected with scorn. Chinese official ignorance of western affairs was near-total; there may have been no more than a few people in the capital who spoke any European language, including Latin. Although the emperors Jiaqing and Daoguang, who reigned between 1799 and 1850, were 'able and vigilant', their seclusion in Beijing and reliance on dubious reports meant that the government had no accurate information on the geography, currencies and customs of these unimportant 'tributary nations'.

Attempting to accommodate themselves to Chinese prejudices, the Whig government despatched a decent but not too senior peer, Lord Napier, with the modest title of 'Superintendent of Trade.' It was useless: no Chinese government official would demean himself to communicate with a mere tradesman, as his title indicated. Nor did a Chinese Foreign Ministry exist: three separate departments controlled trade across the northern and western boarders, and two more the east and south coasts; it is quite possible that they did not communicate with each other, since in 1835 a treaty had been concluded with the Khan of Kokand allowing him everything the British were attempting to request. Lord Napier, after being detained in Canton, died of a fever and Captain Charles Elliot RN took charge of the superintendency. As long as bribes were paid, the trade continued, but the emperor was badgered either to permit the trade, or to ban opium altogether.

In December 1838, after a long debate on legitimizing the trade, the emperor decided to appoint the incorruptible and brave mandarin Lin Tse-hsu to enforce abolition. Lin descended on Canton, threatening Chinese and foreign merchants alike, collected all of the available opium, more than a thousand tonnes, and burned it. He also made the great mistake of attempting to arrest the man he considered the most important trader, Lancelot Dent.

To the foreign secretary Lord Palmerston, this insult to a British subject was an intolerable affront. He accepted the Chinese right to confiscate the opium, but could not tolerate Lin's strong-arm methods and demanded compensation; after all, opium was legal in Britain. During the subsequent months of negotiation the British community was forced out of Canton and Macao to find what shelter it could among the ships moored in the nearby safe haven of Hong Kong. When at last an expeditionary force arrived from England, Captain Elliot, anxious not to protract hostilities, 'with a certain consequence of deep hatred,' offered the Chinese a demonstration of British power. In a single day, with the help of the East India Company's small armed steamer *Nemesis* he destroyed the supposedly impregnable river defences of Canton, laying the city open to a British assault. Within a week, negotiations were in full swing, and a fortnight later the Chinese envoys had agreed to Elliot's demands: $6 million plus the rocky island of Hong Kong to compensate for the loss of the opium. Lord Palmerston was 'greatly mortified and disappointed' that Captain Elliot had won only:

> *'a barren island with hardly a house on it. It seems obvious that Hong Kong will never be a Mart of Trade …'*

Elliot was recalled, and given the least attractive job in the British diplomatic service: envoy to the Republic of Texas. Another year's negotiations were needed before the definitive Treaty of Nanking was agreed: Hong Kong became British in perpetuity, and five ports, including Canton, were opened to British merchants and residents; similar arrangements were made with the USA and France. The very able Chinese plenipotentiary Qiying, an imperial family member, conveyed only a sanitized version of the transactions to Emperor Daoguang for his ratification. Judging from the fact that six years later the emperor was still referring to 'foreign bandits' it seems that the true facts of 19th-century power had not been appreciated, either in Beijing or in the rest of the country. But a growing sense of China's slipping out of control, already apparent by the decay of public works, spreading corruption and violent localized rebellions indicated that Lord Macartney's 'old man-of-war' was drifting dangerously.

'The Volcano On Which We Sit'

Lord Auckland, amiable but lightweight ('a comical dog,' according to his witty sister, the novelist Emily Eden) was sent out as governor-general of India in 1835, a stop-gap appointment with only the vaguest of instructions. In Calcutta, his aggressive and opinionated Council warned of the impending peril of a Russian takeover of Afghanistan. Any attempt to block this must begin by conciliating the powerful Sikh leader, Ranjit Singh, who controlled the Punjab, Peshawar and Kashmir, who would be an essential ally in any Afghan war. The vice-regal party duly paid a visit; Emily described Ranjit as: 'exactly like a mouse, with grey whiskers and one eye' and ' a drunken old profligate', but accurately assessed his importance:

> *'He has made himself a great king; he has conquered a great many powerful enemies; he is remarkably just in his government; he has disciplined a large army; he hardly ever takes away life, which is remarkable in a despot; and he is excessively beloved by his people.'*

Having rallied Sikh support, the Army of the Indus marched into Afghanistan and to the worst military defeat ever suffered by a British Army, with only a few survivors straggling home through the Khyber Pass. Attempting to regain some lost prestige, the brilliantly eccentric General Sir Charles Napier, in what he described as a very 'advantageous, useful, humane piece of rascality' provoked the rulers of Sind into a fight, shattering previously agreed treaties. Public opinion at home was disturbed; the experienced diplomat Mountstuart Elphinstone described the British conduct as being like that 'of a bully who had been kicked in the street and went home to beat his wife.'

Not even Napier would lightly provoke a quarrel with the Sikhs, whose efficient, well-equipped army was the largest in India, but when a succession dispute erupted into civil war after Ranjit's death, conflict was probably inevitable. Two more wars (in 1845–46 and 1848–49), involving hard-fought and costly battles, were needed before the Sikhs surrendered and the Punjab and Kashmir were acquired. The Punjab flourished under British rule, and the Sikhs became invaluable as soldiers and, throughout the empire, as

Snipers observing a column of sepoys as it journeys through the Siri-Kajur Pass in the rugged and inhospitable region of Baluchistan, in the far west of India, in 1839. This confederacy of four princely states, which now straddles Pakistan, Afghanistan and Iran, was brought under British suzerainty in 1876.

police. Kashmir was sold on to a Sikh prince, whose successors governed the largely Muslim province in prosperous tranquillity until partition and Independence. The young Maharaja Dhalip Singh was obliged to present the famous Koh-i-noor diamond to the young Queen Victoria: in his portrait he is shown wearing a miniature of the queen, painted by Emily Eden for her 'little grey mouse.'

Auckland's successor Lord Ellenborough, who initiated the withdrawal from Afghanistan – where Indian troops had already reoccupied Kabul – and who was blamed for the Sind invasion, was recalled, but his successor, Lord Dalhousie, continued the policy of annexation, although less violently. The dubious legal acquisition of the kingdom of Oudh (Awadh) in 1856, with its decadently luxurious but peaceable capital of Lucknow, caused apprehension in Britain and fury across northern India. Once again, Emily Eden was right:

'Given the thinness of the crust over the volcano on which we all sit in this country, the wonder is that it does not explode oftener.'

Sealed by the Plenipotentiaries on board
Her Britannic Majesty's Ship ——
"Cornwallis" this twenty ninth day of August
1842, corresponding with the Chinese
date, twenty fourth day of the seventh month
in the twenty second year of Taoukwang.

Henry Pottinger
Her Mys Plenipotentiary

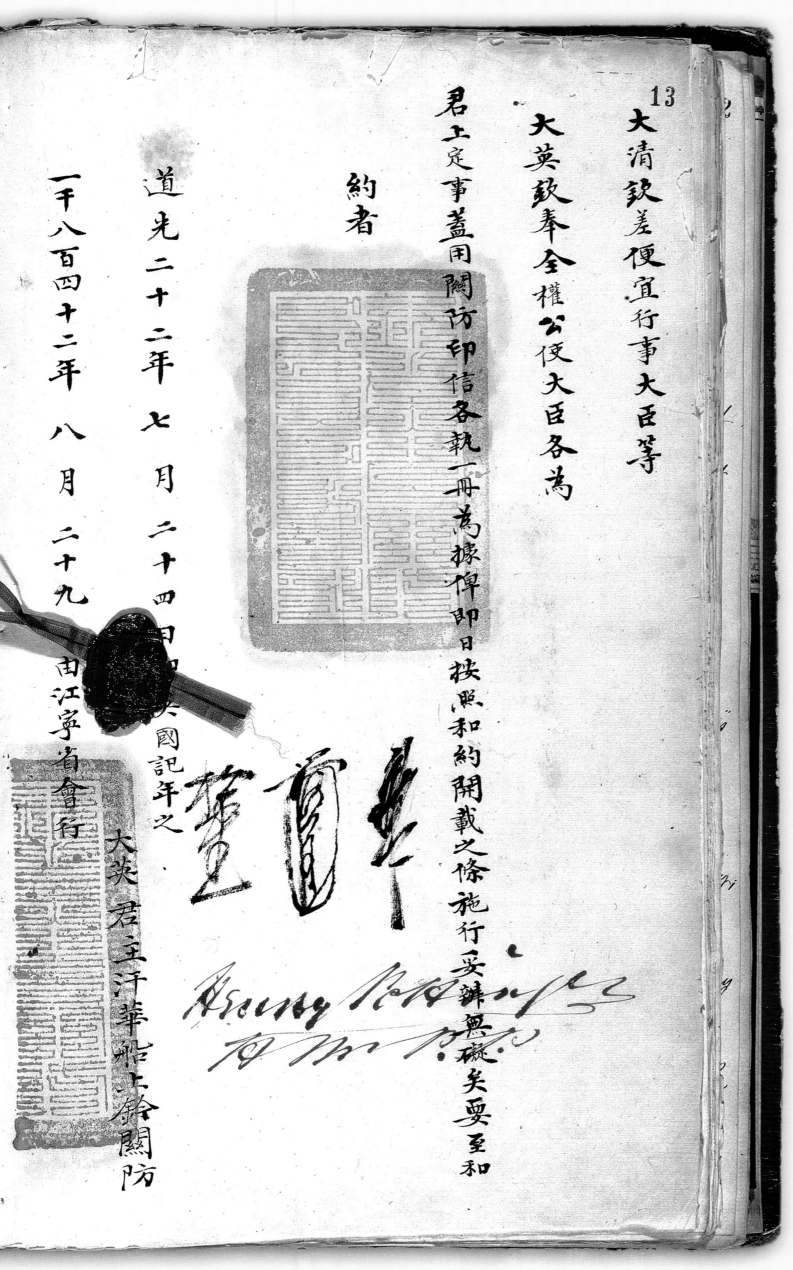

大清欽差便宜行事大臣等

大英欽奉全權公使大臣各為

約者

君上定事蓋用關防印信各執一冊為據悍即日按照和約開載之條施行安辦無礙美要至和

君上定事蓋用關防印信各執一冊為據悍即日按照和約開載之條施行安辦無礙美要至和

道光二十二年七月二十四日即大國記年之

一千八百四十二年八月二十九由江寧省會行

大英君主汗華船大鈴關防

The Nanking Treaty of 1842 was the document that formally ended the First Anglo-Chinese War (or First Opium War), which broke out three years earlier over trade rights. It was couched in terms of 'peace, friendship, commerce and indemnity' but in fact was wrested from a resentful and chastened China.

c.1800 – 1871
Continental Empires

■ Mexican-American War 1846–48 ■ Military campaign secures Caucasus for the Russian Empire 1859 ■ The American Civil War erupts over states' rights and the slavery question 1861 ■ First transcontinental railroad crosses the USA 1863–69 ■ Tammany Hall scandal 1871

By an accident of geography, the two great 19th-century continental empires of Russia and America adjoined one another in Alaska, but were separated by the Atlantic Ocean and Western Europe. One was partly democratic, the other wholly autocratic; both faced similar challenges, of industrialization and the future of a slave population, and evolved in very different ways.

The changes that began in Britain in the mid-18th century, transmitted over the world in the 1800s, permanently transformed all societies. The use of steam power multiplied productive capacity and speeded communication; mass production made manufactures widely available; gas and electric lighting, local railways and sewage systems made life possible and even comfortable in the sprawling and fast-growing cities.

Workshop of the World

But why had it begun in Britain? In the mid-1700s France, a much larger and richer country, had more technically-advanced industries, and was modernizing faster, but many factors, technical and social, favoured Britain. The United Kingdom, although relatively small, formed the largest unified economy, without internal barriers, and with an unmatched capacity for raising finance. Patents and other forms of property were protected by a long-established law, competently administered. Communications were excellent: Macadam's new roads, with tarred surfaces from 1803, the new canal network and well-organized coastal traffic facilitated the movement of goods. Social mobility helped – protected by their patents, working inventors could prosper: John Dalton, Henry Maudslay, James Watt and George Stephenson all became rich and respectable; Richard Arkwright, youngest of 13 and a barber's apprentice, gained a knighthood. Antoine Lavoisier, the great French chemist, designer of the metric system, was executed; while Marc (later Sir Marc) Isambard Brunel escaped to England and flourished.

Britain's major advantage was its widely available coal and mining expertise, developed over hundreds of years: the first successful railway locomotives, safety lamps and breathing apparatus all started in English coalfields. Once coke was established as a substitute for charcoal, the availability of coal for blast furnaces precipitated British steelmaking to world leadership. Engineering advances also depended on machine tools to produce the necessary fine tolerances. John Harrison's 1759 Chronometer, a marvel of precision, was handmade, with the assistance of Vernier gauges, but large scale production demanded mechanical measurements, made possible by Henry Maudslay's screw-micrometer, accurate to 0.0001 inch, working on fine steel produced by the Huntsman crucible process, which permitted such radical improvements as the manufacture of John Wilkinson's horizontal borer of 1775. The impetus provided by war advanced the pace of invention, demonstrated by Brunel's design of an automatic block-making factory for the Admiralty. Pulley-blocks, essential to manage sails and rigging, were needed in great quantity: Brunel's steam-powered Portsmouth factory produced over 100,000 a year, using ten unskilled labourers in place of 110 skilled artisans. When peace came in 1815, Britain really was the world's workshop, but its lead was soon challenged over the Atlantic.

An Experimental Republic

Europe, once it had caught its collective breath after a generation of war, was fascinated by the American experiment. Democracy was generally believed dangerous, and outsiders (and a lot of Americans themselves) were puzzled that slavery was allowed – even advocated – in an advanced society. Alexis de Tocqueville, historian and politician, having visited the United States in 1831 and 1832, produced his thoughtful *Democracy in America*. Some of his observations were quickly outdated – notably his reference to the impossibility of acquiring hereditary wealth – but most remain relevant, such as the popularity and influence of the churches, especially strange to a Frenchman, and the enormous difficulty of ever assimilating the black slaves and the Indians into a culture which claimed to be egalitarian. Charles Dickens visited ten years later, and was equally shocked by the unspoken dislike, even fear, of straying from contemporary accepted thought, even in the great universities. But both of these well-versed foreign observers agreed that the experiment was working and Dickens in particular appreciated the terrible consequences to the rest of the world should it fail – an outcome that appeared quite possible.

The 1820 compromise that allowed the admission of Missouri as a slave state, but with slavery to be prohibited in all other new states north of 36° 30' only postponed the inevitable clash. President-to-be John Quincy Adams believed that it was nothing more than a 'preamble – a title page to a great, tragic volume': 30 years later the text was begun. The trouble started in the new Republic of Texas. It was possible that with British and French help Mexico might be brought to accept Texan independence, but on condition that slavery would be banned. Sam Houston and many others liked the idea, but Mexico prevaricated and the American slave states were horrified at the prospect. President James Polk was determined to bring the republic into the Union as a slave state, and seizing on the doubtful pretext of a border skirmish, declared war on Mexico, denounced by one young officer as:

> *'one of the most unjust ever waged by a stronger against a weaker nation.'*

It was, however, speedily successful, and the 1848 Treaty of Guadalupe Hidalgo ceded not only Texas to the USA, but also what became the states of California, Nevada, Utah, New Mexico and parts of Wyoming and Colorado; as an extra bonus gold was discovered in California the following year.

Manifest Destiny

Within a single lifetime the Thirteen Colonies had expanded from the Appalachians to the Pacific, with the great swathe of Mexican territories uniting the country from coast to coast. To Polk and his supporters, this clearly indicated that it was white America's 'Manifest Destiny' to populate the entire West, reluctantly leaving the colder bits to the Canadians. Transcontinental railroad lines were therefore essential, but their construction raised sensitive issues. Senator Stephen Douglas of Illinois, anxious to secure his potential profits from land purchases, pushed for a central railway line, which involved defining the status of new territories to be known as Nebraska and Kansas, thus questioning the Missouri compromise. And slavery, endorsed by the Supreme Court in the Dred Scott case of 1857, was deemed legal anywhere in the United States. With renewed vigour, Southern states began to press for resumption of the African slave trade.

That other minority, the Indians, also had their rights pushed to one side. One voice from the heroic past spoke up for them when Houston protested that solemn treaties had granted these lands to the Indians 'as long as grass shall grow and water run', but the 'Trail of Tears' pioneered by President Jackson's ejection of the Cherokee and Choctaw continued. Opponents of the Kansas and Nebraska Act formed a new party, taking the name of Republicans. Not primarily concerned with the abolition of slavery, but rather with banning its westward extension, Republicans reflected northern values of smallholdings rather than plantations, and the protection of commercial interests. Their new party came close to winning the 1856 presidential election, which went instead to the Democratic candidate James Buchanan. Shifty and indecisive as Buchanan was, even a better man might have been no more successful in the face of the passions seething in both North and South. Slavery abolitionist John Brown's murderous raid on a federal arsenal at Harpers Ferry, Virginia, in 1859 created a hero for one side and a villain for the other. Writer Ralph Waldo Emerson hailed him as:

'a new saint who will make the gallows glorious like the cross.'

and yet for many Southerners the raid only stimulated fears of a vile northern plan to provoke slave rebellion, always a Southern nightmare. Many Southerners made no secret of their passion to preserve slavery, a general feeling made official when South Carolina issued its own declaration of independence on Christmas Eve 1860, announcing that the Northern denunciation of slavery as sinful had 'invested a great political error with the sanctions of a more enormous religious belief.'

The new Northern leader, the unprepossessing, ungainly, small-town lawyer, little-known to the people at large, Abraham Lincoln, made it clear that the North was not prepared to go to war to abolish slavery, or even interfere with the 'peculiar institution'. Lincoln was as much a white supremacist as most Southerners:

BELOW *A Confederate sharpshooter lays dead in Devil's Den, Gettysburg, 1863. One of the images taken by Alexander Gardener for his* Sketch Book of the Civil War. *The North's greater reserves of manpower and its industrial might were decisive in securing victory over the Confederacy.*

'I am not nor ever have been in favour of bringing about in any way the social and political equality of the white and black races … I am not nor ever have been in favour of making voters or jurors of negroes, nor of qualifying them to hold office, nor to intermarry with white people.'

Lincoln's core belief was that American revolutionary values, of freedom and equality for all citizens (no blacks included!) depended on maintaining the integrity of the Union. Any states unilaterally deciding to leave must be prevented, if not by negotiation then by force.

The war that began by the Charleston artillery's bombardment of Fort Sumter on 12 April 1861 ended on 9 April 1865. It cost over 600,000 lives, more casualties than in all other American wars before Vietnam; most families in the South, and many in the North, had lost members. Much of the fighting was in the very centre of the country, within a 100 miles (160 km) of the northern and southern capitals. Photographers recorded the carnage, speedily engraved for the illustrated papers, and war correspondents such as W. H. Russell of *The Times*, who had learnt his trade in the Crimea, described the battles. Many Southerners prefer to call it the 'War Between the States', but there is no doubt that it was a true civil war, in which families were divided and brother fought brother. More than most wars it was also unnecessary, brought on by the hysterical tones in which debate was so often conducted. The North's superiority in men and material was so great that a Southern victory was near-impossible: the best that might be achieved was a stalemate, nothing more than a postponement, which well-intentioned

foreign observers hoped to achieve. If the war really aimed to liberate slaves, then the Northern cause would, especially in Britain, be supported, but without such an assurance the South was often seen as an underdog bullied by aggressive Yankees. Such equivocation was dramatically ended by Lincoln when, after General Robert E. Lee's invasion of the North, which had threatened to encircle Washington, was halted at Antietam, the President announced that as from 1 January 1863 all slaves in rebel states

> '… shall be, then, thenceforward, and forever free.'

The war was now appreciated as justified, and international opinion mobilized behind the Union. Ironically, slaves in such loyalist states as Delaware and Kentucky remained in bondage for another two years, but when emancipation was formally declared an enthusiastic black population rallied to the Union flag. Fighting with conspicuous bravery, blacks provided nearly 180,000 men to the army, and formed a quarter of the navy's strength, insisting on, and receiving, equal rates of pay. In the final months of the war, entering the southern capital of Richmond Virginia on 4 April, Lincoln was surrounded by cheering blacks, elated at meeting their liberator as he walked through the crowd: a troop of black cavalry escorted him back to the docks. Ten days later the President was shot dead in Ford's Theater in Washington, and the Secretary of State Seward was brutally attacked at his home. Lincoln's personal qualities, his patience and controlled passion, his ability to see beyond the conflict to the political realities, reinforced by a formidable gift for oratory, had carried his country through terrible times, and were never more needed than in the aftermath of war. His successors were lesser men, defective and corrupt, who sacrificed for expediency what thousands had gained for America on the battlefield.

Four score and seven years ago our fathers brought forth, upon this continent, a new nation, conceived in Liberty, and dedicated to the proposition that all men are created equal.

Now we are engaged in a great civil war, testing whether that nation, or any nation, so conceived, and so dedicated, can long endure. We are met here on a great battle-field of that war. We have come to dedicate a portion of it, as a final resting place for those who here gave their lives, that that nation might live. It is altogether fitting and proper that we should do this.

But in a larger sense we can not dedicate—we can not consecrate—we can not hallow this ground. The brave men, living and dead, who struggled here, have consecrated it, far above our poor power to add or detract. The world will little note, nor long remember, what we say here, but can never forget what they did here. It is for us, the living, rather to be dedicated here to the unfinished work, which they have, thus far, so nobly carried on. It is rather

Draft of the Gettysburg Address, delivered by President Abraham Lincoln on 19 November 1863 to commemorate fallen Union troops in the bloody battle that took place near this Pennsylvania town four months before. At the time, he thought his oratory had fallen flat, but history has judged his speech to be one of the most eloquent expressions of the democratic ideal.

Hopes Deferred

After an initial effort at federal support, the millions of freed slaves, enthusiastic for a better life and the chance to put their strength and talents to work, were left at the mercy of State governments, who ensured that the blacks remained an underclass, under-privileged and under-valued. Ingenious 'Jim Crow' laws robbed most blacks and many poor whites of their rights to vote, uniting both in poverty and hopelessness. Open black protest was brutally smothered, forcing blacks to accept their position at the very bottom of the pile. Black creativity was, however, able to express itself in two distinctive ways, both linked by music: Black churches flourished, with their own elected pastor, and gospel music, while in such cities as New Orleans jazz was becoming the progenitor of a new musical art form. Anton Dvorák, who visited America in the 1890s, expressed with consummate artistry the cultural essence of postwar America in his New World Symphony; but the

ABOVE *Cartoon (1871) on the Tammany Hall corruption scandal, by the celebrated US political caricaturist Thomas Nast. All the principal protagonists blame one another; the plump, bearded character on the far left is 'Boss' Tweed, leader of Tammany Hall.*

consequences of a century of oppression are still haunting the USA. New immigrants flocking west, along the trans-continental lines first opened in 1869, paid as little attention to either blacks or Indians as possible. Among those who had already travelled West the hard way, by horse and mule wagon, the Mormons – members of the Church of the Latter Day Saints – were already flourishing, the most successful of the crop of new religions that continue to thrive in the United States.

Inventiveness, another American speciality, was striking. Edison being only one of the most prominent, but America's distinctive contribution was the mass-production of interchangeable parts. The West may not have been won by Colonel Colt's revolving pistols, fabricated in the 1850s by a plant using more than a thousand machine-tools, but without Cyrus McCormick's reaping machine, a star success of the London Exhibition of 1851, easily maintained with interchangeable parts, the prairies could not have been so readily converted into wheatfields.

Disappointments

If any of the Founding Fathers could have visited the United States a century after George Washington's first inauguration they would have been amazed by its extent and prosperity. Its cities – if they kept out of the south and the slums of the northern towns – were populated by healthy families, able to buy inexpensive consumer goods, delivered to them by an extensive railway network. By 1890, the USA was the world's leading industrial power, with 63 million inhabitants, no longer so exclusively Anglo-Saxon, but diversified by great numbers of Germans, Italians, Scandinavians and Irish.

Looking a little closer, however, they would have been horrified at the cost. Prosperity had been obtained by generalized, near-universal corruption, extending into the presidency itself. The grandly named Credit Mobilier of America made millions for the White House and its coterie by awarding itself railway contracts at grossly inflated prices. The Bureau of Indian Affairs officials siphoned off money, while the Whiskey Ring affair and the gold market manipulation of 1869 became notorious scandals. Tammany Hall, the Democratic Party's New York headquarters, ran the city and embezzled

millions of dollars from every public works project, from the construction of the Brooklyn Bridge to local schools. The best organized and most consistent corruption was that of the great family businesses – the Vanderbilts, Morgans and Rockefellers – who combined to drive up prices and keep wages down. Labour attempts to organize were crushed by private armies – 300 of Pinkerton's 'detectives' in the 1892 Homestead strike battle, willingly aided by the state militia.

The reputation of US presidents was at its lowest ebb. If they were not corrupt, it was because they were too insignificant to be worth bribing. Those Virginian gentlemen and New England intellectuals, well-versed in international affairs, would have been astonished by the fat, ungainly, but amiable and honest Grover Cleveland, who had acted as public hangman, had no experience of life outside the United States, and was educationally underprivileged, but nevertheless served two terms as President. They would have to wait until the new millennium before a president such as they had hoped for appeared, in the shape of the well-bred and enterprising Theodore Roosevelt: but by then three presidents had been assassinated within 40 years.

Drive to the East

Another land empire was expanding, on a considerably greater scale than that in North America. The 21-year-old Tsar Ivan 'the Terrible' began the Russian drive to the east in 1551 by invading the Mongol Khanate of Kazan, a much tougher prospect than the Mexicans or Indians. An army of 150,000, with a formidable siege train took six weeks to reduce the city of Kazan and to kill all the fighting men, but it was enough to warn the remaining Tatar states. Astrakhan on the Caspian, giving control of the Volga basin, was quietly handed over and a Russian foothold in the Caucasus obtained. More peacefully, the merchant Grigorii Stroganov was permitted to explore and exploit the region east of Perm. Trading with bands of tribal hunters, Stroganov's men were able to cross the Ural Mountains into Asia. The only organized opposition came from Kuchum Khan's Tatars, defeated in 1579 by Stroganov's small army.

The Russians were now 1,000 miles (1,600 km) east of Moscow and all Siberia lay open before them. Securing so vast an area was left to the Cossacks, that adventurous collection of Tatars, Poles, Lithuanians and Russians who had occupied the northern Black Sea coasts, and offered their services to reliable employers. By 1648, Cossacks had travelled as far east as the Bering Straits and by the end of the century had found their way to Kamchatka.

Administering so raw a territory in any other than the loosest fashion was impossible, and once the Bering Straits were crossed, as they were in 1728, official presence was limited to establishing a base at Okhotsk, and a few fur

ABOVE: *View of the Kremlin, Russia's seat of power, in the early 19th century by Maksim Vorobev (1787–1855). Russia's territorial expansion was impressive, but left its rulers with a constant fear of rebellion by conquered peoples.*

trading stations on the American coast. Russian expansion into the south, however, came across more substantial obstacles, but a short fight with China proved that both countries were more interested in trade than territory. Exceptionally, Russia was treated as an equal sovereign power and a special office in Beijing was nominated to deal with Russian affairs. The first treaty, negotiated in Latin, agreed borders and led to guardedly friendly relations, with a Russian embassy in 1719, which included a military band and a Scottish doctor, arranging for regular caravan passages.

Persia had been brought into contact with Tsarist Russia by the Caucasus invasion, leading to wars concluded in 1826 by decisive Russian victories; but in acquiring the Caucasus, potentially rich and strategically vital, Russia also inherited many future difficulties. Christian Circassians, Georgians, Muslim Chechens, together with Ingush, Ossetians and a dozen other tribes, isolated in mountain valleys, all battled to retain their independence, well after the Persian surrender. The Chechen Shamyl, leader of the fanatically anti-Western Murid Sect, united all Caucasians in a fierce struggle that only ended in 1859. General Alexei Yermolov, the commander charged with subduing the Caucasus met resistance with a campaign of terror. He famously stated:

> *'my word should be a law more inevitable than death.'*

But while Yermolov's policy of brutal suppression quelled insurrection and secured the Caucasus for the Russian Empire, it could never extinguish nationalist aspirations and anti-Russian sentiment in the region, as subsequent events have demonstrated all too clearly.

One hopeful sign in the new regime was the establishment of a new province to shelter that much-harried race, the Armenians. With Persia subdued, the Russian empire was now uncomfortably close to British India, only separated by the unstable buffer state of Afghanistan.

Exploration and Empire-building

■ Cook's First Voyage to the Pacific 1768–71 ■ Burton and Speke search for the source of the Nile 1856 ■ Construction of the Suez Canal 1859–69 ■ Formation of French Indochina 1887 ■ Second Anglo-Boer War ends in British dominance over South Africa 1899–1902

In October 1884, the world was divided by another line, this time drawn not by a pope, but by an international conference sitting in Washington, which decided that the Prime Meridian – 0 – of Longitude should pass through the Royal Observatory at Greenwich. Mortified that Paris was not chosen, to this day the French retain the Paris meridian on their domestic maps. But all the world's time, and the location of any point on the map, is still determined by reference to London.

The Washington delegates had before them a much clearer world map after a century of extensive explorations, which had begun in 1768–71 with Captain James Cook, the only man to 'discover' two continents, Australasia and Antarctica. In recent times, the global importance of Cook's voyages was underlined when NASA named its fifth space shuttle *Endeavour* after Cook's ship (a sturdy but cramped former collier) – an unmistakable allusion, given the British English rather than American spelling of the word.

Cook's Continents

The British Admiralty was anxious to establish the extent of the Southern Continent, already known to exist after earlier Portuguese and Dutch voyages. Parts of what appeared to be a huge landmass east of Longitude 112°E had been sighted, but reports were unanimously unfavourable, and no effort had been made to corroborate them. Then, 4,000 miles (6,400 km) or so further east a more promising coast had been spotted by the Dutch seafarer Abel Tasman in 1642 and named New Zealand. Were these two linked? Or was there another continent somewhere in the millions of square miles of uncharted waters? Cook was charged with the investigation, and in 1769 discovered that New Zealand, was indeed where Tasman had placed it, and carefully charted the islands' coasts. The Maori, proving friendly enough after some initial clashes – due in no small part to Cook's 'very perfect and gentlemanly demeanour,' as one observer later described it – had arrived there only a few centuries previously, making the near-2,000 mile (3,200 km) journey from the eastern Pacific in their

magnificent canoes. It remained to be discovered where that other larger land mass ended, by sailing west to the point Tasman had named Van Diemen's Land. On 20 April 1770, Cook sighted the land he named New South Wales and, as a formality, claimed it for King George III. The next four months were spent charting the Australian coast and identifying a wealth of entirely new species. They did not know it, but the crew of the *Endeavour* had met one of the oldest societies on Earth. Australian Aboriginals had crossed from the Asian mainland before the melting ice had separated off, with the first arrivals probably 40,000 years ago and had preserved their culture almost without outside contact.

Cook was not yet finished with the Pacific. One great southern continent had been discovered. Could it be that another existed, further to the south? Navigators were well acquainted with the high northern latitudes, and assumed that those in the south were similar. Conditions were, however, very different on the far side of the world. Nothing south of 60° was habitable: in the Northern Hemisphere, by contrast, the equivalent line of latitude runs through Helsinki and the Shetlands, with a thousand miles of settlements still further north. On his second voyage, again in former colliers, the *Resolution*

LEFT *The young Scot Sydney Parkinson accompanied James Cook on his first voyage as a botanical artist. In 1770 he made this detailed drawing of 'A New Zealand warrior in his proper Dress, and completely armed, according to their manner.' Parkinson succumbed to illness on the return leg and was buried at sea.*

Captain Cook's ships HMS Resolution *and* Adventure *anchored in Matavai Bay, Tahiti, during Cook's second voyage of exploration (1772–75). Painting by William Hodges.*

and the *Adventure*, Cook spent three Antarctic winters, and reached 71°10' S in January 1774: Midshipman George Vancouver, later to become a noted explorer himself, insisted on climbing out on the jib-boom to claim he had ventured further south than any man in the world.

Having now circumnavigated the Southern Hemisphere Cook had established that no habitable land mass existed south of Australia and New Zealand, but the ships pressed on, charting and naming the Pacific island groups of New Caledonia, New Hebrides and South Georgia and revisiting the Friendly Isles and Tahiti. On his return to London, with an almost intact crew – three had drowned – after three years away, almost certainly with a better health record than any comparable land-based group, it must have seemed to the Admiralty that they had found in James Cook a flawless explorer. Give Cook a decent ship or two, and he could find anything, at minimum cost, it seemed. After a cruelly short interval he was sent to find the elusive Northwest Passage, that sea connection between the two oceans north of the American continent, attempted many times from the Atlantic side, but never from the Pacific, the ocean that Cook knew better than any man ever had. He did not succeed, but filled in more empty spaces on the charts, and in particular a group of islands which he named after Lord Sandwich, First Lord of the Admiralty (the inventor of the ubiquitous snack). And it was there, on

his return voyage, that he met his death, a sad end after so many successful encounters with indigenous peoples.

Not all explorations broke new ground. India had long been occupied, with copious records and descriptions of the whole subcontinent, but the British administration there needed an accurate survey. This entailed an immense geodesic effort, which was carried out in the first 60 years of the 19th century, largely by George Everest, recalled in the name of the world's highest peak.

Africa

Unlike Australia, the rest of the world knew at least where Africa was, but only the coastal areas had been surveyed. In particular, geographers longed to corroborate the Alexandrian writer Ptolemy's claim that the Nile's source lay in two great equatorial lakes. In 1768 the Scots laird James Bruce, set out to test Ptolemy's idea and after 10 years' absence published a sensational book, *Travels to Discover the Source of the Nile,* with tales that the British found incredible – of perpetual battles ending with mass mutilations and killings, of banquets where a beast would be hacked about and its flesh eaten raw. He had, in fact, discovered a source of the Nile, but it was the wrong part, the shorter Blue Nile, which rises in Lake Tana, latitude 12° N.

In the 1840s, Ptolemy's ideas were reinforced by the accounts of German missionaries, Johannes Rebmann and Johannes Krapf, who had walked inland from the East African coast and claimed to have seen snow-capped mountains and heard of a great lake. The Royal Geographical Society (RGS) entrusted the next expedition to Captain Richard Burton of the East India Company's army, one of the most formidable of human beings. 'Ruffian Dick' with his 'questing panther's eyes' was an expert linguist, who had fought face to face with many hundreds of Her Majesty's enemies, but had never been popular with the authorities, partly because of his insatiable curiosity in sexual matters – he had reported that Arab wives prefer African lovers for reasons, as he wrote: 'somewhat too physiological for the general reader.' Burton was already famous, having made the *Hajj* (pilgrimage) to Mecca and Medina incognito, as this was forbidden on pain of death to non-Muslims.

For his Nile venture, Burton was given a more conventional colleague, John Hanning Speke, and it was Speke who discovered the great lake that he named Victoria, since Burton was too ill for the final stages, and was sure that it did indeed form the source of the Nile. Yet there was still no proof; Burton, for one, remained unconvinced. The RGS left the question open for a public debate between Burton, who insisted that the true source was further south, and Speke: dramatically, on the very day of the meeting, Speke was found dying of a gunshot wound, presumably the result of an accident.

As well as investigating the source of the Nile, British expeditions had found slave trading on a massive scale, shared by Arab merchants, each taking slaves on his agreed territory, often with extreme cruelty. Scottish missionary David Livingstone, with 20 years of African experience, abhorred slavery.

'The strangest disease I have seen in this country seems really to be broken-heartedness, and it attacks free men who have been captured and made slaves.'

Livingstone gave a chilling eye-witness account of one raid, when two parties of Arab raiders attacked a village, firing indiscriminately at the crowd in the market place, driving them into the river. The slavers themselves estimated that between 330 and 400 people had died, but all the women were taken. The publicity value of Livingstone's accounts was multiplied by the adventurer Henry Morton Stanley, travelling as a correspondent for the *New York Herald*, whose descriptions of his journey to Ujiji to meet Livingstone, presumed lost in the dark heart of the continent, and his subsequent voyage down the River Congo in a steel boat, carried from the east coast, forced Central Africa onto the world's attention.

Franco-British Rivalry

In the first part of the 19th century, few European countries were interested in overseas expansion. Britain had quite enough of expensive colonial responsibilities, with the expanding Indian Empire, Canada, Australasia and formerly-Dutch South Africa. 'Informal' empire, where profits could be made

LEFT *British gunboats open fire on enemy positions while on their way up the Nile in early 1885 to relieve General George Gordon, besieged by the army of the* Mahdi *in Khartoum. They arrived two days too late to save Gordon and the garrison. Coloured lithograph from* The Illustrated London News.

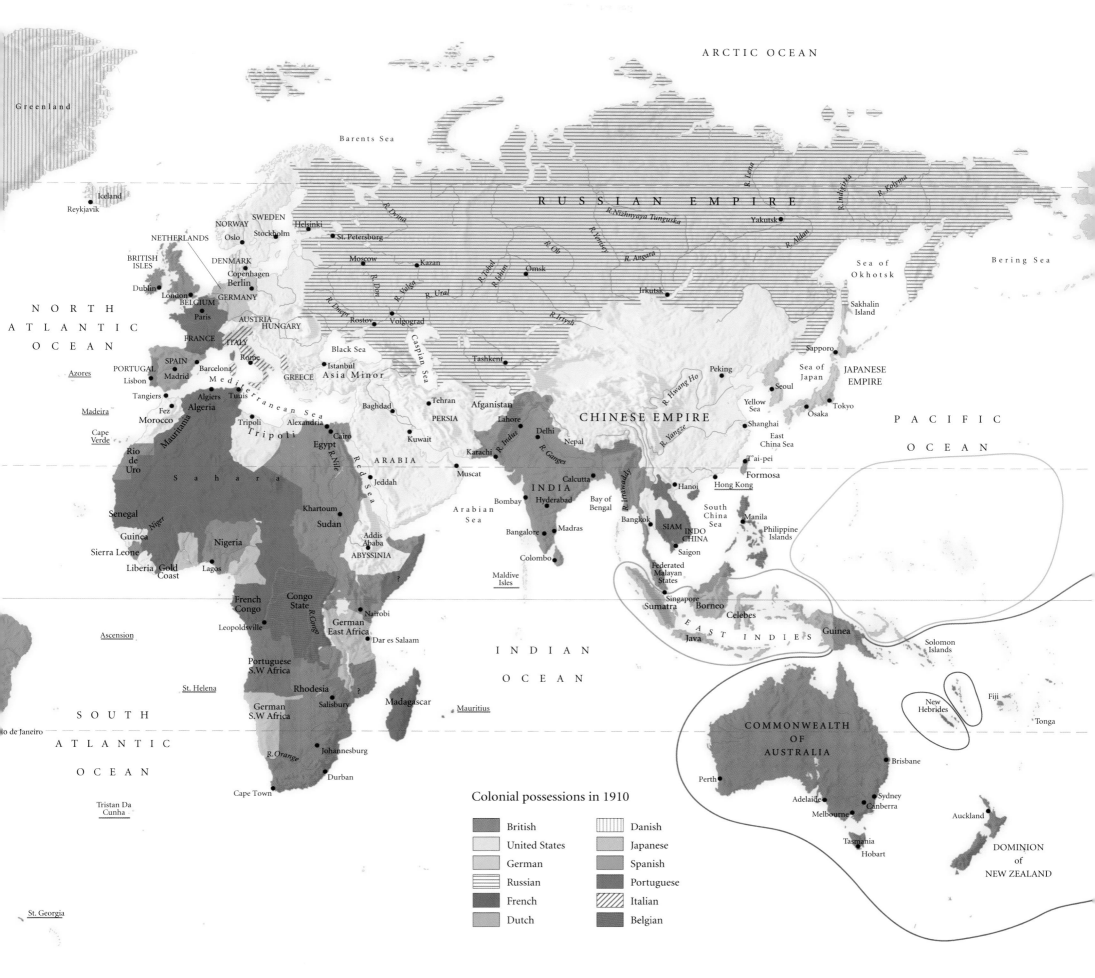

Colonial possessions in 1910

British		Danish	
United States		Japanese	
German		Spanish	
Russian		Portuguese	
French		Italian	
Dutch		Belgian	

from trade and finance without having to take on administrative burdens was infinitely preferable. The only exception was in the vigorous pursuit of slavers, in which the Royal Navy had taken the lead after Britain banned the trade in 1807 and to which British missionaries, especially the great David Livingstone, were dedicated. Of the old colonial powers, only France showed interest, with the invasion of Algiers in 1830 intended to create 'a French Roman Empire.' After spirited resistance led by the Berber Emir Abd'el Qadir, Algeria was formally annexed in 1848, not as a colony, but as an integral part of France.

France also had ambitions, dating from Napoleon I's time, to gain some control over Egypt, where an opportunity was presented by the Suez Canal

Company's project to connect the Mediterranean with the Red Sea. Financed jointly by French investors and the Khedive Ismail, nominally Turkish governor of Egypt but in practice independent, the canal was opened in 1869, with Verdi's opera *Aida*, specially written to mark the occasion.

The Suez Company had sold Ismail an almost fraudulent prospectus which, combined with his own extravagance, drove Egypt to the brink of bankruptcy. Attempting some empire-building on his own behalf, the Khedive employed two Englishmen, Sir Samuel Baker and General Charles 'Chinese' Gordon, to extend the Egyptian state south to the Great Lakes. That was checked by a popular uprising in the Sudan, led by Sheikh Muhammad Ahmad, a charismatic leader who claimed to be the *Mahdi* (the Islamic

Redeemer), which annihilated an Egyptian army in 1883, and was only halted with British intervention in 1898: the young Winston Churchill charged with the 21st Lancers during the final engagement at the Battle of Omdurman. Meanwhile a nationalist uprising in the north, which could have led to the birth of modern Egypt, was stifled by the British, resulting in the establishment of de facto British control of Egypt. Edged out of Egypt, an invasion of Tunis gave France a consolation prize.

Ismail tried to evade responsibility, but was dismissed by the Sultan, exercising his constitutional powers; the former Khedive then retired to Naples with the 300 ladies of his harem. Under British administration Egypt's fortunes were restored, the turbulent Sudan subdued and the vital route to India protected.

After the expulsion from Mexico, the defeat of 1870 and the loss of Alsace and Lorraine, French opinion demanded dramatic success overseas, and this was found in Indochina, when a foothold obtained in Saigon in 1862 was expanded into a French empire of Annam, Tonkin and Cochin China, while the areas now forming Laos and Cambodia were brought within the French sphere of influence: a slice of the world equivalent in size to France itself, stretching 1,000 miles (1,600 km) south from the border with China, came under French control. On a smaller scale, a French protectorate over Tahiti was proclaimed in 1844 and seven years later New Caledonia was annexed.

The Scramble for Africa

Africa became the prime target of ambitious colonizers, beginning with the avaricious and unscrupulous Leopold II, King of the Belgians, who planned to have his own private company take over the whole of the Congo Basin, nearly a million square miles of Africa. This prospect galvanized the French, whose young naval cadet Pierre de Brazza had already struggled from the coast to raise the flag at the most strategic spot on the Congo, alarmed the Portuguese, whose old colony of Angola came within a few miles of the river's mouth and worried the British, concerned that a royal company would stifle competition. Then, converting concern to crisis, in May 1884 a German gunboat planted the imperial flag in South West Africa, Cameroon and the coastal territory of Togo, all bordering on formal or informal British interests. An international conference was held in Berlin in 1884–85 to resolve these issues. King Leopold succeeded in his aims, with his Congo Free State taking the lion's share of that very profitable area. European spheres of influence in Africa were marked out and some boundaries fixed; Britain's main concern was not to acquire territory but to ensure that freedom of trade – of which the majority would be British – was guaranteed; the continent was now laid open for foreign exploitation.

Germany, which came late to the race for overseas colonies, now went all-out to secure its 'place in the sun', snapping up a slice of East Africa by the simple expedient of sending warships to Zanzibar. All German Africa was governed with extreme brutality: labour obligations, enforced by often-fatal floggings, provoked rebellions that were suppressed with pitiless severity. When the Herero of South West Africa rebelled in 1904–07, they were virtually wiped out, while over quarter of a million perished in German East Africa. German genocide was not invented by Hitler's Third Reich.

One country was left aggrieved. Italy, newly united, also began acquiring colonies, beginning in 1885 with the Red Sea port of Massawa, which was intended to be the springboard for an invasion of Abyssinia, the ancient kingdom of Axum. When that was attempted ten years later it proved disastrous, with the Italian force destroyed at the battle of Adowa, and King Menelik increasing his own kingdom substantially, the only traditional African society to survive the hectic 20-year Scramble for Africa.

British colonial policies had become a party issue; Conservatives were imperialist, welcoming new colonies, while most liberals were anxious to avoid new responsibilities and deplored the subjection of native communities; free trade for all and the eradication of slavery were their priorities. As in India, the flag followed the traders. British Chartered Companies, reinforced by missionary societies, penetrated present-day Nigeria and Uganda, using their own small forces together with local allies to subdue opposition before London would consent to take over. The Colonial Office rejected the first proposal that Nigeria, potentially the richest state on the continent, should become a protectorate, since the cost was likely to be £5,000 a year. Much depended on having the right man on the spot, in both countries the decisive and persuasive Captain Lugard.

In British South Africa, Cecil Rhodes carried through a protracted campaign of mixed idealism, greed, force and deceit, again using a Chartered Company, but here with total lack of scruple, to establish two eponymous countries, Northern and Southern Rhodesia, today's Zambia and Zimbabwe, as well as securing Bechuanaland (Botswana) as a British Protectorate. Colonial South Africa had grown immeasurably since the first British troops took over the Dutch settlement at the Cape. The original inhabitants, the Khoikhoi and San, had been absorbed into the colonial society while those other newcomers, the Bantu tribes coming to the end of their long migration south, were forced to choose between compliance and resistance. Border wars continued for many years, but in 1853 a coherent government was established in Cape Town, with the typical colonial constitution of an elected assembly and council. The right to vote was limited by a property qualification, as in Britain, but specifically kept low enough to allow:

'those of the coloured classes who in point of intelligence are qualified for the exercise of political power.'

The same conditions were meant to apply in the other British colony of Natal, but were simply ignored; there, as in the rest of southern Africa, whites aimed at complete domination.

Only in the Cape Colony and in the British Protectorates of Bechuanaland, Basutoland (Lesotho) and Swaziland could blacks have a voice in their own government. With his usual insight Livingstone put their case:

'We are not advocates of war, but we would prefer perpetual war to perpetual slavery. No nation ever secured its liberty without fighting for it …the true Negro family was entitled to its place in the general community of nations.'

ABOVE *The Battle of Isandlhwana during the Anglo-Zulu War of 1879, as portrayed in a painting from the period. An entire regiment was virtually wiped out in this engagement. Just before this defeat, during the siege of a mission at Rorke's Drift, a small British force of 150 held out bravely against a Zulu army of 4,000.*

The explosive expansion of the Zulu people, which swept right through southern Africa, was eventually contained, after a spectacular British defeat at Isandlhwana in 1879, but the emigrant Boers were a tougher proposition. These descendants of German, Dutch and French settlers, chose not to accept British rule, the ban on slave-holding being a particular irritant. They had trekked to the interior, carving out their own republics, forming that dogged and talented people since known as Afrikaners. With the discovery, first of diamonds then of gold in great quantities, the local economies were transformed. While the diamond mines could – just – be claimed by the

British colonies all the gold belonged unequivocally to the the Afrikaner Transvaal Republic; but the capital and expertise had to be imported and a railway constructed. The small Boer farming community was overwhelmed by a rapacious crowd of entrepreneurs, the 'Randlords' or *Uitlanders*. Coexistence would have been possible, given some goodwill, but Rhodes, then Prime Minister of the Cape Colony, was determined on a coup to be made with the connivance of the Conservative government in London. The first attempt, the Jameson Raid, failed, but in 1899 major hostilities began, which would continue for three years. The outcome was to prove decisive for the whole future of Africa.

The Energy Revolution: The East Reacts to a Changing World

■ The Meiji Restoration in Japan 1868 ■ Queen Victoria becomes Empress of India 1876

■ Edison and Swan invent the electric light bulb 1879 ■ Spanish-American War 1898

■ Boxer Uprising in China 1900–01 ■ Russo-Japanese War 1904–05

The Industrial Revolution continued in the 19th century, in what might be termed the Energy Revolution, as electricity, on both small and large scales, transformed industries and urban life.

Russia and Japan both successfully developed modern industries and attempted political change, but China, constantly jolted by foreign pressures, remained slow to adjust. After the profound shock of the 1857–58 Mutiny, Britain began to introduce her unwieldy Indian Empire to the modern world.

The Electrical Age

Coal remained Queen in industry, transport and city life, whether for production of coal gas, raising steam in industry, coking for steel production and municipal lighting, but from 1850 the twin products, paraffin and kerosene, were invented, making small-scale domestic lighting and heating economic. Both depended on dry distillation of oil-bearing rocks or shale, but in 1858 the first oil drillings in Pennsylvania provided an easier source for distillation, which could not only produce kerosene and fuel oil or lubricants but also petrol (gasoline), at first regarded as both dangerous and useless.

It was not, however, America, but Russia that took the lead in the oil industry, beginning with wells in the Caspian region in the 1870s, using superheated steam and continuous distillation patented by the Swedish Nobel brothers – famous for their invention of dynamite. By 1901, Russia was the world's largest oil producer with 11.75 million tons, shipped direct from Batumi on the Black Sea to London by Nobel tankers.

Internal combustion engines, powered by coal gas from the early 1800s, were developed to run on petrol by the German Nikolaus Otto in 1876, but applied only slowly to transport. The horse continued to rule the roads, but the future of the oil industry as a competitive international enterprise with the USA, Germany and Russia vying for leadership was defined. Wars, previously fought for territory, became equally concerned with oil.

Early electrical research was international, with the names of the Italians Volta and Galvani, and the French Andre Ampère commemorated in all languages, but the 19th-century development of industrial electricity became an Anglo-American and German speciality. Michael Faraday was the first with his invention in 1836 of an electric motor, and therefore the dynamo, a method of converting mechanical power into electrical power. Small steam-driven dynamos invented by the Belgian Zénobe Gramme were used for powering electric arc lamps in such varied locations as railway stations, theatres, department stores and art galleries. The real breakthrough came with the development of the filament bulb, the joint invention of Thomas Edison and Sir Joseph Swan, which made domestic lighting practicable. Large scale generation was pioneered by Sebastian de Ferranti, commissioned in 1887 at the age of 23 to build what was then the largest power station in the world, at Deptford in East London, generating 10,000 volts AC, an alarming output for the time, and supplying electricity to the whole district. The work was completed in just 15 months, and the station became the prototype of all subsequent steam-powered generators, which

LEFT *Oil derricks at Baku on the Caspian Sea, photographed in around 1890. Russia was an early leader in oil exploration. By the beginning of the 20th century, this region (in present-day Azerbaijan) was producing more than half the world's oil supply.*

revolutionized steel and chemical production. In factories, electric engines were first used as steam had been, to provide a central supply, but small electric motors were soon being integrated with machine tools. All this development shot ahead at an unprecedented speed – less than 25 years from the first small generator installed in the Paris Gare du Nord to Ferranti's Deptford station coming on stream.

Urban transport was still almost all horse-drawn by the end of the century, with the attendant street pollution, but electric tramways were coming into use, and in 1890 the first electric trains ran on the City and South London tube: ten years later two more lines were operating. Combined with improved sewage systems, efficient urban transport immensely improved city life, but coal-firing and the dank climate of the Thames Valley made London fog a notorious phenomenon. Rapidly increasing urbanization and industrialization created a class of more educated and articulate artisans, and new social and political organizations appeared. By the 1870s most major European countries had active trade unions and social democratic parties. Unlike the continental groups, with their strong middle-class and intellectual element, the British Labour Party, a late arrival in 1906, developed from the Trades Union and Cooperative movements, with a dash of evangelical religion, leaving theory to that small but influential group, the Fabian Society.

Russia and Japan

Karl Marx, who died in 1883, would have been astonished to see how quickly Russia developed the proletarian organizations that he had believed would emerge in more industrialized societies The Russian tradition of government – strongly persistent for much longer – of autocracy enforced by a brutal

ABOVE *Elevated trains roll over the busy streets of New York's Bowery district in 1895. Not only did the railroads change the nature of New York street life, but also were a sign of the increasing urbanization of the big American cities.*

police, sporadically obliged to acknowledge the need for change by violent protests, was challenged by rapidly increasing industrialization. Alexander II's reign (1855–81) had been marked by real reforms, including the liberation of the serfs and the establishment of provincial representative authorities, but his assassination – literally blown to pieces by anarchist bombers – re-established a period of autocratic rule. Tsar Nicholas II, who succeeded in 1894, edged towards reform. After a wave of mass protests and strikes in 1905, he permitted the election of a parliament, the *Duma,* in September of that year, which first met in May 1906. It proved too much for the reactionaries; the franchise was restricted, and a second *Duma* elected. Even this proved too liberal, and more adjustments to the ballot were needed before a third, more biddable, *Duma* was able to meet in November 1907. Clearly, Russia's path towards democracy was going to be stony.

A tough police state can control the home front, but international humiliation undermines any militarist government, and Russia suffered a crushing defeat by an unlikely enemy, Japan.

When Commodore Matthew Perry USN politely asked to open trade negotiations with Japan in 1858, the Tokugawa Shogunate, in power since 1600, hesitated, but realized that resistance was useless. Treaties similar to those signed by China were made, although much resented by many suspicious *samurai*. Within a few years, the Emperor Komei combined with

the two most powerful noble houses to depose the Tokugawa Shogun and restore direct executive power, assumed next year by the 15-year-old Emperor Mutsihito, who took the reign name Meiji. The next 30 years saw a new society emerge in what must be the most dramatic development of a nation ever recorded. With minimal disruption, apart from one violent rebellion by some Satsuma *samurai*, quelled by a force stiffened by the new Tokyo police, Japan became a modern nation, with a representative constitution, the rule of law, international standards of education and urbanization. A new army was trained by France and a navy supplied by England. The territorial magnates, the *daimyo*, were deposed and the *samurai* disbanded.

The first clash came with China, after a number of incidents in Korea, for long a cause of dissension. Within months the Chinese armies were crushed by the better-equipped and trained Japanese, and their navy sunk. The Treaty of Shimonoseki (April 1895), was harsh, making greater demands on China than any of the Western powers had formerly exacted. All of Formosa (Taiwan), the Pescadores Islands and the Liaodong Peninsula of Manchuria were ceded to Japan and an indemnity of 230 million taels demanded – more than ten times that paid to Britain in the terms of the Treaty of Nanking. Russian intervention succeeded in modifying the conditions, but Russia was the next empire to feel the weight of the new Japan.

ABOVE *A Japanese print of 1895 showing an infantry clash between French-uniformed Japanese and poorly armed Chinese during the Sino-Japanese War. This brief conflict saw regional dominance shift from China to Japan, and dealt a terminal blow to the moribund Qing Dynasty, already weakened by decades of internal unrest and foreign intervention.*

When Russia bullied the Chinese Empire, now sliding towards final extinction, into granting it the right to establish a military base and ice-free port at Port Arthur (Lushun) in Manchuria, Japan protested, Russia prevaricated, and a naval war ensued, watched with great interest by all countries. Admiral Togo, who commanded the Japanese fleet, was a particularly fine seaman, who had been trained at the Dartmouth Royal Naval College, and his British-built ships had no difficulty in destroying the Russian fleets dispatched against him (the Baltic Fleet was even sent halfway around the world from St Petersburg). This defeat of a European power boosted Japanese confidence and established the country as the leading force in the western Pacific. The Treaty of Portsmouth, which ended the war, gained new territory for Japan, including a protectorate over Korea. Embodying the new Japan, her representative at the negotiations was Harvard-educated, while the fact that President Theodore Roosevelt chaired

plenipotentiary Lord Elgin. In retaliation for the murder of some Europeans, including the *Times* correspondent Thomas Bowlby, who had been starved then beaten to death, Elgin ordered the Imperial Summer Palace to be destroyed, an act of vandalism that fuelled lasting Chinese resentment. Free travel and trade throughout the realm was now permitted to all foreigners, who were to remain subject only to their own nation's laws. Almost as an aside, the mainland shore opposite the capital town of Hong Kong, part of the Chinese city of Kowloon, was transferred to British sovereignty in a personal deal between Parkes and the Chinese Governor-General of Canton; the cost was $500.

Effective Japanese-style reform demanded a more receptive attitude than the Chinese could adopt. Officials argued that since 'intelligence and wisdom of the Chinese are necessarily superior to those of the various barbarians,' China, with a little application, would be able to reassert herself as the world's centre. Much was, however, achieved, with the help of a steady income from the (foreign-administered) Imperial Customs, but constructive action came not from the Manchu élite but from the thousands of young Chinese who studied abroad, in Europe or Japan – Chinese being excluded from the USA, as 'dangerous to our peace and welfare,' bringing as they did 'seeds of moral and physical disease, of destitution and death.'

Knowledge of the outside world reached even the Emperor Guangxu, who in the summer of 1898 asserted his authority by issuing the Hundred Days Reform programme, a comprehensive list of modest and practicable measures affecting the constitution, administration, army and education It was too much for the Dowager Empress, who erupted from her retirement, put the emperor under house arrest, and had his more prominent advisors executed. In June 1900, Cixi finally quashed all hopes of moderate constitutional reform by openly supporting the Boxer Rebellion, a violent anti-foreign uprising staged by a secret society known as the 'League of Righteous and Harmonious Fists.' After the siege of the foreign embassies, the famous '90 Days at Beijing,' the revolt was crushed by a combined foreign military force. The International Protocol of 1901 exacted an enormous sum in reparations and established a foreign garrison in the Legation Quarter of Beijing. The end of the Qing dynasty was assured, but what would take its place was far from clear.

America's New Colonies

The United States was not averse to a little empire-building on its own behalf. The Sandwich Islands, now better known as Hawaii, was the first target in January 1893 when a force of US Marines and sailors overthrew the popular Queen Liliuokalani. Subsequent Congressional reports worried over the legality of the move, but the question was simply settled by the annexation of the country as the 49th state, whose history is commemorated in the state ensign, which has the Union flag in its canton.

An attack on Cuba, Spain's last American possession brought with it two more colonies, almost by accident. Regular rebellions, which had troubled Cuba throughout the century, culminated in a 10-year war that ended in 1878, with promises of reform. In 1895, a new revolt was suppressed with great brutality – the Spanish General Weyler invented the concentration camp system – and perhaps a quarter of the population was killed. As Cuba was an offshore island, less than 100 miles (160 km) from Key West, the American press reported the fights in detail, with much passionate support for the rebels. When, in 1898, the USS *Maine* was mysteriously destroyed

the meetings symbolized the return of America to international affairs. After the final battle, a major engagement in the Straits of Tsushima in May 1905, only three Russian ships out of 37 returned to base. When the news reached Russia, the crew of the battleship *Potemkin* mutinied. The ensuing widespread unrest of 1905 turned out to be a dress rehearsal for the October Revolution of 1917.

The Last Dynasty

China attempted its own version of renewal, but was hampered by simultaneous violent and persistent revolts, by the Taiping, who adopted a curious version of Christianity and attempted to establish an ideal state, by the Nian, old-fashioned bandits in the Yellow River, and by Muslims in the north and west. Not until the 1870s was most of China reunited under Qing rule, in which the dominant personality was that of the Dowager Empress Cixi, who had assumed a regency on the succession of the Emperor Tongzhi in 1861, and after his death in 1875, for her nephew Guangxu.

In the south, the governor of Hong Kong, Dr John Bowring, and Harry Parkes, the British consul at Canton, jointly provoked a war that was only terminated in 1860 after the occupation of Beijing by a force under British

in Havana harbour, anti-Spanish feeling grew hysterical, and in spite of Spain's effort to comply, President McKinley was forced to declare war.

The war was very brief and economical – fewer than 300 American dead – and included one dramatic charge by Theodore Roosevelt's volunteer 'Rough Riders' (who, contrary to popular myth, actually fought on foot) but its consequences were momentous. Spain ceded Cuba, the Philippines, Guam and Wake Island to the USA, establishing a chain of US bases across the ocean to within a few hundred miles of China and Japan. The small island of Puerto Rico also became an American possession, and something of an embarrassment. The Philippines were also an embarrassment, since the rebellion already taking place against Spanish rule was extended to the Americans. President McKinley had announced the aim of 'Christianizing' the inhabitants, apparently not realizing that most had been devout Catholics for four centuries. The aim of the US troops was summed up in their song:

'Beneath the starry flag, Civilize 'em with a Krag.'

– the Krag being the standard .30 calibre army issue rifle.

The New India

The explosion predicted by Emily Eden came in 1857 with the Indian Mutiny, sometimes called the First National War of Independence. It had been provoked by the sheer pace of change; thousands of books had been printed in Bengali between 1810 and 1820, introducing new and provoking ideas, while the brisk imposition of new regulations horrified traditionalists. Once the last rebellious sepoy had been killed the British government was forced seriously to consider its responsibilities on the Subcontinent.

In fact few other European countries were as poorly equipped to run a great empire as Britain. British law was incoherent and outdated – trial by battle was abolished as late as the 1820s – and there was no police service until 1827. Local and regional government were still in the hands of medieval corporations and lord lieutenants. At a time when France and Germany both had well-designed national systems, English education was largely irrelevant to national needs. The army was small and unprofessional: commissions were bought and sold. The only two first-class organizations were the Royal Navy and the City of London, the twin pillars that supported the British Empire.

India could not be governed by such a muddled system. The East India Company's services were taken over by the government of India, and the Indian Civil Service, which Rudyard Kipling described as 'the first fighting line' of imperial rule, became a byword of thorough and incorruptible administration of a quality never seen before in either India or Britain. Under its aegis, India was brought into the world economy. Enjoying the highest possible credit rating, low-interest Indian loans enabled communications to be constructed to a standard unparalleled elsewhere in Asia: by the

"NEW CROWNS FOR OLD ONES!"

(ALADDIN *adapted.*)

LEFT *In 1876, the celebrated* Punch *cartoonist John Tenniel (famous for his* Alice in Wonderland *illustrations) depicted Prime Minister Benjamin Disraeli as a magician offering Victoria the crown of India.*

end of the 19th century India had 24,000 miles (38,600km) of railway compared to China's 340 miles (550km). Such traditional industries as metalworking and cotton-spinning declined, affected by the industrial revolution, but the Indian cotton industry was now one of the world's largest. By 1900 Tata was already one of the world's biggest industrial groups.

There were to be no more conquests or dispossessions; no legal distinctions were to be made between races or religions and public posts were to be open to all. Although it was accepted that, sooner or later, Indians must govern themselves, the British regarded that as, at best, a distant prospect. Britain's responsibility was to:

'establish peace, order and the supremacy of law, the prevention of crime, the redress of wrong, and enforcement of contracts … [and] the construction of public works.'

India was a concept, a tradition, the ancient land of Hind rather than a political entity, divided as it was among many races and religions, and even more languages. Symbolizing the new order, Queen Victoria became Empress of India in 1876, a position she took very seriously. But the new social fabric, with schools, colleges and a thriving vernacular press, ensured that a concept of Indian nationality emerged, and with it came demands for self-government.

The *Fin de Siècle*

As the end of the 19th century approached, Europeans sensed the end of an era. Within a single lifetime – Queen Victoria, still on the throne of England, had been born in 1820 – the middle classes had moved from a time of boot-blacks and chamber pots, coal fires, draughts, muddy streets, agonizing surgery and gas flares, to fast and comfortable travel, warm houses, luxurious hotels, electric light, trains, telephones and anaesthetics. Hot baths and clean clothes were now commonplace (as late as 1890 the Duke of Westminster had reproved his grandson for the extravagance of insisting on a clean shirt every day). Although starched shirts, frock coats and crinolines were necessary formal wear, loose tweeds and soft shirts – even bloomers – were acceptable at weekends. The Prince of Wales was often seen in a soft Homburg hat, tweeds and gaiters. In the United States, the tall, softly-contoured 'Gibson girl' had become the female ideal.

Social changes were mirrored in the arts. Those typical London clubmen Dickens and Thackeray were dead: the current favourites were Robert Louis

ABOVE Portrait of Adele Bloch-Bauer I *by Gustav Klimt (1862–1918). The work of this Austrian symbolist painter heralded a new liberalism in art and society and particularly in work by Klimt.*

Stevenson, languishing in the South Seas, no distance from Paul Gauguin on Tahiti, Arthur Conan Doyle, introducing skiing to Switzerland, or Henry James, painstakingly putting his sentences together in Rye in Sussex. Intellectuals enthused about Ibsen, Chekhov and Turgenev, while less serious playgoers flocked to the latest productions from Oscar Wilde, Bernard Shaw or Arthur Wing Pinero.

In painting, the work of James McNeill Whistler and the French impressionists had become respectable by the 1890s, and fashionable attention was turning east, to the exotic elegance of Gustav Klimt and Alfons Mucha, but there were signs of harsher times ahead. Writer Emil Zola's brutal realism was deployed to expose French militarism and anti-Semitism in the Dreyfus case, while Kaiser Wilhelm II's belligerent posturing in Berlin angered his grandmother Victoria and alarmed the British military establishment, especially the navy.

From the other German-speaking capital, Vienna, the works of Dr Sigmund Freud began to pour out, beginning in 1895; and there too in 1911 some, watching Richard Strauss' new opera *Der Rosenkavalier* must have felt that when, after the Marschallin renounces her love for the young Octavian and her little black page skips back on to the deserted stage to retrieve her handkerchief, a whole era was ending.

A CENTURY OF WARS

	1900	1910	1915	1920	1930	1940
EUROPE	**1904** *Entente Cordiale* signed between Britain and France **1906** First elected Russian parliament (Duma)	**1912–13** Balkan Wars **1914** (28 June) Assassination of the Austrian Archduke Ferdinand in Sarajevo **1914** (Aug) Outbreak of the First World War: Germany and Austria (the Central powers) fight Russia, France and the British Empire LEFT *German troops mobilized, 1914*	**1915** Armenians massacred by Turks: first 20th century genocide **1917** (Apr) The USA declares war on the Central powers **1917** (Nov) Bolshevik revolution in Russia **1917** (Dec) Bolsheviks sign armistice with Germany **1918** (Nov) Armistice is signed between Germany and the Allies **1918–21** Civil war in Russia	**1920–21** War between Poland and the Soviet Union **1920–22** War between Greece and Turkey **1921** Irish Free State founded **1922–23** Formation of the Union of Soviet Socialist Republics (USSR) **1923** France occupies the Ruhr **1923** Kemal Ataturk becomes first president of Turkey	**1936** Germany occupies the Rhineland **1936–39** The Spanish Civil War **1938** Germany invades Austria **1939** (Aug) Stalin signs the Nazi–Soviet Non-aggression Pact **1939** (Sept) Germany and the Soviet Union invade Poland; France and Britain declare war on Germany	**1940** (May) German forces invade France and the Low Countries. (September) Defeat of German Luftwaffe in the Battle of Britain **1941** (Jun) Germany invades the Soviet Union **1943** (Jan) German army surrenders at Stalingrad **1943** (Sep) Italy surrenders **1944** (July) Soviet forces enter Poland. (June) Allied forces invade at Normandy (D-Day)
THE AMERICAS	**1900** US annexes Puerto Rico **1906–07** Revolts in Cuba are suppressed by US intervention	**1910** The Mexican Revolution, an uprising against autocrat Porfirio Díaz, begins **1914** Panama Canal opens; Canada enters the war against Germany	**1917** The US declares war on Germany **1919** The US Senate rejects the Treaty of Versailles	**1920** Prohibition starts in the US **1929** Wall Street Crash; beginning of the Great Depression		**1941** Pearl Harbor attack brings the USA into the Second World War LEFT *An unemployed worker, photographed in Chicago, during the Great Depression*
THE MIDDLE EAST	**1909** Jews establish their first kibbutz in Palestine	**1916** Arab revolt against the Ottomans	**1917** Balfour Declaration commits Britain to the creation of a Jewish 'national home'	**1920** French forces invade Syria to impose their League of Nations mandate **1925** Reza Khan begins the modernization of Iraq	**1932** The Kingdom of Hejaz and Nejd is renamed the Kingdom of Saudi Arabia	**1942** German forces defeated in the Western Desert marking a turning point in the war
ASIA AND INDIA	LEFT *A Japanese print of the surprise attack on the Russian fleet, anchored at Port Arthur, 1904* **1900–01** Boxer uprising in China against foreigners **1904–05** Russo–Japanese War	**1911** Chinese Revolution overthrows the Qing dynasty **1914** Japanese troops land on the Shandong Peninsula, China	**1919** Japanese fire upon a demonstration by Koreans calling for freedom from Japanese rule	**1924** Ho Chi Minh begins directing rebel activities in his native Vietnam, against the ruling French	**1931** In India a protest march by Muslims is fired upon. It will be known as the Kanpur Massacre **1932** Japan annexes Manchuria **1937** Japan invades China: the 'Rape of Nanking'	**1941** (Dec) Japan attacks Pearl Harbor, the Philippines, Hong Kong and Malaya; USA enters the Second World War **1942** (Feb) British forces in Singapore surrender to Japan
AFRICA	**1902** Second Anglo–Boer War ends as the British overcome the Boers	**1910** Union of South Africa established, the first modern African country **1914** Egypt proclaimed a British protectorate	**1915–1918** British and South African forces fight Germans in West and East Africa	**1922** Egypt gains independence	**1935–36** Italian forces invade Abyssinia (Ethiopia)	**1943** (May) Defeat of Germans in Tunisia, ends the North African Campaign LEFT *German and Italian prisoners of war in Tunisia*

174

1900–PRESENT

| 1945 | 1950 | 1960 | 1970 | 1980 | 1900 | 2000 |

1945 (May) Germany surrenders; United Nations Organization established

1947 Sovietization of the governments of Eastern Europe

1948–49 The Berlin airlift supplies food and material to the isolated city after Soviet Union closes land routes

1954 Treaty of Rome establishes European Economic Commission

1955 Warsaw Pact inaugurated

1956 Anti-Soviet uprising in Hungary quelled

1961 Berlin Wall built

1968 Czechoslovakian 'Prague Spring' ends with Warsaw Pact invasion; students riot in Paris

LEFT *East German troops erecting the Berlin Wall*

1974 Greek and Turkish coups divide the island of Cyprus

1979 John Paul III is first non-Italian pope for 450 years

RIGHT *Serbian troops withdrawing from Kosovo in 1999*

1980 Solidarity union in Gdansk, Poland, begins erosion of Soviet power

1989 Berlin Wall torn down; regimes in Hungary, Poland, East Germany, Bulgaria, Czechoslovakia and Romania fall

1990 East and West Germany reunited

1990–92 Slovenia, Croatia and Bosnia-Herzegovina break away from Yugoslavia

1991 Soviet Union breaks up

1993 European Union established

1993 Czechoslovakia splits into the Czech Republic and Slovakia

1998–99 War erupts in Kosovo

2002 Single European currency issued

2005 London hit by Islamic terrorist bombings; the IRA announces it is officially ending its violent campaign for a united Ireland

---

1959 Marxist Fidel Castro takes over Cuba

LEFT *Fidel Castro and fellow revolutionary Camilo Cienfuegos in Havana, 1959*

1961 Attempt by Cuban exiles, backed by America, to invade Cuba

1962 Cuban missile crisis; J. F. Kennedy assassinated

1973 Chile's president Allende is killed in a US-backed coup

1974 US president Nixon resigns following the Watergate affair

1982 Argentine invasion of the British controlled Falkland Islands repulsed

1983 US forces invade Grenada

1994 Four convicted of World Trade Center, New York, bombing in 1993; US forces invade Haiti to overthrow the military regime

2001 Terrorists attack New York City's World Trade Center and the Pentagon

---

1948 Proclamation of the state of Israel, followed by an attack by its Arab neighbours

1951 Iran nationalizes the oil industry

1956 Egypt nationalizes the Suez Canal

1967 Israel's defeat of Egypt, Syria and Jordan in the Six-Day War gives Israel control of Sinai and the West Bank

1969 Muammar Gaddafi overthrows King Idris in Libya

1973 Egypt launches an attack on Israel

1979 The Soviet Union invades Afghanistan

1979 Islamic republic in Iran; Saddam Hussein takes power in Iraq

1980 Iraq invades Iran

1982 Israel invades Lebanon

1989 Soviet troops leave Afghanistan

1990 Iraq invades Kuwait

1991 An American-led UN coalition defeats Iraq

2003 US and Britain launch war against Iraq

2008 Egypt brokers a cease-fire between Israel and Hamas

1945 (Sep) Formal Japanese surrender

1947 Independent state of Pakistan established after India partitioned on the basis of religious demographics

1948 The states of North and South Korea established

1949–50 Creation of the People's Republic of China

1950 North Korea invades South Korea

1953 Korean Armistice ends the Korean War

1954 The French surrender at Dien Bien Phu, Vietnam; Laos and Cambodia become independent; Vietnam is divided

1961 The US becomes involved in the war in South Vietnam

1966–70 The Cultural Revolution in China

1971 Independence for Bangladesh

1973 US troops leave South Vietnam

1976 North and South Vietnam reunited

1976 Cambodian genocide by Khmer Rouge begins

1979 Military coup in South Korea

1989 Student-led pro-democracy movement crushed at Tiananmen Square, Beijing

LEFT *Chinese Red Guards with the* Little Red Book, *containing writings by Mao Zedong*

1997 Hong Kong returns to Chinese rule

ABOVE *Students demonstrate in Tiananmen Square, Beijing*

1949 Apartheid introduced in South Africa

1954 Algerian National Front declares war on the French

1960 Belgian Congo gains independence

1962 Algeria achieves independence from France

1967 Biafran civil war

1974 Emperor Haile Selassie ousted by Marxists in Ethiopia

1976 Central African Empire proclaimed by Jean-Bédel Bokassa

1980 Robert Mugabe wins election in Southern Rhodesia (Zimbabwe)

1994 Nelson Mandela becomes president of South Africa after first democratic election

2011 Popular uprisings occur in Tunisia, Egypt, Libya and other Arab countries

1906–1919
Stumbling into War

■ Balkan Wars increase tension among Europe's Great Powers 1912–13 ■ Assassination of Archduke Franz Ferdinand is the catalyst to the First World War 1914 ■ Tsarist rule in Russia is ended by revolution 1917 ■ Treaty of Versailles 1919

The series of wars that devastated Europe in the 20th century, and spread to other parts of the world, began in that troubled region, the Balkans. Unlike most previous conflicts, which had generally been based on territorial or dynastic disputes for which rational causes could be found, 20th-century wars were inflamed by nationalist and ideological passions which observers found incomprehensible or even ridiculous; but the savagery with which they were waged was terribly real.

For much of the 19th century Italians and Germans still thought of themselves as belonging to pre-unification states, as Prussians or Saxons, or Neapolitans and Tuscans. Catalans, Galicians or Basques acknowledged themselves as Spanish only in an official context rather than accepting Spain as a homeland.

The Tinder-box of Nationalism

The late 19th century, however, saw a brisk rise in nationalist feelings, especially among those whose past history had been submerged in that of larger states. Norway's independence from Sweden was effected, with only moderate ill-will, in 1905: Finland continued to protest against Russian oppression, and succeeded in winning its own parliament in 1906, with votes even for women, only shortly after Australia (1902) but lagging behind New Zealand, where both Maori and white women had secured the franchise since 1884. The Baltic States of Estonia, Latvia and Lithuania struggled to preserve their own languages against both Russian and German denigration. In spite of William Gladstone's efforts, Irish demands for Home Rule were encouraging violence; the first terrorist bomb in London was detonated in December 1867, killing and injuring more than 40 passers-by.

Internationalist organizations moderated nationalist passions to some extent, in particular the Hague Conventions of 1899, which banned the most contentious methods

of war, including poisonous gases and the launching of projectiles from balloons, and established the still-flourishing Court for the Pacific Settlement of International Disputes. Its value depended on the willingness of sovereign countries to cooperate, but was soon proved by the settlement of a dispute between Britain and the United States over the border between British Guiana (now Belize) and Venezuela. Objections mainly came from Germany, refusing to discuss either armament limitation – surely a warning signal in 1907 – or compulsory arbitration.

An awareness of individual cultures flourished, most distinctively in music, as the Czech composers Dvořák, Smetana and Janácek outdid the Russian masters in the originality of their work. Liszt in Hungary, Greig in Norway and Sibelius in Finland all expressed national aspirations as Chopin had done so magnificently for Poland. Provençal literature and language was revived by Frédéric Mistral (Nobel prize winner in 1904), whose contemporary Henrik Ibsen brought Norwegian literature to the world's attention.

The Balkans, that complex area of different languages, races and religions, was jealously watched by the Habsburg, Russian and Turkish empires. The Congress of Berlin in 1878, intended to stabilize the region, had been a complete failure.

LEFT *Gavrilo Princip, a member of the Serbian 'Black Hand' terrorist group, assassinating Archduke Franz Ferdinand and his wife in Sarajevo on 28 June 1914. This outrage sparked the First World War.*

Even those two seasoned diplomats, Bismarck and Disraeli, were concerned only with their own national interests, and the Congress settlement left the Balkan countries frustrated. Serbia, Bulgaria, Romania, Greece and Montenegro waited for an opportunity to expand further, primarily at Turkey's expense, but with considerable mutual distrust. The first act in the series of 20th century wars began over a two-day period in October 1908, when Bulgaria renounced Turkish sovereignty and Austria annexed Bosnia-Herzegovina, still nominally a Turkish province, confided to Austrian protection at the Berlin Congress. Europe was startled, Russia and Turkey indignant and Serbia, now encircled, furious.

Turkey was then undergoing the Young Turk revolution which led to the Sultan's deposition in 1911, while Serbia's new dynasty, coming to power after murdering the previous monarch, felt humiliated by Austria's annexation of Bosnia. Greece, badly defeated in their previous war with Turkey in 1897, had a new government, dedicated to expanding the country's borders. In October 1912, the First Balkan War was declared: with more than a million men in the field it proved to be the most serious conflict since 1870. By May the next year, the Turkish forces had been decisively beaten, but within days another war broke out, between Serbia and Greece, joined by Romania and Turkey, against the Bulgarians. Although hostilities lasted for only a month,

the regional balance of power shifted decisively. Russia, previously supported by their co-religionists in Bulgaria, was now left with Serbia as her main ally: Greece and Romania were already firmly tied to Britain and France, leaving Bulgaria and Turkey to side with the two German empires.

In the face of Serbian resentment and following a savage conflict that had ended only a few months before, the Bosnian visit of Archduke Franz Ferdinand, the heir to the Austrian throne, was ill-advised. His subsequent assassination at Sarajevo shocked the world, but was not seen as likely to lead to a general war. Royal and presidential assassinations were not uncommon: the Archduke's own mother and King Umberto of Italy, to say nothing of President McKinley, had all been killed recently. The Serbians had murdered their own king only 13 years previously, and a warning had been given that violence might be expected during the Archduke's Bosnian visit. A brusque Austrian demand for apologies would probably suffice, and at worst yet another of those now-common Balkan wars. It might be that Russia would object, but Serbia was unconvincing in the role of victim, and generally regarded as an aggressive nuisance: Britain had cut off diplomatic relations for several years after 1903. The nations stumbled into a wider war through a series of misunderstandings, diplomatic gaffes, sheer stupidity and, on the part of the Germans, an insatiable appetite to assert their new imperial power.

An Infallible Plan

The German general staff had prepared an infallible plan to deliver a massive blow on France through Belgium, feigning an attack on the French frontier near the Swiss Border while the Austrians held off the Russian armies in the East. It was expected that Britain would object, but hardly, the Germans argued, to the point of war. Then with France out of the war, the German armies could be switched to help the Austrians. It should all be over by Christmas. What might have been just another European conflict, like 1866 and 1870, developed into a world war when Britain decided that her commitment to defend Belgian neutrality must be maintained. The German Chancellor, Theobald von Bethmann-Hollweg, was furious when the British ultimatum arrived, and stormed at the British ambassador:

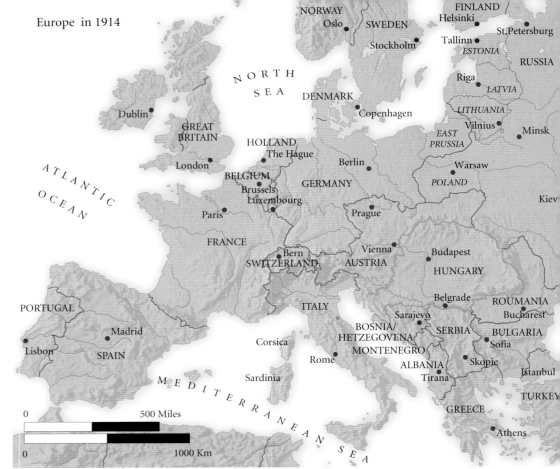

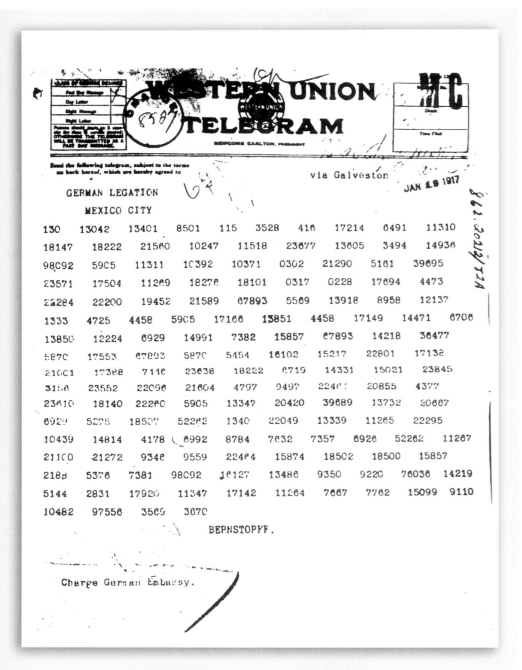

The infamous encoded Zimmermann telegram, forwarded on 19 January 1917 by Count Bernstoff, the German Ambasssador in Washington, D.C. to the German Imperial Minister in Mexico, instructing him to offer that country help in waging war on the United States.

'The war is only turning into an unlimited world catastrophe through England's participation …Compared to the disaster of such a holocaust does not this neutrality dwindle into a scrap of paper?'

Bethmann-Hollweg had a point. Why should Britain let itself be drawn into a European war with Germany, let alone Austria? The countries had traditionally been allies for centuries. Britain had no treaty obligations to France, but only a friendly understanding: Sir Edward Grey, the Foreign Secretary would have settled for neutrality, but – and it was a big but – only if Belgium remained inviolate, a British commitment since 1839. And since the infallible German plan demanded a quick strike through Belgium, this was impossible. Encouraging one another, the German and Austrian general staffs practically declared war on their own accounts, with the excitable Kaiser Wilhelm hopping from hysterical aggression to nervous apprehension.

Few of those politicians and monarchs who made the decision – or rather, avoided making decisions but drifted with events - had any experience of conflict. Edward Grey, dedicated fly-fisher and bird-watcher, believed that even if Britain was forced into war the Navy would ensure that it did not become too serious. The only British minister with military experience, Winston Churchill at the Admiralty, was also convinced that the fleet would secure Britain: he was to learn, leading a regiment on the Western Front, that German gunners were not the Sudanese he had charged at the Battle of Omdurman in 1898.

As so often happens, things did not go according to plan. When war came the plan's creator, Graf von Schlieffen was dead, and his successor, General von Moltke, hedged his bets. The German initial assault was indeed staggering, but the French and British armies retreated in good order, to make a stand beyond the River Marne, within a few miles of Paris itself, with French reinforcements being rushed to the front by rail, road and even Paris taxis. For the next four years northern France and Flanders became one vast battleground, as nearly immobile armies attempted to wrest a few hundred

Europe in 1922

500 Miles

1000 Km

President Woodrow Wilson. In February, the tsar's government had been overthrown, replaced by a shaky parliamentary government headed by Alexander Kerensky, which endured until October, when Lenin, smuggled back into the country with German help, masterminded the Bolshevik October coup, subsequently much romanticized since in fact the Kerensky government fell without a murmur. An election was held, in which the Bolsheviks gained only a quarter of the vote. In December, Russia pulled out of the war, and in March agreed to the Treaty of Brest-Litovsk, which lost Russia swathes of territory, including a high proportion of the most advanced industrial and agricultural areas.

One of the original Allies, who had pinned down Austrian and German armies in the East, had now dropped out of the war, and at a critical time, since after the remorseless slaughter around Verdun, whole regiments of the French army were mutinying. Very fortunately, another more powerful nation took Russia's place.

American Intervention

None of Britain's former colonies, now independent Dominions, had any formal obligation to join in a European war, but all immediately followed Britain. An attempt at rebellion was made in South Africa, but promptly crushed by Jan Smuts, one of the Boer commanders 12 years previously, and the South Africans were left to deal with the German African forces. Australian and New Zealand (ANZAC) forces were to suffer grievously in the disastrous Dardanelles campaign against Turkey in 1915–16.

If there were few strategic reasons for British Dominions to become involved in the war, there were even fewer for the United States. Many Americans were originally from Germany, although they may well have left to escape persecution or hardship; the affable Professor Fritz Bhaer, who marries Jo in Louisa May Alcott's *Little Women* (1869), represented the typical German to

BELOW *The shattered landscape of the Western Front between Bapaume and Arras in 1916. A German artillery battery moves along rutted tracks to take up position before what became known as the Battle of the Somme which saw the British Army suffer the worst one-day losses in its history, with nearly 60,000 casualties.*

yards of ground. The world's attention has always focussed on the Western Front, where most of the French and British army, and all the American and Canadians were fighting – the Australians were everywhere – but battles just as deadly were being fought in the Balkans, Russia, Germany's African colonies, the Middle East, the Dardanelles, and even in Siberia.

The Russian attack on the Eastern Front was quickly halted by the Germans, taking 100,000 prisoners, but the Austrians had trouble with the Serbians and were pushed back by the Russian attacks in Galicia, and, after May 1915 when Italy came 'hurtling to the aid of the victors', an Italian Alpine offensive. Under such pressure the Austrian army, whose soldiers came from many different national groups, held together remarkably well, but resolution wavered on the death in 1916 of Emperor Franz Josef, whose stubborn piety had been combined with a genius for personal rule.

In 1917, the whole course of the war, and of subsequent history, was changed by two events: communist revolution in Russia and the intervention of US

generations of young Americans, though Mark Twain, in *A Tramp Abroad* (1880) exposed some deeply unattractive Teutonic traits, such as the ritual scarring proudly practised by German student duelling fraternities.

Since the Founding Fathers' generation American presidents had been a provincial collection, rarely setting foot outside the United States. Theodore Roosevelt (1901–08) was the first with any foreign experience, and Woodrow Wilson (1912–20) benefited from the advice of the Texan Colonel Edward House, whose assessments had been formed in talks with both British and German leaders. Wilson became enthused by the prospect of designing a new, democratic and pacific postwar world (the 'Fourteen-Point Plan'), but first the war had to be brought to a close, and the Germans were fast losing American support. Already angered by German attacks on American shipping, the public was infuriated by the revelation of an intercepted note from the German Foreign Minister, Arthur Zimmerman, promising German help to Mexico in recovering her lost provinces. President Wilson's efforts to change the world were boosted by the downfall of the disreputable autocratic Tsarist regime, an embarrassing partner in the crusade for democracy.

President Wilson's speech to Congress on 2 April 1917, requesting a declaration of war against Germany, displayed both his idealism and its tangential relation to political facts. The President declared:

> *'We shall fight for the things which we have carried nearest our hearts – for democracy, for the right of those who submit to authority to have a voice in their own governments for the rights and liberties of small nations.'*

The President concluded by hoping that this would bring with it a 'universal dominion of right by such a concert of free people as shall bring peace and safety to all nations and make the world itself free'. His aspirations were hardly realistic, considering that only a few months previously the USA had launched two armed attacks on Mexico, were facing revolts against their occupation of the Philippines and Puerto Rico, and the colonial powers would only agree if the small nations were comfortably in Europe, and not in their own widespread empires.

Assembling, equipping and training a great army needed all the legendary American energy and genius for organization, but it was still nearly a year after the formal declaration of war on 6 April that the first American soldiers saw action. Subsequently, on 26 September 1918 a massive, well-trained, and superbly equipped US force of nearly a million men launched an all-out offensive against the Germans. America's greatest contribution to an Allied victory had in fact already been made. Germany's unrestricted U-boat war had been fearfully effective, sinking nearly 900,000 tons of merchant shipping in one month alone: the US Navy, escorting convoys of ships of all nations, reduced this dramatically and enabled food, men and munitions to flow to Europe.

Prince Max of Baden, upright heir to all the liberal traditions of his family, was appointed as Chancellor by the Kaiser on 3 October, in the hope that his well-known opposition to the conduct of the war would enable him to conciliate the Allies, and the following day asked President Wilson – selected as the 'softest touch' – to arrange an immediate armistice and begin

THE TECHNOLOGY OF DEATH

The French, Germans, Austrians and Russians went to war without having learned the lessons of previous conflicts. Officers had their swords sharpened, heavy cavalry wore their brass helmets and cuirasses, novelties such as machine guns were viewed suspiciously and allocated sparingly. Only the British army was entirely professional, the others relying on conscription, and had at least profited from the fight with the Boers to become very proficient in massed rifle fire: even so, British commanders still prided themselves on having designed the perfect all-purpose sword, the 1907 pattern. Lacking such experience, the French relied on 'élan' the irresistible charge driven by the *fureur française,* that had so impressed observers in the Italian wars.

Once in the trenches different skills were needed: telephone communications, dugout construction and fortification, trench design, but most importantly in artillery where the Germans had the edge. And guns need shells: one critical factor was to be the supply of the enormous quantity of munitions devoured in an artillery barrage.

peace negotiations. The president responded eagerly and for three weeks American–German discussions continued, with Germany accepting Wilson's famous Fourteen Points, at least two of which were totally unacceptable to the other Allies. Meanwhile the fighting went on.

The Allies themselves were divided. President Wilson hoped that peace terms would ensure that it had really been a war to end all wars: French (and to a lesser extent, British) politicians wanted rigid conditions: realistic soldiers like Haig pointed out that the German army had not been defeated, and was capable of holding on, probably over the winter, even although Austria, Turkey and Bulgaria were already counted out. Prince Max's efforts were annulled on 9 November by the outbreak of a revolution in Berlin: trying to make things easier for his successor, the Prince announced the Kaiser's abdication and appointed his Social Democrat colleague Friedrich Ebert as Chancellor.

On 7 November a German delegation was told the agreed terms: there was no point in further negotiation and at 5 a.m. on 11 November 1918 the Germans agreed to accept the Allies' conditions, which were exceptionally severe, with the intention of allowing no room for argument when it came to settling a final peace.

The two prime ministers, David Lloyd George and Georges Clemenceau, dominated the subsequent peace negotiations at Versailles, pushing for massive reparations from Germany and an admission of total war guilt. The new German Republic, symbolically based in Goethe's adopted home town of Weimar, could do little but point out the dangers of Bolshevism, demonstrated by a shortlived Soviet in Bavaria. Wilson was obliged to compromise and the settlements pronounced in June 1919 satisfied nobody. Germany was saved from starvation by American Food Aid but remained deeply resentful, seriously considering the resumption of war. Wilson's great idea, the League of Nations, was incorporated into the peace settlement, but since the United States failed to ratify it and withdrew from the League, it was doomed never to fulfil its lofty ideals.

Lloyd George saw the dangers clearly enough, expressed in his Fontainebleau Memorandum: the peace terms ought not to be dictated to 'a proud and intelligent people, with great traditions, in a spirit of savage vendetta:' if not, a resentful Germany had the power rapidly to recover and reorganize. Although his views were supported by Jan Smuts and the influential young economist John Maynard Keynes, the French were implacable and Germany was faced with French occupation of the Rhineland and a huge bill for damages. Forced to comply, the German government signed the Treaty of Versailles on 28 June, and promptly resigned.

Clearing Up

One war was over, but fighting continued for another two years, following the Allies' decision of July 1918 to support the White Russians in their struggle against communism. There remained, too, the question of the Baltic States, ceded to Germany by the Treaty of Brest-Litovsk. Latvia and Lithuania declared their independence in 1918, and Estonia agreed a treaty with Russia two years later, assisted by an Allied campaign commemorated by a plaque in Tallinn thanking the Royal Navy for securing Estonian freedom. Poland was also forced to fend off a powerful Russian attack, which it did with great courage and success, in warfare almost on the scale of Great War battles, restoring Poland to the map of Europe after 200 years.

Dealing with Turkey sparked off another war, which very nearly led to a general resumption of hostilities. The peace terms dictated by the Allies were so severe, entailing not only huge indemnities but the dismemberment of the Ottoman Empire, as to provoke a nationalist revolt led by the decisive Mustafa Kemal, later known as Atatürk ('Father of the Turks'). Greece was

ABOVE *Vladimir Ilyich Ulyanov, better known as Lenin, was the principal architect of the Bolshevik Revolution in October 1917. Following the February Revolution, he returned to Petrograd from foreign exile and began to agitate for the overthrow of the Menshevik government by the proletariat.*

authorized to force the terms on Turkey, but after an initial success was expelled from the mainland with considerable loss A final treaty, acceding to most Turkish demands, was made at the expense of the Armenians and Kurds, now divided between Turkey, Russia and Iraq.

Some internal problems caused difficulty. The tricky settlement of Ireland's divisions, between Ulster Protestants, Anglo-Irish and Irish Nationalists was contested by extremists, leading to a civil war, the birth of the IRA and the creation of the Irish Free State.

RIGHT *The 'Irish Question' was a constant headache to British politicians throughout the 19th and early 20th centuries. This cartoon of 1913 satirizes the difficulties encountered in persuading Ulster to accept Home Rule.*

1920–1939
The Interlude

■ Establishment of the Mandated Territories by the League of Nations 1920 ■ Benito Mussolini comes to power in Italy 1922 ■ Adolf Hitler becomes German Chancellor 1933 ■ Spanish Civil War 1936–39 ■ Hitler appeased by Chamberlain in the Munich Agreement 1938

The frontiers settled at Versailles transformed the map of Europe and the Middle East, and most survived the huge upheaval of the Second World War. Attention was focussed on Europe, but the division of the Ottoman Empire's Asian territories has proved the more contentious. The modern states of Iraq, Syria, Israel and Jordan all originated as League of Nations' Mandates, and the definition of borders was adjusted to accommodate Britain's insistence on controlling the most important oilfields.

Germany's prewar Western frontiers were not greatly altered, but two new large Slavic states were carved out of the Habsburg Empire. Czechoslovakia comprised the ancient kingdom of Bohemia-Moravia, with its substantial German populations, extended through Slovakia into Ruthenia, while Serbia, Bosnia, with its substantial Muslim population, together with Croats and Slovenes, each regarding the other with sentiments ranging between distaste, distrust and downright hatred, were bundled into Yugoslavia.

Turkey, Persia and Palestine

Kemal Atatürk's successful resistance enabled him to establish a republican government at Ankara, with himself as life president. Genuine public support, encouraged by a vigorous personality cult, endowed him with dictatorial powers to establish Turkey as a modern, secular and effective nation-state with secure borders. The remaining Asian Ottoman territories were assigned to Britain and France as Mandates, giving authority to supervise what would in due course be recognized as independent nations. After heated arguments, Britain arranged for their wartime allies, the Hashemite sheikhs of the Hejaz, hereditary guardians of Islam's sacred sites, to provide rulers of Trans-Jordan and Mesopotamia/Iraq, with the Palestine Mandate remaining a British Colonial Office responsibility. Both Turkey and Britain, as Mandatory for Iraq, disputed the still-undeveloped Mosul oilfields. The League of Nations decided in favour of Iraq, but the terms of agreement between the Iraq Petroleum Company and the new Shah Faisal I, skewed heavily in the company's favour, proved a constant source of friction. The new boundary divided the Kurdish population between Turkey and Iraq, a division which the Kurds themselves have never fully accepted. British rule was enforced when needed not by an expensive ground force, but by bombers of the Royal Air Force; it was economical, although frowned on by the more humane.

Persia, which had kept out of the war, was the second major source of oil, with exploitation rights contracted to the Anglo-Persian Oil Company, the originator of British Petroleum. Much-delayed stability had been brought to Persia by the 50-year reign of Naser Shah, but the chaos that followed his murder in 1895 had been followed by the 'Constitutional Revolution' ten years later, a period of short-lived and harried governments, British occupation and financial support, stultified by hesitant and contradictory policies, culminating in 1921 by the appointment of the Cossack Brigade commander Reza Khan as Prime Minister. Following a similar pattern to Atatürk in Turkey, Reza, who became Shah in 1925 set about modernizing and to a lesser extent laicizing what was once again to be known as Iran. But whereas Atatürk valued personal power as an instrument for restoring Turkey's former prominence, Reza was at bottom little more than the modern version of the ancient Persian autocrat, and less effective as a modernizer.

While the oil supplies, essential to the Royal Navy, now converted from coal- to oil-firing, were well-protected, the Palestine Mandate landed Britain with the intractable Jewish/Arab hostility exacerbated by the commitment known as the Balfour Declaration. A vague undertaking to 'use their best endeavours' to 'facilitate the establishment' of a 'national home for the Jewish people,' the Declaration was made in an informal letter to Lord Rothschild by Foreign Minister Arthur Balfour in November 1917. At the same time, it was made clear, the interests of the Arab population had to be protected: sorting out the multiple ambiguities of this commitment were to prove a constant frustration for successive British governments.

RIGHT *Mural by the Catalan artist Josep Maria Sert for the League of Nations building in Geneva. The ideal of unity collapsed when Japan, Germany and Italy withdrew from the organization in the 1930s.*

The Balfour Declaration of 2 November 1917, expressing the British government's support for the establishment of a Jewish 'national home' in Palestine. Arab hostility to Jewish immigration caused a constant problem to successive British governments.

The principle was established that limited Jewish immigration be allowed only in the area of present-day Israel, where for many years industrious European Jews had been demonstrating how poor land could be made to flourish. The Arabs, perhaps themselves descendants of the ancient Canaanites, were not impressed, seeing this as a different form of colonization and resenting the implied – and unfortunately justified – settler superiority.

The Dictators Analyzed

Hampered as it was by the absence of both the USA and Russia, the League of Nations was able to settle a number of acerbic territorial disputes, and did good work in helping refugees and fighting slavery: but when disputes involved major powers the League quickly ran out of steam. Any international contribution was only possible when American interests were concerned, as in the Washington Treaties of 1922 when relative American,

British and Japanese naval strengths were agreed, submarine attacks on merchantmen banned, and the Japanese withdrew from the Chinese territories acquired after the war.

Not only had the USA failed to sign the Treaty of Versailles or to join the League of Nations or the International Court of Justice, but it continued throughout the 1920s to withdraw from all international affairs, fortifying isolation by severe tariffs on imports, increasing her relative economic advantage over the rest of the world. Financially speaking, the United States had a good war, with their gold reserves increasing by £278 million. Britain's, by contrast, fell by £42 million, with £800 million owing to the United States. Considering that this had all been spent on the common cause, British opinion was outraged by President Coolidge's refusal to renegotiate the terms of payment; 47 years after the end of the First World War, Britain was still allotting one percent of national income tax receipts to repaying the United States: the even larger payments due to Britain from Russia, France and Italy were quickly written off.

The League was powerless to intervene in any internal matters, however serious the abuse of human rights might be. Democracy was quickly abandoned in many countries, and the 1920s and 1930s became the age of dictators, differing considerably in methods, ideas and toxicity. Some, like Marshal Pilsudski of Poland, were given and retained popular support, and worked within the constitution. Admiral Horthy, officially Regent, was appointed Hungarian Minister of War in 1919, after the short communist regime of Bela Kun, and ensured that no dangerous socialist ideas were permitted to emerge. The Iberian dictatorships of Franco and Salazar were joint enterprises with the Catholic Church, providing a moral authority accepted by a quiescent majority; in Spain this was easier, since so many of the opposition had been killed or had fled during the ferocious civil war of 1936–39. Other totalitarian regimes did not survive the Second World War, but Spain and Portugal emerged unscathed, if miserable, which is some sort of tribute to their founders.

The most toxic, unpredictable and brutal dictator was Joseph Stalin, in complete control of Soviet Russia between 1926 and 1953. Numbers cease to have much meaning when evaluating tyrants' responsibilities, but it is estimated that Stalin was directly or indirectly responsible for some 20 million deaths. Any potential enemy, or indeed anyone arousing suspicion, was shot or sent to slow death in a Siberian *gulag*. Many more perished in such foolish experiments as forced collectivization, which devastated agriculture, bringing severe and widespread famine.

By far the most inventive of the dictatorships was that of Benito Mussolini in Italy, who provided the ideological basis of fascism. The Italian economy had surged ahead in the early 1900s, leading the world in some of the most modern industries, but parliamentary groupings failed to consolidate, and the division widened between the prosperous and liberal north and the impoverished, often corrupt, south. Italy's final triumph, the defeat of the Austrian army in 1918, had stimulated a patriotic demand for Italian self-

ABOVE *Mussolini in characteristic declamatory pose, addressing a rally in 1935. The Duce liked to style himself as a successor to the emperors who had brought power and glory to Rome in its heyday, but his foreign military adventures were unmitigated disasters.*

The dark side of Fascism, which had always been visible to critical observers, was dramatically revealed in 1935 with the Italian invasion of Abyssinia, the only African country that had retained its independence right through the Scramble, and, with its history of nearly 3,000 years of civilization from the Kingdom of Axum, was perhaps the world's oldest surviving state. Abyssinia appealed to the League of Nations, which responded only by establishing committees of arbitration and enquiry, while Italian troops using poison gas embarked upon, according to the Duce's instructions, 'a policy of terror and extermination.' A clear signal had been given that dictators need not fear international intervention: and Italians applauded their new military glory.

Like Mussolini – although less convincingly, never having a majority in the Reichstag – Adolf Hitler had come to power in a constitutional fashion, but in the process had made no secret of his contempt for democracy and his reliance on violence. Unlike Fascism, Nazism had no philosophy, but only a lust for power and absolute commitment to two causes, the destruction of communism and the expansion of German settlement in Eastern Europe, where the Slavs were regarded as an inferior species, destined to fill the same place as the blacks had done in the German African colonies, and treated with the same brutality; it was hardly a coincidence that the Nazi deputy leader, Hermann Goering, was the son of a governor of German South West Africa. Powering these deplorable, but not irrational, policies was a hysterical dedication to the extermination of European Jewry, based upon absurd theories of 'racial' purity. The existence of a Nordic 'Aryan' race was a complete fiction – 3,000 years of immigration and interbreeding since the first Indo-Europeans arrivals had made Germans, like all other Europeans, genetically complex – but, it might be added, was the same theory that was upheld by the American Supreme Court in October 1922 in its decision that anyone 'of a race which is not Caucasian' was not eligible to become a citizen of the land of liberty. On becoming Chancellor in 1933, Hitler gained the authority to rule by decree and made no secret of his ruthless intentions: the rule of law was suspended and by the end of the year some 100,000 Germans were imprisoned, mostly in newly built 'concentration' camps.

The combination of centralized decision-making, and the financial support of industrialists, together with the enthusiastic readiness of most of the people to follow any leader who sounded totally confident, enabled the Nazis to achieve an economic miracle, and to begin an unparalleled expansion of armaments. Hitler's own disdain for the democracies' leaders was often well deserved. France, Britain or the United States might have halted Nazism, but France was divided between supporters of the left-wing Popular Front, and militant right-wing associations. Ministry succeeded ministry at sometimes near-monthly intervals – four between May 1937 and April

RIGHT *1933 election poster supporting the uneasy alliance of conservative President Paul Hindenburg (the 'Marshal') and 'Corporal' Adolf Hitler, leader of the NSDAP.*

assertion, bitterly disappointed by the division of enemy territories made at Versailles, provoking the poet Gabriele D'Annunzio to invade the city of Fiume, which had been allotted to Yugoslavia. With postwar unemployment soaring, a communist revolution seemed entirely possible.

Fascism began as a popular movement of armed bands attacking perceived enemies, whether Slavs or Socialists, which was adroitly captured by Mussolini. In November 1922, following the Fascist March on Rome – in which he took no part – Mussolini was appointed prime minister and proceeded to create a new State that would not be based on the liberal doctrines inherited from the French Revolution. Fascism was to be purely Italian, a return to Roman virtues, indicated by the choice of the *fasces*, the symbol of Roman lictors. The more unruly elements were discouraged, and popular support consolidated: in the April 1924 elections, fascists gained over two thirds of the vote. Although basically pagan, with the person of the Duce near-deified, claiming infallibility (*Il Duce ha sempre raggione!*;'The Duce is always right!') the fascists enlisted the support of the Church by 'a concordat between two totalitarian regimes, as Pope Pius XI himself' pointed out. Striving for international respectability, Mussolini dispatched such presentable emissaries as the aviator Cesare Balbo to America, hailed by a million citizens of Chicago, many giving the fascist salute. They could well have been forgiven, for Italian fascism had a stylishly glossy finish, and Mussolini himself could exert great personal charm. The German Nazis were, the Duce considered, a barbarian imitation of the real thing.

1938. Leon Blum's first administration brought major reforms – the 40-hour week and paid holidays – but did nothing to improve the economy, racked by industrial conflict. At least French politicians were acutely conscious of the rising German threat, contrasted with the almost incredible purblindness of Neville Chamberlain's British government, capable, as late as March 1939 on insisting that 'Europe was settling down to a period of tranquillity.'

America had opted out of world affairs, desperately attempting to recover from the Depression, to extricate itself from the consequences of the absurd 'Prohibition' episode and to provide its people with the same social protection that had been commonplace in Europe for half a century. Franklin Roosevelt's heroic, and ultimately successful efforts, were viciously attacked by conservatives, and such rabid isolationists as Colonel Frank McCormick, bracketing Roosevelt with Hitler and Mussolini.

An example of what might be expected in a future war was given by General Francisco Franco's rebellion against the Spanish Republican government in 1936. Nazi Germany and Fascist Italy eagerly joined in on Franco's side, sending squadrons of warplanes to attack troops and civilians alike. The Luftwaffe raid on the northern town of Guernica, in April 1937 was reported everywhere and immortalized in Picasso's great painting: but fewer than 200 died in Guernica, while a few years later more than 200 times that number were killed in a single 43-minute bombing raid on Hamburg. Russian support for the Spanish government was more restrained, but volunteers also arrived to form the hard-fighting International Brigade, encouraged by Ernest Hemingway, and the Irish Brigade, fighting for Franco. Legally, the attack on a properly constructed democratically elected government should have aroused universal condemnation, but the League of Nations was powerless to intervene.

After three years of vicious fighting – some 30,000 were killed in arbitrary executions, in addition to the military and civilian casualties – Franco emerged as an unquestioned autocrat, fully supported by the Church; every Spaniard, he decreed, was obliged to be Catholic. He was, however, something of a disappointment to his fellow dictators, obstinately staying neutral, considerably encouraged in this by some £10 million of bribes paid by Britain to Spanish generals. Spain remained stable, if internally oppressed and culturally stagnant.

Faced with such hesitant European resistance, Hitler's strategies were masterly, producing the maximum effect with economy of effort, taking what would have been great risks if faced with even slightly more resolute opponents. His unilateral renunciation of the Versailles rearmament restrictions, announced in 1935, was followed by fretful complaints, but also by a speedy Anglo-German Naval Treaty, implicitly validating German rearmament. Hitler's quick move into the demilitarized Rhineland in March 1936, apprehensively watched by German generals well aware that France could have intervened decisively, was accepted almost approvingly. Two years later Austria's chancellor, Kurt von Schuschnigg, abandoned by France and Britain, was bullied into acquiescing to German annexation (*Anschluß*).

No attempt was made to disguise the fate of those forcibly brought into 'Greater Germany'. Summary execution or despatch to concentration camps

LEFT A Catalan poster from the Spanish Civil War urges Republican volunteers to join in the fight to protect the Basque region in the north from fascist aggression.

was the fate of all potential opponents. Jews were singled out, deprived of all civil rights, brutally attacked, with the acquiescence, or even connivance, of the populace. Newsreel films brought some of the facts home, but the British press was discouraged from reports that might jeopardize relations with Germany. A stand might have been made in 1938 when Czechoslovakia was threatened. It was true that millions of German-speakers disliked Slav rule, as they had for 500 years, a fact seized on by Hitler to present what seemed like a possibly reasonable demand for at least local autonomy. President Edvard Benes' government was Europe's most liberal and the Czech army , with 35 divisions, was perhaps Europe's most effective. France and Britain could have stood firm, but fears of what war might mean, now so clearly demonstrated in Spain, and an almost comic inability to appreciate the true nature of Nazi Germany, led to Chamberlain's appeasement of Germany, and betrayal of a great nation, which he airily described as a 'faraway country of which we know little.'

A TAIL-PIECE

With the advent of 'talkies' in 1926 and full colour in 1935, cinema audiences rapidly expanded. Walt Disney's animations created a new art form: Mickey Mouse made his first appearance in 1928, and *Snow White* set a standard rarely surpassed. Hollywood was unbeatable for the grand epic, such as *Gone with the Wind* in 1939 and for creating the star system which presented unnaturally well-groomed exemplars, faithfully imitated wherever films were shown. French and German directors aimed higher and sometimes succeeded: Sergei Eisenstein's *Alexander Nevsky,'*with a score by Prokofiev, is perhaps the most memorable of all films. Both the Soviets and Nazis were adept at cinematic propaganda: Hitler used the 1936 Berlin Olympics to showcase the new Germany, and Leni Riefenstahl's film of the occasion, *Triumph of the Will,* enthused German audiences, but in the end Charlie Chaplin and the Marx Brothers were infinitely more influential. British films, including *Fire over England* and *Mrs.Miniver,* engaged the sympathies of American audiences at a crucial time.

Mickey Mouse, who was originally given the far less catchy name of Mortimer Mouse, made his first talking appearance in the short animation Steamboat Willie *in 1928.*

The Second World War and After

■ Japanese invasion of China 1937 ■ Nazi–Soviet Non-Aggression Pact 1939 ■ Battle of Britain 1940 ■ Attack on Pearl Harbor 1941 ■ Battle of Stalingrad 1943 ■ Atomic bombing of Japan 1945 ■ Indian independence 1948 ■ Korean War 1950–53

The First World War in Europe ended as it had begun, with the enemy armies not far removed from their original positions; the German forces were in disarray, but not finally defeated. Strategically, the Second World War proved very different; after fighting for thousands of miles across Europe and Asia, Germany and Japan were both shattered, while the Allied nations of France, China, Russia and Britain were impoverished, leaving the United States as the world's first, unchallenged superpower – or so it seemed.

Given its clear origins in the unsatisfactory resolution of the Great War, the Second World War can be thought of as the second act of an ongoing conflict lasting 40 years. And Act II opened not in the traditional theatre of Europe, but in the Far East, in the early 1930s.

Prelude in China

The start of the Asian war was signalled in 1932 by Japan's annexation of Manchuria and establishment there of a puppet state (Manchukuo) headed by the last Qing Emperor, Pu-Yi. Japan, previously a reliable supporter of the League of Nations, had been radicalized by acute poverty exacerbated by the Depression and discriminatory American legislation. Two prime ministers and a finance minister were assassinated in 1931–32, with democratic government becoming increasingly impossible as frustrated army commanders, who could rely on support from discontented younger men, struck out on their own.

The Chinese Republic was led by Chiang Kai-shek's Guomindang administration, based in Nanking, Beijing being occupied by the Japanese. The undeclared war that began at the Marco Polo Bridge, just south of Beijing, in July 1937 was followed by a full-scale Japanese advance on Nanking. Atrocities equal to the 'Rape of Nanking' had occurred before in China – less than a century ago, in the same place, in fact, during the Taiping Rebellion – but Japanese brutality there was recorded in such shocking detail on newsreels and

in newspapers that the world shuddered, shocked into incomprehension. Japan, the land of the Chrysanthemum and Kimono, feted by the West – Emperor Hirohito was loaded with British decorations – had suddenly gone mad, it seemed. Orders to kill all prisoners – to be shot in groups of 12 – had been obediently followed, although some soldiers amused themselves by decapitating or bayoneting the captives. Japan suddenly became a pariah state with which no civilized accommodation was possible. Inevitably this uncompromising attitude led to advances from the more liberal and pacific sections of Japanese opinion being rebuffed by the West, ensuring the triumph of the militarists. Supplies were sent to China from Hong Kong, but even these ended in January 1939: the world regretted 'a passive and shameful acquiescence in the wrong that is being done', but was more concerned with Europe.

Europe in Flames Again

The alliance against Hitler was fluid: only Britain and the Dominions stuck it out from the start. Russia, which was to be the most committed of the anti-Nazi forces, began as a German ally, forced into war by Hitler's unexpected invasion in June 1941, before the USA was precipitated into action by the attack on Pearl Harbor. Italy, which started as a German ally, switched sides after the

LEFT *US poster of 1942 solicits aid for China in its long-running struggle against the Empire of Japan. Japan sought to present its rape of the Far East as a common Asian alliance against Western interests.*

Allied invasion. Hungary, Romania and Bulgaria joined the Axis in the winter of 1940–41, and contributed substantially to the war with Russia. All three changed sides in 1944, although Hungary was forced to continue, bringing the near-destruction of Budapest in the final Soviet offensive.

The Second European War started, as had the First, with the German invasion of a country protected by France and Britain. Relying on the same supine attitudes that their leaders had previously shown, Hitler did not expect either country to react: and even if they did, there was little they could do, given the geographical isolation of Poland. The vital condition of success had been ensuring that Russia did not intervene, and this was more than achieved on 23 August 1939, with the mutual 'Non-Aggression Pact' between Nazi Germany and Communist Russia, previously pilloried for the benefit of capitalists and the pious as the great adversary. It was, however, a fraud, since Hitler had every intention of destroying Soviet Russia as soon as possible. On 1 September, Poland was attacked: two days later Britain and France declared war, and on 17 September Soviet troops invaded Poland from the east: the victors, at a very modest cost, began to divide the spoils. Italy was not included: Mussolini was taken aback by the German offensive in Poland. He had bragged about the size and aggressiveness of his forces, which were however completely unready and poorly led: but surely the war would be over before he was called upon for any real effort?.

ABOVE *National Socialist delegates greet Hitler at a sitting of the German Reichstag in 1939. By this stage, parliamentary democracy had long been dismantled by the Nazis, with political opponents incarcerated in purpose-built labour camps, or reduced to apprehensive silence.*

After the 'Phoney War', an interval that should have given Britain and France a chance to prepare, real action only began in May 1940, but despite material superiority in both tanks and guns, the Allies' performance in the field was lamentable. The *Blitzkrieg* ('lightning war') began on 9 May; within five weeks France had surrendered, placated by the promise of a puppet regime and the hollow pledge that France could keep her colonial empire: some suspect that a deal had already been struck between Hitler and the French leaders Pétain and Gamelin. Most of the British Army and many French were evacuated at Dunkirk and Britain was left alone to face the planned German invasion, although individual Czechs, Poles and French, organized by the majestically unyielding General de Gaulle, were forming their own units. The defeat of the Luftwaffe by the RAF in the Battle of Britain avoided the danger of invasion, but left the German armies free to operate on other fronts.

Seizing the moment, Mussolini committed Italy to the war on 10 June and attacked British Egypt and Somalia from bases in their North and East

African colonies. The Italian armies rapidly collapsed, obliging the annoyed Hitler to send German forces to their aid. Mussolini had also decided, without consulting Hitler, to invade Greece: once again the Italians had to be rescued by the Germans. Both these forces had been intended to support the surprise German attack on Russia (Operation Barbarossa), planned for May 1941, which had to be postponed for a month. Their absence did not affect the impetus of the *Blitzkrieg*, which in June swept through the unprepared Russian armies to the suburbs of Leningrad and the Sea of Azov. But that month's delay brought the offensive into a harsh Russian winter. Hitler acknowledged 'we started one month too late.' In one December day 14,000 German soldiers had frost-bitten limbs amputated; it was a foretaste of what became the most appallingly harsh campaign in the history of warfare.

America Joins the War

On 7 December. the surprise attack by Japanese carrier-borne aircraft on Pearl Harbor changed the whole course of the war. President Roosevelt had previously supported the British war effort within the bounds of legality: the gift of 50 elderly destroyers to Britain, and the Lend-Lease Act of March 1941 aroused much isolationist indignation, but now Americans dedicated themselves to the fight, and ended 20 years of self-imposed absence from world affairs. The direction of the war rested with two men, Winston Churchill and Franklin Roosevelt, with attempts to liaise with Chiang Kai-shek and Stalin being sporadically successful. Their first strategic meeting in August 1941, in Ship Harbour, Newfoundland, produced the Atlantic Charter, a statement of war aims, which promised postwar sovereign rights and self government on the widest scale: more decolonization was inevitable.

The speed and power of the Japanese attack surpassed even the German Blitzkrieg. Within weeks all the British, French, Dutch and American colonies in South East Asia were overwhelmed. British and Chinese troops were driven out of Burma, to end beyond the Indian frontier and in New Guinea the Australians were just holding on. The fight-back began at sea, with American naval victories at the Battles of Midway and Coral Sea, continued in August by a landing on the Solomon Islands, at Guadalcanal. But the Pacific War was aimed primarily at containing Japan, the most important issues being settled in Europe. The first checks came in October 1942 when the British victory at El Alamein began the German withdrawal from Africa at the same time that the Russian resistance halted the German advance at Stalingrad. Much more hard fighting remained to be done before Hitler's German armies started their retreat from Stalingrad in January 1943 and from Africa in May, leaving hundreds of thousands of prisoners. From now on Axis forces were obliged to mount a steady rearguard action over the regions that had so quickly been occupied.

Warplanes and tanks, prisoners and corpses covered the headlines, but some of the most decisive contributions were by civilians. The British population had to cope with the 'Blitz', but could rely on enough decent food being available; in fact, wartime children deprived of sweets and sugar, were the healthiest generation for many years. In Europe starvation threatened. Hitler could use the resources of the vast occupied territories to provide food and fuel for his armies, but with them also came more mouths to feed and

LEFT *Sailors in a motor launch rescue a survivor from the water alongside the sunken USS* West Virginia *shortly after the Japanese air raid on Pearl Harbor. President Roosevelt called 7 December 'a date which will live in infamy'.*

ABOVE *Troops and supplies began to pour into France after the opening of a 'second front' against Nazi Germany on the Normandy beaches on 6 June 1944.*

prisoners to be guarded. Ruthlessness could go only so far, labour being needed in agriculture and industry, and, as in Napoleon's wars, the seas were blocked by the Royal Navy. But below the surface the U-boat was master, and during 1942 the success of 'wolf-packs' was threatening to cut off all supplies, of food and arms, upon which Britain and the Allies in Europe were dependent. More than 30,000 British and 8,000 American merchant seamen were killed on the Atlantic and Russian convoys combating what Churchill believed to be the greatest threat to survival. The eventual defeat of the U-boats came with the final decrypting of the German naval codes by the heterogeneous team of analysts at Bletchley Park – including the brilliant Cambridge mathematician and father of the computer, Alan Turing. The German encryption machine, Enigma, had been handed to the Allies by Polish cryptographers before the outbreak of war, and was worked over at Bletchley to penetrate almost all the enemy codes: by 1944 the Allies could read Hitler's most secret messages. In May 1943, the U-boats were withdrawn, making Allied victory near-certain. Unless, that is, the Germans developed some entirely new secret weapon.

The Pacific War had become a brutal succession of island-hopping, hand-to-hand warfare with grenades, flamethrowers and cold steel, in contrast with the mobile armoured warfare ranging over the European plains or the slog through rugged Italian hills, which followed the invasion of Sicily in July 1943 and of the mainland a few weeks later. In Burma, British and Indian troops, aided by the Burmese leader Aung San, were learning how to master the Japanese in a miserable jungle war. The long-awaited invasion of France on D-Day, 6 June 1944 was history's best-planned and most spectacular event, with thousands of ships and aircraft swooping across the Channel to land the Allied armies in Normandy. Thanks to cryptographers and spies convincing the Germans that the invasion was to take place further north, the defenders were taken by surprise, and a bridgehead was successfully established.

With American troops now in Rome, Germany had to fight on four fronts – in Russia, Italy, France and the Balkans. They were facing not only the regular Allied armies, but partisans equipped with captured weapons and where possible by RAF supplies. German atrocities had infuriated the civilian population, and the resulting conflict was brutal and unsparing. Nowhere was this more so than in Yugoslavia, where the mainly Serb partisans, led by the Croat Josip Broz, better known as Tito, had secured consistent British support. Tito's men had to fight not only the Germans but also against the Croat *Ustase*, a particularly unpleasant Fascist movement dedicated to the extermination of Jews, Serbs and gypsies.

After D-Day British and American troops, accompanied by a Free French armoured divison pushed on to reach Paris in August: there was some delay with the French organization, since it was thought better that not too many of the troopers should be black. German resistance was tenacious and more hard fighting was needed before the Rhine was crossed, causing some very anxious moments for the Western Allies, now under the cool and emollient General Dwight Eisenhower. The European war ended in May with a final surrender, very different from that in 1918. This was no armistice, but unconditional surrender, with the whole of Germany occupied and its armies totally defeated: but almost immediately another conflict began between Eastern and Western allies. Before this could develop, however, the Pacific War had to be settled, which was done even more finally in August, with the atomic bomb raids on Hiroshima and Nagasaki. There was much disquiet about the horrifying effects of the blasts, but those faced with the probability of years of fighting were relieved: those who had sown the wind had indeed reaped the whirlwind.

The Aftermath

The first General Assembly of the United Nations was eventually opened in London by King George VI on 9 January 1946. Many earlier League of Nations' institutions were retained, including the International Court of Justice. There were no absentees: the United States was there, as one of the permanent members of the Security Council (the others being Russia, China, France and Britain). It was soon made clear that Russia was to be disruptive: one month later Stalin warned that a peaceful international order was impossible and that the Soviets would immediately rearm; but the discussions continued.

France and Holland were both determined to hold on to their colonial possessions in Indonesia, Africa and Indochina. It took four years before Holland accepted the inevitability of an independent Indonesia, but did little to facilitate an eventual handover in 1950. President Sukarno then led the country to economic disaster, to near-open war with Britain and Australia in an increasingly wild series of adventures, until his deposition in 1967 by a coup that resulted in at least half a million deaths. The remarkable success of de Gaulle in securing a place for France in the Big Five, after the Vichy government's collaboration with Germany, was diluted by fractious governments; after 1947 the average administration's lifespan was six months, which did not encourage calm policies. Accepting the facts of the post-war world was to prove a painful process for France, and also, as it turned out, for America.

Before the war Britain had begun to prepare for Indian self-government with a conference in 1930. Then there was no idea of haste, but 15 years later, with a war-damaged economy and a Labour government pledged to colonial independence, the process was pushed forward at what was probably reckless speed. No agreement was possible between Muslims and Hindus, and the partition between Pakistan, East and West, and India took place amid large-scale disruption and violence, which cost the lives of up to a million people. In an ironic footnote, Mahatma Gandhi, whose advocacy of nonviolence and intercommunal tolerance had done so much to make Indian independence possible, was murdered by a Hindu extremist in January 1948. India and Pakistan, however, inherited a fully-functioning state, with democratic institutions and a tradition of political debate, an experienced civil service and a respected judiciary.

Plans were also made for Burmese self-government, with the first democratic elections held in 1937. Aung San, whose party won a majority in the first postwar election, was murdered before independence was proclaimed in January 1948. As in India, violence followed, but Burma was free to work out her own destiny. The future of the Straits Settlements, that collection of nine

Hitler's military advisor General Alfred Jodl (centre) signs the document of surrender of Germany's armed forces (right) at General Dwight Eisenhower's HQ in Reims, France on 7 May 1945.

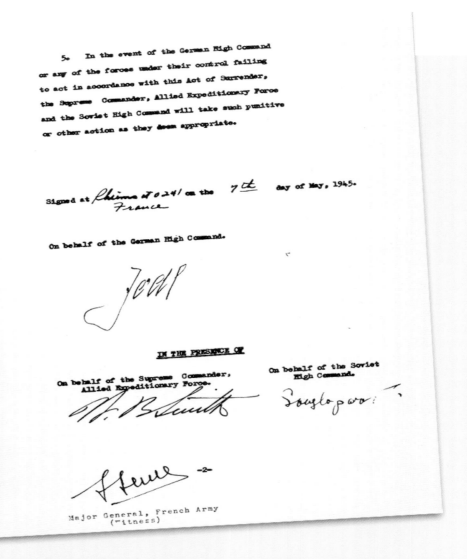

ABOVE *Virtually the only building left standing after an atomic bomb was dropped on Hiroshima 6 August 1945 was the Prefectural Products Exhibition Hall. Unofficially known as the 'Atomic Dome', it has become the city's Peace Memorial.*

regional states and two British colonies, was determined by the creation of the Republic of Malaysia – Malaya plus the small ex-colonies of Sabah and Sarawak, and the separate city-state of Singapore. Both Chinese communists and Indonesians attempted unofficial armed insurrection, but popular support and an effective military response ensured the new countries' survival.

Germany and Japan had been defeated, but fighting continued. China was divided between the republicans and Mao Zedong's communist armies until December 1949, when the Guomindang government, sympathetically supported by the USA, was evacuated to Formosa (Taiwan). In Korea a period of post-war confusion, which included one brutally suppressed rebellion in the South, was followed by the division of Korea between an oligarchic and corrupt South and a totalitarian communist North, both with real grievances. In June 1950, Northern troops, encouraged by Russia, began their invasion of the South, giving the United Nations the opportunity to act, which it did (thanks to the temporary absence of the Soviet delegate) by appealing to all members for armed assistance. Sizeable American forces already stationed in the area responded immediately, forcing back the invaders. Over the next three years the Korean conflict developed into a major war, with over one and a half million UN and South Korean troops involved. The biggest United Nations contributors were the United States, with some 500.000 and the British Commonwealth with 100,000, but with detachments from a dozen other nations. After Chinese 'volunteers' flocked to join the north, a war of nerves ensued, as the US commander General Douglas MacArthur strove for permission to use atomic weapons against enemy supply lines. Neither President Harry Truman, who succeeded

Roosevelt in 1945, nor Clement Attlee, the British Labour prime minister, would agree; the war was won and the status quo restored by persistent and punishing infantry actions. The UN had proved its efficacy, but only if member nations were prepared to put force behind its decisions.

In Europe, the 'Iron Curtain' foreseen by Churchill had descended, and acted in some ways as a protective barrier. Greece and Yugoslavia slipped from underneath, but Czechoslovakia, very unwillingly, became part of the new Soviet bloc, all politically and economically subservient to Russia. American Marshall Aid, rejected by Stalin for states under his sphere of influence, enabled the rapid economic recovery of Western Europe and discouraged the strong communist parties in France and Italy, which might otherwise have threatened the new Western alliance. In spite of the horror generated as the concentration camps revealed the secrets of the 8 million dead, Germany was not punished further, but, liberated from years of uncertainty and capricious tyranny, and restored to international society, with a functioning democratic government, was a nation reborn, but only in part. The Western (US, British and French) zones became the Federal Republic of Germany, with its capital at Bonn, in September 1949: six months later the first European economic associations, which were to form today's European Community, were initiated; even Spain, hitherto a pariah, was admitted to the United Nations.

In 1949, the Western Alliance was institutionalized by the formation of NATO, the North Atlantic Treaty Organization, acting as an American guarantee to allied nations. Beyond the Curtain, Russia was able to build up a central state, surrounded by a core of obedient satellites, grateful for their rescue from the German occupation, and reaching out to valuable potential allies in Asia, Africa and even Latin America. When the first Russian atomic bomb was exploded in 1950, followed by the launch of the world's first artificial satellite, *Sputnik I*, in 1957, it became apparent that the world had two superpowers and that caution was advisable.

New Nations

■ Foundation of the State of Israel 1948 ■ Ghana becomes Africa's first independent state 1960 ■ Vietnam War 1964–75 ■ Chinese Cultural Revolution begins 1966 ■ Assassination of Martin Luther King and Robert Kennedy and the Prague Spring 1968

The postwar decolonization of India and Africa was speedily recognized as inevitable, but Southeast Asian independence became embroiled in Cold War rivalries, leading to the Vietnam War. Urbanization and industrialization increased the demand for oil, concentrating attention on the Middle East, where tensions heightened after the creation of the state of Israel.

Although Stalin was responsible for more deaths than Hitler, the peculiar horror of Nazism was its doctrine of Aryan supremacy. Reasons, however tortuous, could be advanced for slaughtering political opponents or prisoners of war, but the Nazis systematically liquidated as many as 8 million innocent civilians simply by virtue of their race, sexuality or religion. By far the most numerous group were the Jews of Central and Eastern Europe, some of the world's most cultivated and industrious people. Antisemitism was rife in the 1930s. At best, as in England, Jews were tolerated as they had been since Cromwell's time: one of the 19th century's most famous figures was the Jewish-convert prime minister Benjamin Disraeli, admired by Bismarck. Antisemitism in France, however, was an explosive political issue, illustrated in the famous Dreyfus case, and further east more or less organized pogroms were commonplace. Peculiar to Germany was the conviction that Jews were an inferior, parasitic race, polluting the pure German flesh and spirit. Hitler's deliberate singling out of Jews for persecution and eventual destruction struck a sympathetic chord with a very great number of Germans. For the first time in history, the resources of a modern, industrialized nation were devoted to killing an entire people, as economically and quietly as possible: the enormity of the *Shoah* (Holocaust) remains incomprehensible.

The State of Israel

Compassion for the thousands of uprooted, homeless and traumatized Jewish survivors (combined with admiration of the outstanding achievements of earlier Zionist settlers in Palestine)

led to demands for unrestricted Jewish immigration to Palestine after the war. Yet this brought with it a seemingly intractable set of difficulties.

Since Turkey remained neutral there had been little fighting in the Middle East apart from a brush with the Vichy French in Syria, but Britain remained saddled with the twin commitments of the Palestine Mandate and the Balfour Declaration, now made more urgent by pressure from displaced European Jews. Anything more than the controlled admission of limited numbers would certainly provoke more violence from the Arabs. Many British troops were already tied down, attempting to keep the peace and subject to constant attacks from both sides, making regular government difficult. Hard-pressed Britain saw no reason to continue accepting responsibility and handed the issue back to the UN, where it was agreed that a Jewish state would be established in a divided Palestine. Six months' notice was given and in the interval terrorist attacks continued, but on 14 May 1948 the new state of Israel was proclaimed – and immediately attacked by all its Arab neighbours. The war continued for nine months; it would have finished sooner had the UN mediator Count Bernadotte not been murdered by Jewish terrorists. With thousands of Arab refugees and no internationally agreed borders it was clear that a solution was no nearer.

LEFT *Anti-Vietnam War march in New York in 1969. US involvement in Vietnam, plus the failure to grant its Black citizens full civil rights, seriously damaged the country's international standing.*

Obsession with the 'Domino Effect'

Since China remained preoccupied with her own domestic problems, the postwar world was dominated by the two superpowers, armed with atomic weapons and the ability to deliver them. Neither France nor Britain, although permanent members of the UN Security Council could act independently, but both NATO and the European Economic Community were developing their own policies. America should have been the unquestioned leader of the free world, with such wary and experienced presidents as Harry Truman (1944–52), who succeeded after Roosevelt's death, and General Eisenhower (1952–60). The country's prestige had been reinforced by its effective leadership during the Korean War and the sympathetic fashion in which General MacArthur, as proconsul, was helping a chastened Japan back into the community of nations. But the US was badly damaged by the anti-communist witch-hunt conducted by Senator Joseph McCarthy and the continued failure to address Black grievances. The promise of American

ABOVE A ship laden with European Jewish refugees, many of them survivors of the Holocaust, docks at the port of Haifa in 1947. Wishing to settle in Palestine, the ship is impounded by the British Mandate authorities and the settlers returned to Europe.

leadership, however, was therefore forfeited by policies which identified communism as an economic system with Soviet imperialism, largely in fact sated by Russian control over Eastern Europe, while disappointment at Chiang Kai-shek's failure to hold on in China led to an irrational refusal to recognise the Communist regime. The Republican State Department, headed by John Foster Dulles from 1952, abetted by his brother Alan in charge of the Central Intelligence Agency, the CIA, blundered about in a series of destructive initiatives. Unaccountable and irresponsible by statute, the CIA had much greater powers than the British Secret Intelligence Service, being specifically authorized to employ and recruit paramilitaries and assassins to destroy perceived enemies of the USA, in defiance of international law. Some

毛泽东选集

革命无罪
造反有理

A cover design for an edition of Mao Zedong's works shows a Red Guard brandishing a copy of Mao's thoughts, the so-called 'Little Red Book'.

ever-larger numbers of troops, and finally with the most protracted and destructive bombing campaign ever seen. The conflict that inspired Martin Luther King to call the USA 'the greatest purveyor of violence in the world' continued for nearly 15 years, with great savagery on both sides; American forces used such reviled tactics as defoliation with the toxic chemical Agent Orange and the widespread use of napalm. The result was hundreds of thousands of casualties and eventual humiliation for the world's most powerful army. Neither Kennedy, assassinated in 1963, nor his successor Lyndon Johnson was able to extricate America from this tragic sequence of events.

When the true facts were revealed the American people were appalled at the deceit of their leaders. None of the original war aims, although these were hard to define, were achieved. Some 60,000 Americans had been killed, along with untold numbers of Vietnamese, Laotians and Cambodians. Since military action in Vietnam had not been authorized by the United Nations, America was joined only by small detachments from Siam, Australia and New Zealand, while the rest of the world looked on uncomprehendingly.

By April 1975, after a war that had devastated three countries, spawned the genocidal Khmer Rouge regime in Cambodia, and deeply divided the United States, the last American soldier left. Combined with the resignation of President Richard Nixon, charged with high crimes and misdemeanours in August 1974 in the wake of the Watergate Scandal, the political reputation of America had sunk to the level of the 1920s.

In the Soviet Union, the harshly repressive atmosphere softened gradually after Stalin's death in March 1953 as Nikita Khrushchev and his successor Leonid Brezhnev won foreign friends outside the Soviet empire, in particular India, Egypt, and on America's doorstep, Chile and Cuba. It was much easier for foreigners to graduate in Russian universities than to gain

of its operations were successful and even justifiable, but it was the failures that became public and prompted damaging investigations.

When the young and personable Democratic candidate John F. Kennedy won the presidency in 1960, it seemed the dawn of a new era, but it was Kennedy who was responsible for enmeshing his country in the most conspicuous postwar failure of American foreign policy, the intervention in Vietnam. After the French attempt to hold on to Indochina had failed, the civil war between the communist North and the anticommunist South was settled in 1954 by the Geneva Convention's division of the country. Obsessed with communism's 'domino effect', America refused to accept the agreement and supported the South, at first with supplies and advice, but then with

access to the United States, but their experience did not necessarily increase their admiration for Russian communism. The limits of either superpower's ability to project its force was demonstrated in two incidents in 1961 and 1962 when a failed American-planned invasion of Cuba, at the Bay of Pigs, and a Russian attempt to equip the communist government there with nuclear missiles led to the brink of war; but both Kennedy and Khrushchev sensibly backed off.

The policies of the third Great power, China, were determined by the whims of Mao Zedong, who as the leader of the heroic fight against the Japanese and the unquestioned founder of the new Communist China, wielded absolute power. Although statistically the most successful mass-murderer with perhaps 30 million – mostly Chinese – victims, Mao was not an unsympathetic character, combining as he did egalitarian communism with Chinese Confucian tradition: the Mandate of Heaven had been granted to Mao. It had to be shared, however, with four other members of the Central Committee of the Communist party, the two best known being Zhou Enlai, a prudent statesman, and Deng Xiaoping, who eventually ushered China into the modern world. Mao was the creative thinker, producing such radical ideas as the Great Proletarian Cultural Revolution, which saw thousands of China's most distinguished scholars murdered or imprisoned and destroyed much of her cultural heritage, and the Great Leap Forward, intended to boost productivity by communizing local farming cooperatives, but which resulted in the most terrible famine, killing at least 20 million. Throughout such massive follies the Chinese people carried on, rebuilding their country. In one distant corner they showed what might be achieved, given stability and the rule of law: the British colony of Hong Kong was becoming one of the world's most prosperous cities, coping with millions of refugees looking for sanctuary from violence and misgovernment.

Winds of Change in Africa

Europe's sub-Saharan African colonies had not been disturbed by the conduct of the war, but the commitments of the Atlantic Charter and the United Nations placed decolonization firmly on the agenda. France had a clear idea of the future: colonies were to become an integral part of the French state (as overseas *départements*), with representation in Paris, a common currency, and acknowledgement of the free and equal status of all French citizens: in theory, at least. Britain preferred to think of colonies progressing towards independence, as Australia had done, moving in a century from prison colony to Dominion, developing their own representative institutions, education and social systems. In a couple of generations, or at most a century, the Foreign Office believed this would ensure a prosperous future for Africa. Their timing was wildly adrift, for African leaders were insisting on immediate action. Riots in Accra, the Gold Coast capital, in 1948 persuaded the London Labour government to bring forward the programme, with direct elections to a parliamentary system, which were won by the visionary Kwame Nkrumah, who proclaimed the new republic of Ghana in 1960. Events then followed what became the usual West African pattern: democracy was briefly introduced, followed by a one-party state and rule by a 'big man', subject to coups and nourished by corruption. Change in the eastern states of Northern and Southern Rhodesia and Kenya was complicated by the existence of powerful White minorities, keen enough on independent institutions but determined not to share these with the Black majority. Few colonial states were natural political or economic entities, their boundaries often being arbitrary lines, encompassing people of different languages, ethnicities and traditions. Many vicious but limited civil wars were fought before relative stability was possible.

The two major exceptions to the general rule were the Belgian Congo and South Africa. That monstrously inflated state, the Congo, had no pretensions to unity, nor had Belgium, occupied by the Germans during the war, any real control. Left to civil servants and missionaries the Congo had become prosperous, with primary education and health services in advance of any other African colony, and immense natural resources. When independence came, in 1960, it was marked by extreme violence, division and international attempts at interference, which have continued ever since. Today the Democratic Republic of the Congo shares with Zimbabwe – ex-Southern Rhodesia – the dubious distinction of being officially classified among the

ABOVE *A major figure in Congolese independence was the pro-Western president of the breakaway province of Katanga, Moise Tshombe, who was later made prime minister of the unified Congo, only to be ousted when Joseph Mobutu seized power in 1965.*

world's poorest and most repressive countries, whereas they had once been ranked as the richest and most advanced of all African states.

South Africa followed a different route. The union of British colonies and Boer republics had only been achieved by eroding Black political rights to near-extinction. In 1940, the Afrikaner nationalists secured a parliamentary majority, which enabled them to implement their racial policy of *apartheid* or 'separate development'. Leaving the Commonwealth, South Africa became a republic in 1961 and enforced its policies with brutal effectiveness. Such blatantly discriminatory legislation made South Africa a pariah state, but for many years the country was too valuable as a bulwark against communism for the West to interfere, and at least judicial independence and the freedom of the press were to some degree safeguarded.

A Year of Revolutions

The 'baby boomers', the sudden postwar increase in births, came of age in 1968, when their influence was felt worldwide. Western European capitalism began to seem dangerously attractive to the Eastern Soviet satellite states. The strongly fortified and guarded border between East and West Germany was reinforced in 1961 by the construction of a wall dividing the Russian sector of Berlin from the West; the explanation given was to stop 'fascist infiltration',

LEFT *In May 1968, violent clashes took place on the streets of Paris between student protesters and workers on the one hand, and the* Compagnies Républicaines de Sécurité (CRS), *the French riot police, on the other.*

'neutralize' suspected opponents, in which more than 20,000 were shot as a climate of apprehensive suspicion spread through that unfortunate country.

Anti-Vietnam protests continued for some years until the final surrender, but the Prague Spring was brought to a brutal end in August as a quarter of a million Soviet and Warsaw Pact troops invaded the country. Czechoslovakia was dragged back behind the Iron Curtain, but another country, Albania, took the opportunity to renounce its allegiance to the Soviet bloc.

Television acted as a subversive force in the Eastern bloc, especially in East Germany, where West German broadcasts and popular America soap operas depicted a prosperous society, replete with consumer goods, which the Easterners hankered after. The highest ambition of all was to own the locally-manufactured car, the *Trabant*, a noxious and uncomfortable 2-stroke-engined vehicle with a delivery time of several years. Official relationships were improving, however, leading to an atomic Non-Proliferation Treaty and Soviet recognition of West Germany: small steps, but indications that the end of the Cold War was on the way.

RIGHT *Martin Luther King waves to the crowds from the Lincoln Memorial during the Civil Rights Movement's 'March on Washington' on 28 August 1963.*

but in fact, it was clearly intended to prevent the steady haemorrhage of East German citizens, decamping to join their cousins in the West.

On 5 January 1968, the agreeable Alexander Dubček came to power in Czechoslovakia and set in motion that brief period of liberal optimism known as the 'Prague Spring.' Students gathered in excited groups listening to the ubiquitous loudspeakers broadcasting not martial music but pop, with the Beatles, and Rolling Stones favourites: I remember '19th Nervous Breakdown' and 'Yellow Submarine' drifting over the Charles Bridge. In March, student protests against arbitrary government interference swept through Poland: muddying the issue, the ancient scapegoat – the Jews – were blamed and the police were able to restore Stalinist order. Young Germans began a campaign of strident extra-parliamentary opposition (a splinter group of which later became the terrorist Baader-Meinhof Gang). The most significant student revolts were in France, which were taken up by militant workers, not demanding higher pay but joining in protests against what was seen as an insensitive and materialistic society: even President de Gaulle panicked, and secretly fled Paris for the Army headquarters before order was restored. Meanwhile, Mexican students, seeing the Olympic Games of that year as an opportunity for publicity, were massacred by uniformed police and *agents provocateurs:* hundreds were killed and injured.

In the United States frustration with the slow progress on civil rights and anger with the Vietnam War burst out, exploding after the assassination of Martin Luther King, the most inspirational defender of black rights, a Nobel Prize winner, by James Earl Ray. Barely two months later, Senator Robert Kennedy, brother of the president assassinated in Dallas in 1963, was shot dead by a Palestinian. Television, now commonplace in the West, brought such events into the family home. The stark images of Vietnam that fuelled indignant horror were the photos of a naked child running screaming from an American air strike, scorched with napalm, and a South Vietnamese police chief shooting an opponent in the head. Not recorded at the time was the start of 'Operation Phoenix', a joint CIA/South Vietnamese operation to

NEW FREEDOMS

A period of new sexual freedom, which dawned with the availability of the first oral contraceptives in the early 1960s, lasted until the onset of AIDS in 1982. This was an epoch when, as Wordsworth had put it in a rather different context, 'to be young was very heaven'. Mini skirts and hot pants encouraged a cult of emaciation, but the pill gave women a new control over their own bodies and lives.

The 1960s were also an age when austerity gave way to consumerism. Cheap transistor radios became essential equipment for the young, while Vespas and Lambrettas, Italian motor scooters immortalized by Audrey Hepburn in the film *Roman Holiday,* became the epitome of youthful urban chic. Better sound quality came with the introduction of long-playing records and 7-inch 45-rpm singles. When audio cassettes were marketed in the early 1970s, followed by the Walkman personal stereo in 1977, near-permanent access to pop was made possible, and sometimes, as parents found, achieved.

1970–1994
Cautious Optimism

■ President Richard Nixon visits China 1972 ■ Soviet Union invades Afghanistan 1979
■ Islamic Revolution and establishment of theocracy in Iran 1979–80 ■ Fall of the Berlin Wall
and collapse of Soviet communism 1989–90 ■ First free elections in South Africa 1994

As China's equilibrium was restored after the Maoist excesses, dialogue opened between government and
citizens, uneven and inconsistent, but making a return to previous totalitarian rule difficult. Social changes
in Western countries sharpened the contrast with more traditional societies, but assisted one notable
advance, the emergence of South Africa as the most powerful African state, and a promising true democracy.

After the long-drawn-out agony of Vietnam and Cambodia and the shock-waves of Mao's delirious enthusiasms had ended, Eastern Asia began a steady recovery and under the steadying influence of Deng Xiaoping a stable pattern of government evolved in China, welding society together in a tightly-bound organization. Since some flexibility was essential, this did not necessarily make for efficiency and certainly did not improve individual freedoms, but the population was at least fed and educated. The rule of law rather than the dictates of Maoist theory stimulated legislation, as young people began to agitate for more democracy, and made the Democracy Wall in Peking the hub of young reformers' complaints. In what seemed to be a reversion to former open brutality student demonstrations in Beijing's Tiananmen Square in 1989 were crushed by troops and tanks, with hundreds of casualties. Yet the storm of protest this action unleashed, especially in Hong Kong, served to deter the Chinese government from any blatant repetition.

Asian Stability

Chinese attention focussed particularly on Hong Kong as the lease on the mainland 'New Territories' was due to expire in 1997. Serious discussions between London and Beijing in 1984 had resulted in an agreement that the whole colony would be handed back to China, but that all existing Hong Kong colonial laws, a free press and an independent judiciary would be maintained, and that in due course a fully democratic system would be introduced. China would at a stroke recover the last part of her territory still in foreign ownership, but her reputation was

clearly at risk if the promises were seen not to be kept: a peaceful transition was absolutely essential.

Before the collapse of his administration in a cloud of deceit Richard Nixon had removed the albatross that had hung around the State Department's neck since 1945 by recognizing the People's Republic of China, and permitting its representatives to take their place on the Security Council. Sealed by the President's visit to Beijing, guardedly friendly official relations were established, finalizing the delicate question of Taiwan's future, which was eventually to be as part of China. The joint Sino-American communiqué of February 1972 marked not quite the beginning of détente, but the acknowledgement of diplomacy rather than war as the normal relationship.

Rebuilding the economies shattered after the Vietnam War was a titanic task: even today Laos and Cambodia are among the region's poorest countries. Postwar Vietnam started badly, relying on collectivizing agriculture and industry, well-tried methods guaranteed to fail and, when they did, prompting the flight of millions of desperate Vietnamese. It took until 1986 for common sense to reassert itself and for the country to edge back into international acceptance. In South Korea a coup in 1979 was followed

LEFT *Soviet troops withdrawing from Kabul, Afghanistan in May 1988, after a conflict lasting 8 years, which cost the Red Army 15,000 dead. Like many armies before and since, the Russians could not subdue this wild and largely ungovernable country.*

by nearly 20 years of military rule, but the economy continued to grow. In what might be an object lesson of capitalism's merits, South Korea shot ahead to become one of the world's most prosperous countries, ranking just behind Japan in the UN tables of human development, while by contrast the North (under the eccentric and ruthlessly oppressive dictators Kim Il-Sung and his son Kim Jong-Il) has become perhaps the most deprived of human societies. The Philippines underwent over 20 years of rule by the able, but despotic and phenomenally corrupt Ferdinand Marcos, kept in power with US economic aid and a surprising degree of popular support, but never achieving the same success as its neighbours or a similar degree of unity.

By 1970, Russia had achieved parity with the United States in the atomic arsenal, prompting the Nuclear Non-Proliferation Treaty of 1970. Although extreme right-wingers (a fair supply always available in the USA) continued to press for a pre-emptive strike as late as 1980, governments accepted the necessity of limiting confrontation. The message was forced home by the failure of Russia's invasion of Afghanistan in 1979. Under the acceptable rule of King Zahir, Afghanistan had enjoyed probably its most tranquil period. Foreigners and Afghans politely jostled each other in the bazaars, women could, if they wished, go unveiled, and girls freely attended school. Taittinger and even Afghan wines (drinkable) were available in the Intercontinental

Hotel. Russian aid, demonstrated by the fine Salang Road Tunnel, assisted by Western investment had made this possible. The king's deposition by a coup in 1973 left Russia unperturbed, believing her influence impregnable, but after the Iranian Revolution of 1979 President Leonid Brezhnev acted, faced with the possible Islamization of the country, invading Afghanistan and thereby adding to his existing difficulties in Soviet Central Asian territories. For most of the next decade, Afghan opposition forces, aided by the West, transformed the country into the Russian Vietnam.

Oil and Diplomacy

All Western prosperity depended on ever-increasing supplies of oil, and the richest source of oil was in the Middle East. Western governments were therefore usually ready to employ any methods, however dubious, to ensure that their major oil companies were able to operate profitably: if this involved propping up unpleasant regimes, or undermining constitutional governments, it would still be done.

The trigger to the Afghan explosion had been an Islamist revolt in Iran which deposed Shah Reza, for many years a reliable supporter of the West. Britain and America had united in opposing Prime Minister Mosaddeq's nationalization of the oil industry in 1951, and failing to secure an adequate settlement, engineered the downfall of the constitutional government in 1953. After at first following constitutional procedures, the Shah moved to autocratic government, ultimately enforced by a particularly brutal state police, SAVAK. Iran was however transformed. Women were enfranchised and liberated from Islamic restrictions and education expanded to produce a generation of well-informed, and critical, young people. Supported by an expanding oil income and remaining on good terms with both Russia and America, the Shah saw himself as another Cyrus the Great, restoring the former magnificence of Persia.

He failed, however, to command the loyalty of any major section of Persian society, and both the educated and unemployed youth, and the conservative clerics were restive. By 1977 demonstrators were demanding the Shah's overthrow, hoping to gain social justice, employment, affordable housing and democratic freedoms. What they got two years later was an 'Islamic Republic' to be governed by Sharia law under the guidance of Ayatollah Khomeini: and the law was to be whatever the elderly clerics decided in the light of Quranic doctrine. Islam has no Magna Carta, no Institutes of Justinian, no centuries of recorded case law, nor an authorized collection of statutes: all of which makes it a very convenient framework for a repressively authoritarian state.

On the other side of the Shatt al-Arab waterway, the former British protectorate of Mesopotamia was demonstrating how absolute power could be maintained by total disregard for any laws. After a 1958 military coup against King Faisal I, in which the royal family were murdered, the Revolutionary Council flexed its muscles, nationalizing the Iraq Petroleum Company, largely British-owned, and threatening the Shi'a Iranians. In 1979, rule in the Republic of Iraq was assumed by Saddam Hussein, who as vice-president had actually held the reins of power. Although Saddam ruled as a murderous autocrat, his opposition to the Islamist regime in Iran won him friends abroad, and when in 1980 he declared war on the 'Persian cowards and dwarfs,' he could rely on extensive financial support from many Western countries and from the USSR. After eight years of bitter warfare, in which Iraq deployed a variety of chemical weapons, an uneasy peace was agreed.

BELOW *Supreme Leader of the Islamic state of Iran, Ayatollah Ali Khamenei, greets pilgrims at the shrine of Ayatollah Khomeini during a ceremony to mark the 20th anniversary of his death. Ayatollah Khamenei said speeches alone would not change the image of the United States in the Middle East.*

During the conflict the ancient quarrel between Iraqi Sunni and Persian Shi'a brought an added bitterness to the fighting, and enabled Iran to celebrate those some half million dead who had been privileged to enjoy the 'exquisite elixir of martyrdom.' Both countries were left impoverished, with the Iranian Islamic revolution more firmly entrenched, and Saddam looking desperately for some source of prestige and dollars.

Apart from bombing an Iraqi nuclear reactor in 1981, Israel kept out of this war. Since its foundation in 1948 and the initial fight against all the Arab nations, Israel had mounted a successful attack on Egypt and Syria and Jordan in 1967, the Six-Day War, and occupied the remainder of the Palestine Mandate – the West Bank and Sinai. Although a peace treaty with Egypt, after another, more evenly-matched conflict in 1973, was agreed, the Israeli occupation of the West Bank remained an unsettled issue, encouraging Palestinian resistance. The Palestine Liberation Organization, the PLO, headed by Yasser Arafat, did little to attract sympathy for the Palestinian cause by a widespread series of terrorist attacks, which also hardened Israeli attitudes.

Finding a solution to the Israeli/Palestinian conflict became a prime objective of the USA, but between Israeli intransigence and Palestinian incoherence, attempts floundered. American support for Israel, even when clearly in the wrong, added fuel to smouldering Arab resentment.

An Israeli-Egyptian peace treaty, guaranteed by continuing large payments from America, ensured the neutrality of the largest Arab country, but signs of militancy appeared even in the West's most reliable ally, and the world's major source of oil, Saudi Arabia. A demonstration of the joint power of the oil suppliers was given in 1973 when deliveries of oil were embargoed, rocketing the price. Algeria, Morocco and Tunisia remained on the sidelines, but Libya, under the eccentric Colonel Gaddafi from 1969, was unpredictable. The smaller states of the Persian Gulf provided an unusual example of tranquillity as the old Trucial States, in a formal relationship with Britain since 1820, evolved into the United Arab Emirates.

A New Age?

Away from the turbulent Middle East, the rest of the world was relaxing The United States was waking up to the attractions of sex. Films, hitherto strictly controlled by the Hayes Code of censorship, were allowed to suggest that couples sometimes went to bed for other purposes than sleep – although even as late as 2008 a discreet female nipple on television could provoke a national scandal. Most surprising was the widespread acceptance of homosexual equality – 'gay rights' – and the affirmation of homosexual relations as normal. Women, too, demanded recognition of equal rights, and in one famous case the Supreme Court decided that abortion could be legal. Such – by other standards quite restricted – liberalism scandalized much religious opinion, both Catholic and Protestant, and made abortion a particular touchstone of political affiliation. The generation of 1968 were now often parents, their radical ideas doubtless modified, but also more readily accepted by society at large. By the end of the 1980s it seemed that a New Age might be arriving.

Africa

Very few of Africa's newly independent countries had survived without undergoing violent alterations of government, and few of the changes were for the better; the cult of the 'big man', surrounded by corrupt associates and

ABOVE *Voters hold aloft a banner proclaiming their support for Nelson Mandela, leader of South Africa's African National Congress, in the country's first democratic elections in 1994. The ANC won an overwhelming majority in this contest.*

their followers the 'WaBenzi' – named for their predilection for Mercedes cars – was almost universal. Compared with the steady, sometimes spectacular, economic advance of Southeast Asia, African economies failed to deliver the advantages of growth to their citizens. Despite attempts at democracy and the presence of an educated élite, oil-rich Nigeria, one of the continent's wealthiest states, was governed by successive kleptocracies, and only South Africa offered any prospect of stability; but South Africa laboured under the stigma of apartheid.

South Africa had, however, two other advantages not possessed by any other country on the continent: an acceptable government in waiting and a parliamentary tradition. Democracy itself was not enough: free elections

ABOVE *Mikhail Gorbachev being greeted by enthusiastic crowds on a visit to Prague in 1987. 'Gorbymania' swept Eastern Europe in the late 1980s, as people realized that reforms in Russia might lead to freedom in the satellite states.*

could easily lead to a dictatorship, as Mussolini and Hitler had proved. An independent judiciary, a reasonably free press, and the acceptance of constitutional opposition were essential. All these, albeit somewhat shop-soiled, existed in South Africa. South African governments had always depended on maintaining a majority in a parliament elected, by however unequal a franchise, according to the constitution. And in 1989 the Nationalist majority in Parliament was crumbling. If President F.W. de Klerk could not rely on a parliamentary majority, 100 years of tradition demanded a fresh election, and world opinion would not countenance a whites-only franchise. De Klerk accordingly accepted that the African National Congress, led by such respected figures as Oliver Tambo and the imprisoned Nelson Mandela, as well as more militant communists, must be allowed to function. On 11 February 1990, Mandela was released: in March, Namibia, formerly controlled by South Africa, was declared independent. It took another four years, many negotiations and much violence before South Africa's first fully democratic elections were held, but the process was unstoppable.

Even more surprising events were unfolding in Eastern Europe. Mikhail Gorbachev had come to power in 1985 with two principal policies – *glasnost*– 'openness' – and *perestroika* – 'reconstruction'. Treading warily, since Stalinist opposition persisted in Russia, the most radical steps were taken by the satellite governments. In the summer of 1989, Hungary opened all its frontiers, creating the first gap in the Iron Curtain. The East German leadership was given strong hints on the need to reform, and obediently removed travel restrictions: the Berlin Wall began to disappear in November. The most dramatic change was in Romania, where demonstrations forced the tyrant Nicolae Ceausescu to flee: he was captured and shot. In the other satellites, the transition was more peaceful, but equally decisive. By 1990 East and West Germany had been united to form the largest state in Western Europe, Georgia, Lithuania, Latvia and Estonia were independent and Gorbachev had been awarded the Nobel Peace Prize. Within another twelve months the Soviet Union had been dissolved, replaced by the Commonwealth of Independent States: the 'independence' was perhaps debatable.

What had been Western Europe was now considerably expanded eastwards. After the heavy hand of General de Gaulle had been lifted the European Economic Community was able to move ahead, and by 1990 all Western European countries except Norway and Switzerland, had joined. Certain standards of good governance were demanded from new members, but it was evident that many, if not most of the former satellites, would be eligible as newly-unified East Germany had already become.

Dictatorships in Latin America were slackening their hold. Military rule in Argentina had been given its death blow by Britain's successful defence of the Falkland Islands in 1982: succeeding governments, threatened from both left and right, had been fragile, but the 1989 victory of Carlos Menem promised at least a less gloomy future. By contrast Brazil's generals had been able to preside over an 'economic miracle' of growth and edge towards a restoration of democracy, fully achieved in 1989, by which time the ebullient Lula da Silva had emerged as the coming man. Chile had survived both the military coup of 1973 which had overturned the elected Marxist government of Salvador Allende, and the experience of General Pinochet's economic experimentation, to the first free elections in December 1989. All three of South America's largest economies therefore entered 1990 in good heart. In Central America, Mexico continued its peculiar system of one-party government, skilfully controlled by satisfying basic social demands and well-entrenched corruption, which had maintained consistent growth at the price of international reputation and heavy debt. The administration of Carlos Salinas as President in 1986 began radical reforms, negotiating debt-relief in 1990 and discussing a free trade agreement with the USA and Canada.

The international climate, however, soon clouded over, beginning in that old trouble-spot, the Balkans. Tito had firmly restrained the separate nationalities that form Yugoslavia, but after his death in 1980 the country began to disintegrate. Slovenia was the first to declare independence in July 1991, closely followed by Croatia. The central government in Serb-dominated Belgrade, resisted, but real trouble began in Bosnia, with its mixed Serb/Croat/Muslim population, when past resentments and jealousies dating back to the Turkish occupation, were revived. Authorized to use force by the United Nations, NATO troops attempted to keep civilian supplies moving, and later after some shocking massacres bombed military installations.

Kosovo, the southern province of the new Yugoslavia (Serbia plus Montenegro) demanded independence. When this was sharply rejected by Belgrade, resulting in desperate refugees harassed by Serbian forces, another war in 1998–99 was needed; this included a NATO air raid on Belgrade itself, the first time a European capital had been bombed since the end of the Second World War. The repercussions of this action still persist.

The other limited war was briefer, but a good deal more deadly. After the Iraqi invasion of Kuwait in 1990, a UN-authorized force, mainly American, British and French, expelled the invaders and forced an inconclusive settlement on Iraq. Saddam Hussein remained in power, but with an even more damaged infrastructure and harassed population. Since Saddam's forces had also threatened Saudi Arabia, that country agreed to receiving US troops as a guarantee against further Iraqi aggression; that was to prove a grave error.

RIGHT *On 9–10 November 1989, the hated Berlin Wall, erected in 1961 to stop East Germans from leaving the country, came down. Joyous scenes greeted the relaxation of travel restrictions, which heralded the demise of Soviet communism.*

2000–
Towards the Third Millennium

■ Expansion of the World Wide Web 1990s ■ Formation of the G-20 group of major economies 1999 ■ Terrorist attacks on the United States 2001 ■ US-led invasion of Iraq topples Saddam Hussein 2003 ■ 'Arab Spring' popular revolts across North Africa and the Middle East 2011

As the Third Millennium approached, the world seemed to be shrinking. New methods of communication brought people from all parts of the world together and made available an enormous quantity of information. International sport, broadcast on television, provided new excitement and perhaps popularized standards of fair play. The dominance of Europe and America in international politics and economics was, however, increasingly and widely resented.

The small portable telephone that could be linked with a wireless network was pioneered in Scandinavia by the Nordic Mobile Telephone network in the 1980s, as a method of communicating over large stretches of poorly-inhabited country. Initial growth was modest – some 1 million sets sold over the first ten years – but in the 1990s, with the extension of network coverage, sales rocketed. Today over half the world's population possess a mobile phone and in African countries, where fixed-line systems are sparse, it has transformed communications. In 1996, the first 'smartphones' appeared, enabling connection with the Internet.

Social-networking services developed in the 1980s, at first used mainly for games, and by 2004 culminated in the 'Facebook' webpage, now ubiquitous especially among the young. With the use of texting allowing messages to be received at any time, near-constant communication is possible. Widespread use of smartphones with cameras affords instant coverage of any striking event, natural disaster or social unrest. For repressive regimes, this has proved troublesome, as information could be instantly transferred to any part of the world; the 'Arab Spring' uprisings of 2011 proved the power of the new IT media.

Birth of the Internet

The first computer interchanges were developed during the 1960s in the USA, based on principles evolved in the British National Physical Laboratory. By 1975, the first American system was opened for public use, but it was not until the 1990s that international interest in computer networks was sparked by the World Wide Web project. Tim Berners-Lee, working at CERN (*Conseil Européen pour la Recherche Nucléaire*) in Geneva, later famous for its Large Hadron Collider that straddles the Franco-Swiss border, changed the whole course of modern history by his concept of the World Wide Web. The whole episode was extraordinary. Very much like Bletchley Park during the Second World War, CERN had gathered together an eclectic group of talented individuals who bounced ideas of each other.

Berners-Lee's concept was simple enough, to marry hypertext – the multiplicity of information, including images, that can be displayed on a computer – to the Internet, the international network of computer links. Anyone with access to a computer would be able to consult a phenomenally wide variety of information, and through 'Wikis' – collaborative websites – help to create references, the most successful being Wikipedia, that essential quick-reference resource for baffled writers. Just as the young found mobile telephones essential, so their harried seniors relied on their laptops or smartphones to continue working at all hours. Anyone eager to express their ideas in public, and with enough spare time, could publish a 'blog', a web log, inviting comments and supplementing newspaper coverage.

LEFT *The launch of Google shares on the NASDAQ exchange in New York in 2004. Since its inception in 1998, this Internet search service has become the world's most recognized brand, and an enormously profitable concern.*

The results of these discoveries were far-reaching. Information was accessible throughout the world and at any time, and could be exchanged across the continents. Without such drastic action as closing the Internet or banning all communications equipment, governments could not prevent their people from discovering what was going on in the rest of the world. Intercepting correspondence – the origin of the 18th-century British Secret Service – and tapping telephone lines became unprofitable, and monitoring the millions of mobile telephone communications, especially by text, demanded sophisticated surveillance systems. What began as a limited local demonstration of discontent could flare into a full scale rebellion orchestrated by mobile telephone. Berners-Lee made his work freely available: 'to be a pool of human knowledge and human culture, which could allow collaborators in remote states to share their ideas.' Yet with the advantages came dangers. If the Internet collapsed or was maliciously attacked, a country's infrastructure could collapse; regional banking systems, energy-providers or national defences could be damaged, and false information channelled as easily as the truth.

Fair Play

In the half century since the Second World War, Britain changed from being the hub of the most extensive empire the world had ever seen to a respectable second-division power – although by an odd quirk of geography Queen

ABOVE *South Africa's international Rugby Union team – the 'Springboks' – celebrate their victory in the World Cup Final in Paris in 2007. Their cup final win on home soil in 1995 was hailed right across the newly post-apartheid state.*

Elizabeth II is now sovereign of more of the world's surface than anyone except the President of the Russian Federation (as Queen of the United Kingdom, Canada, Australia, New Zealand etc). Countering the decline of British power, however, was the growth of the English language as the world's medium of communication, as an official language for some 2 billion people and the second language for most of the rest. As with Latin in the ancient world, English may be in the process of splitting into regional variants. American, British and Australian English, most closely allied as they are, have developed different lexicons and degrees of acceptability. Irony, for example, essential in Australian, has to be treated delicately in the United States.

The other more evident indicator of a shrinking world is international sport, again with regional differences. North American team games, basketball, baseball and American football, are almost limited to that area. Cricket is – again almost, for its popularity is spreading – confined to British Commonwealth countries, Australasia, the Indian Subcontinent and South Africa, but not including Canada. Few other countries could seriously contemplate a game where a single match can last for five days.

Rugby Union football is somewhat more widespread, extending through Europe and the Commonwealth to South America, where the Argentinians are formidable, but again, not to the North, although American football is a variant. The one truly international team game is, however, Association Football – 'soccer' in 19th-century university slang. Throughout Black Africa, South America and Europe soccer is a passion. International contests have hundreds of millions glued to their televisions, radios or mobile phones, following every dramatic minute.

Tennis and golf, the most closely followed individual games, attract a geographically limited audience, although still one counted in multi-millions. And the common factor to all these sports is that they are products of 19th century Britain, where the rules and standards were evolved, even though 'lawn tennis' is actually a variant of the much older game, and golf has been played since the 16th century. With the laws came standards of conduct, the ideals of fair play and the admiration of professional skills, whatever the player's race or nationality. All the world has embraced sporting ideals, first evolved in a liberal society. South Africa's transition to democracy, although in part enforced by financial pressures, was fired by humiliation at being excluded from international sport. Subsequently White and Black have united to support the national teams; as one Black rugby fan said: 'They may be Boers, but they are *our* Boers'.

Globalization

The world's affairs seemed to be – and indeed largely were – controlled by small group of rich countries. Three permanent members of the United Nations Security Council, with a combined population of some half a million, could veto any action or resolution that any country might propose: China and Russia, the other two permanent members certainly had much greater numbers, but that still left more than half the world's population on the sidelines. World economies were also settled in discussion held at the rich countries' club, the G-6, consisting of the United States, the United Kingdom, France, Germany, Japan and Italy, which became with the addition of Russia and Canada the G-8. Very nearly all the international organizations were quartered in Europe or the United States: those that were not, such as the International Research and Training Institute for the Advancement of Women (Dominican Republic) and the University of Peace (Costa Rica) were hardly front-rank institutions. Discontent with the system fuelled violent protests at the annual meetings of the G groups, mostly organized by young activists. Even after the G-8 was expanded to become the G-20, it was hardly representative: the only sub-Saharan African country included was, almost inevitably, South Africa.

Official international efforts to moderate human misery were supplemented by many International Non-Governmental Organizations (INGOs), usually charities, funded by donors. Corruption and incompetence have swallowed up much of what has been given, but INGOs – some 40,000 at one recent count – remain formidable, constantly able to challenge, and sometimes –albeit indirectly – to destroy governments. Although most INGOs are sectional and small, perhaps a dozen are outstanding, defined by those agreeing to an Accountability Charter, which includes Action Aid, Amnesty International, Greenpeace, Oxfam, Save the Children, Médecins Sans Frontières and BRAC, the admirable institution inspired by Sir Fazle Abed, assisted by Bill Gates. BRAC employs some 120,000 people with projects in Africa and Bangladesh, the world's third-largest Muslim country and one of the poorest.

ABOVE *Members of the international aid organization Oxfam wearing masks representing the foremost world leaders of the period – Chancellor Merkel of Germany, PM Tony Blair of Britain, and presidents George W. Bush and Jacques Chirac – protest in favour of a fairer system of world trade.*

Modern INGOs are divided between 'helpers' and 'challengers,' the organizers of good works in despairing societies – Africa being a priority – such as Oxfam, BRAC and Save the Children, and the challengers who scarify abusive governments: Amnesty International is the most active of these. There is no lack of opportunities for both, and since the work done by helpers often exposes official brutality and corruption, both are often unpopular, reviled as post-colonial, neo-imperialistic, superior Westerners interfering in other nations' domestic affairs. By contrast, however, local INGOs often support this officially unpopular interference: Kenya, Zimbabwe and Israel are only a few examples.

Apart from the risk of being seen as yet another way in which the rich nations exert power, the possibility that aid might suddenly be cut off, for either political or economic reasons, adds another factor of uncertainty, making long-term planning near impossible. The world's oldest INGO, the Catholic Church, under its remarkably energetic but firmly reactionary Polish Pope John Paul II found itself often at odds with the charities, especially those concerned to limit the spread of AIDS. Since condoms, the most effective method of preventing infection, were banned, much of the Church's missionary effort was wasted.

Into a New Era

On 18 September 2000, the General Assembly of the United Nations had issued its Millennium Declaration, signed by all members. Six fundamental values were defined, among them:

> ***Freedom.*** *Men and women have the right to live their lives and raise their children in dignity, free from hunger and from the fear of violence, oppression or injustice. Democratic and participatory governance based on the will of the people best assures these rights.*

'Best assures', hardly amounted to a ringing declaration of human rights, carefully drafted to be acceptable to the many authoritarian rulers. The fourth value 'Tolerance' also carefully avoided commitments.

> *Tolerance. Human beings must respect one another, in all their diversity of belief, culture and language. Differences within and between societies should be neither feared nor repressed, but cherished as a precious asset of humanity. A culture of peace and dialogue among all civilizations should be actively promoted.*

It was all a far cry from the American Declaration of Independence, or even the Magna Carta.

As the millennium approached the international climate seemed, if not exactly set fair, at least only moderately unsettled. The Kosovo crisis having passed, no major war was being fought. Europe was consolidating, with a common currency, the Euro, established among the western countries – Britain always excepted. Combined with the existence of a no-passport free-travel zone – Britain again excepted, and the accession of Hungary , Poland and the Czech Republic to NATO – European unity was becoming more than a pious aspiration.

The Union Flag having been lowered in Hong Kong in 1997 under the steady guidance of the last governor, Chris Patten, a new era was ushered in. China kept faithful to its obligations, if slow in progressing to full democracy, and

the former colony continued to be peaceably prosperous, an example of what the economically liberal New China might become.

The Middle East continued to smoulder. Saddam Hussein's Iraq, suspected of harbouring weapons of mass destruction, was resisting United Nations inspectors. Some American right-wing 'hawks' campaigned for a pre-emptive strike, but President Bill Clinton continued to support the United Nations' patient policy of containment.

South Africa continued to be democratic, although struggling under Mandela's idiosyncratic successor, Thabo Mbeki, who insisted, among other eccentricities, that a fruit diet could cure AIDS. The process of reconciliation gently administered by the Anglican Archbishop of Cape Town, Desmond Tutu, succeeded in healing the old wounds, a remarkable achievement which could have proved an example to the rest of Africa .

Even the Near East's prospects seemed to be brightening, as Israeli troops withdrew after more than 20 years in southern Lebanon. They proved fleeting, however, after Ariel Sharon, the hard-line opposition leader, who

BELOW *US Marines in central Baghdad in April 2003 at the culmination of the Iraq war, prepare to topple a statue of Saddam Hussein. President of Iraq from 1979 until 2003, Saddam was executed for crimes against humanity in 2006.*

Republican, dependent on right-wing votes, Bush was expected to introduce domestic policies that in Europe would be regarded as reactionary, but his choice of a distinguished soldier as Secretary of State suggested a cautious, even liberal, foreign policy. General Colin Powell, born in the United States of Jamaican parents, had made a reputation as a humane and cautious commander, always ready to prefer diplomacy to war, but at the same time not one to criticize political decisions. More aggressive cabinet members discussed the possibility of a pre-emptive strike on Iraq to remove the still-undiscovered weapons of mass destruction, but it was not Iraq that threatened American security.

The enormity of the concerted attacks on prominent targets in the United States on 11 September 2001 ('9/11') horrified the world. Captured live on television, the images of two hijacked airliners, deliberately flown into the soaring Twin Towers of the World Trade Center, the buildings' subsequent collapse, and the

ABOVE *Protestors demonstrate in the city of Benghazi against Colonel Moamer Kadhafi's oppresive regime in Libya. In early 2011, the 'Arab Spring' of revolts swept North Africa and the Near East; the protests were greatly aided by the free exchange of information on the Internet and by e-mail.*

sight of doomed victims jumping to their death are etched on the world's collective memory. Another plane crashed into the Pentagon in Washington DC. As the recordings of the final telephone calls, and the successful attempt of the passengers on another hijacked plane to divert their captors from their intended target (thought to be the Capitol or the White House) were heard, another dimension of drama was added; but only a visit to the site, to appreciate how great an area in the heart of New York was devastated, gave the full effect of the tragic event.

had previously been blamed for a particularly nasty massacre in Lebanon, led several hundred Israeli police on to the Jerusalem Temple Mount, the third of the Muslim sacred places; the provocation duly unleashed the Second Intifada uprising among the Palestinians. When, on 6 February 2001, Sharon became Prime Minister of Israel, an escalation of violence was inevitable.

Israel was now faced by three separate militant Palestinian forces. Hamas, an off-shoot of the Egyptian Muslim Brotherhood, centered in Gaza, and the more moderate Fatah in the occupied West Bank. Hezbollah, which had emerged in Lebanon during the Israeli occupation, was strategically well placed, adjacent to both Syria and Iran. As a Shi'a party it was opposed by the mainly Sunni Arab states, but had considerable support from Iran, which enabled it to build up a powerful political organization. But the assault, when it came, was from an unlikely quarter, the reliable Western ally, the Kingdom of Saudi Arabia. Although one of the world's richest nations, Arabia's wealth was distributed very unequally. The royal family were phenomenally wealthy, and some members blatantly squandered their money in the West, while paying lip-service to a particularly severe version of Islam, in which personal freedoms were severely restricted, public executions frequent and literacy well below that of the neighbouring Arab Emirates. Disgust at the hypocrisy and corruption of a state that had the high responsibility of guarding Islam's most sacred places had been amplified by the fact that the American troops and aeroplanes had been allowed to station themselves in the land where the infidel should not be tolerated.

On 20 January 2001, George Walker Bush, son of the former president George Bush, succeeded to the Presidency of the United States, after a contested result, eventually decided by the Supreme Court. As a conservative

As the meticulous planning of the plot was uncovered, the attackers' motives were made clear. The World Trade Center was chosen as a target to represent the West's dominance of the global economy: its position in New York, housing one of the world's largest Jewish populations, was aimed at America's constant support of Israel. And, most shockingly, the perpetrators were not from Hamas, Hezbollah, the PLO or any identified terrorist group, but citizens of America's closest ally in the Middle East, Saudi Arabia – no fewer than 14 of the 20 conspirators were from that country, signalling their detestation of their own government's support for the 'Great Satan'.

President Bush was faced with a country in shock, but with sympathy expressed from all over the world: within days he had forfeited much of this by declaring a 'war on terror', described as a 'crusade', a word with sinister connotations for many Muslims, with the equivalent threat of a 'holy war'. It was also short-sighted in that many leaders acceptable to the United States were themselves former terrorists, such as Prime Minister Menachem Begin of Israel (once a member of the Irgun in British-mandated Palestine). The 'War on Terror' was to lead in due course to the second Gulf War, and a skewing of American foreign policy resembling that after the Second World War , with Muslims instead of communists now pilloried as the enemy.

RIGHT *Scenes that the world will never forget: as the North Tower of the World Trade Center blazes, hit by a hijacked airliner, another plane plunges into the South Tower. In all, 9/11 claimed 2,937 victims, from 70 countries.*

6000 BC	2000 BC	100 AD	1000	1250	1500	1700

c.6000 BC First use of copper in Middle East. Development of the plough in Mesopotamia

c.5500 BC First farming communities appear in Central Europe

c.4400 BC Egyptians weave cloth on a loom

4236 BC The first 365 day calendar is introduced in Egypt

c.4000 BC Domestication of horses in the Ukraine. The development of planked wooden hulls for boats in Egypt

c.3500 BC Invention of the wheel, used for casting pots, in Mesopotamia

3500 BC–3100 BC Writing developed in Egypt and Mesopotamia

c.3200 BC Wheeled vehicles appear in Middle East

c.3000 BC The use of hieroglyph numerals in Egypt. Abacus first used in China

c.2800 BC The Egyptians make papyrus

c.2700 BC Silk developed in China

c.2600 BC The first glass is made in Mesopotamia

c.2700 BC Physicians in Egypt practising surgery

2300 BC The earliest known map is produced in Iraq

c.2000 BC Medicine based on astrology is practised in Syria and Babylon

1750 BC Babylonian astronomers catalogue the stars and planets

c.1700 BC The first phonetic alphabet is developed in Syria

1350 BC Sundials and water clocks developed

400 BC Hippocrates records human anatomy

340 BC Difference between arteries and veins distinguished by Praxagoras in Greece

250 BC Archimedes develops the screw pump for raising water for irrigation

ABOVE *A medieval woodcut shows an Archimedian screw lifting water for irrigation*

150 BC The precession of the equinoxes and the distance from the moon to the Earth are calculated by Greek astronomer Hipparchus

50 BC Hero of Alexandria develops the first steam engine

45 BC The introduction of the Julian Calendar in Rome

30 BC Glass blowing technique developed in Syria

AD 100 Chinese farmers develop the seed drill. The first maps with grid references are created by Greek geographer Marinus of Tyre. The wheelbarrow is used in China

AD 105 Paper is made using tree bark and rags in China. Chinese develop first insecticide

AD 132 Chinese astronomer Zhang Heng invents a seismograph for detecting earthquakes

AD 175 Greek physician Galen uses the pulse for the first time to aid diagnosis

AD 300 Recipe for gunpowder recorded in China

AD 495 Development of paddle boat in China

AD 615 Petroleum used as fuel in Japan

AD 618 Printed newspapers using woodblock printing produced in China

AD 800 The use of blast furnaces to produce cast iron in Europe

AD 964 The Andromeda Galaxy and the Large Magellanic Cloud identified by Arab astronomer Abd al-Rahman al-Sufi

AD 976 Chain drive mechanism invented by Chinese engineer Chang Ssu-Hsun

AD 984 Systems of canal locks invented in China

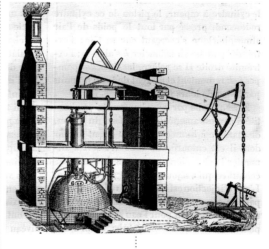

ABOVE *A page from a treatise by astronomer Abd al-Rahman al-Sufi on astrology and the fixed stars*

1021 A treatise is published on optics, curved mirrors and light refraction by Arab mathematician Alhazen

1075 Arab astronomer al-Zarqali proposes that planet orbits are ellipses and not circles

1086 The magnetic compass is first described by Chinese scientist Shen Kua

1105 Chinese potters make porcelain. The first use of windmills recorded in Europe

1180 The first ships which use rudders to steer are built in Europe

1220 Gunpowder bombs with outer casings first used by Chinese military

1260 Pulmonary circulation of the blood first described by Arab physician Ibn al-Nafis

1267 English scientist Roger Bacon describes the magnification of objects by lenses and suggests they could be used to improve weak sight

1269 French scientist identifies the polarity of magnets

1288 First gunpowder cannons built by Chinese military

1320 French surgeon Henri de Mondeville first suggests the cleansing and stitching of wounds to aid healing

1395 Printers in Korea use metal type

1425 German Nicholas of Cusa postulates that the Earth rotates on its axis once a day and orbits the sun once a year

1430 German mechanics introduce a fly wheel to even out the motion of rotating machinery

1461 Breech loading cannons introduced in Europe

1485 Leonardo da Vinci produces a parachute design

1492 In England graphite is used for writing in lead pencils

1573 Dane Tycho Brahe invents the sextant to measure the angles of the stars and aid navigation

1628 The circulation of blood around the body explained for the first time by Englishman William Harvey

1631 Pierre Vernier invents the Vernier measuring scale, allowing very precise measurements to be made

1642 A mechanical calculating machine is built by French scientist Blaise Pascal

1649–59 Capillary blood vessels, red blood cells and the lymphatic system identified by Henry Power, Jan Swammerdam and Thomas Willis

1665 English scientist Robert Hooke proposes the wave theory of light. English physician Richard Lower performs the first blood transfusion between two dogs

1676 Dutch scientist Antonie van Leeuwenhoek reports observations of bacteria. Robert Hooke invents the universal joint

LEFT *The first manned hot air balloon takes off from the Bois de Boulogne, Paris, in 1783*

1701 First smallpox inoculations given by Italian Giacomo Pylarini. Jethro Tull invents the mechanical seed drill

1709 Gabriel Fahrenheit invents the alcohol thermometer and the Fahrenheit temperature scale

1712 Thomas Newcomen invents the atmospheric steam engine

ABOVE *Newcomen's atmospheric engine, used for pumping water from a mine*

1735 English clockmaker John Harrison designs a chronometer to keep accurate time at sea

1764 James Hargreaves invents the Spinning Jenny

1765 James Watt builds a steam engine with a separate condenser

1772 Oxygen is discovered by Karl Scheele

1783 The Montgolfier brothers invent the hot air balloon

1786 The threshing machine is invented by Scottish inventor Andrew Meikle

1796 Lithographic printing is developed by German printer Aloys Senefelder

LEFT *A Greek vase of the 4th century BC depicting a chariot race*

6000BC–PRESENT

1800 The battery is invented by Italian Allessandro Volta. The discovery of infrared radiation by William Herschel and of ultraviolet light in 1801 by Johann Ritter

1810 Food canning invented by Nicolas Appert, a French chef

1815 Scottish engineer John McAdam devises a method of making paved roads

1817 Frenchman René Laennec invents the stethoscope

1820 Electromagnetism discovered by Danish physicist Hans Orsted

1822 The 'Difference Engine' – a mechanical adding machine – is invented by English mathematician Charles Babbage

1825 First public railway runs between Stockton and Darlington, England

ABOVE *A section of Charles Babbage's* Difference Engine

1826 The first photograph using a metal plate is taken by Joseph Niepce in Paris

1838 Samuel Morse demonstrates the electric telegraph in New York

ABOVE *The* Planet *locomotive that ran on the Liverpool-Manchester railway in 1830, typical of the early steam locomotives*

1839 Charles Goodyear develops the process of vulcanizing rubber to harden it

1840 German pathologist Jacob Henle theorizes that germs cause infection

1845 Isambard Brunel launches the *SS Great Britain*, the first successful propeller driven ship

1854 English physician John Snow finds a link between contaminated water and cholera

1856 Henry Bessemer develops the Bessemer converter to make steel out of iron

1859 Charles Darwin publishes *On the Origin of Species* describing his theory of evolution

1867 Carbolic acid is used as a disinfectant in operating rooms by English surgeon Joseph Lister. Swedish chemist Alfred Nobel patents dynamite

1876 The telephone is patented by Alexander Graham Bell

1876 The four-stroke internal combustion engine is built by German engineer Nikolaus Otto

1877 Electric light bulbs are developed by English physicist Joseph Swan and, independently, by American Thomas Edison

1879 Discovery of DNA (deoxyribonucleic acid) and RNA (ribonucleic acid) by German biochemist Albrecht Kossel

1886 German Gottlieb Daimler produces a car fuelled by gasoline

1887 Radio waves are identified by German physicist Heinrich Hertz

1889 The first motion-picture is made by English inventor William Friese-Greene

1893 First open heart surgery performed by African American surgeon Daniel Williams

1895 The first X-ray is taken by German physicist Wilhelm Röntgen

1897 The first subatomic particle, the electron, is identified by English physicist J.J. Thomson. A new pathogen named as a 'virus' is identified by Dutch botanist Martinus Beijerinck. Cathode ray tube developed by German Ferdinand Braun

BELOW *Alexander Graham Bell demonstrates his first telephone*

1901 Italian Guglielmo Marconi makes the first transatlantic radio transmission

1903 The first flight in a powered airplane is made by American brothers Wilbur and Orville Wright

ABOVE *The* Wright Flyer *takes to the air, piloted by Orville Wright, for the first heavier than air powered flight*

1905 Theory of relativity by German Albert Einstein is postulated

1923 Scotsman John Logie Baird invents a television system using mechanical scanning

1926 The first successful launch of a liquid fuel rocket by American Robert Goddard

1927 Belgian astronomer Georges Lemaiter proposes the Big Bang theory for the origin of the universe

1928 The antibiotic penicillin is discovered by Scottish bacteriologist Alexander Fleming

1930 An analogue computer is built by American engineer Vannevar Bush. The first frozen foods are marketed by Charles Birdseye

1931 Hungarian László Bíró makes the first ballpoint pen. He patents the design in 1938

1932 Nuclear fusion is achieved by English physicist John Cockcroft and Irish physicist Ernest Walton

1935 Radar is invented by Scottish physicist Robert Watson-Watt

1937 Photocopying is invented by American physicist Chester Carlson

1938 A binary digital computer is constructed by German Konrad Zuse

1944 American engineer Igor Sikorsky designs the modern helicopter

1943 Alan Turing and Thomas Flowers build Colossus, an all electronic stored-program computer

1945 First test of the atomic bomb

1947 The first supersonic flight is made by Chuck Yeager. The Polaroid instant camera is demonstrated by American Edwin Land

1951 The contraceptive pill is developed by American biologist Gregory Pinkus Djerassi, Miramontes and Rosenkrantz in America

1953 The gene code is unravelled by James Watson and Francis Crick

1957 The first space satellite, *Sputnik*, is launched by the Soviet Union

RIGHT *Neil Armstrong steps down from the Lunar Module on to the Moon's surface during the Apollo 11 mission*

1960 The ruby laser is developed by Theodore Maiman

1967 South African, Christian Barnard performs the first heart-transplant

1969 Neil Armstrong becomes the first man on the moon

1970 The pocket calculator is developed simultaneously by Sanyo, Canon and Sharp

1971 Email is developed by Ray Tomlinson. The use of MRI scanning (magnetic resonance imaging) is developed for diagnostics in medicine by Raymond V. Damadian

1977 The mobile phone is developed by Bell Labs

1981 NASA's space shuttle *Columbia* makes its maiden flight. Hewlett Packard launch the 32 bit silicon chip for computers

1982 Communications satellites are placed in space by re-usable space shuttle *Columbia*

1984 English geneticist Alec Jeffreys perfects genetic fingerprinting

1989 Boeing researchers produce a photocell that converts solar radiation into electricty

1990 NASA launches the Hubble space telescope

1993 Englishman Tim Berners Lee, launches the world wide web for international computer communications

1996 Scottish biologist Ian Wilmutt clones Dolly the sheep

1997 Huntingdon Willard successfully replicates an artificial human chromosome

1998 Human stem cells are successfully grown by American researchers at Johns Hopkins University

2001 American researchers clone a human embryo

2004 The first commercial rail service using magnetic levitation trains starts in Shanghai, China

2005 American researchers grow human eggs in the laboratory

BELOW *A communication satellite is launched from the cargo bay of the space shuttle* Challenger *in 1984*

Epilogue

Looking back over more than 30,000 years of human history, some conclusions seem obvious. Progress, for example, is not inevitable. Life in the Indus Valley around 4,000 years ago was quite probably more secure, sanitary and pleasant than it is in much of the modern state of Pakistan. European art today is not notably superior to that of well, of almost any preceding period you care to specify.

On the other hand, even with their country's current problems of drug-related violence, few modern Mexican citizens would welcome the return of Aztec human sacrifices. Medical advances have eliminated some diseases, but others have developed, many self-inflicted through alcohol, drugs and obesity. In politics, in spite of fine phrases and new doctrines, the cry of the Cambridge True Blue Club in the 1780s for 'Civil and Religious Liberty, all over the World' is still far from being universally accepted or enacted. Magna Carta demanded, and has usually secured, in Britain and her heirs, free passage for traders, the right to be tried by one's peers and by the laws of the land: those privileges, too, are still far from universal.

What is undeniable is that humanity has coped with the sudden and enormous rise in population – which has nearly doubled in the last half-century – without general disaster. Widespread famine is rare, even if undernourishment is not, while children have a better chance of survival in most parts of the world than their grandparents. They have too much greater access to intellectual stimulation through literacy, but also through radio, television and the Internet.

Even if the benefits remain unevenly distributed, the pace of human development has been enormously accelerated in the last two centuries. Selecting 1820 as a starting-point, to give time for Europe and America to recover from revolutionary wars, and choosing the most advanced societies – Britain, France, Northern Germany and New England – the picture that emerges is of people living with their active days shortened by lack of lighting, suffering (especially in cities without effective drainage) illnesses that today could be cured by a few pills, and enduring surgery without anaesthetics. Anywhere except the northern American states – further south they were quite likely to be Black, and so have no civil rights at all – citizens were likely to have only a limited local franchise, and exercise very little direct influence on their country's future. Travel was expensive and uncomfortable: most people rarely went further than the next market town, unless they were unwillingly displaced by wars. For the literate, books and newspapers were accessible but expensive, and libraries rare (here North America again fared better). Houses were poorly heated, with open coal fires and industrial engines (Britain the biggest culprit) producing foul emissions, blackening both the countryside and human lungs. And these were the most highly developed countries, in the forefront of scientific and technical change, where the doctrines of the French and American Revolutions were widespread, if not always enthusiastically accepted; life in the rest of the world continued much as it had for the previous 1,000 years.

Move forward a lifetime, to 1890, and life has improved radically. Gas and electric lighting had doubled the length of a winter's day, for work or leisure. Adequate drainage and clean running water had all but eradicated such earlier killers as cholera. Streets were still filthy, but cheap and punctual railways made travel popular. Restrictive laws and union pressures had improved working people's conditions; literacy was common and free libraries abundant. London workers could afford to escape to Southend or Margate. Medical practice, after Florence Nightingale's shake-up of hospitals, the developments of anaesthesia and aseptic surgery, had enormously improved. Queen Victoria made birthing anaesthesia respectable in 1853 and the use of cocaine as the base for a local anaesthetic, which was to make dentistry so much less painful, had been proved. Postal services were efficient – the novelist Anthony Trollope had a hand in that – and inexpensive; telegraphic communications now covered the developed world. Further advances had already been signalled as the German physicist Wilhelm Röntgen began his work on X-rays.

Such developments were confined to European-based cultures, including North America and Australasia, with the rest of the world altering little. Some barbarities were abolished: German and Belgian colonies aside, many Africans were finding chattel slavery and human sacrifice less common, at the price of submitting to colonial rule. India, although its administration was the fairest and most competent ever experienced there, was still subject to devastating, and possibly avoidable, famines. China was racked by internal war and foreign exploitation, with its ancient culture fast decaying.

By 1960, another lifetime on, and to a date within living memory, the quality of life in the richer nations had improved again. Antibiotics had reduced the risks of infection for minor injuries and helped to end diphtheria, tuberculosis, syphilis and many other diseases. In Europe, unemployment and retirement pay was now universal, as was free or inexpensive healthcare, although of varying quality. The United States remained suspicious of

such 'socialism'. Radio had brought information and entertainment to the remotest corners of the world, and television – in colour from the 1950s – was becoming widely available. Passenger aircraft crossed the Atlantic in a few hours (but anyone with time and money would still find the great liners much more agreeable). Household drudgery had been reduced by inexpensive appliances; the mangle, washtub and flatiron disappeared. Cheap and washable clothing not only reduced labour but helped to remove the more obvious class distinctions. But new anxieties had gathered. For the first time in history mankind had the ability to destroy all life on the planet, a possibility which sometimes seemed frighteningly near.

ABOVE *New skyscrapers tower over the commercial and financial centre of Shanghai. In just over 70 years, the People's Republic of China has become one of the world's fastest growing economies.*

Although sanitary improvements lengthened life expectancy in what were optimistically termed 'developing' rather than 'poor' countries, and malaria was controlled by DDT, rapid increases in population entailed more pressure on food resources. To some extent supplies were permanently improved as the 'Green Revolution' began in the 1950s. India was the first country to develop the techniques pioneered in Mexico, beginning in 1961 when new

high-yielding varieties of wheat and rice were introduced. Bolstered by irrigation, artificial fertilizers and pesticides, the results were dramatic. Within a few years yields tripled, and fears of famine vanished, but later the limitations and disadvantages became apparent. Pesticides, herbicides and fertilizers required sophisticated products, produced in the richer countries, using fossil fuel, and needed careful handling in the field, storage, distribution and advice, all demanding effective administrations locally. Since many of these qualities were lacking in Africa, the Green Revolution has rarely been successful in the region where it was most needed. Success had its own dangers, as forest areas were cut down and cropped for animal feed or even bio-fuels, severely damaging the environment and disrupting established societies. Reliance on a single major crop led to dietary limitations, the erosion of some traditional farming skills, and the disappearance of valuable cultivars.

Improvements were sometimes rejected, even when available. Conditions in Afghan villages in the 1960s were much as they would have been in Ancient Persian times: food was cooked over an open fire or in a wood-fired oven, and houses were still built of mudbrick and stone as they had been since the Indus Valley civilization. Fabrics and furniture readily available in the Kabul bazaar were disdained and hospitals always fearfully avoided: penicillin was however much appreciated. The only obvious signs of 20th-century influence were in the men's weaponry: they all carried a long Khyber knife, but the matchlock *jezail* had been replaced by a magazine rifle.

That, however, is far from being the end of the story. Even assuming only modest population growth from *c.*7 billion today to 9 billion in 2050, food production will need to rise very considerably, even to double, within the next generation to avoid under-nourishment and keep pace with the demand for an increased variety of diets inseparable from growing urbanization; carnivores are on the increase and meat is a thirsty product, requiring some eight times as much water as the production of a equivalent weight of cereals. Many hazards stand in the way of a complete solution. Most suitable and still-uncultivated areas are concentrated in South America and Africa. Brazil and Argentina still have considerable extents of potentially productive land, which could provide a proportion of future needs, if not used in the extravagantly wasteful production of bio-fuels, now demanded by international agreements. If American maize, currently converted into petrol, sold domestically at prices half the international norm, was used for food, the world supply would increase by 14 percent, feeding many millions. Using African land is more difficult, partly because much is already of poor quality, following over-cropping and lack of access to fertilizers and better techniques, but also due to government inefficiency and consistently corrupt handling of aid funds. Genetically modified crops might help, but objections to their potentially damaging effects remain to be answered, and have led to their being banned in many European countries. Water supply is another constraint. Major rivers are already drying up and in some regions such as the Middle East water supplies can be a major political issue: future wars may be as much about water as land.

A surprisingly high proportion – between one-third and a half – of food is wasted, in poorer countries by poor transit and storage facilities, which could be corrected and in rich countries by simple extravagance, in quantities that, at present, amount to a shocking 1,000 million tons a year: if this were only to be halved, the extra 2 billion people expected to populate the planet by 2050 could easily be fed. And the food that is eaten brings its own health problems, with obesity, grotesquely evident, increasing in North and Central America and Europe.

Overhanging anxieties over food security are aggravated by concerns on possible climatic alterations. Rapid climate changes have been experienced previously, even if the last one was several thousand years ago, and it seems that another might have to be expected very soon. In the last century, average world temperatures have risen by nearly one degree centigrade, and most of that rise has been since 1960. Today the latest projection indicates a further increase during the current century of anything up to another six degrees, which would increase sea levels considerably and greatly extend desertification. Droughts and floods would become more common, with often extreme effects on agriculture. Nothing is inevitable, but all the evidence points to these conclusions, and every year new examples of the possible results become evident.

Some of this warming is due to human activity producing carbon dioxide, methane and other gases in hitherto unknown concentrations – unknown that is for the last 20 million years or so. Deforestation for stock farming and agriculture and the combustion of fossil fuels has been responsible for most of the increase. Opinions differ as to what may be expected in the future, but most accepted studies indicate that decisive action is essential to avert the escalation of these 'greenhouse gases'. In October 2010, the Kyoto Protocol, an agreement to limit and reduce the quantity of damaging emissions, was ratified by 192 states, concluding the negotiations that had been begun in late 1990s. Hitting the targets was going to be difficult and not without cost; cleaner but more expensive forms of power generation and increased taxes on fossil-fuel usage were inevitable, and the accord constituted a remarkable display of intranational responsibility.

An Uncertain Note

There was, however, one exception to this impressive unanimity. The United States of America, by far the biggest polluter, refused to ratify the Protocol, the only country in the world to back out. In 1998, President Bill Clinton had signed the initial agreement, but one of the first acts of his successor George

W. Bush's presidency was to withdraw his country's assent: it was not, he said, right for America. The rest of the world was appalled, but carried on, with some measure of success: but even President Obama, in spite of accepting the urgency, has continued to do nothing.

America's detractors see this as just another example of monumental selfishness, and store up more resentment to fuel the next outrage, but her NATO allies tend to shrug it off as another example of Transatlantic exceptionalism, parallel to Americans' propensity to shooting each other – an annual death rate very much higher than that of the Vietnam War – or locking people up, with 0.75 percent of the population in gaol in 2009, a much higher rate than in any other country in the world. Moreover, in some states, a number of these prisoners await execution, a punishment long since abolished in all other Western democracies.

One explanation offered is the remarkable level – by any other advanced culture's standards – of American religious credulity. Reputable opinion polls indicate that over a 20-year period to 2004 nearly half (44–47 percent) of the adult population believed that humanity was created some 10,000 years ago, and that, perhaps more alarmingly, a third of postgraduate students do not believe that Charles Darwin's theory of evolution is well-supported by the evidence. Balanced against these idiosyncracies is the recognition of enormous American generosity, and especially the personal generosity of the very rich and the contribution of American scientists to the world's benefit: but the United States remains an uncomfortable leader for a world with such different values.

Leadership, however, does not depend entirely on economic strength; Russia, although still only a modest economy, effected a dramatic change in Europe under Mikhail Gorbachev's leadership. Recently, in the last 20 years or so, there has been a general shift in economic strength, of which the clearest example has been Japan's displacement by China as the world's second largest economy, with a rate of growth that indicates it may overhaul the United States within a generation. Other countries, notably Russia, India and Brazil but also Indonesia and Mexico, are showing signs of growth that might by 2050 displace Japan, Germany and the United Kingdom, currently (2010) lying in third, fourth and fifth place, in Gross Domestic Product (GDP) rankings. The total GDP of all African countries is at the moment only about half that of the UK, but both Nigeria and South Africa have the potential to become high-performing economies. An indication of the scale of Africa's problems is the fact that half the population have no access to that most basic of human needs, safe drinking water. In some African countries only some 10 percent have proper sanitary facilities, and even in India public defecation is common.

One of the most successful institutions, the nation-state, evolved over tens of thousands of years, appears to be mutating. Supra-national authorities, of which the European Community is the largest and most coherent, have assumed previously national sovereign rights. Unilateral, country-to-country treaties have been replaced by participation in multilateral groups, a process now more than a century old. The International Court of Justice, sitting at The Hague, traces its descent from the Hague Conventions of 1899. All countries, except the United States, which limited its accord to selected judgements, have agreed to accept the court's judgement, which may be enforced by the United Nations Security Council.

At the same time as this transfer of authority outwards, some nation states are becoming regionalized. Spain has devolved extensive self-governing powers to its provinces, especially Catalonia and the Basque region. Scotland, Wales and Northern Ireland have been granted Parliaments or Assemblies, and are pressing for more. Czechoslovakia and Yugoslavia have formally divided into their constituent states, Georgia and the Ukraine have become independent. One major Italian political party is pledged to establish a Northern Italian state, and even France, historically the most centralized of all nation-states, is experienced mild stirrings of regional independence.

BELOW *Flags of the European Union (EU) member states outside the European Parliament building in Strasbourg. From a core of six countries in 1958, the European Community has grown to embrace 27 countries. Yet full political integration is a contentious issue.*

Index

222

Picture credits

Quercus Publishing Plc
21 Bloomsbury Square
London
WC1A 2NS

First published in 2011

Designed and edited by BCS Publishing Limited, Oxford.

A catalogue record of this book is available from the British Library

UK and associated territories 978 0 85738 476 8

Canada 978-1-84866-156-1

Printed and bound in China

10 9 8 7 6 5 4 3 2 1